D1560417

Object-Oriented Development at Work

Fusion In the Real World

Hewlett-Packard Professional Books

Object-Oriented Development at Work

Fusion In the Real World

Ruth Malan
Reed Letsinger
Derek Coleman

For book and bookstore information

http://www.prenhall.com

Prentice Hall PTR
Upper Saddle River, NJ 07458

Malan, Ruth.
    Object-oriented development at work: fusion in the real world /
Ruth Malan, Reed Letsinger, Derek Coleman.
        p.   cm. -- (Hewlett-Packard professional books)
    Includes bibliographical references and index.
    ISBN 0-13-243148-3
    1. Object-oriented programming (Computer science) 2. Computer
software--Development.   I. Letsinger, Reed.   II. Coleman, Derek.
III. Title.   IV. Series.
QA76.64.M347   1995   95-42331
005.1'2--dc20   CIP

Editorial/production supervision: **Ann Sullivan**
Cover design: **Paul Gourhan**
Cover manager: **Jerry Votta**
Manufacturing manager: **Alexis R. Heydt**
Acquisitions editor: **Karen Gettman**
Editorial assistant: **Barbara Alfieri**

Published by Prentice Hall PTR
Prentice-Hall, Inc.
A Simon and Schuster Company
Upper Saddle River, NJ 07458

The publisher offers discounts on this book when ordered in bulk quantities.
For more information, contact:

Corporate Sales Department
Prentice Hall PTR
One Lake Street
Upper Saddle River, NJ 07458

Phone: 800-382-3419
Fax: 201-236-7141
email: corpsales@prenhall.com

Printed in the United States of America

10 9 8 7 6 5 4 3 2 1

ISBN: 0-13-243148-3

Prentice-Hall International (UK) Limited, *London*
Prentice-Hall of Australia Pty. Limited, *Sydney*
Prentice-Hall Canada Inc., *Toronto*
Prentice-Hall Hispanoamericana, S.A., *Mexico*
Prentice-Hall of India Private Limited, *New Delhi*
Prentice-Hall of Japan, Inc., *Tokyo*
Simon & Schuster Asia Pte. Ltd., *Singapore*
Editora Prentice-Hall do Brasil, Ltda., *Rio de Janeiro*

Contents

2   Using Fusion on a Hewlett–Packard Medical Imaging Project: Analysis Phase Retrospective   79

Ron Falcone, Jacob Nikom, and Ruth Malan

PART 2 APPLICATIONS 101

12 Extending Fusion: Practical Rigor and Refinement   314

Desmond D'Souza and Alan Wills

Preface

This book is about best practices in object-oriented software development. The focus is on the process by which software is developed and in particular the use of the Fusion object-oriented analysis and design method (Coleman et al. 1994). The book contains a collection of papers on the practical aspects of Fusion. The authors come from a wide variety of backgrounds including product development organizations, research laboratories, academia, software houses, and consultancies. From the book the reader will learn about the benefits of using Fusion, how to introduce the method, and how to customize it to meet the needs of a project. Overall, the papers testify to the level of interest in Fusion and the great variety of projects and situations in which the method is making a real and significant contribution.

Audience for Book

The target audience for this book is software engineers and project managers with some familiarity with object-oriented methods. It should be particularly useful to those charged with evaluating methods or introducing a method onto a live project. The book is self-contained and includes an introductory overview of Fusion together with full reference documentation. It is stressed however that the experiences documented in this book are likely to be of general interest to object-oriented practitioners and research workers and not limited to Fusion aficionados.

Evolution of the Fusion Object-Oriented Method

Until the late nineteen eighties, only structured methods, such as structured analysis and design (SA/SD), were available for systematic software development. Of necessity, developers who wanted to approach the new object-oriented paradigm systematically had to apply structured techniques. In most cases these attempts were at best only partially successful because it was not easy to map the concepts of SA/SD to objects.

The problem is that there is a fundamental clash between the computational models that underlie the two paradigms. Structured methods lead to software which is structured as a collection of procedures, all of which can access global state. The object-oriented computational model is fundamentally different because there is no global state and software is structured as a collection of objects, each of which has its own encapsulated state. The objects interact solely by passing messages. Consequently using structured methods for object-oriented development necessarily requires a translation from the structured computational model to the object-oriented model. Packaging the global state of the structured model into objects is, in essence, the same task as designing object-oriented software in the first place. In both cases the developer has the difficult conceptual task of "finding the objects," i.e., partitioning functionality across appropriate object classes.

The problems with the use of SA/SD for object-orientation were soon recognized and prompted investigation into object-oriented analysis and design (OOA/D) methods. By the early nineteen-nineties there were a large number of such methods available. In 1992 the Object Management Group (OMG) compiled a list of nearly thirty OOA/D methods (OMG 1992). Of course, not all of the methods had entered widespread use. Many were speculative research ideas that were not supported by books or training courses. However, there was much commonality between some of the methods; for example, many incorporated some form of object model, or class diagram, based on entity-relationship modeling. Some used models and notations borrowed from structured methods. There were also important differences; some methods emphasized expressiveness of notations while others gave more support for a particular phase of the software life cycle.

For object-oriented software development, unlike traditional software development, there was a wide choice of methods. The great variety of methods, which was growing all the time, caused problems for practical software developers. Before a project could use a method, it was faced with the prospect of carrying out a methods evaluation to ascertain which to use. The prospect of choosing the "wrong" method also increased the risk of using object-oriented techniques.

These problems were very apparent in Hewlett-Packard (HP) company. Many projects embarking on the use of object-oriented techniques were unsure which method should be used. They did not know the strengths and weaknesses of the various methods and did not know which one would best meet their individual needs. In order to alleviate these problems, a research project was begun in 1990 at HP Labs, Bristol, in order to develop OOA/D method training and consultancy suitable for use by the many and diverse HP projects developing software.

The project began by surveying HP's object-oriented projects in order to understand their needs (Coleman and Hayes 1991). The project also conducted an extensive and systematic evaluation of the leading methods (Arnold et al. 1991). At that time, only a few methods had attracted significant numbers of users. The most prominent were Object Modeling Technique (OMT) (Rumbaugh et al. 1991), Booch (1991), Responsibility Driven Design (RDD) (Wirfs-Brock 1990), Shlaer-Mellor (1988) and Coad-Yourdon (1991a, 1991b).

The results of the method evaluation and the studies of user needs confirmed that there was no single best method. It was clear that the best way to meet the needs of software developers was to synthesize a new method based on the best aspects of existing methods. This work lead directly to development of the Fusion OOA/D method, which is a seamless combination of techniques from a number of different methods.

The analysis stage of Fusion is based on OMT, with the addition of a formal methods technique known as pre- and postconditions (Jones 1990). Pre- and postconditions are an essential tool for precisely capturing the desired behavior of software. The analysis stage also employs scenarios which are closely related to the use case concept in Objectory (Jacobson et al. 1992). The Fusion design stage is based on the Class-Responsibility-Collaborator (CRC) (Beck and Cunningham 1989) technique, which is the core component of the RDD method. The design stage also incorporates elements of the Booch method. The different models are integrated to form a systematic process spanning the analysis and design phases of the software life cycle. The Fusion method evolved through several iterations via experimental use in the research labs and on live software development projects. This culminated in the publication of the reference text on Fusion (Coleman et al. 1994) that was published in late 1993.

Since its introduction, the use of Fusion has spread rapidly within HP. It is now being used to develop a broad range of products including printers, network management software and embedded firmware. Today, many companies worldwide are employing Fusion on an even wider range of domains including MIS, telecoms and defense systems. The contents of this book represent just a small fraction of this growing use.

Structure of Book

The book starts with an overview of the Fusion method. This chapter together with the reference material contained in the appendices will give the reader who is unfamiliar with Fusion sufficient context to understand the rest of the book.

The book has four sections. The first section contains in-depth reports of case studies. Chapter 1, by Jerremy Holland, is an account of an HP project developing a distributed telecom test system. The main thrust of the paper is the lessons learned in introducing a method to a team inexperienced in object-oriented development. The lessons are presented as some highly useful guidelines and lists of "dos and don'ts." The second chapter, by Ron Falcone and his colleagues, explains how the analysis stage of Fusion was applied by an HP project developing a breakthrough medical imaging product. The chapter places particular emphasis on project management and how Fusion was customized to meet the circumstances of the project.

Section 2 deals with how Fusion can be applied in a variety of domains and circumstances. Paul Jeremaes, one of the original team that developed Fusion, shows in Chapter 3 how the method can be applied in the face of bottom-up constraints. This chapter tackles one of the key issues for all OOA/D methods—how to apply them to non-greenfield situations. The paper uses the development of telecom network management applications as its motivating example.

In Chapter 4, Laurence Canning and Richard Nethercott report on the application of Fusion to the development of bespoke software, where cost control is a major concern. The authors focus on how Fusion contributes to managing the development process and how it relates to incremental development, project staffing and cost estimation.

In the era of business re-engineering, process modeling is an area of growing importance. This is the subject of Chapter 5 by Colin Atkinson and Michael Weisskopf. The chapter is based on experiences gained working on the development of software for NASA and takes the software maintenance process as the motivating example. The chapter also introduces some interesting and powerful extensions to the Object Interaction Graph notation.

Project management is the key to successful software development and this is the theme of Section 3. In Hewlett-Packard, Fusion is almost universally used in the context of evolutionary development. This combination has been spectacularly successful since it allows a project to systematically tackle business and technical risks. In Chapter 6, Todd Cotton, a principal developer of Evolutionary Fusion and one of HP's internal software consultants, explains how the steps of the Fusion method can be effectively mapped onto an evolutionary and incremental project life cycle.

In Chapter 7, Kris Oosting explains how metrics and defect tracking can be introduced into the management of a project using Fusion. The work is based on Kris's extensive experience as a consultant and software developer using Fusion and other OOA/D methods.

Section 4 of the book focuses on practical extensions to Fusion. Chapter 8, by Andrew Blyth of the University of Newcastle Upon Tyne, introduces a requirements engineering front-end process for the Fusion method. The work has been developed as part of a research project funded by the European Union on Informatics in Healthcare.

Chapter 9 is authored by Howard Ricketts, a designer of the *Fusion*CASE tool and a software consultant. The chapter proposes some extensions to the design phase of Fusion based on Howard's experience as a consultant. The extensions are aimed at making design more systematic through refinement of the object model. The chapter also introduces notations and guidelines for handling concurrency.

Distributed computing is of growing commercial interest and importance.

Many projects today are using Fusion to develop client/server and distributed software. In chapter 10, Kris Oosting extends the Fusion notations to allow the development of client-server applications. The paper is based on the author's extensive experience developing NextStep/OpenStep applications using Fusion.

In the transition to using object technology, education and training of software engineers in OOA/D is of key importance. In Chapter 11, Gabriel Eckert discusses the issues raised in training university students in the use of Fusion. The chapter presents a critique of the Fusion analysis phase based on the observations of student progress developing software in a laboratory project.

The Fusion method was significantly influenced by the ideas and concepts of formal methods. In Chapter 12, Desmond D'Souza and Alan Wills take this a step further by introducing a new methodology which incorporates a more formal notion of refinement into a Fusion-like development methodology. The chapter indicates the extent to which ideas and concepts that were pioneered by Fusion are being incorporated and extended in new experimental methodologies.

Fusion and the Future of OOA/D Methods

From the outset, the originators of Fusion believed that OOA/D methods must be based on the experiences and needs of software developers. Of course, as the challenges facing software developers grow, and understanding of the software development process improves, OOA/D methods themselves must evolve. Users will not benefit from a "fossilized" method which fails to take account of the lessons of experience.

An important aim of this book is to facilitate the evolution by documenting best-practices with Fusion. We also hope that the book will make a contribution beyond Fusion by promoting the cross-fertilization of methods with ideas that work.

As this book shows, the Fusion method is an open "school of thought." Although we at HP Labs are actively working on extending and improving Fusion, we do not consider that we own the method. On the contrary, we enthusiastically welcome all contributions on how Fusion can be developed. We believe that openness must be the watch word for the future evolution of object-oriented analysis and design. The software development community will be best served by methods evolving and converging according to the experience of what works and what does not. This book is a step in that direction.

Derek Coleman
Ruth Malan
Reed Letsinger

REFERENCES

Arnold, P., S. Bodoff, D. Coleman, H. Gilchrist, and F. Hayes. 1991. Evaluation of five object-oriented development methods. In *Journal of Object-Oriented Programming: Focus on Analysis and Design*. pp. 101-121. New York, NY: SIGS Publications.

Beck K. and W. Cunningham. 1989. A laboratory for teaching object-oriented thinking. In *ACM OOPSLA'89 Conference Proceedings*.

Booch, G. 1991.*Object-Oriented Design with Applications*. Redwood City, CA: Benjamin/Cummings.

Coad, P. and E. Yourdon. 1991a. *Object-Oriented Analysis*, 2nd edition. Englewood Cliffs, NJ: Yourdon Press.

Coad, P. and E. Yourdon. 1991b. *Object-Oriented Design*. Englewood Cliffs, NJ: Yourdon Press.

Coleman, D., P. Arnold, S. Bodoff, C. Dollin, H. Gilchrist, F. Hayes, P. Jeremaes. 1994. *Object-Oriented Development: The Fusion Method*. Englewood Cliffs, NJ: Prentice Hall.

Coleman, D. and F. Hayes. March 1991. Lessons from Hewlett-Packard's experience of using object-oriented technology. In *Tools 4*. pp. 327-333. Paris.

Jacobson, I., M. Christerson, P. Jonsson, and G. Övergaard. 1992. *Object-Oriented Software Engineering*. Reading, MA: Addison-Wesley.

Martin, J. and J.J. Odell. 1992. *Object-Oriented Analysis and Design*. Englewood Cliffs, NJ: Prentice Hall.

OMG. October 1992. Object Analysis and Design Survey of Methods 1992. *Technical Report*. Framingham, MA: Object Management Group.

Rumbaugh, J., M. Blaha, W. Premerlani, F. Eddy, W. Lorensen. 1991. *Object-Oriented Modeling and Design*. Englewood Cliffs, NJ: Prentice Hall.

Shlaer, S. and S.J. Mellor. 1988. *Object-Oriented Systems Analysis - Modeling the World in Data*. Englewood Cliffs, NJ: Yourdon Press.

Wirfs-Brock, R., B. Wilkerson, and L. Wiener. 1990. *Designing Object-Oriented Software*. Englewood Cliffs, NJ: Prentice Hall International.

Acknowledgments

Since its launch in 1992, many people inside and outside of Hewlett-Packard have played an important role in establishing Fusion as an essential success factor in numerous real-world projects. We want to thank the HP engineers who have adopted Fusion, as well as Todd Cotton, Wendell Fields, Bill Crandall, Mark Davey, and Mike Ogush of the HP Software Initiative for the part they have played in making Fusion the dominant object-oriented development method used within HP. We would also like to thank Paul Jeremaes and Chris Dollin for, even though they now working on different projects, they continue to take an active interest in Fusion.

We also thank Patricia Gill, Lisa Guinn, David Bell-Lee, Wolfgang Demmel, Dennis Todd, Tim Ryan, Betty Lin, Wulf Rehder, Steve Mock, Gregson Siu, Larry Marran and Padma Sreenivasan for their support of Fusion as an integral component of HP's training and consulting services.

Fusion has received strong support outside of Hewlett-Packard, and we would like to thank Dr. Lekkos and Carlos Carvahal at ProtoSoft, Howard Ricketts at *Soft*CASE Consulting, Kris Oosting at SHARED OBJECTIVES, Graham Glass and David Norris at ObjectSpace, and Viktor Ohnjec at Semaphore. Special thanks go to all those engineers who have championed the use of Fusion in their organizations, and used Fusion on their projects. It is their experience that forms the basis of this book.

From the initial call for papers to the final production of this book, we have had strong support and encouragement from many people in Hewlett-Packard and the broader Fusion community. We would like to thank them all, and especially Mary Loomis, manager of the Software Technology Lab in Hewlett-Packard Laboratories, for sponsoring our time as editors on this project. We also thank all those who submitted abstracts for the book, but had to withdraw due to work conflicts. We especially thank Justin Murray, whose paper went all the way through the review process receiving high praise from the reviewers but had to be withdrawn at the last moment due to concerns about project confidentiality issues.

Many people participated as reviewers of the papers in this book, including Colin Atkinson, Andrew Blyth, Todd Cotton, Bill Crandall, Lew Creary, Chris Dollin, Gabriel Eckert, Paul Jeremaes, Justin Murray, Kris Oosting, Michael Weisskopf, Kevin Wentzel and Bill Kent. We thank them all.

We would also like to thank Alan Apt for his enthusiastic support for the book concept and Mona Pompili and Sophie Papanikolaou for their advice and assistance with formatting the book. Thanks also to Karen Gettman, Barbara Alfieri, and Pat Pekary for shepherding the book through the publication process, and to Ann Sullivan for coordinating the production. We would like to thank Louise Herndon and William Thomas who did a wonderful job in copy editing this book.

Finally, we would like to thank Paul Malan, Glenna Letsinger and Victoria Stavridou for their support.

Overview of Fusion

Reed Letsinger

Hewlett–Packard Laboratories

INTRODUCTION

Fusion is a step-by-step process that leads a development team from an initial requirements document through to the implementation of an object-oriented software system. During the process, various models are constructed, each providing a view of the software system that highlights certain issues and encodes a well-defined set of decisions. The purpose of this paper is to introduce the main features of the process steps and models in Fusion. The goal is to give the reader enough detail of the method to serve as background for the papers that follow. Further details can be found in Appendices A and B. For a comprehensive treatment of the Fusion method, the reader should consult Coleman et al., 1994.

The method distinguishes three stages:

- **Analysis**—which produces a declarative specification of *what* the system does
- **Design**—which produces an abstract object-oriented model of *how* the system realizes the required behavior
- **Implementation**—which encodes the design in a programming language

Fusion starts with an informal requirements document. Analysis transforms the information in the requirements document into a set of models that more precisely characterizes the way the software system interacts with its environment. These analysis models are then input to the design process, which produces another set of models describing how the system is structured and how the system's behavior is realized in terms of that structure. The structure is represented as a set of classes, and the desired behavior is characterized by patterns of messages flowing between instances of these classes. Finally, the classes and

1

methods identified during design are implemented in an object-oriented programming language.

Figure 1 shows the principal models produced during the Fusion process. Throughout all the phases of software development, important concepts and assumptions are recorded in a *data dictionary*. The other models are partially ordered according to their dependencies, indicated by arrows in Figure 1. The Fusion process guides the developers through the construction and evaluation of the models in an order consistent with their dependencies. Of course, in practice, iteration and backtracking will always be necessary. Any model can be revisited. Earlier models can be left in a partial or tentative state while work on later models gets under way. However, keeping to the process as much as possible minimizes the need for rework because the steps are ordered according to the logical dependencies between the models that are produced.

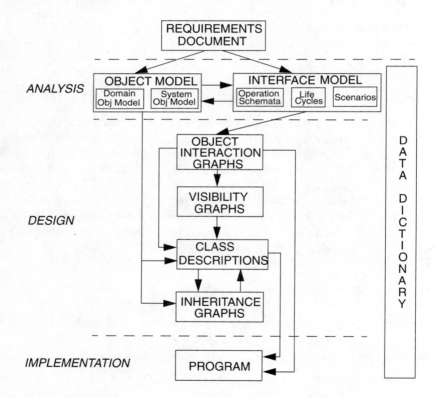

Figure 1 The Fusion Process

The basic notations and process steps in Fusion can best be illustrated by walking through a simple example. We will consider the development of a data management system to assist a technician in a clinical biochemistry laboratory in carrying out chemical tests on samples of body fluid and tissue drawn from patients in a hospital. The example will necessarily be artificially simple, and we will make no effort to develop all the models that would be called for even in this simplified version. The point is to illustrate each step and the modeling notation used in the Fusion analysis and design phases.

ANALYSIS

The starting point of Fusion is an informal requirements document. This may take many possible forms, but it typically includes a natural language description of the problem to be solved, possibly supplemented with structural diagrams, example output reports, and mock-ups of user input screens. Figure 2 shows the requirements document for the Clinical Lab example.

The output of analysis is a set of models that together specify how the system interacts with its environment. The *object model* provides an abstract characterization of the possible states of the system expressed in terms of object classes and their relationships. During analysis, objects are used only to represent possible system state; no effort is made to describe how they behave. It is the task of design to determine how the behavior of the system is to be realized in terms of the behavior of objects. For this reason, objects at analysis time have no methods.

The *interface model* provides a declarative description of the system's behavior, specifying the possible patterns of interaction between the system and its environment and the impact those interactions have on the state of the system. The interface model is actually a collection of simpler models. The *operation model* breaks down the system behavior into discrete system operations and events. Each system operation is described declaratively, using preconditions and postconditions expressed in the vocabulary of the object model. Complex temporal patterns of behavior can be explored using *scenarios*—which are related to the *use cases* in Objectory (Jacobson et al. 1992)—and formally defined by writing a *life-cycle model*, which is essentially a grammar that defines the allowable sequences of system operations and events.

Effort spent during the analysis stage provides three major benefits to the software development team:

- It helps identify and resolve ambiguities, inconsistencies, and gaps in the requirements documentation.
- It establishes an understanding of the problem—as well as a vocabulary for talking about the problem—that can be shared among the diverse parties that have a stake in the software development—customers, designers, implementers, testers, managers, and so on.
- It develops a good foundation for the design activities to build on.

Requirements for a Clinical Lab Information System

Clinical biochemistry is a branch of pathology in which body fluids are subjected to tests in order to facilitate diagnosis, prognosis, and monitoring of treatment. The increasing demand for medical testing has led to the introduction of automated analyzers for carrying out tests. An analyzer can carry out tests on body fluids such as blood, urine, and swab specimens and then send the test results across a network for printing or input to another system. Most analyzers have a single slot where samples can be queued up waiting for processing. A new generation of advanced analyzers have multiple sample slots; that is, they are capable of carrying out tests on more than one sample simultaneously.

The task is to develop a computerized data management system for a laboratory comprising a mixture of standard and advanced analyzers. In such a system, a technician enters a batch of samples from a single patient by first entering the patient's identification and then indicating, one at a time, the tests that need to be performed on the samples. A "batch end" message informs the system that there are no more samples for the current patient.

The system decides which analyzer—and, in the case of advanced analyzers, which slot—will be used to process the sample. Details of each requested test, the sample it is to be performed on, and the analyzer slot to be used are sent to a labeling machine that produces a label that the technician attaches to the sample. The technician is responsible for loading the labeled samples into the correct analyzer slots, and a bar code reader on each analyzer reads the label to determine what to do with the sample. When all the test results for a patient have been returned, they are collected together into a patient report, which is sent to the technician.

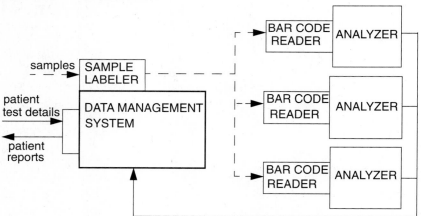

The system can perform test requests for more than one patient at a time. The technician may ask for a report reflecting the current status of a patient's tests before they are completed. The tests for a patient may also be aborted, in which case a patient report containing just the test results collected up to that point is generated and all further tests on samples from the same patient are ignored.

Figure 2 A Requirements Document

Object Model

It is convenient to start analysis by constructing a list of the different kinds of entities mentioned in the requirements document. A possible list for the Clinical Lab example includes *Technician, Analyzer, Sample, Patient, Test, Patient Report,* and *Test Request.* The next step is to go through the list, determining for each entry what information about entities of that kind is needed to understand the requirements. These decisions are captured in the *object model,*[*] which is expressed using a generalization of entity-relationship diagramming notation. For example, information that might be important to capture includes the time a sample was taken and the patient it was taken from. An object model summarizes these decisions, as illustrated in Figure 3.

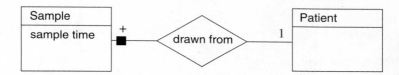

Figure 3 Classes and Relationships in an Object Model

A class of entities is drawn as a rectangle labeled with the class name. Attributes of the class members are listed inside the rectangle below the class name. (Object-valued attributes are introduced during design and should not be included during analysis.)

The diamond connecting the two class rectangles represents a relationship that can hold between patients and samples. Relationships can have cardinalities that specify the number of objects that may be associated with each other in a relationship. The allowable annotations are a number, a range (e.g. 1..4), * denoting zero or more, and + designating one or more. In Figure 3, the + indicates that each patient may have one or more samples taken from him, while the 1 on the other end of the relationship expresses the requirement that a sample may only be drawn from one patient. The black box at the **Sample** end of the **drawn from** relationship is called a totality marker. It is used to emphasize that every sample must be drawn from some patient.

Relationships may connect more than two classes. Technicians are responsible for loading samples into sample slots on analyzers, as represented in Figure 4.

Some entities are naturally viewed as having parts configured into a particular structure. In the Fusion object model, such composite entities are called aggregates. The classes and relationships that represent the structure of an

---

[*] These diagrams are sometimes referred to as domain object models, to distinguish them from the system object models generated from them. When the distinction is not important, the extra modifier will be dropped.

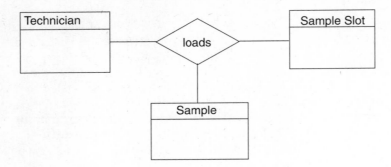

Figure 4 A Ternary Relationship

aggregate are embedded inside the aggregate class box. Figure 5 illustrates how this is done. This model of the **Test Request** class describes the structure of test requests. Each test request contains the representation of exactly one sample and exactly one test. The cardinality constraint is expressed by the numeral 1 occurring at the upper-left corners of the **Test** and **Sample** boxes. By including the **carried out on** relationship inside the aggregation, the modeler expresses the constraint that the test in a test request must be the test applied to the sample in the same test request. In other respects, the aggregate **Test Request** is just like any other class; it can have its own attributes, such as **request time**, it can be linked to other classes through relationships, and it can be embedded inside other aggregate class boxes.

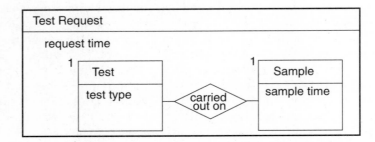

Figure 5 An Aggregation

A more complex example of aggregation is illustrated in Figure 6. This diagram shows that a patient report consists of any number of test requests related to the same patient. The test requests are also paired with their results. At intermediate stages of processing the tests for a patient, some test requests may not yet have results, so the cardinality constraint 0..1 is used.

Sometimes a class can be usefully specialized into a set of classes, each with its own additional detail. The requirements document indicates that two differ-

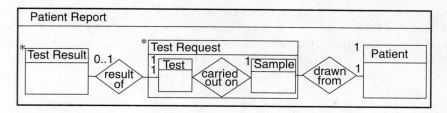

Figure 6 Nested Aggregation

ent kinds of analyzers are relevant to the Clinical Lab problem—the regular and the advanced analyzers—and that three different types of sample should be distinguished—blood, urine, and tissue swabs. It is also possible to work the other way and introduce a more inclusive class to generalize common properties from classes that have already been modeled. The relation between a class and its specializations can be expressed in an object model, as illustrated in Figure 7.

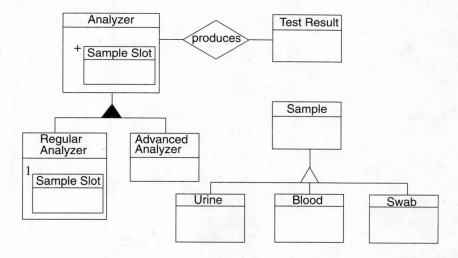

Figure 7 Examples of Subclass Notations in Object Models

All analyzers are either regular or advanced, but not both. The division of the class of analyzers into regular and advanced analyzers is both complete (there are no other cases) and disjoint (there is no overlap among the cases). This is a common situation, which can be captured in the diagram by filling in the triangle as shown in Figure 7. The triangle under **Sample** has not been filled, since the modeler wants to leave open the possibility that other kinds of samples might be added later.

The relationship **produces** is shown relating the class **Analyzer** to the class **Test Result**. Since all regular analyzers and all advanced analyzers are analyzers, these subclasses are also related to the **Test Result** class through the **produces** relationship. These connections need not be explicitly drawn, since they can easily be inferred from what has already been shown. Notice also that the **Analyzer** class has been shown as an aggregate containing one or more **sample slots**, a condition that applies to regular and advanced analyzers, since they are also analyzers. However, regular analyzers must also satisfy an additional cardinality constraint stating that they have exactly one sample slot. Advanced analyzers are only subject to the more general constraint included on the **Analyzer** class.

The process of building the object model introduces vocabulary that the development team needs to agree on. Some of the terms are used to denote classes, some to express attributes, and some to name relationships. All these terms should be logged in the data dictionary, as shown in Figure 8. Additionally, if there is information that the analyst feels that it is important to capture, but which the object model notation cannot express, the analyst is free to add this extra information in the data dictionary or as annotations in the object model. As other models are built, new vocabulary that is introduced will also be added to the data dictionary.

DATA DICTIONARY		
Name	**Kind**	**Description**
Sample	class	a tissue or fluid sample to be tested by an analyzer
sample time	attribute	time the sample was taken—used to check that the sample is sufficiently fresh for testing
Patient	class	a source of samples to be tested
drawn from	relationship	relationship between a patient and the patient's samples
Patient Report	class	a report to be printed out for the technician indicating the status of tests on a particular patient

Figure 8 The Start of a Data Dictionary

A diagram for the Clinical Lab object model is presented in Figure 9. It may not always be feasible to develop a diagram with a readable layout without including more than one box for the same class. In Figure 9, **Test Request**, **Analyzer**, and **Sample** each occur twice. Both occurrences represent the same class. Boxes representing the same class can also occur on different diagrams when the object model is too complex to draw on a single sheet of paper.

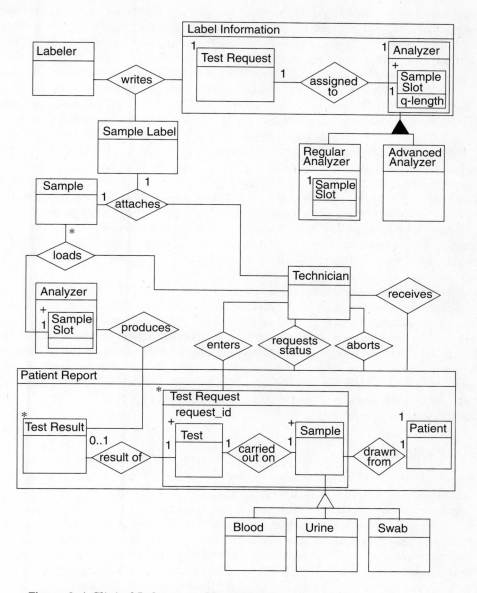

Figure 9 A Clinical Laboratory Object Model

System Object Model

The object model in Figure 9 represents the entities and relationships in the domain that the clinical laboratory information system will operate in—it does not describe the system itself. The first step in building a representation of the system is to add a *system boundary* to the object model. The system boundary is a line forming a closed curve that separates those classes and relationships that are part of the system from those that belong to the system's external environment. Including a class inside the system boundary indicates that the system will maintain information about the entities of that class. Similarly, if a relationship is included within the boundary, the system is expected to record information about which entities are related according to the relationship. When drawing the system boundary, developers should concentrate on deciding what information the system needs encode, and not on how the information should be encoded, which is a problem addressed during design.

Classes on the outside of the system boundary may represent agents, human or otherwise, that interact with the system. Relationships connecting agents outside the boundary with classes inside the system may represent types of interaction that the system must be able to support. Classes and relationships that fall outside the boundary but do not represent agents or interactions can safely be deleted from the model once the system boundary has been finalized. The new object model that results from adding the system boundary is called the *system object model*. Figure 10 shows a possible system object model for the Clinical Lab example.

Note that the **Analyzer** class box occurs once outside the boundary to stand for agents interacting with the system, and once inside the boundary to show that the system must maintain information about the analyzers. This is an ambiguity that frequently arises when constructing object models. In general, the ambiguity is harmless, since context makes clear which meaning is intended. However, some modelers adopt a practice of introducing new names to distinguish the class of information objects, which occur inside the system boundary, from the class of entities that the information objects represent, which fall outside the system boundary.

Interface Model

The interface model specifies how the system should interact with its environment. The first step in constructing the interface model is to write down the list of *agents* that the system will interact with. An agent can be anything that communicates with the system. Agents can be people, such as users or system administrators, or equipment, such as printers or manufacturing machinery, or other software systems. The agents in our example are all included in the system object model. They are the technician, the various analyzers, and the labeler. The data management system will need an interface to each of these.

The second step is to iterate through the list of agents and, for each one, to identify the kinds of interactions that can occur between the system and that agent. The technician can initiate behavior in the system by *entering* a request for tests, by requesting the *current status* of a patient's tests, or by *aborting* a series of tests on a patient. The system will respond by *sending* a patient report back to the technician. All these types of interaction can be read off the system object model. Similarly, the analyzers *produce* test results that are sent to the data management system, and the system instructs the labeler to *write* label

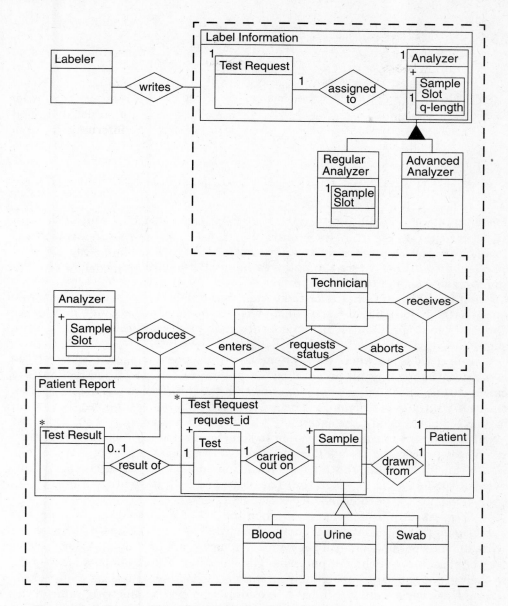

Figure 10 A System Object Model for the Clinical Laboratory

information on sample labels. Figure 11 shows a context diagram that summarizes these observations.

The purpose of building the interface model is to refine and document the understanding of these system interfaces.

Some important interactions may not have been captured on the object

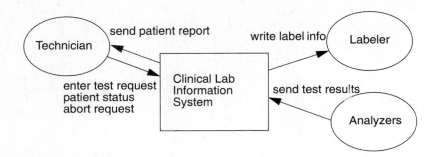

Figure 11 Context Diagram for Clinical Lab Information System

model, and some of the interactions that have been identified may have sub-structure that is important to capture. When we read the requirements docu-ment, it is clear that entering a request for patient tests is not a simple action. The technician first enters the patient's name, then repeatedly enters descrip-tions of samples and tests to be performed, and finally sends a message indicat-ing that the batch of samples for the patient has finished. The processing of tests for a patient does not happen all at once—other system activity may occur between the original entry of the patient's name and the final *batch end* mes-sage.

Interactions between the system and the external agents that can be treated as happening all at once (at an appropriate level of abstraction) are called *events*. These are the units out of which the interface model is built. When the agent initiates the action, the action is called an *input event*; when the action is directed back toward the external agent, it is called an *output event*. An input event is designed to cause the system to behave in some manner. It may change the object's state, and it may give rise to one or more output events. The collec-tion of an input event and all its effects, including state changes and output events, is called a *system operation*. The input and output events and the system operations need to be identified for each agent.

Scenarios are useful aids to building the list of input and output events. A scenario is a time-line diagram representing the system, the agents it interacts with, and one possible ordering of events. Scenarios are useful for exploring com-plex or special-case behavior patterns. They also help the developers locate gaps in their event lists by focusing their attention on concrete situations. Figure 12 is a sample scenario for the Clinical Lab information system, showing some of the possible orderings of input and output events.

Operation model

The operation model defines the behavior of the system by specifying how each system operation affects the system state. Each specification includes informal preconditions and postconditions that describe the effect of the operation on the object model. Even though they are informal, preconditions and postconditions

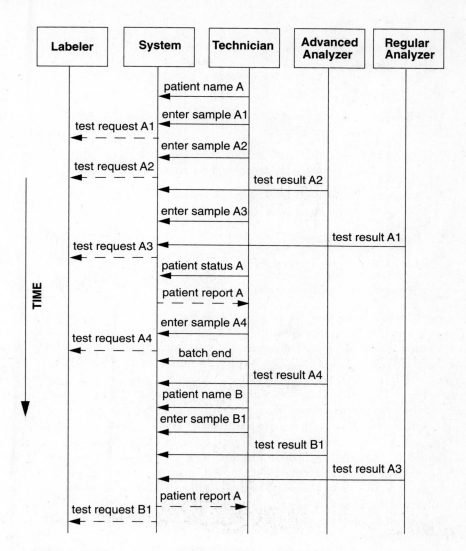

Figure 12 A Scenario for the Clinical Laboratory

must be purely descriptive statements that are either true or false. The specification of a system operation is captured in a table called an *operation schema,* the format of which is shown in Figure 13.

The preconditions and postconditions describe the state of the system in terms of the objects, attributes, and relationships of the system object model. The precondition, which is stated in the **Assumes** field of the operation schema, specifies a property of the system state that must be true if the operation is to have its intended effect. If an operation is invoked in a situation where the pre-

Operation	: name
Description	: informal description of the operation
Reads	: parts of the system state that are read, but not changed
Changes	: parts of the system state that are read and maybe changed
Sends	: messages that are sent by the system to agents in the environment and the agents they are sent to
Assumes	: preconditions—what is assumed about the state before the operation is invoked
Result	: postconditions—how the system changes after the operation completes

Figure 13 Template for an Operation Schema

condition is not true, the effect is undefined. For the operation used to enter a test request to have its intended effect, it must occur between the entry of a patient name and a *batch end* message. During this period, one patient report is marked as current, and all test requests are added to it. The precondition for *enter test request* is simply that there be a current patient report. If there is no current report, the test information cannot be associated with a patient, and the results of the operation are undefined.

A system operation can change the state of the system by creating new objects, by changing the values of an object's attributes, or by adding or deleting tuples from a relationship. These changes are captured in the postcondition, which is recorded in the **Result** clause of the operation schema. The **Result** clause should also specify messages sent to other agents in the environment as a result of the system operation.

The intended effect of the operation for entering test requests is that a new test request object has been created and added to the current patient report, that an analyzer and a slot on the analyzer have been selected for processing the requested test, and that the labeler has been sent information describing the test, the sample, and the analyzer slot that the sample has been assigned to. These effects need to be spelled out explicitly in the **Result** clause of the operation schema.

After the **Assumes** and **Result** clauses have been filled out, objects that play a role in the operation are identified and categorized. Objects that the **Result** clause indicates are either created or modified are listed in the **Changes** field. Newly created objects are marked by adding **new** before their name. Objects referred to in either the **Assumes** or **Result** clauses, but not modified, are listed in the **Reads** field. If an object was supplied as an argument to the system operation, the word **supplied** is added before its name. Finally, any messages that may be sent to agents as a result of invoking the system operation are listed in the **Sends** field. All these features are illustrated in the operation schema for the *enter test request* in Figure 14.

Operation	:	enter test request
Description	:	Enter information about a sample and the test to be performed on it.
Reads	:	**supplied** sample_info **supplied** test_info analyzer
Changes	:	**new** sample **new** test **new** test_request **new** label_info current_patient_report sample_slots of analyzers
Sends	:	labeler:{send_label_info}
Assumes	:	There is a patient report that has been selected as current, current_patient_report.
Result	:	A new test request has been created to hold information about the requested test type and sample; A slot on an analyzer has been selected for use in processing the requested test; The length of the queue for the selected analyzer slot has been incremented by 1; A description of the sample, the test to be performed, and the analyzer slot to be used has been created and sent to the labeler; A new entry for sample and test to be performed on it has been added to the current_patient_report.

Figure 14 Operation Schema for *enter_sample*

Writing the specification for a system operation forces developers to study the requirements closely. Constructing the operation model has been shown in practice to be a powerful tool for revealing problems with the requirements document, enabling developers to identify problems early and to resolve them with the customer, avoiding costly design rework.

Life-cycle expressions

Often the requirements for a system constrain the temporal ordering of system operations and events. The operation schemata can be used to capture some of these constraints through appropriate use of the **Assumes** and **Result** clauses, but in all but the simplest cases, this approach is inadvisable—in part because temporal relations between operations are difficult to see by comparing their pre- and postconditions. Scenarios are a useful alternative for describing ordering among events. However, since they only describe particular sequences, scenarios are not sufficient for delimiting the set of all patterns the system might engage in. This is the role of *life-cycle expressions,* which are essentially regular expression grammars. Figure 15 contains part of a life-cycle expression for the example system. The syntax of life-cycle expressions is presented in Appendix B.

lifecycle ClinLab :   Batch* || Results* || Status*

           Batch =   patient_name .

                            (enter_sample)* .

                            batch_end .

                            [abort]

          Results =   (test_result)*

           Status =   (status_request)*

Figure 15 Life-cycle Expressions

Checking the Analysis

After constructing the object and interface models, the developer must check them for completeness and consistency. The analysis models should be checked against the requirements. In particular, it is important to ensure that all the system operations have been found and that there is no missing functionality. This check can be done by investigating different scenarios; however, since the requirements are informal, there can be no foolproof way of checking them.

The analysis models can be checked for consistency and completeness. The most important check is on the completeness of the object model and operation schemata with respect to each other. Because the interface model is based on the object model, every class, attribute, or relationship mentioned in the operation descriptions must appear in the object model. If this is not the case, the analysis is incomplete and the defect must be remedied. This check has proven to be a very effective way to judge the adequacy of object models. On the other hand, if a class, attribute or relationship in the system object model is never referred to in an operation schema, either it is not needed after all and should be deleted, or the definition of the operation schemata is incomplete, or a special justification for keeping the feature should be documented in the data dictionary. If the analysis models pass these checks, they can be used as the basis of the design.

By the end of analysis, the development team has worked out a detailed understanding of what the software system is to do. The object model gives the team a vocabulary for talking about the system and its environment, and it also provides a starting set of classes to use in designing the system structure. The interface model specifies the interface to the system and describes how the operations on the system relate to each other and how they affect the system state.

DESIGN

The interface model produced during analysis describes the behavior of the system as a whole. A principal task of design is to work out how the system behavior will be realized by the interaction of individual objects. The analysis-time system object model gives the designer an initial collection of classes to describe the possible states of the system. However, much of the system state is represented in relationships between objects, and not in the objects themselves. The design phase is also concerned with allocating responsibility for holding the state expressed by relationships to individual objects. The performance, robustness, and maintainability of the system are greatly affected by how the system behavior and state are broken up and distributed among objects. New objects may also be introduced at design time in order to address nonfunctional system requirements.

The Fusion approach to design focuses first on deciding how the system operations are to be realized. Only toward the end of the design phase, when detailed models of the system behavior have been developed, does the focus return to the structure of the classes. *Object interaction graphs* are constructed to show how objects cooperate to provide the system-level functionality specified by the operation schemata. *Visibility graphs* are used to work out how objects refer to each other, as required by the patterns of communication recorded in the object interaction graphs. *Inheritance graphs* are built to finalize decisions on the generalization/specialization relations between classes, and the results of all the design models are finally summarized in *class descriptions*.

Object Interaction Graphs

An object interaction graph is constructed for each system operation to show what objects are involved in the computation and how they cooperate to realize the functionality specified in the schema for the operation. The goal of developing object interaction graphs is to work out the high-level structure of the computation, to allocate responsibility for parts of the computation to individual objects, and to map out the pattern of communication between the objects required to achieve the overall effect of the system operation.

An object interaction graph describes a pattern of messages flowing among a set of objects. The nodes in the graph represent individual objects or collections of similar objects. Solid rectangles represent individual objects, and dashed rectangles stand for object collections. Every node includes the name of the object and the name of the class that the object belongs to. Objects may be created during the interaction, in which case they are given the annotation **new**.

The arcs in the graph represent messages passed between objects, where the direction of the arrow is from sender to receiver. An arc is annotated with the name of the method, information about its parameters, and where appropriate, the type of the return value. The messages sent by an object are typically constrained to occur in a certain order. *Sequence numbers* are attached to the arcs to indicate which messages must occur before which—lower numbers are associated with messages sent before those having higher numbers.

The first step in constructing an object interaction graph for a system operation is to identify a starting set of objects (and possibly agents) that will be accessed during the execution of the operation. These include the objects mentioned in the **Reads**, **Changes**, and **Sends** clauses of the operation's schema. As the object interaction graph is developed, additional objects may be introduced to help achieve design goals. Examples of such *design objects* include objects whose only purpose is to control the behavior of other objects, objects that serve as interfaces between the system and the user or between one subsystem and another, objects that translate between different protocols or provide a common interface to a heterogeneous collection of servers, and so on.

The next step is to select an object to play the role of *controller*. The controller object receives the request to perform the system operation and then sends messages to other objects, its *collaborators,* as needed to access information or delegate subtasks. The controller may be one of the objects mentioned in the operation schema, or it may be a new design object introduced specifically for the purpose. Figure 16 shows a partial object interaction graph for the *enter test request* operation.

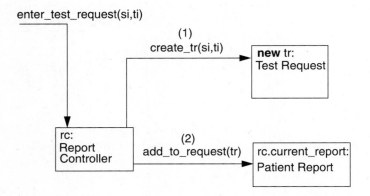

Figure 16 A Simple Object Interaction Graph

A special controller object has been introduced to receive the incoming message. This object, **rc** in the diagram, serves in part to keep track of the patient report that is currently selected, if any, and in part to carry out the highest levels of the algorithm followed for entering test requests. The object interaction graph in Figure 16 shows the **enter_test_request** message routed to the object **rc**. The method evoked in response to this message has, of course, not yet been designed; however, the graph shows that this method will first create a new **Test Request** object, called **tr**, and then, sometime later, it will pass **tr** as an argument to **add_to_request** along to the **current_report** object, which is accessible from **rc**.

Sometimes, two messages are alternatives—only one will actually be sent. When this happens, the same sequence number is assigned to both, distinguished only by primes. An arc can be made conditional by adding a guard clause. A message is sent only if the associated guard condition holds. Also, a collaborator may respond to a message from the controller by sending messages to other objects. In this case, the sequence number of the originating message is attached to the front of the sequence number of the resulting message.

These additional features of object interaction graphs are illustrated in Figure 17, an elaboration of the graph in Figure 16, in which two changes have been made. The **Test Request** object **tr** is now responsible for the creation of the new **Sample** object and the new **Test** object that serve as its parts. The sequence numbers **1.1** and **1.2** indicate that both messages flowing out of **tr** are part of **tr's** response to the incoming **create_tr** message, which has sequence number **1**. The second change is the addition of the error message sent out of the controller **rc** under the condition, expressed by the guard in square brackets below the arrow, that **rc** does not know about a current report. The controller object sends the error message instead of creating a new test request if the guard is true. Because sending the error message and creating the test request are alternatives, they

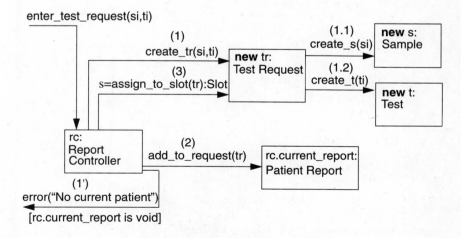

Figure 17 An Elaborated Object Interaction Graph

are both given the sequence number **1**, differentiated by the use of a prime.

In the examples shown so far, all the nodes in an object interaction graph represent individual objects. It is also possible to introduce nodes that designate collections of similar objects, shown as dashed rectangles. In the case of collections, the object name acts as a variable ranging over the members of the collection. An arc flowing into a collection node indicates that the message is sent to all the objects in the collection satisfying any guards on the arc. When an arc leaves a collection node, all that is indicated is that some object in the collection might send the message.

Figure 18 shows the final version of the object interaction graph for the *enter test report* operation. Two collection nodes have been introduced, one representing the collection of available analyzers and the other standing for the collection of sample slots for a particular chosen analyzer, designated as **a**. These collections are involved in deciding which analyzer slot should be used for processing the test request. In the design captured in Figure 18, the responsibility for choosing an analyzer slot has been assigned to the new **Test Request** object, which queries the available analyzers to discover their status. The analyzers in turn ask their sample slots for information about the length of their queues, which they return as integers. The analyzers send the relevant status information back to **tr**, which uses the information to make its choice. The selected sample slot is finally returned to the controller, which passes it on to the labeler, along with information about the test request.

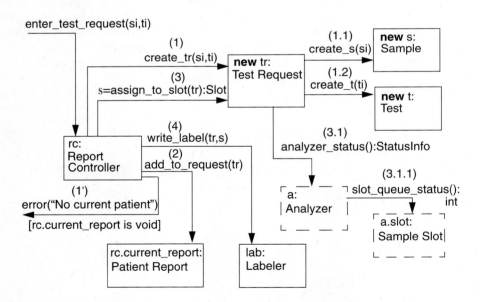

Figure 18 A Complete Object Interaction Graph

The object interaction graph for the *enter test request* system operation is now complete. Much work remains before the system operation is implemented. Nothing has been said, for instance, about the algorithm for selecting an analyzer slot once the status of the analyzers is known. However, we now know all the objects that will be involved in the implementation, how the program logic is to be divided up and parceled out among the objects, and what possible message flows will need to be supported. The design is complete in that it has assigned responsibility to specific objects for all the state changes specified during analysis in the schema for the operation.

Visibility Graphs

When an object interaction graph is constructed, it is assumed that all objects are mutually visible. In an implementation, objects only have limited visibility and the sender of each message requires a reference to the receiver object. Several options are available for storing and managing object references, and the next step of the design process deals with these.

A visibility graph is constructed for each class, including those design classes introduced while building object interaction graphs. The visibility graph for a class shows the links between instances of the class and other objects. A *link* is a reference held by one object to another object that it communicates with. A link is represented in a visibility graph by a directed arrow from the class to a referenced object or object collection. Objects and collections of objects are represented with the same syntax used in object interaction graphs. Each arc in an object interaction graph must be associated with a link in a visibility graph; however, the same link may be used for several arcs, possibly contained in different object interaction graphs.

Links to objects can be permanent or dynamic. A permanent link is represented by a solid arc and a dynamic link by a dashed arc. A link is *dynamic* if it is only required in the context of one execution of the system operation. *Permanent* links indicate that the class requires a reference to the server object beyond the duration of the execution of the system operation. Thus permanent object links are used when an object of a class needs the same reference in several contexts. A dynamic link corresponds to an object identifier that is passed as a parameter or is computed at runtime when a new object is created, while a permanent link is likely to show up in the implementation as an object-valued attribute.

In the example object interaction graph of Figure 18, the link between the **Report Controller** object **rc** and the test request is dynamic—**rc** will never need to send a message to the same test request after it has finished processing the call to the system operation. However, the link between **rc** and the current patient report is permanent, since it must be maintained throughout all the test requests in the same batch.

Another feature of a reference that can be captured in visibility graphs is its *mutability*. Some references, once initialized, cannot be changed, while others can. A reference from a **Sample** to the **Patient** it was drawn from is *constant*—a sample cannot change its patient over time. A reference is marked as constant in the visibility graph by including the word **constant** before the name of the referenced object. In the example shown in Figure 19, the link between the report controller and the labeler is marked as constant, since the identity of the labeler will not change between the times the report controller is created and destroyed.

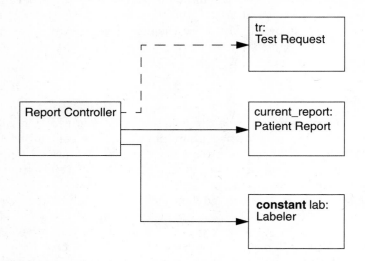

Figure 19 A Visibility Graph for Report Controller

   In addition to documenting the duration and mutability of links, a visibility graph indicates whether the server object is referenced *exclusively* by the client or whether it is shared (i.e., whether other objects can have a reference to it at the same time). If one object has an exclusive reference to another, then all communication to the referenced object must pass through the object that holds the reference; the server object depends on the client object for all its communications.

   Sometimes the relation between two objects is even closer. The existence of one object may depend on the existence of another. In this case, the dependent object is said to be *bound* to the other. If an object depends on another both for its communication and its existence, it can be implemented as part of the structure of the other object, rather than as an object with its own identity.

   Exclusive objects are denoted in visibility graphs by double borders. When one object is bound to another, its box is drawn inside the box of the other. The visibility graph for the **Analyzer** class in Figure 20 shows that analyzer objects have exclusive reference to the **Sample Slot** objects, since no other class has need to access them, and that sample slots are bound to their analyzers.

   By the time the visibility graphs have been completed, information expressed during analysis as relationships has been allocated to objects or to the messages flowing between objects. Some relationships have turned into object-valued attributes, some have become parameters in messages or local variables

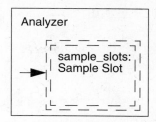

Figure 20 A Visibility Graph with a Bound and Exclusive Reference

in methods, and some have been realized by physically embedding one object structure inside another. These design decisions were driven by the needs of the objects to support the system behavior, as represented in the object interaction graphs.

Class Descriptions and Inheritance Graphs

Developers make most of their significant design decisions while constructing the object interaction graphs and the visibility graphs. They spend the final stages of design repackaging information from the models into a form more suitable for implementation. They build *class descriptions* to collate information from the object model, the object interaction graphs, and visibility graphs. Then they develop *inheritance graphs* from the class descriptions to clean up the class inheritance hierarchy. Finally, they update the class descriptions to take the new inheritance structure into account.

A class description is a textual summary of design decisions that affects the implementation of a class. After the visibility graphs are complete, a class description is produced for each class mentioned in an object interaction graph. Data attributes are read off the system object model for those classes introduced during analysis. Object-valued attributes are gathered from permanent links on the visibility graphs, annotated as appropriate. Methods and parameters are extracted from the object interaction graphs, as modified where necessary from dynamic links in the visibility graphs. Physical aggregation is also detected by reviewing the visibility graphs. When all this information about a class has been gathered, it is written down, as illustrated in Figure 21.

At analysis time, some classes may have been described as generalizations of others. Now that classes have taken on the results of a great many design decisions, the question of what classes should be generalized or specialized needs to be revisited. The class descriptions are examined to see if the specialization/ generalization relations recorded in the object model represent significant opportunities to share attributes and methods between different classes. New opportunities for generalizing are also identified at this stage, which may lead to the introduction of additional design classes. The same notation used in the object model to express generalization/specialization relations is now used to construct

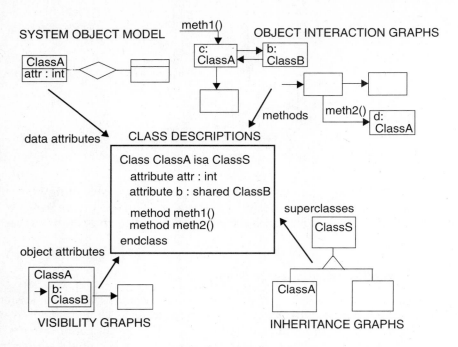

Figure 21 Class Descriptions Collect Information from Other Models

an inheritance graph that shows all the classes in the system and how they inherit from each other.

The final step in design is to add class descriptions for any new classes introduced during construction of the inheritance graphs and then to add information in all the class descriptions about which classes inherit from which. The class descriptions, now completed, are readily mapped into the class declarations of an object-oriented programming language. The object interaction graphs provide sketches of the algorithms needed to implement the methods on the classes. It is these two sets of design documents—the class descriptions and the object interaction graphs—that will drive the implementation activity.

Checking the Design

The most important check of the design models is to ensure that each object interaction graph satisfies the specification given in the operation schema for the corresponding system operation. This check can be performed through design reviews. The scenarios developed during analysis can be used to check that sequences of system operations work correctly. Also, all the classes in the system object model should appear in at least one object interaction graph. If a class does not play a role in realizing any system operation, there is no reason to implement it.

Visibility graphs should be checked for consistency with the system object model and the object interaction graphs. Relationships inside the system boundary in the system object model are realized by links in the visibility graphs. If a relationship exists that does not correspond to any links, either the relationship was not relevant after all, or something may be missing from the visibility graphs. The visibility graphs should also be compared with the object interaction graphs to check that every method that needs to be sent is supported by a link. Visibility graphs must also be internally consistent. For instance, if a class has an exclusive link to an object, then no other class should have a link to the same object.

Class descriptions and inheritance graphs should be checked together to make sure that classes have all the attributes and methods required by the object model, object interaction graphs, and visibility graphs.

CONCLUSION

The Fusion process has been presented as a sequence of steps designed to take the software development team through the construction of various models in an order in part dictated by the dependencies between the models. In practice, customizations of the method are frequently justified—certain models may be skipped, others introduced, and variations on the suggested ordering may be appropriate (Malan et al. 1995). The Fusion models do not cover all important design decisions for all classes of software. Some of the missing elements that Fusion practitioners have found useful for dealing with real-time requirements, concurrency and distributed systems, for instance, are described in the following papers. Also, Fusion is not intended to address all issues pertaining to defining a good product development life cycle. Several of the papers discuss how Fusion can be effectively embedded in project management processes. Fusion will evolve as the results of experience in using it are collected. The papers in this book are a sampling of that experience.

ACKNOWLEDGMENTS

This Fusion Overview is based on an earlier description of Fusion written by Derek Coleman, Paul Jeremaes and Chris Dollin.

REFERENCES

Coleman D., P. Arnold, S. Bodoff, C. Dollin, H. Gilchrist, F. Hayes, and P. Jeremaes. 1994. *Object-Oriented Development: The Fusion Method*. Englewood Cliffs, NJ: Prentice Hall.

Jacobson, I., M. Christerson, P. Jonsson, and G. Övergaard. 1992. *Object-Oriented Software Engineering*. Reading, MA: Addison-Wesley.

Malan, R., R. Letsinger, and D. Coleman. 1995. Lessons from the Experiences of Leading-edge Object Technology Projects in Hewlett-Packard. To be published in *Proceedings of OOPSLA'95*, October 15–19, Austin, Texas.

Case Studies

*F*usion use has grown considerably since OOPSLA'93, when it was first made available to the objects community. In that time, many projects have used Fusion and gained invaluable insights into successful practices, pitfalls, and the real benefits of object-oriented analysis and design (OOA/D) in general, and Fusion in particular.

The two case studies in Part 1 do more than describe experiences with Fusion. They provide a rare opportunity to look closely at real-world projects that begin with a loosely defined notion of a product and have to surmount a variety of technical and organizational challenges as progress is made toward getting the product out. Both papers offer candid pointers to pitfalls encountered in these projects' first use of OO development methods, implementation languages, and tools. They share with the reader hard-won lessons about what works well and why, and how to address many of the challenges that arise in OO projects. Practitioners just embarking on OO development will find the discussion and insights rewarding preparation; practitioners who have already engaged in OO development will likely find some helpful new insights, along with validation of lessons already learned.

In "Transition to Object Technology Using Fusion Pilot Projects: A Case Study," Jerremy Holland relates the experiences of an object technology pilot project that he initiated and championed at a Hewlett-Packard division. The paper provides guidance on planning and conducting the first pilot project and will be of interest to those considering the move to OO development. It also deals with the pragmatics of OO development, including project management and reuse considerations, tips on how to round out the Fusion process in the area of requirements analysis and testing, assistance in tool selection, and advice on setting up standards and templates. Of course, these topics provide vital guidance to those just embarking on OO projects, but they are also of interest to managers and engineers who have already gained some exposure to OO development.

Another Hewlett-Packard project is the subject of the second case study. "Using Fusion on a Hewlett–Packard Medical Imaging Project: Analysis Phase Retrospective" provides a blow-by-blow account of the challenges and successes of a medical product development team that adopted Fusion to help analyze and design a breakthrough product. Focusing on the analysis phase, Ron Falcone and his co-authors report the team's experiences in dealing with the challenges associated with producing a revolutionary product and using object technology for the first time. The paper describes organization and process issues encountered by the team and practices they found successful in dealing with those issues. It also covers technical areas, for example describing the extensions to Fusion that the team found helpful.

In both case studies, Fusion was viewed by the teams as key to managing the risks associated with the move to object technology.

Transition to Object Technology Using Fusion Pilot Projects: A Case Study

Jerremy Holland

Hewlett–Packard

1.1 INTRODUCTION

Object technology was introduced into one of the Hewlett–Packard telecommunications divisions via a pilot project that delivered network simulation and test tools to internal customers. The success of the pilot project led to the use of object technology in the development of production systems. This paper describes the pilot project and draws on the lessons learned in both the pilot project and the mainstream OO development efforts to present an approach to successful object technology adoption. Specific examples from the case study are used to illustrate what was learned in applying Fusion to pilot the use of object technology.

1.1.1 Overview

The goal of this paper is to help managers and engineers tackle the problems that arise in the transition to object technology.

The use of pilot projects and Fusion are central to the approach to object technology adoption developed in this paper. Pilot projects demonstrate the benefits of an object-oriented approach and help control the risks associated with introducing a new technology. The Fusion method helps reduce the risks associated with object-oriented developments by providing a road map to drive software development from requirements analysis through to implementation. The paper details other techniques to help minimize development risks, including the utilization of incremental development and subsystems.

The approach taken throughout this paper is forward-looking so that the project management and software development scaffolding put in place for the pilot projects can be used as evolutionary stepping-stones toward organization-wide object technology utilization. This paper also provides some practical suggestions for testing object-oriented software. All the tips presented in this paper can be applied to new and existing OO developments to reduce risk.

Target audience

If you are, or could be, a champion of object technology in your organization, you will find the information, experience, and recommendations that are provided in this paper useful. In particular, this paper is targeted to

- Managers or software development engineers who want to know how to reduce the risks of object-oriented software development
- Managers or software development engineers who are considering a first attempt at using object technology
- R&D or division managers considering the introduction or adoption of object technology to their organization

Structure

The paper is organized into the following major sections:

- Introducing object technology into a software development organization
- Project management
- Complementing the Fusion development process
- Development environment
- Reuse
- Results of the pilot project

Each topic that is covered is composed of three parts: an introduction to the topic, results from the pilot project case study, and recommendations based on what was learned addressing the topic in a real development environment.

1.1.2   Pilot Project Overview

Hewlett–Packard is a large corporation consisting of many organizations, each containing a number of divisions. Across these divisions, experience with object technology varies. A few divisions were very early adopters of object technology. A greater number have moved to object technology in more recent years. This case study describes the use of Fusion in the first object technology pilot developments completed in one of these "early follower" divisions.

Project description

The object technology pilot project developed two related products, a telecommunication network simulator and an automated test network, for in-house use. Both are software tools for system-level testing of a distributed system. These tools were used to automate what had been a manual process, so the projects were important, but any delays delivering the tools would not affect customer shipments or the quality of testing already underway.

Development and execution environment
The pilot developments consisted of distributed processes on HP Workstations executing HP-UX and were implemented in C++.

Development team
Figure 1.1 shows the staffing profile for the pilot project. Initially, I was the only member of the development team. I spent time up front, collecting requirements for the system and getting buy-in for the use of object technology. The next person to join the team was an engineer experienced in object technology. She spent a couple of months contributing to the development of the analysis models and some prototype work before being moved to another project. At this time, the first external recruit, a contract software engineer, experienced with objects and C++, joined the team. He contributed to the review and refinement of both analysis and design models and then began implementation of one subsystem. Two months later, the second external recruit, a student working on her masters thesis for a software engineering degree (focusing on object technology) joined the team and began development of the next subsystem. One month later, two external recruits who were experienced object practitioners joined the team, each focusing on a subsystem. Two integrations of the subsystems were completed before the staffing was reduced. Mainstream use of the products of the pilot was initiated only 10 months after the project began.

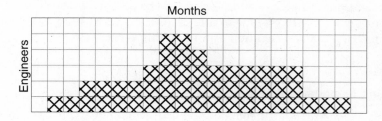

Figure 1.1 Pilot Project Staffing Profile

Results
The pilot project succeeded in delivering two tools that met the needs of their internal customers. These products were delivered on schedule and have proved to be both flexible and extensible—they are still in use and have been modified and extended in functionality without redesign.

Following the pilot project, there has been increased support in the division for the use of object technology. The engineers involved in the initial pilot were seeded into other development teams, and some of them are involved in mainstream application development projects that use object technology exclusively.

The Fusion method has been carried over from the pilot and is now being used in the mainstream projects. Both the third-party and internally developed class libraries have been utilized in the follow-on object technology projects.

In summary, the pilot development using Fusion resulted in wider use of object technology and the decision to use the technology on products developed for external customers.

1.2 INTRODUCING OBJECT TECHNOLOGY INTO A SOFTWARE DEVELOPMENT ORGANIZATION

A number of steps[*] are required to successfully introduce object technology in a software development organization. The first step is gaining management approval to pursue new, and therefore "risky," technology in an organization that needs to make money. As part of getting management buy-in, the benefits of object technology are explained in general terms, and a broad-brush plan for reducing any risks is outlined. Next, specific examples of where object technology is appropriate for use within the organization's domain of development are identified. A pilot project is selected from the candidate projects. In preparation for the pilot, an OOA/D method must be chosen. With this foundation in place, the pilot team can be created and trained. As the pilot project progresses, its successes need to be made visible to enlist long-term support for object technology. Each of these steps is discussed in the sections that follow.

At the outset, an Object Technology Champion is needed to help motivate the introduction of object technology and guide the organization through the transition. This role will have its ultimate rewards, but if you take on the challenge, be patient and diligent—there is much work ahead. As the Object Technology Champion, you will have to spend a lot of time addressing the concerns of various people in your organization and becoming a respected object technology resource.

1.2.1 Getting Management Buy-in

Management authorization is needed for object technology to be test driven in an organization. Getting management support involves showing that the use of the new technology makes good business sense and that any perceived risk is being minimized.

The following questions illustrate some of the issues managers face when approving the use of new technology:

- What are the benefits? Will it be cost effective?
- Will the delivery of the product be delayed?
- Will there be any friction in the organization due to unfamiliar practices associated with the new technology?

---

[*] See also Edward Yourdon's chapter entitled "The OO Battle Plan" (Yourdon 1994), which describes a set of steps that may be taken to help introduce object technology into an organization.

- Will the lack of management experience with the technology cause any problems?
- Are there other risks associated with the new technology?

Case Study

Convincing management to take a risk
Although we did not have to provide a detailed business case for the introduction of object technology, we had to show that the use of the technology would benefit the kinds of projects our division undertakes.

First I solicited the support of my manager. He, in turn, suggested that I prepare a white paper describing the advantages of object technology. In this paper I focused on advantages that object technology would bring to our organization's specific problem domain. I presented the paper to the R&D manager and the division manager.

The following factors convinced management to try object technology:

- The enthusiastic support of my manager
- The suitability of object technology for a number of suggested applications
- I worked very hard to champion the use of object technology

Existence of systematic OOA/D methods strengthened the case
Another big factor in getting management buy-in was our decision to adopt a systematic OOA/D method. Early in my campaign to get support for the use of object technology, I began to survey the methods supported in the software development community. The existence of methods for applying object technology was seen to be a risk-reducing factor. By presenting some of the approaches to developing object-based software as well as describing the advantages of object technology, I was able to achieve a high enough "feel-good factor" that further investigation was approved.

Recommendations
One of your first tasks as Object Technology Champion is to gain management buy-in by providing information and addressing concerns about the role of objects in your organization.

Get approval at two levels
The main thing to remember is that you should be trying to get at least two levels of management buy-in:

- Get your manager to support your use of object technology.
- Go to the top. Make the head of your organization aware of the advantages of object technology. Also make sure that he or she is aware of the risks associated with applying any new technology for the first time. Make every effort to get high-level management support.

Host an object technology mind-set course

You can start by hosting a mind-set course that presents some of the business and technical advantages of object technology without going into the details of how it is applied. Although all managers should be strongly encouraged to attend, it is a good idea to include developers to help build a ground swell of interest in object technology.

Set the vision—think globally, act locally

Know where you are heading before you start your journey.

It pays to develop a vision of how you expect object technology to pay off in the long run. If you bear in mind that a pilot project is just the first step toward the goal of organization-wide adoption of object technology, you will take steps early that will pay off in the long run. But if you try to solve *all* the organizational issues related to its adoption, you are sure to fail. Establish and maintain the vision of where you want your organization to end up (e.g., everyone using object technology or having an established reuse program) and make sure everything you do on the pilot is in alignment with a path toward that ideal vision.

Don't try to change the world...yet.

Feed the hype machine—carefully

Feed the hype machine carefully; if you are not careful it can backfire.

Make sure that you are setting everyone's expectations correctly. Dispel OO myths, but show that the organization's object technology vision and strategy will, if followed, realize some of the longer-term OO advantages. For example, do not promote reuse as anything but a long-term benefit of object technology that has a start-up cost. Be very clear about what you and others (especially your manager) can expect to get from object technology in the short term and long term. Don't kid yourself—it will take lots of time and energy to get things moving. So feed the hype machine, but feed it carefully with realistic information.

1.2.2   Selecting a Pilot Project

Like all new technology, object technology needs to be validated and demonstrated to the organization (Yourdon 1994). A pilot project is the best way to prove that it can succeed and also serves to build a strong team of object technology practitioners. Immersing a team in object technology for at least six months will do more than any theoretical study or investigation to prove the value and appropriateness of the new technology.

Case Study

Why pilot object technology?

By this time, object technology was seen to be important to the future of our organization. However, introducing object technology in a major product development effort was too risky because there was limited experience with it in our division and the delivery pressures for developments destined for external customers was too great. Therefore, approval was granted to pilot object technology on a project with internal customers.

What was the best project for the pilot?

A set of system-level simulation and test tools being developed from the ground up for internal use seemed the ideal proving ground. Our goal was to develop a system that would allow the automation of tasks that were being done manually. Although this project was very important and very visible, it did not face the same sort of delivery risk that would be associated with an external development.

We received approval to apply object technology on this internal test tool because it met the selection criteria for the pilot:

- It was not mission critical.
- It did not have committed customer delivery dates (yet).

Also, object technology was well suited to the product because

- Its requirements would be quite dynamic over the lifetime of the development, so extensibility was important.
- It had to be of high quality and provide reasonable performance.
- Encapsulation, inheritance, and polymorphism can all be useful tools in the modeling of network elements and protocols.

Recommendations

If you do not have complete support from the management at your company for the use of object technology, you should pilot the technology to provide examples of success. Remember,

- If you put your effort into telling others what they should do to succeed in applying object technology, they probably will not listen.
- If you successfully apply object technology, others will want to know how you did it.

Choose a project of the right size

Size is an important consideration in the choice of a pilot project. One that is too big will add undue risk and will undoubtedly be under considerable pressure. On the other hand, if a very small project succeeds in using object technology, there will be people who discount the success by saying "Yes, it worked, but that wasn't a *real* development project." Make sure that your pilot *is* a real project with real (internal or external) customers. The pilot project should ideally require at least six months of calendar time and involve three or more engineers.

Establish success criteria for the pilot

Before starting, you should define the success criteria for the pilot project, making it clear to the engineers on your team, peer development teams, and management how the success of your project will be determined. You do not want to reach the end of the pilot project not knowing (and not being able to explain to others) why the project either was or was not a success.

Watch out for political pitfalls before you start

As you are looking for candidate pilot projects, choose your testing ground carefully. If there are clear signals that some part of your organization is hallowed ground that is not to be disturbed, it is probably not a good idea to even suggest that object technology be piloted in that area—even if it is the perfect proving ground. When hunting for a fit for object technology, try to find an environment where change would be welcomed from the start; there you will be much more likely to succeed.

1.2.3   Adopting an OO Development Method to Minimize Risk

An OO development method like Fusion helps reduce risk by providing the models and steps that allow appropriate separation of concerns and sequencing of engineering decisions. By applying an object-oriented analysis and design (OOA/D) method, errors that would otherwise have far-reaching ramifications and costs can be caught early in the development life cycle.

Moreover, Fusion is a very good method to choose for a first effort at applying object technology because it prescribes a specific approach to get from requirements analysis to implementation. It defines deliverables for each stage along the way and provides initial checklists for the deliverables that assist developers and managers in deciding when to progress to the next step of the development process.

Thus, besides providing a reasonable set of notations to capture object-oriented analysis and design models, Fusion presents a road map for software development. The "Fusion Process Summary" in Appendix A of the book by Coleman et al. (1994) provides a good overview of the steps, deliverables, and checks in the Fusion process. The steps can fit either a spiral or "V" development life-cycle model. Therefore, the Fusion road map leads developers and managers along a route that will easily support incremental/evolutionary development approaches, which can be used to minimize risk.

Because the steps and deliverables of Fusion are clearly defined, integrating the use of Fusion into an organization with an established development life cycle should be simplified.

Case Study

Choosing the method

Prior to the pilot project kickoff, some time was spent reviewing several OOA/D methods. Fusion was chosen to be the least-risk path because it provided a clear set of steps and deliverables to help manage the development life cycle.

For the first pilot project using Fusion, we chose to use Lightweight Fusion as described by Coleman et al. (1994), because the project had quite short time scales. Also, the team members had not used Fusion before, so the lightweight version entailed less of a learning curve.

Integrating Fusion with existing development life cycle reduces risk
Because Fusion recommends an approach and defines deliverables, we were able to reduce the work needed to integrate Fusion into the existing software development life cycle in the division. This reduction in effort increased our chances of successfully using Fusion.

Fusion helps to maintain momentum
Having a definition of the deliverables and checklists for those deliverables provided a framework that helped us maintain development momentum. The team did not experience the "stall" phase that often occurs when figuring out how to apply a new technology, concept, or approach.

Recommendations

If your organization uses software development methods to help control development, adopt an OOA/D method as part of your OO kickoff. If your organization has not used development methods in the past, make sure that you definitely, for a fact, adopt an existing OOA/D method to start you off in the right direction. Your use of an OOA/D method will be seen by management as a concrete step that you have taken to reduce the risk that you add to a project by adopting a new technology. You get an added bonus in that the use of a method can actually make your life easier by providing a notation and a plan of attack.

Don't try to change too many things at once
You may have a list 27 pages long of things that you would like to change to improve the efficiency or effectiveness of your team—but don't try to change too many things at once. In particular, if your organization does not use software development methods, does not have documented processes, and does not use object technology, don't try to change all these aspects in your first pilot project. Approach the adoption of object technology as an evolutionary activity. Try to identify the actions that will have the biggest impact on the success of your project. Follow through on these and focus on the success of your project. If you feel that you are spreading yourself too thin, you probably are—try to do less, better.

Using Fusion can help you focus your energy. Adopt the notation and process recommended in the Fusion book and focus on applying the method successfully. If you have processes in your organization, fit what you learn about Fusion into your existing software development process. Whatever you do, don't try to write or rewrite all your organization's processes while you are trying to learn and apply object technology.

Take the time to become a respected object technology resource
As Object Technology Champion, you will need to invest the effort required to become an object technology resource capable of providing guidance in applying the chosen OOA/D method. You will be most effective if you have been through courses and workshops yourself, know your own limitations, and have a knowledgeable consultant to call on when the going gets rough. You don't necessarily have to have all the answers, but you will need to know where you can find

answers quickly if you don't already have them. Plan on spending quite a large amount of extra time making sure that you know what you are talking about and have applied the techniques that you are recommending.

1.2.4   Creating the Team and Developing Momentum

For the first OO project in an organization, there are two primary options for creating the pilot project team:

- Hire experienced object technologists
- Get experienced software engineers that are already in the organization and turn them into object technologists

Because experienced object technologists are still somewhat scarce, it is less likely that new hires will have domain experience too. A combination of the two options allows the pilot project to bring some domain experts up to speed on objects, while infusing the team with OO experience.

In addition to finding the right staff for the pilot project, some further groundwork will allow the new team to become productive quickly. This includes planning the training program (covered in the next subsection). It also involves establishing the development infrastructure (e.g., setting up appropriate standards, templates, processes, top-level system models, or plans) so that the development team never feels that it is floating without direction or support. Establishing this framework is especially important on the pilot project because the use of new technology alone can be discouraging for a development team.

Case Study

Creating the development team
The creation of the team that was to work on the pilot object technology development coincided with growth in our division. With the exception of myself as the team leader, it worked out that the team was built entirely of engineers who were new to the organization. We recruited permanent and contract staff with strong object technology experience. Although everyone on this newly formed team had experience with objects, none had experience with Fusion.

Developing momentum
Prior to the creation of the team, work had begun on specifying the system requirements, performing the system-level analysis, and establishing a system architecture. This groundwork was especially important for us, because the other team members were new to the product domain.

Recommendations

Creating the team
For the pilot project, a mix of domain experts and experienced object technologists is desirable, but not essential. As long as you can find engineers who either know objects or are willing and able to learn about them, your team is ready to

go. The main thing to remember is that if you are trying to create object technologists you will need some help.

Provide the project groundwork early

In parallel with your team-building efforts (or prior to building the team), it is a good idea to take the time to lay a foundation for the team. Put in place as much scaffolding as possible to support the development effort. Your goal should be to put in place everything that the team will need to be immediately productive.

Assuming that you already have an initial project plan, you should also prepare a development strategy document to provide a high-level vision of how the project is going to get from day 1 to shipment release. Even a bullet-point strategy with reasoning will give team members a clear and concrete vision that will supplement the project plan and the development process defined for the project.

You should also take a first pass through some of the high-level analysis and system decomposition. It is often a lot easier to review, criticize, and improve something than to create it in the first place. Providing a new team with a framework for the system will give them the vision of how the pieces of the project might fit together. It is better to have some model of the system on day 1, even if it is totally rewritten on day 2.

Find a consultant who you know is an object technologist and not just a hype monger. As object technology becomes more and more popular, many people will bill themselves as object experts, without knowing much more than some of the terms and catch phrases. Watch out for these people! If you have the luxury of time before your team joins the project, a trusted consultant (with a signed nondisclosure agreement, of course) can help you put together some of the initial analysis models and system decompositions.

Whatever work you can do to provide a foundation for the rest of the development needed on the project will certainly give your team a jump-start. By developing draft processes, strategies, models, decompositions, and the like, you will allow your team to hit the ground running.

1.2.5   Developing OO Skills

The need to invest in training was one of the most important lessons cited by early adopters of object technology (Taligent 1994). Gaining experience is also vital. Love (1993) says that "qualified object-oriented software engineers can be created in a year." This is because effective use of objects is something that is learned by applying the concepts of object technology again and again. Often people mistakenly believe that sending a good C programmer to a C++ course will make that person an object technology specialist. Success will only be achieved when the practitioner is able to recognize objects and patterns of objects that lead to strong object-oriented designs. Such insight into OOA/D requires practice, and once the penny drops you will never look at software problems again without seeing objects.

Case Study

Training

We did not organize any training during the pilot developments. Lack of training did not cause any catastrophes because all the engineers were experienced with object technology and the group was relatively small. However, building a common foundation in object technology would have been useful.

After the completion of the pilot projects, I brought in an external consultant to present a mind-set course for anyone interested in object technology. This course was well received.

The go-ahead was given to apply object technology on a mainstream application being developed for external customers. The team that was created for this mainstream development contained some engineers from the original pilot and some engineers who were relatively new to object technology. I organized a one week tutorial/workshop on OOA/D for this team. The course was held in-house and was also attended by engineers on other development teams. This workshop very effectively pulled the team together and got everyone thinking and, more importantly, talking in common terms.

Recommendations

Failure to provide training at the start of the project will just waste time and money. Prior to starting an object technology pilot project, you should find an object technologist who can provide training and consultancy. For team members who are new to objects, an OO concepts or mind-set course is a good idea.

As soon as the team is on board, you should get the consultant in to run an object technology workshop with the goal of applying OOA/D to a vertical slice through the actual project that the team is working on. Focusing the workshop on solving problems that are part of the project will help in two ways:

- The time spent in the workshop actually contributes to progress on your project and is a great way to build up momentum quickly.
- As a team, you work through concrete examples in *your* problem domain, instead of the problem domain chosen by a book or an instructor.

Get everyone speaking the same language

Whether you are building a new team from experienced object technology engineers or from engineers who have never used object technology, the workshop should involve all team members and the team manager. Often people who are "experienced" with object technology have used a variety of methods or an ad-hoc approach in applying the technology. Focusing on a single method and running a workshop is the best way to get the team's terminology and views in sync. For a team to work effectively, it is essential that everyone on the team understand what the other team members are talking about. A workshop is a great way to get everyone on the team sync'ed up and storming ahead.

Budget for consulting assistance

You should have experts available for consultation throughout your initial efforts to apply object technology. The ongoing use of consultants is important not only to provide a sanity check on the work being done, but also to show management that you are taking steps to reduce risk.

Steps to becoming fluent in objects

The following steps will help you accelerate the creation of an object-oriented software engineer:

1. *Start off with a qualified software engineer.*

2. *Learn the fundamentals.*
   - Attend an object technology mind-set course.
   - Read an introduction to object technology; see Booch (1994), Cox and Novobilski (1991), Jacobson et al. (1992), Love (1993), Taylor (1990) and Yourdon (1994) for good introductions to objects with plenty of useful ideas.
   - Learn the steps for OOA/D using Fusion; read Coleman et al. (1994). The Fusion method provides a good road map that describes how to apply object technology.
   - Read books on other OOA/D methods; for example, Booch (1994), Rumbaugh et al. (1991), and Martin and Odell (1992). Coleman et al. (1994) present a brief overview of several methods.
   - Attend a week-long workshop on object-oriented analysis and design.
   - Learn an object-oriented language, but don't fall into the trap of driving the OOA/D by the limitations of the language.

3. *Learn from the experience of other object technology practitioners.*
   - Spend some time understanding the classic examples of object technology (e.g., the Smalltalk-80 environment; see Goldberg 1985).
   - Read about object technology idioms and design patterns that can be utilized in object-oriented developments; see Gamma et al. (1995).
   - If you are using C++, study C++ tips (Meyers 1992, Taligent 1994) and idioms (Coplien 1992), and get a good toolkit class library (e.g., tools.h++ from RogueWave).
   - Join local object technology interest groups to network with others who are or have been in your position.
   - If you work in a large corporation, search for others in your company who may be pursuing object technology.
   - Follow network news groups that discuss object technology and object-oriented languages.
   - Acquire e-mail addresses of experienced object practitioners and utilize their knowledge when troubleshooting problems and discussing object-related issues.

4. *Gain experience.*
   - Practice, practice, practice. Apply the object technology concepts to

things around you—don't just keep rehashing the infamous automated teller machine (ATM) example.

- Get an object technology expert to help with analysis and design through review or workshop-oriented development of analysis and design models.
- Apply everything you have learned on several small projects.

1.2.6 Ensuring Long-term Support

Ensuring ongoing, long-term support for the use of object technology involves finding opportunities to promote managers' and engineers' understanding of OO development and its associated benefits. Therefore, as the pilot progresses and particularly upon its completion, successes should be made visible. Measures taken to avoid or overcome any pitfalls that the pilot team encounters should also be shared.

Case Study

Provide management with object technology success stories
During the pilot project, we took steps to demonstrate the successes of object technology. We provided demonstrations of intermediate system integrations for both functional (R&D) and divisional managers. The demonstrations helped to increase the visibility of our team's successes.

All members of the team kept an eye open for external success stories, both during and after the pilot, so that we were able to give a constant stream of information to management to identify the advantages and costs of object technology. Our goal was to provide management with justifications for using the technology so that they could effortlessly field questions from their managers.

Present an object technology vision to strategic groups
Following the pilot project, I presented information about object technology to a high-level strategy team in our organization. My presentation included both the short successes already seen in the division and some of the longer-term benefits of object technology, as well as the costs associated with those benefits.

Provide a retrospective presentation following the pilot project
Unfortunately, we did not undertake a retrospective review and presentation following the object technology pilot. Not providing closure on the pilot was a mistake. The lessons learned were not documented and presented for all to learn from. Equally, the clear successes were not summarized and presented for all to see.

The lack of a final retrospective on the pilot project meant that information about the successes and failures of the pilot was disseminated in an ad-hoc manner, by word of mouth. By not broadcasting our successes and not highlighting the hurdles that we overcame, we missed an opportunity to promote the long-term success of object technology. Be sure that you do not miss this opportunity!

Recommendations

Provide ongoing object technology education

Continue the flow of information and education opportunities beyond the initial buy-in. Don't think that because you got the green light your job as an Object Technology Champion is over. Actually, it has only started. You must make every effort to educate everyone in your organization about object technology, and you must keep information flowing throughout the organization.

Don't get labeled as a religious zealot

Make sure that you are not the only one pointing out the benefits of object technology. Encourage others, especially experienced team members who are new to object technology, to publicize successes. The views of well-respected engineers who are new to object technology will be highly valued by management. To continue to strengthen the organizational buy-in for object technology, people in the organization other than yourself must become enthusiastic about objects. If you end up getting labeled a religious zealot, you will find that people will have learned to ignore you.

Actions are stronger than words

Not many people will listen to hype. Conversely, not many people can argue with proven success (although some will try). Be sure to keep management informed of all the progress being made. You should become the ultimate PR person when it comes to advertising the success of your project.

   If you find yourself always saying "Check this out. This is the ultimate deal!," then give it a rest for a while. Spend your energy ensuring the success of object technology by making the pilot succeed. Then run around saying "Check this out. This proves it's the ultimate deal—object technology has paid off!"

Make all successes visible

Take all steps to make any and all successes of the pilot development visible to both management and to peer development teams. Be very careful that you are presenting the successes in an informational way, instead of with a "you see, I told you it would work" attitude.

Hold project reviews at the end of the pilot

Once the pilot project is complete, you should hold a private project review with the development team to discuss what worked well and what could be improved if the pilot were to be redeveloped.

   Call an external review for peer development teams and management to review the results of the pilot project. At this review, present the results of your private project review, both positive and negative. Make sure that everyone sees both the advantages of object technology and the problems that were tackled when adopting the new technology. For each problem that is presented, make sure that steps to overcome the problem are also presented. This will show other development teams how to avoid the pitfalls you encountered, and it will show the management team that you know how to reduce the risk of continued use of object technology.

1.3 PROJECT MANAGEMENT

Turning our attention from the concerns and activities involved in introducing object technology, we focus now on two important topics relevant to object-oriented (OO) project management. First, the incremental development life cycle and its implications for OO projects are considered. Next, subsystems and their role in staffing OO projects are discussed. Both provide approaches to breaking down the work to be done in a project. In the former, the work breakdown allows multiple sequential short "design, implement, integration/test" cycles. In the subsystems approach, work is partitioned along structural lines. These approaches are not necessarily mutually exclusive.

1.3.1 Incremental Development

The use of object technology enables software systems to be developed incrementally. Incremental development allows high-risk areas to be addressed early on in the development of a software project.

The basic steps involved in an incremental development are as follows:

- Definition phase
  - Do analysis
  - Prototype risk areas
  - Choose sets of features

- Development phase, made up of multiple cycles each consisting of
  - Review and update analysis
  - Develop design
  - Implement
  - Test
  - Review results

The definition phase would ideally produce a workable model of the system and a full set of system operations. The highest-risk operations (e.g., related to the *user's conceptual model* [Collins 1995], or performance-critical operations) are then prototyped. The prototype is meant to prove out the analysis model, system architecture issues, and/or system limitations, thus acting as a sanity check before proceeding to development.

Evolutionary Fusion[*] is a specific method of using Fusion to help manage an evolutionary product development life cycle.

---

[*] See "Evolutionary Fusion: A Customer-Oriented Incremental Life Cycle for Fusion" by Todd Cotton, in Chapter 6 of this book.

Case Study

Early prototyping

We used early prototyping during the definition phase to prove out the overall architecture and performance of the system. Initially, the communication subsystem was profiled for acceptable performance. Then we created a minimum system framework to test the overall system architecture. Just a small subset of the operations for two subsystems was built. This initial prototyping was used to establish the feasibility of the system. The team knew that poor performance could cause our model to "blow up," so this really was viewed as an early prototype instead of a development iteration. As it turned out, the system framework that was completed for this early prototype evolved into the first iteration of the system.

Early results

The first iterations produced early, visible results:

- Working classes
- Some subsystem development
- Incremental development allowing a proof-of-concept release

Early system integration

Early and frequent integrations paid off by eliminating the "big-bang" effect seen when performing a single integration of system components just before entering the system test phase. Tackling system integration in steps helped us make the integration prior to the main system testing almost trouble free. The periodic integrations definitely minimized integration risk during the pilot developments.

Recommendations

Prototypes

You should develop prototypes to prove out or test high-risk aspects of your system or model. Typically, prototypes can be used to verify the ability of a system to meet performance constraints or to test usability and the user's conceptual model of the graphical user interface.

Prototypes should not be developed with complete disregard to standards and methods. It is desirable to develop a prototype that implements some components that could possibly evolve into components of the actual system. As part of prototype development, existing class libraries should be checked to see if any existing classes can be used to accelerate the development of the prototype.

Prototypes are not evolutionary steps in the development phase, because they are used to prove out some aspects of the system definition. Even so, it is not desirable to build prototypes that will be thrown away entirely.

Planning is required

People often think, incorrectly, that evolutionary developments cannot be planned. All software development activities should be planned and tracked. Use of the Fusion method can simplify the planning process because it suggests specific steps to get from system analysis to implementation and defines analysis and design deliverables.

Planning feature-sets for each incremental step

Features that should be developed and integrated during each incremental step should be carefully chosen and planned. Because design using Fusion is driven by system operations identified during analysis, Fusion is very well suited to an incremental development life cycle. Features for each incremental development step may be selected by choosing system operations from analysis models and only performing the complete design, implementation, and test cycle on the selected operations.

Complete features and components of phased features may be selected for a given incremental step. The feature-set selection may imply that only a subset of the operations for a given system or subsystem need be developed further.

Plan high-risk features in early releases

Determining feature-sets for the various integrations can be difficult when using incremental or evolutionary development methods. Often the best approach is to try to prove high-risk areas as early as possible; therefore, user interface components and performance-critical components should be developed early in the development cycle.

Use feature-set lists and phased-feature time lines to plan integrations

It is a good idea to create a list of all the features to be supported by the final release when you start to plan the feature sets of the various integrations. Often, many features may be phased across several integrations. Phased-feature time lines may be used to capture the development steps taken to deliver a feature and to capture the relative order of potential phases in which nonatomic features may be developed. Frequently, early phases of a phased-feature time line include limitations or compromises that allow only a part of the feature to be developed and integrated into the system.

Figure 1.2 shows an example of a phased-feature time line. The phased-feature time line should capture the incremental developments leading up to and including customer deliveries of a given feature. In this figure, a thick solid circle (above b,c) indicates the required partial feature set that identifies the fall-back feature set; without this part of the feature, the customer would not be satisfied with the product. The narrow solid circle indicates the development of the feature that is highly desirable to deliver to the customer—this is the real target. The dashed circle indicates a feature that is viewed as a bonus—if you get this done, the customer will be extremely pleased with your product.

A description of each development step should accompany the phased-feature time line. It is acceptable if some development steps are mutually exclusive, but care should be taken to point this out when specifying the feature sets of the various incremental developments and the necessary verification effort.

When you are planning the product verification effort, you should develop test cases and tests for both the target phase and the fall-back phase of a given feature. This way, if, due to delay in development, only the fall-back feature set

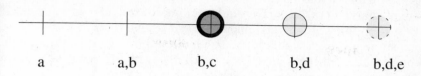

Figure 1.2 Phased-feature Time Line

is developed, tests exist for the system, and it can still be tested and shipped. Imagine if no tests were developed for the fall-back—besides being behind schedule, you would be struggling to verify the correct operation of the system.

1.3.2   Use of Subsystems

Many examples presented in books use analysis and design models that can fit on one page. If you want a model to be both readable and comprehensible, there is a limit to what should be placed on a single page (the old rule of thumb is that the brain can only effectively keep track of 7 ± 2 things at one time). Most systems in the real world are too large to fit entire analysis or design models onto a single page. In large systems, the models must be viewed at several levels through the use of decomposition.

Subsystems are a tool that the object technologist can use to create models that are both understandable by normal humans and possible for a development team to tackle. A subsystem should be viewed as a cluster of classes sharing some common properties or serving a common purpose. A typical system would be described at a high level as a cluster of related subsystems. Each subsystem may then be recursively expanded until, at the lowest level, the models contain details of the clusters of classes comprising the subsystem (see Figure 1.3).

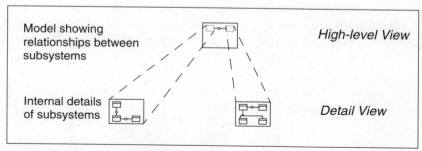

Figure 1.3 Example of Different Subsystem Views

A subsystem should be viewed as having public objects and interfaces that are visible to other subsystems and objects outside the subsystem. A subsystem also has internal classes, interfaces, relationships, objects, object interactions, and the like, which make up the detailed analysis and design of the subsystem.

When analyzing a large system, you should first identify the subsystems and produce high-level analysis models that describe the relationships between the subsystems. The goal should be to identify the interfaces, responsibilities, and dependencies for each subsystem so that parallel development teams may tackle the detailed analysis and design of each subsystem.

The detailed analysis and design of each subsystem will undoubtedly produce some inconsistencies in the high-level model. You should be prepared to revisit, update, and refine the high-level model many times as each iteration of analysis and design is applied to the detailed views of the subsystems.

Case Study

Identifying subsystems

Identifying subsystems can often be difficult and seem like black magic. There may not be any hard-and-fast rules for identifying subsystems, but during the pilot developments, we identified subsystems in two ways:

- Objects that were very complex internally were identified as subsystems to which all the steps of the Fusion method were applied.
- Clusters of objects that served a common purpose were grouped into a subsystem.

Another tool you can use to identify subsystems is to categorize the classes on the candidate class list[*] or the qualified class list. This categorization, combined with the object model, may suggest subsystem boundaries.

Apply Fusion recursively

In the top-level view of the system, we treated the subsystems as objects themselves. We applied the standard Fusion analysis and design steps to the top-level models and developed operations for the subsystems. Each "class" that represented a type of subsystem in the top-level model was then described with its own set of detailed analysis and design diagrams. When performing detailed analysis and design on a subsystem, the subsystem was viewed as a system itself, and the operations identified by the top-level design became the system operations for this subsystem.

Subsystem descriptions and models

During the analysis and design of the pilot developments, we used standard Fusion models to capture the high-level view of the system, with the symbols for objects and classes being used to represent subsystems and subsystem types, respectively. In lower-level, more detailed diagrams, we used dotted lines to demarcate subsystem boundaries.

An annoying problem that we ran into was the lack of subsystem support in the CASE tool that we were using. We addressed this deficiency by entering each

---

[*] See Section 1.4.

subsystem into the CASE tool as though it were a separate system. The top-level view was entered as one system with classes used to represent each subsystem. Each subsystem was then individually entered as a stand-alone system. This approach was problematic because the development team had to manually maintain consistency between subsystems and between the subsystems and the top-level view.

Managing the parallel development of subsystems

After we created the top-level models and identified the subsystem operations, responsibilities, and dependencies, separate teams of engineers started to work in parallel on the detailed analysis and design for each subsystem. Managing the parallel development of subsystems proved to be nontrivial. The major issues included

- Keeping the team members up to date with the big picture
- Planning appropriate synchronization points in the system evolution
- Keeping all team members abreast of changes made to each subsystem that would affect other subsystems
- Keeping the top-level view of the models up to date

Teams of one to two engineers then tackled each subsystem. Working with an initial set of required operations, each team developed analysis models for its subsystem.

Periodically throughout analysis and design of the subsystems, the whole team got together for interactive review and rework meetings. These meetings were in part cooperative analysis and design sessions, with all team members contributing to walk-throughs and proposals of how subsystems might be modified to solve larger system-wide issues. The review and rework meetings were almost always productive and contributed greatly to synchronization of the developments taking place on each subsystem.

Recommendations

Use subsystems to simplify the top-level view of the system

When developing top-level models of a system, treat subsystems as objects and develop top-level object models and object interaction graphs. By treating subsystems as objects at this level, you are abstracting away the details of how the subsystems perform the operations implied by the object interaction graphs (OIGs). Your top-level analysis will capture the relationships between the various subsystem types and the system operations. Developing object interaction graphs for the system operations using the top-level model will capture the way the subsystems collaborate to satisfy system operations and, as a result, identify the operations that each subsystem must support.

Ideally, you should be using a CASE tool that will support subsystems and maintain consistency between the top-level view and the internal analysis and design of each subsystem.

Use Fusion to drive the development of each subsystem

The "zoom-in" approach should be used to focus the system context around each subsystem identified in the top-level model. When appropriate, any new information or modification to existing information that is identified as a result of the subsystem analysis and design should be reflected in the top-level models of the system.

Once the top-level object interaction graphs (documenting the interactions between subsystems) have been completed, each subsystem may be treated as a system itself. You should simply change the system context to focus on a specific subsystem and decrease your level of abstraction.

The operations for each subsystem (identified by the OIGs) may be used as the system operations for the subsystem. The other subsystems that interact with a given subsystem become agents outside the system context. Your goal then is to identify and capture the analysis and design models that describe the internal structure and behavior of a given subsystem. It may be appropriate for a subsystem to contain subsystems of its own. If subsystems contain subsystems, then Fusion may be recursively applied to develop the detailed analysis and design of each subsystem.

Management of parallel subsystem development activities

The management of parallel subsystem development efforts can be tricky. It requires that the big picture be clear in everybody's minds, as well as documented clearly and early in the project life cycle. A good way to keep everybody in sync is to make sure that engineers representing each subsystem development team are involved in all analysis and design reviews.

Some of the techniques described in Section 1.3.1 on incremental development will help plan the coordination of multiple streams of development. Planning synchronization points in the development of the subsystems, as well as planned team reviews of the analysis and design of each subsystem, will increase the probability of success in parallel subsystem development.

Cooperative analysis and design

All the engineers in the team, standing together around a whiteboard and cooperatively developing an analysis or design model, can be much more effective than any one of the engineers working away in solitude at his or her desk. To ensure an effective cooperative development session, it is good to begin with a base-line work, prepared by one or more of the team members, as a starting point to stimulate discussion.

Although cooperative development may not always be practical, it should definitely be used at the following key points in the development life cycle:

- Developing and/or reviewing and refining the initial analysis model
- Developing and/or reviewing and refining high-level system models that reflect decomposition of the system into subsystems
- Developing and/or reviewing models of objects used by multiple subsystems
- Developing and/or reviewing first-draft subsystem analysis and design models

1.4 COMPLEMENTING THE FUSION DEVELOPMENT PROCESS

Next, we focus on some of the pragmatics associated with object-oriented project management. Rather than revisiting topics that are covered well in the Fusion text (Coleman et al. 1994), this section focuses on development life-cycle activities that are not covered by the Fusion process. These include preliminary steps leading up to Fusion's analysis phase, models that are useful for capturing additional information that the Fusion analysis and design models do not represent, and testing of object-oriented software.

1.4.1 Requirements Analysis

The steps presented in this section will help you generate object models and form a front end to the Fusion method. If you have a tough time identifying classes and knowing how to start building an object model, then read on. Here is a plan of attack to get you from customer requirements to a Fusion analysis model:

- Collect and catalog customer requirements
- Generate a System Requirements Specification (SRS)
- Generate a requirements database by extracting atomic requirements from the SRS applicable sources
- Begin the data dictionary by creating a candidate class list
- Qualify classes by analyzing their responsibilities
- Follow the analysis steps specified by Fusion (Coleman et al. 1994)

Analysis overview

The analysis process is used to map user requirements onto components of a system that will satisfy these requirements. When performing object-oriented analysis using Fusion, the deliverables of the analysis phase include system context diagrams, object models, and interface models (system operations and schemas). This section describes some steps that can be taken to get from user requirements to the Fusion analysis deliverables. This section also includes useful tips to keep in mind while you perform analysis.

Building an analysis model of a system that is representative of the real-world problem domain is central to developing a successful object-oriented system or application. It is very important to focus analysis on the problem that you are attempting to solve or the system that you are modeling in software. Sometimes engineers try to look at how the system will work (the design) and this convolutes or derails the analysis effort.

Engineers can also be tempted to focus too narrowly on the problem that they are trying to solve. It is always a good idea to step back during analysis and try to capture the whole picture in an analysis model. The focus on how the system will work should really be saved for the design phase.

Analysis example

Here's an example of how the big-picture view can pay off:

You are asked to develop a system that monitors telephone use. You know that telephone calls are controlled by a set of messages to set up and tear down the call. During analysis, you decide that to satisfy the customer requirements your system should focus on telephone calls—by modeling calls as your lowest-level object. Now your system can do anything. It's the ultimate system! You build the system and ship it. Everything seems great until your customers get involved in mobile telecommunications and want to know about the identification messages that mobile phones send out periodically while they are switched on (whether or not a call is in progress). "Hmmm," you say to yourself, "This is a problem. Our system only knows about calls. It doesn't have message objects, only call objects. We've got a lot of work to do."

Had you taken a step back and looked at the big picture, you would have realized that it is significant that all calls have relationships to the messages that set up and tear down the calls. And since there are call setup messages in the real world, you should include message objects in your system. You may not use (or even implement) these message objects now, but the fact that they are in your analysis model will reduce the risk of missing a step when the system gets designed.

Customer requirements
The customer requirements should be captured in a database of some description. It is most useful for them to be captured in a computer-based database or spreadsheet and for each requirement to be uniquely identified.

Software Requirements Specification
The Software Requirements Specification is a document that specifies all the requirements and constraints of a software system. The functional requirements section of the SRS often captures the system requirements in a somewhat coarse level of detail. Often, the functional requirements imply requirements (that are not to be tested) without stating them. Constraints also imply requirements of the software system.

If your organization does not have a standard format and content for a Software Requirements Specification, a good starting point is the set of guidelines produced by the IEEE (IEEE 1994).

Requirements database
The requirements database is meant to hold all the atomic software system requirements. Often a single functional requirement in the Software Requirements Specification may imply several requirements. The requirements database is used to capture all the stated and implied requirements of the software system with very fine detail. It should be populated from the Software Requirements Specification and any other source of requirements, such as local system development requirements referenced by the SRS.

Data dictionary
A data dictionary is a central repository of definitions of terms and concepts. A goal of analysis should be to populate this dictionary with all the information known about the classes, system operations, agents, relationships, and the like, in the system.

Candidate class list

The first step in building the data dictionary is to create a candidate class list that enumerates all potential classes. The idea is to use a "scan the requirements database and brainstorm a list of possible classes" approach to populate the candidate class list. You should be looking for all the "things" in the problem domain that might be represented by objects in the software system. Shlaer and Mellor (1988) identify the following categories as starter ideas for identifying objects:

- Tangible things
- Roles
- Interactions
- Events
- Specifications

As you build the dictionary you should review the entries continually to make sure that each item is really necessary. The next step, responsibility analysis, will help you weed out items from your candidate class list.

Responsibility analysis

By identifying the responsibilities of each class on your candidate class list, you can start to see classes that appear to be classes, but actually are not classes at all. As part of the description for each class on the candidate class list, write down the responsibilities of that class. Any class on your list that does not have any responsibilities should probably not be created as a class. Only the classes with responsibilities should move on to the list of qualified classes.

Object Model and beyond

Use the qualified class list to populate a Fusion object model. Then apply all the steps described by the Fusion method.

Traceability is important

Traceability is a tool used to make sure that the system or application that is created and tested actually meets the customer requirements. Traceability from customer requirements through to implementation and back to customer requirements should be captured initially during analysis and updated and propagated throughout the entire development cycle (see Figure 1.4).

Traceability is particularly useful for object-based systems

Traceability is a particularly useful tool to help manage the evolution of object-based solutions. Because the responsibilities and behavior of objects often evolve over the lifetime of a system, it makes sense to maintain traceability links between requirements and the objects that collaborate to satisfy the requirements.

Case Study

During the pilot project development, we developed an initial set of requirements through the informal questioning of the internal customers. Next we generated a proposed set of user requirements in the form of a text-based document, which was reviewed by the internal customers.

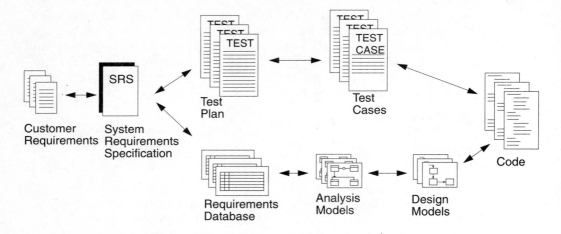

Figure 1.4 Paths of Traceability

We created a requirements database from the signed-off user's requirements. This database was captured using a computer-based spreadsheet and
included fields for requirement categorization, subsystem categorization, scheduled feature-set release reference, requirements cross reference, and traceability.

We brainstormed a candidate class list that was also captured using a computer-based spreadsheet. The candidate class list contained fields for the class
name, responsibilities, class cross reference, logical categorization, subsystem
categorization, and traceability.

We performed responsibility analysis and initial modeling to weed out what
appeared to be classes but actually were not. The entries in the candidate class
list that were not used as classes in the system were marked accordingly.

The major subsystems were recognized from the start by using a top-down
approach to sketch object models while brainstorming the candidate class list.
Some sub-subsystems were identified through the categorization and responsibility analysis of the classes on the candidate class list. Once we had derived a
solid set of classes, we used the Fusion method to drive the development effort
from capturing analysis models, generating design models, and then carrying
the effort through to the development of class descriptions and implementation.

Our intention was to maintain a separate document (linked to the requirements database) to capture sign-off dates for the completion of the various development life-cycle phases for each requirement in the requirements database.
However, this was performed in a less rigorous manner by informally reviewing
which requirements were satisfied (in more general terms) for each new feature
release.

We did not use traceability to a great extent in the pilot project. Initially,
forward traceability was provided from the requirements document to the
requirements database and then to the classes used in the system analysis

model. Traceability was not carried on to the design documents and implementation.

Recommendations

Class identification and naming are often difficult

One of the hardest parts of analysis is identifying the real objects (and classes) in a system and naming them appropriately. Naming can be very difficult. If an object in your model has a direct counterpart in the problem domain, name it after its counterpart in the problem domain. Get others to review your names. Your model will not be effective if you are the only one who knows what the names mean.

Allow enough time for a thorough analysis

You should plan to spend a considerable amount of time in the analysis phase of your project—especially on a pilot project. With experienced object technologists, the analysis phase can easily take 30% of the development time leading up to an initial delivery. The biggest problem with spending so much time up front on a pilot project is that the management in your organization may not be used to this. Managers may get nervous when the only tangible products they see are analysis diagrams and documents. Often managers feel better when they see executing code (and often it doesn't matter that this code might be garbage). Section 1.3.1 (on incremental development) describes how you can use prototypes during the analysis phase to prove out your analysis model and comfort nervous managers.

Maintaining traceability is difficult without automation

In practice, traceability proved to be a problem to maintain. The drawing tools, documentation tools, and CASE tools did not have good support for adding and accessing fields that might be used for maintaining traceability. Also, without a tool that could automatically maintain forward and backward traces, the maintenance and usefulness of the traceability information became questionable.

In summary, for traceability to work for a software development team, tools must exist to automate the creation and maintenance of both forward and reverse traces from user-requirements capture all the way to implementation.

1.4.2   Capturing Analysis and Design Information

Although Fusion does a good job of meeting general OOA/D needs, sometimes complementing the Fusion models with additional models or notations adds to the understanding and documentation of the system. This section covers diagrams that the pilot team found useful and points to some areas where Fusion needs enhancements to capture specific design decisions.

Case Study

The Fusion method defines the following models for capturing the analysis and design for your system:

- System context diagram
- Object model
- Interface model
- Object interaction graphs
- Inheritance graphs
- Visibility graphs

We found that we needed some extra diagrams and documents to fully describe our system. The following subsections describe additional information that was captured on paper.

State diagrams

Fusion does not recommend a notation for documenting state diagrams. This does not mean that you are not meant to use state machines. In the pilot developments, state diagrams were captured using simple electronic drawing tools, because the CASE tool that we were using did not have a mechanism to allow the entry of state diagrams.

In the object technology pilot, state diagrams were developed between the analysis and design phases. They were used to document state machines that were developed within classes and subsystems. Typically, state diagrams were used when modeling objects that, in the real world, function by moving through a series of states (e.g., the states of a telephone call or the states of a database transaction). State diagrams captured the overall intended behavior of the software model. Design models were then developed to satisfy the state diagrams. During the design phase, any necessary refinement was incorporated into the state diagrams.

Physical design diagrams

Physical design diagrams are used to show diagrammatically how objects are mapped onto the processors and processes in the system (as illustrated in Figure 1.5). Fusion does not recommend a notation for capturing this mapping of logical design to physical design.

During the pilot development, ad-hoc diagrams were used to capture the physical design. Dashed lines were used to show boundaries of processes. IPC mechanisms such as shared memory were also identified on the diagrams.

The physical design diagrams capture the location of the various objects in the object models. Standard Fusion object models capture relationships, and object interaction graphs describe how objects collaborate to perform a task. The physical design diagrams capture details that specify how objects in the logical design will be mapped onto processes and machines in the physical implementation. The notation used is not particularly important, but having some diagram that shows the system context in which objects will exist is important.

Recommendations

Capture the analysis and design of your system even if Fusion does not recommend a notation

The Fusion notation provides no way to denote

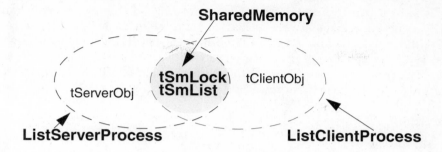

Figure 1.5 Physical Design—Object Mapping Example

- Process/thread/synchronization issues
- IPC (shared memory, semaphores, etc.)
- Asynchronous message passing
- Which objects are located in shared memory

Additional models and notations can be added to your process to fill these gaps, as long as care is taken to document the syntax and semantics of the additions. Also, just because Fusion has no specification for state machines does not mean that you should not use them when they are of value in your problem domain.

1.4.3   Testing Object-oriented Systems

This section focuses on functionality testing used to verify that systems and system components behave correctly. For complete test coverage, there are many other areas (not covered in this paper) that should be considered, including load and stress, performance, reliability, and volume.

Several levels of testing have been found to be useful:

- Unit tests (class and class cluster tests)
- Subsystem (integration) tests
- System tests
- Regression tests

The unit tests are applied to software components in isolation. Subsystem integration tests are applied to the collection of classes in a subsystem and focus on verifying the correct interaction of the various units making up the subsystem. System tests test the entire integrated system or application. Regression tests are all the tests that are maintained as a system develops to verify that the performance of the system or system components has not degraded from one release of the system to the next.

It is important to remember that many tests may be made such that they can be used as regression tests. A regression test is used to retest a software component after some changes have been made to verify that it still performs correctly and that the changes have not degraded the system.

It is important to realize that the granularity of the lowest-level unit test applied to object-based software is coarser than the granularity of low-level unit testing that might be applied to function-based software. With object-based software, typically the finest-grain software component is a class: a collection of state, methods, and instance variables. With function-based software, the finest-grain software component is typically a single function.

Case Study

Test harnesses
Automated test harnesses were created for most tests, allowing them to be versioned and stored in the source code repository. The automated test harnesses could then be kept up to date as changes were made to the various classes. Because of the development of automated test harnesses, regression tests were possible for most classes in the system.

Unit tests
Class-level unit test harnesses were developed for most classes in the system. The unit tests were most often developed as applications that instantiated the class-under-test. Any other class that was referenced by the class-under-test was either used as is or replaced with a dummy proxy controlled by the test harness application. With some test harnesses, input test data files were used to drive the tests. The tests were either designed to exit with a success or failure code, or to write output to a file that could be verified against the expected results.

All class-level unit test harnesses were stored in the same version control system as the classes themselves. The class and test source files were marked with the same symbolic version names so that consistent sets of class source and test harness source code could be retrieved easily from the source repository. As changes were made to classes, the test harnesses were modified to track the changes in the class source code.

Keeping track of dependencies on classes and class libraries
The update of the test harnesses was not strictly reviewed, and some test harnesses became out of date. A dependency diagram or chart was not developed for all the classes in the system. This would have helped to maintain the test harnesses.

Recommendations
A very good goal would be to build class-level unit test harnesses that test every path through every method of every class and test all boundary cases for each method. If the class-level test harnesses are created as stand-alone programs or scripts, they may be maintained as regression tests for the classes.

The following approaches can be used to create automated tests that may be maintained as regression tests:

- Create an executable program that instantiates the object and applies test cases to the object.

- Create an executable program that instantiates the object, reads test data for each test case from a text file, and applies the test cases to the object.
- Create test scripts using a Tcl interpreter and an interface library that provides access to the objects methods. Implement the test cases using the Tcl scripting language (Ousterhout 1994).

Documentation of the test cases should be embedded within the test script or input test data. Embedded documentation is especially useful for tests that are meant to be used as regression tests, as these tests will have to be maintained over the life of the unit under test.

Develop class-level unit tests and test harnesses

The unit test is the lowest level of testing performed during software development. In an object-oriented development, the lowest-level unit that should be tested is the class. Class-level unit test harnesses should be developed for each class in the system. If your organization does not typically test to this level of granularity, you should at least develop class-level unit test harnesses for any class that you intend to make reusable. The unit test harnesses should be stored under configuration management so that a consistent set of class implementation and tests may be extracted from the configuration management system.

Class-level unit test harnesses should be

- Developed when the classes are developed
- Used initially to verify correctness of class implementations
- Used later for class-level regression tests

Testing object-oriented software presents some interesting problems. At first it might seem that encapsulation should simplify the task of testing object-based software. It might seem that all you have to do is create a test harness for each class that instantiates the class, tests every possible path through each method, and tests all boundary cases for each method call.

Developing a class-level unit test harness may be simple for some classes, such as a class that implements a list. When a **list** object is created, the **list** object itself may service all requests to add, remove, and get the objects in the list. Because the **list** object does not call any methods of the objects contained in the list, a class-level test harness for the **list** object is relatively easy to develop. The class-level unit test harness should be able to satisfy all test cases for the **list** object by inserting, removing, and accessing objects managed by the **list** object. The only objects the test harness needs to create are passive objects managed by the **list** object (and at least one instance of the **list** object itself).

The class-level unit test gets much more complicated very quickly when objects collaborate in performing an operation. Consider the situation where several objects interact to perform an operation. If you plan to provide a class-level test harness for each class involved in the collaboration, every class, except the unit under test, would have to be incorporated into the test harness (e.g., instead of the class being tested talking to an instance of class **X**, should it talk to a class that is actually part of the test harness? or possibly a subclass of class **X** that can verify that class **X** is being used appropriately?). Complex collaborations of objects make test harnesses complex and difficult to maintain, because the classes that are part of the test harness must be maintained as all the real classes that they represent change.

A simple rule to use when assessing the complexity of the required test harnesses is that objects that act as atomic servers (i.e., do not interact with objects other than aggregate objects to perform operations) are likely to require less complex test harnesses than clusters of objects that collaborate to perform operations.

Subsystem test harnesses

The goal of subsystem testing is to verify the correct behavior of the clusters of classes that will collaborate to perform the operations supported by an entire subsystem. The execution and generation of results of the subsystem tests should be automated in the form of subsystem test harnesses.

A Tcl interpreter provides a good solution as the standard "test executive" for all subsystem and system-level tests. Widespread use of a common mechanism for implementing test cases will facilitate the maintenance of all the test harnesses. You should create test scripts that include both the definitions of the test cases and their implementation. This approach of using a single document to capture both specification and implementation of the test cases will make them easier to maintain.

System tests

System tests should be developed for verifying the correct collaboration of the subsystems to perform system operations.

Use of Fusion helps to simplify the testing effort

In Fusion, during the development of the operation model, a schema is developed for each system operation. This schema specifies the preconditions (**Assumes** clauses) and the postconditions (**Results** clauses) for each operation. These clauses can be used as input to the any white- or black-box testing efforts. Also, asserts can be used in the code to test that the preconditions and postconditions have been satisfied.

1.5   DEVELOPMENT ENVIRONMENT

For the object technology pilot and subsequent projects, a number of aspects of the development environment need to be adapted to better support OO development. In particular, tools that facilitate OOA/D model drawing and maintenance need to selected and purchased, and software development standards and templates need to be added or extended to support object technology. This section describes how the use of various tools, standards, and templates can help to ensure the success of an OO project, illustrating tips and insights by reference to the pilot project case study.

1.5.1   Computer-based Drawing Tools and CASE Tools

Computer-based drawing tools can be a useful way to capture OOA/D models. Pencil and paper may be fast to start off with, but redrawing the diagrams soon becomes tiresome. A drawing tool is much less powerful than a CASE tool for developing and maintaining analysis and design diagrams. A CASE tool is able to maintain consistency across multiple diagrams referencing the same object, so changes can be made on one diagram and ripple through all related views of the same object. Also, since a simple drawing tool does not have any knowledge of a method, it cannot test for completeness or correctness of analysis or design diagrams. However, general-purpose drawing tools are typically much less expensive than CASE tools and budgetary considerations may force a project to accept a compromise on the tool it uses.

Drawing tool checklist
The following list describes some of the features that are desirable if a drawing tool is to be used to capture OOA/D diagrams:

- Support for libraries of shapes or templates
- The ability to "glue" lines to other graphical objects
- The ability to allow lines connected to objects to stretch if the objects are moved
- The ability to attach text to graphical objects

CASE tool checklist
The ideal CASE tool should support the object-oriented analysis and design method and development life cycle such that it

- Provides an accessible data dictionary containing all information entered into the tool to describe objects, relationships, methods, etc.
- Maintains consistency between different views of the same object (e.g., a change made in one view propagates throughout all views automatically)
- Provides consistency and completeness tests on analysis and design models
- Is easy to enter all information
- Understands the semantics of method parameters so that parameters of methods in object interaction graphs may be checked for type, visibility, etc.
- Supports system decomposition by supporting the development of sub-systems
- Supports teams of people working on a single model (implies locking and versioning)
- Supports reverse engineering so that interfaces to class libraries may be imported into the CASE tool
- Allows analysis and design components of other existing systems to be referenced and used
- Allows for the creation and use of fields to maintain traceability information
- Provides a mechanism to allow links between the requirements and the analysis and design diagrams

- Supports the archiving and maintenance of analysis diagrams that are not tied to the design diagrams and can be maintained as ideal system models (i.e., changes made during design that affect analysis models cause the creation and modification of branches off the analysis diagrams, instead of directly modifying the original analysis diagrams)
- Supports the ability to update analysis models during design, so that a representative set of analysis and design models may be generated to represent the current system
- Allows components of models to be hidden in some diagrams and shown in others
- Allows for hierarchical diagrams to be entered and automatically maintained
- Captures logical and physical designs of a software system
- Generates code that can be used to actually implement the design
- Provides integrated class browsing and source code editing support
- Provides integrated configuration management support
- Allows the import and export of analysis and design diagrams, class descriptions, etc., so that they may be stored in an external configuration management system
- Provides for documentation templates to be created so that documentation may be produced automatically
- Provides the ability to generate complete reports (including headings and textual descriptions) that include the analysis and design documents
- Allows each diagram to be exported to its own uniquely named file in a format that can be imported (e.g., encapsulated postscript or MIF), by reference, into a standard word processor or desktop publishing package (allowing external documentation systems to be used to capture report material other than the diagrams)
- Is affordable

As you might have guessed, it is impossible to find an OOA/D CASE tool that does everything listed here (I have yet to find it). But it is possible to find CASE tools that have many of the desired features.

Case Study

Drawing Tools

In the early stages of the pilot developments, computer-based drawing tools were used to capture Fusion analysis and design diagrams. This proved to be an effective way of capturing the information and making it look presentable. Using a drawing tool was not effective when it came to updating the diagrams to reflect changes in the models, especially when the change was a global name change.

The use of a computer-based drawing tool meant that the initial diagrams took longer to create than if they had been created with pencil and paper. Updates to the diagrams, in most cases, were quicker with the computer-based drawing tool.

Throughout the early stages of analysis, several computer-based drawing applications were used. The use of a computer-based drawing application continued until a CASE tool was selected for use on the project.

Using a CASE tool

At the start of the pilot development effort, several CASE tools were evaluated. None of the CASE tools we evaluated was ideal. Even so, the use of the CASE tool greatly reduced the effort and time required to enter and maintain the Fusion analysis and design diagrams.

Recommendations

It is a good idea to use some form of computer-based tool to capture analysis and design diagrams. The first time you have to change or update a diagram, the extra time it took to enter the diagram into a computer (rather than drawing a quick pencil-and-paper sketch) will pay off. The best option, though, is to use a CASE tool that can maintain consistency between various diagrams that reference the same objects.

If it is initially not possible to purchase a CASE tool, you should at least get a computer-based drawing package that allows for the creation of object templates from which diagrams may be created. Visio (from Shapeware) is one such Microsoft Windows-based drawing package that is reasonably good for drawing OOA/D diagrams because it allows libraries of shapes to be created and allows text and stretchable lines to be attached to these shapes.

Also, if you are planning to choose a CASE tool, you can use a simple computer-based drawing application to keep work progressing while a CASE tool is being selected.

Choosing a CASE tool

In the short term at least, it seems that finding the ideal CASE tool is unlikely. Therefore, it is a good idea to decide up front on the key areas in the software development you want the tool to help with. The following is a list of general areas in which some tools seem to be strong:

- Requirements capture and traceability to class description
- Verification of analysis and design models (consistency, completeness, etc.)
- Code generation, modification, and reverse engineering
- Diagram capture
- Team working
- Documentation generation and maintenance

For our project the most-needed features were support for teamwork, diagram capture, and analysis and design verification.

1.5.2 Standards and Templates

Any sensible effort to collect and create standards and templates that will be needed during the pilot object technology development will realize a short-term return on investment—especially the development of class templates and template analysis and design documents and diagrams. If the project is a reasonable size for an object technology pilot, then time spent establishing coding and development standards and developing template classes and documents will more than pay for itself by the end of the project.

Case Study

Pilot project standards and templates

Applicable standards that existed prior to the object technology pilot were used without modification. Some standards, however, were modified or enhanced to better support the object technology pilot. For example, C++ coding standards were developed for the pilot, and the development life cycle was modified to include the deliverables prescribed by Fusion.

Throughout the pilot project, template documents were used for most of the development life-cycle deliverables. The template document consisted of a skeleton deliverable that simply (or sometimes with great effort) needed to be filled in to create an actual deliverable. This approach is not unique to object technology, but it does reduce the overall risk in developing and delivering a software system. So where templates of deliverables existed in our organization, they were used. Where the use of Fusion and C++ suggested the need for a template that was not standard within the organization, we took the time to develop one.

Coding standards

When the test network project started, our division did not have a set of C++ coding standards. We started with the C coding standards that did exist in the division and added the recommendations and requirements that were needed for C++. Most of the requirements and recommendations were based on the developers' experience with C++ and on many of the rules described by Meyers (1992). Some additions have been made to the C++ coding standards recently based on the experience of our own developers as well as some tips from the Taligent design guide (Taligent 1994).

We included the following in our coding standards:

- Basic coding rules and tips
- File and function header comment templates
- Variable naming convention
- File content recommendations
- Brace placement convention

Development standards

Development standards were also documented for the use of object technology. They specified all aspects of the development tools and environment.

The development standards addressed two major concerns:

- Creating a development environment that would facilitate the pilot development
- Creating a development environment that would help other teams in reusing classes developed during the object technology pilot

Canonical class

A canonical class was developed early in the pilot project. The structure of this class changed only slightly throughout the pilot. Use of the canonical class improved the consistency of classes developed on the project.

Document templates

Document templates were created and maintained for many of the documents developed on the project. Initially, a basic document template was used to simply provide standard paragraph formats, title pages, change history logs, page headers and footers, and the like. The basic template evolved to include standard recommended sections (e.g., introduction and scope) and their formats. Finally, templates for specific types of documents (e.g., requirements specifications) were created. These document templates did not take much time to develop initially (although they have continued to evolve through review and update). The time saved through the development of the templates was significant, especially when new engineers joined the team and when new documents were created.

Recommendations

Makefile templates

If your organization does not already have template makefiles, it is a good idea to create templates for your project. The template makefile should be used as the standard starting point whenever a new makefile is needed.

If your project is of a reasonable size, it is also beneficial to create a hierarchy of makefiles. If you create a makefile hierarchy, you should try to create a base makefile that includes all the project-specific and site-specific rules, variables, dependencies, and targets. This makefile should be included in the makefiles that build the specific targets associated with a particular area or subsystem of your project.

Use standards

If your organization has standards for coding, documentation and development, use them. You may have to customize some of the standards for your project, but start with existing standards. Do not try to invent your own. Introducing new technology may provide the opportunity to customize some of these standards so that they support the use of the new technology.

If your organization does not yet have standards for coding, documentation, development, etc., it is a good idea to take the time to document the expectations you have for the development of your project as early as possible. For the pilot project, providing at least a skeleton set of standards before building up the team will help ensure consistency, facilitate learning, and speed development.

For example, a source code documentation standard that provides enough information so that classes may be documented automatically by extracting all necessary information from the source files themselves will save time later. If you plan to use any tools to automatically generate class documentation, you should understand the conventions of such a tool (e.g., identifying keywords), and recommend the use of such conventions in your coding standards.

Development standards

Development standards should capture information about the development environment, including the configuration management system, the build tools, the source code directory structure, and file naming conventions. If your organization has a set of development standards, it is a good idea for you to create a development standards document that captures the specific requirements of your team's development environment.

Software development templates

Once the standards you are going to use have been identified or created, you should try to build a set of template deliverables that supports the standards. For example, if your C++ coding standards specify a format for file header block comments, function header block comments, and required functions for classes, then you should build a canonical class that can be used as a template on which to base any new class that is created. In this context, the word "template" is used to refer to a standard starting point or base deliverable to be used whenever a new deliverable is being created.

One way to improve the chances of success of any project is to spend some time up front creating generic template solutions for all the work products that are developed repeatedly throughout the development life cycle. Any class of deliverable for which more than three are created during the development life cycle is a candidate for template development. In any project, the following standard templates or skeletons would be very useful:

- Document templates
- Makefile templates
- File header templates
- Function header templates
- Test harness templates

If your software development organization has templates for all these items, then definitely use them. If you are not lucky enough to have all the work done for you, then build some templates now. Any time you spend creating useful templates will undoubtedly pay for itself by the end of the project.

Canonical class template

Object technology projects present a good opportunity to dramatically reduce development effort through the creation of a canonical class template, which should include

- Canonical class header file
- Canonical class code file
- Standard include directives
- Standard methods (e.g., operator, constructor, destructor, and copy constructor declared but not defined; see Meyers (1992) for some useful tips)
- Standard system interfaces (e.g., error handler support and debug handler support)
- Standard file block comments

- Standard method block comments

In past projects, I have used canonical C++ classes that were 300+ lines of combined source code and comments. Think about the time saved not having to type those 300 lines each time a new class is added to your system. Here are a couple of examples of how to use canonical class templates:

- The canonical class template can be copied from the template, and search-and-replace editor commands or macros can be used to set the class name, date, author, etc.
- A script can be developed to generate a new class from a supplied class name combined with a user-specific resource file, a common canonical class template, the system date, etc.

Fusion-specific templates

For projects using Fusion, templates of the following diagrams and documents will be invaluable:

- Object model
- Schema
- Object interaction graphs
- Visibility graphs

Don't waste energy hyping your templates and standards

Don't expend too much energy trying to hype your standards and templates to others in your organization. If the standards and templates you have developed are useful, others will *want* to use them. Making newly developed standards and templates visible to all interested individuals will do more to promote their adoption than investing effort in achieving formal organization-wide acceptance or support for each new standard and template.

1.6 REUSE

Object technology promises to usher in an era of greater reuse, including increased availability of software components from third-party vendors. This section considers reuse of third-party class libraries and library classes developed in-house, as well as issues associated with developing a reuse program. The case study highlights lessons learned in the pilot project, where the two tools that were produced shared a number of third-party and internally developed classes.

1.6.1 Class Libraries

Already a number of class libraries are available commercially. Although many are fairly low-level generic classes, they can help jump-start a reuse effort by populating a starter library with these commonly used classes. Using the purchased library classes helps accelerate OO projects and encourages a reuse mind-set.

Domain-specific class libraries offer the potential to achieve much higher levels of reuse across related products. There has to be an up-front investment in making the classes reusable and an ongoing investment in maintaining them. This investment will pay off if the classes are reused multiple times (the rule of thumb is at least three times). As the organization builds up its domain-specific library over time, the proportion of each product that is made up of reused classes will rise, and corresponding productivity increases and reduced development times can be anticipated.

Case Study

During the pilot project, emphasis was put on identifying and acquiring or developing building-block classes or software components. High-level components and subsystems were then developed using these building-block components. Initially, the tools.h++ library was purchased from Rogue Wave. This class library provides many generic building-block classes, including classes to manage collections, factories, streams, persistence, and time. Later in the development, a Tcl interpreter library was used to provide powerful script interpreting capabilities.

Emphasis was put on identifying building-block classes and many were identified and developed early in the pilot and used throughout the project. Class-level unit tests provided a means of verifying and regression testing the internally developed class libraries. The quality standards for the building-block classes was generally very high. Most of the internally developed and some third-party class libraries are being used as building blocks in current object-based development projects.

The pilot project found the following internally developed class libraries valuable:

- Shared memory factory class library
- UNIX IPC class library
- Logging and parsing class library
- Error handling and debug class library

Recommendations

Use third-party class libraries to jump-start development
Don't start any object technology project without a good class library that at least has some support for maintaining collections of objects. When you are starting to apply object technology, it is a good idea to have a bag of tricks you know how to use. A good class library, supported on UNIX and PC platforms, is the tools.h++ class library developed by RogueWave.

The Smalltalk language is good place to look for examples of useful foundation classes. Smalltalk offers quite a large library of useful classes which manage collections, separate user interaction from underlying implementation (à la Model, View, Controller), and so on.

But don't just assume that third-party class libraries are based on solid object models

When using third-party class libraries, you should not assume that the class libraries have been developed using a sound object model. When you decide to use a third-party class library, it is a good idea to reverse engineer at least the object model and the inheritance graph. You should review these diagrams and understand any flaws, inconsistencies, and compromises that your review uncovers—avoid blind acceptance of a class inheritance hierarchy just because you paid for the class-library product.

Develop Class Libraries

When building components of your system, you should develop your own class libraries. If you take the time to create class libraries during the initial development of your classes, you will make it just a little bit easier to reuse those classes in a subsequent project.

Think ahead when grouping classes into libraries

Your goal should be to develop class libraries that contain groups of compiled and tested classes targeting a particular area of the problem domain. For example, you might have classes that are used to wrap operating system features. These classes should be grouped together in a library. Another library might be created to contain classes that can process events and another library for error handler and debug handler classes. Generally, usable classes should be grouped into libraries based on their area of use, instead of the subsystem or process in which they are used in the current project. If the classes are packaged well, any new application development that uses an existing class need only include the appropriate header file and link in the appropriate class library.

Some classes may be developed that are very specific to a particular problem domain or subsystem. If these classes do not appear generally applicable, there is no need to try to force fit them into a general class library. In this case a library specific to a subsystem or process may make the most sense.

Try to eliminate coupling between class libraries

Try to eliminate or at least minimize coupling between class libraries. You should try to keep your class libraries independent of each other. It may make sense to have one (or possibly more) very general class library upon which most others depend. You should not, however, develop dependent class libraries that are targeted toward different specific problem domains.

For example, you may have a standard mix-in class that provides common interfaces to make all objects persistent. This base class definition may be in a general class library that is required for the library containing both persistent sensor modeling classes and classes providing persistent screen widgets. It is desirable, however, that there not be unnecessary dependencies between the sensor class library (containing the persistent sensor class) and the widget class library (containing the persistent screen widget). Without careful thought and planning, you may find that all class libraries must be linked into any application that needs just a single class. Take the time to plan the organization of your class libraries—especially if you plan to reuse the classes you have developed.

Develop tests for classes in class libraries

You should develop tests that at least test the functionality of each class in the class library. These tests should be stored in the configuration management system with the class library source files so that, when changes are made to the classes, the necessary test programs can be easily identified and rerun as regression tests for the classes. The test programs should also be enhanced and maintained as changes are made to the classes in the class libraries.

1.6.2 Promoting Software Reuse

High levels of software reuse and the associated productivity gains are not an automatic by-product of OO development (Griss 1995). For classes to be reused, the organization must have a culture that understands the value (and cost) of reuse. Also, reusable classes must be

- Visible to all engineers and architects
- Tested and known to be of high quality
- Documented so that they are easy to understand
- Stored or packaged so that they are easy to use

Case Study

Reuse was considered from the start

In the pilot project, reuse was considered from the start. Automated test harnesses were developed for each class, and classes were packaged in libraries based on their area of use.

Early in the project, we addressed the needs of client developers using the class libraries developed during the project. The development environment facilitated reuse by providing a single directory for all header files and a single directory for all built libraries. Links were automatically created from these common include and library directories to the build tree containing the header files and built libraries.

Benefits of considering reuse

Some of the original work was generic enough to be reused (almost as is) in other developments. A current effort is under way to develop and maintain a library of reusable software components. The main problem continues to be a lack of resources to provide ongoing development and support of the reuse library components.

After the pilot, some class libraries were reused. In most cases, this reuse required more effort than should have been required because a global view was not taken at the onset of the pilot development. Some aspects of the class libraries that had to change after the pilot project included the location in the configuration management source code repository and naming conventions.

For example, some of the naming conventions used during the pilot project proved to be much less than ideal when reuse was put into practice. During the pilot project, project-based class name prefixes were used. When the move was made to organization-wide reuse, these prefixes were no longer appropriate because there was a desire for organization-based prefixes.

In most cases, the grouping of classes into libraries (discussed in Section 1.6.1 on class libraries) proved to be effective when classes were reused on new projects. In some cases, several libraries proved to be too tightly coupled together, and some work was undertaken to clean up some of the libraries.

Automated test harnesses were developed for most classes. They provided a mechanism that allowed classes to be regression tested following any change. The existence of regression tests for classes in a reuse class library is a necessity if you expect other developers in the organization to believe in the quality of internally developed class libraries.

Class documentation

During the pilot project, a PC-based class library was created. A utility application was created to extract C++ code and comments from class header files and automatically populate the database. The automated extraction utility removed much of the mundane work required to make documentation usable. This mechanism was very effective in generating printed documentation and providing class browsing capabilities for engineers considering the use of the classes developed. The one major drawback was that few engineers had access to PCs, so the class browser was not very accessible.

Following the pilot, one of the engineers originally on the project created HTML-based class documentation for a class library that he had developed. The HTML-based documentation proved very effective and accessible, especially because it could easily be made accessible to engineers at other sites.

Recommendations

Consider reuse early

During your pilot development you should try to produce classes for reuse on future projects. This forward thinking will give you a head start on the next object-based development and will help your organization to realize reuse (typically a long-term benefit of object technology) as soon as possible.

You should consider and evaluate the potential reusability of everything you develop. Your development standards and methods should promote or at least enable reuse. Every time you make a decision, you should ask yourself, "How might this decision relate to software reuse?"

Especially if your organization does not have a software reuse group, you should take steps to facilitate the eventual reuse of the software components and classes that you develop for your pilot project. You will thank yourself a thousand times over for any steps that you take now to facilitate reuse in the future.

Develop class-level unit test harnesses

You should develop and maintain class-level unit test harnesses. No one (including your own team) will reuse software that has not been verified and known to function correctly. Class-level unit tests (if properly maintained) can be used as regression tests to verify that changes to classes do not affect their ability to behave properly in existing applications.

Ideally, you should have criteria that define the level of test coverage that your class-level unit tests should achieve. Tools exist to measure and analyze the level of test coverage being provided by a test harness. If your organization does not have standards to guide the development and measurement of class-level testing, you should use your best judgment to determine important areas to concentrate on. Whatever you do to decide what to test, make sure that you document the decisions and assumptions you have made in the test harness documentation (and as comments in test case implementation).

Think about your customers—make your classes visible and accessible
If your organization does not have a culture that supports software reuse, then you should take whatever steps you can to make it as easy as possible for others to understand and use the classes that you develop.

Create HTML-based documentation for the classes you develop
If your organization has a standard mechanism for documenting classes, you should use it. If you are not currently using World Wide Web servers to provide class documentation, you should consider this approach. The development of HTML-based documentation will allow you to

- easily support hypertext links between pages of class documentation
- provide printing support for free
- provide an architecture/platform-independent mechanism for accessing the documentation
- support remote access to class documentation
- make the information easily available

Invest in software reuse
Software reuse is a long-term benefit of object technology. For software reuse to really work, your organization must understand the value and costs of reuse. Your organization should attach more value to designs that appropriately reuse existing software than to designs that reinvent the wheel. It should reward engineers for reusing software.

Your organization should also invest in software reuse. Typically, the testing and support of reusable software will cost more than software components or classes that are only used in a single product. Also, if your reusable classes and software components are by-products of customer-focused developments, some reengineering will probably be needed to make the software generally useful. Your organization should also invest in a reuse librarian who acts as the gatekeeper and manager of the reuse library. Eventually, a team focused exclusively on creating and maintaining reuse assets will prove very useful in ensuring the long-term success of software reuse.

Understand the lessons learned by others setting up reuse programs
We have learned a number of lessons since the completion of the pilot project:

- The company culture must support reuse and engineering resources must be invested in the reuse effort before it will have a major impact in a software development organization.
- Simple things like naming conventions should be thought through at a global-level prior to starting the pilot project.
- Carefully evaluate the use of third-party class libraries in any reusable software components—decide up front if you want to require the use of the class library and, at the very least, separate components that depend on third-party libraries from components that do not require their use.
- Group classes into libraries that provide some basic framework or functionality (e.g., all classes needed for communications support and wrapper classes for UNIX functions).

Here are some tips related to starting a reuse program:

- Learn about other organizations that have successfully (and unsuccessfully) started reuse programs.
- Start the reuse library by building a control process around the use of third-party class libraries. This control process should be used to manage changes, log defects, and support a registry that maintains a list of projects dependent on each class library in use within the organization.
- Your first step should be to build up general utility class libraries by re-engineering classes developed for the pilot project.
- Develop automated test harnesses that can be used as regression tests for every class involved in the reuse program.
- Add a step in the development life cycle that requires developers to check the class library and sign off on what classes were or were not found.

1.7   RESULTS OF THE PILOT PROJECT

1.7.1   Summary of Project Successes and Lessons Learned

Results

The pilot object technology project was a success in every respect. The software developed during the pilot met the original requirements and has proved to be very easy to maintain and enhance. Maintainability of the simulation tools developed in the pilot was in part due to the clean and well-documented analysis and design that were developed using Fusion. The coding and development standards and templates also helped to maintain a high standard of consistency across code developed by the team. The final integration was trouble free and the system was delivered on time.

Besides the pilot project succeeding in meeting its requirements as a software development project, the pilot also succeeded in pioneering the use of object technology. Even before the final delivery of the pilot project, object technology was adopted for a mainstream development. Since the pilot project, more software engineers with object-technology experience have been hired by our organization, and several of our engineers have received training and are now applying object technology.

Today, both the software developed during the pilot project and object technology itself are seeing more use within our organization. The pilot of object technology using Fusion has clearly led our organization's transition to object technology.

Here is an overview of the results and lessons of the pilot:

- The systems worked! In fact, they worked well and proved the viability of OO development in our product domain.
- The systems were extensible and accommodated changes in requirements easily.
- Better traceability would have helped efforts to identify the work needed for intermediate integrations, track the development, and assess the impact of new and changing requirements.
- Early partial integrations paid off—the final integration was virtually problem free, since any problems had been previously identified and addressed.
- Establishing measurable metrics and success criteria for the pilot project should have been done at the beginning of the pilot.
- Complete use of Fusion (in particular, preconditions and postconditions) would have helped the development of test cases.
- Cooperative analysis and design are more effective than solitary work.
- Time spent developing template deliverables was time well spent—return on investment was seen by the end of the pilot.
- The use of subsystems proved to be effective.
- Efforts invested during the pilot project to develop reusable class libraries was justified when some of this work was used on the first mainstream object technology development to follow the pilot.

1.7.2   Transfer of Object Technology to Mainstream Development

After the completion of a successful pilot project, you will have a number of experienced object technologists who have tasted success with objects. The next step is to apply object technology in a mainstream development, building on the experience gained in the pilot to bring the advantages of object technology to other development projects. However, some caution does need to be exercised, and it is better to keep the pilot team together on the first mainstream object technology project than to dilute the core of expertise by spreading the object technologists too thinly across multiple projects.

Case Study

The development team was seeded into the organization
As the pilot development was winding down, the organization recognized that there was value in the use of object technology. For various reasons, one of them

being the desire to "grow" object technologists in other groups, the team was split up. This split actually diluted the effort to increase the use of object technology. Some of the original team members were seeded into projects that were not actively applying object technology. It was not surprising that the use of object technology in these seeded groups did not begin magically.

The one team that has continued to actively apply object technology recruited experienced permanent and contract object technologists and is moving ahead on a mainstream project that is applying object technology. One team seeded with a single member of the original pilot is making slower progress, but is moving toward the adoption of object technology for another mainstream application. The other single member that was resourced into a team not using objects is still frustrated by the prospect of a slow journey toward adoption of the technology in her group.

Object technology was applied to mainstream applications

After the success of the pilot object technology developments, the next step was to apply the technology to a mainstream project being developed for external customers. This mainstream application of object technology received even wider management support than the pilot project. To date, the development has been very successful and has resulted in the development of several class libraries that are strong candidates for widespread reuse.

Recommendations

Try to avoid the seeding syndrome

Do not split up teams effective at applying object technology. It is a fallacy to think that seeding your organization with object technologists will lead to successful adoption of object technology. The best way to grow object technologists is through immersion. You should maintain the critical mass of any object technology team and plant engineers into the team to grow the experience base.

If your organization feels that it must seed object technologists into groups that are not using objects, you should make sure that some mass is maintained by the object technologists. Moving a single object technologist into a group of people using objects is not a good way to promote the use and success of object technology. If seeding must follow the pilot project, don't split the team up into groups smaller than two or three engineers.

Facilitate organization-wide adoption of object technology

When your organization moves to more widespread use of objects, you may need to take some time to enhance the development scaffolding that you put in place for the pilot. The tools (e.g., templates, standards, and class libraries) for working with objects created for the pilot provide a good starting point. However, despite foresight and hard work, some modifications and enhancements are likely to be needed before these tools are ready for general use. Plan to spend some time during the early stages of the first mainstream object-based development on reengineering some of these tools, taking into account lessons learned on the pilot. This investment will encourage and enable the successful adoption of object technology by your organization.

1.8 CONCLUSION

If you or your organization decides to make the transition to object technology, you should pilot the technology to prove its value. Many ideas have been presented in this paper to help increase the chances of success both for pilots of object technology and the mainstream acceptance and use of the technology. In fact, the case study documented in this paper provides concrete examples of how an object technology pilot has successfully led a transition to object technology.

The transition strategy relies on Object Technology Champions to lead the transition, using a pilot project as the key vehicle to prove the benefits of object technology. Management buy-in, the use of Fusion (a systematic OOA/D method), training, an appropriate pilot project, the advice of experienced object practitioners, project planning, development groundwork, and vision are all important for a successful transition to object technology. This paper has presented ideas that provide a pragmatic approach to succeeding with objects.

There is no magic way and there will always be Luddites who need to be won over. However, Fusion provides a proven path through the quagmire of object-oriented software development. By embracing the power of Fusion and taking on-board some of the ideas presented in this paper you will improve your chances of a successful transition to object technology and position your organization to benefit from its advantages.

OBJECT TECHNOLOGY ON-LINE RESOURCES

List servers

- Fusion Forum
  To subscribe, e-mail a message to:
      listserv@hplsrd.hpl.hp.com
  in the body of message put:
      subscribe fusion_forum <your name>

Internet news groups

- comp.object
- comp.c++

World Wide Web sites

- www.taligent.com
  - General object technology info
  - Object technology resource list
- http://st-www.cs.uiuc.edu/users/patterns/patterns.html

REFERENCES

Booch, G. 1994. *Object-Oriented Analysis and Design with Applications*, 2nd ed. Redwood City, CA: Benjamin/Cummings.

Coleman, D., P. Arnold, S. Bodoff, C. Dollin, H. Gilchrist, F. Hayes, and P. Jeremaes. 1994. *Object-Oriented Development: The Fusion Method*. Englewood Cliffs, NJ: Prentice Hall.

Collins, D. 1995. *Designing Object-Oriented User Interfaces*. Redwood City, CA: Benjamin/Cummings.

Coplien, J. O. 1992. *Advanced C++ Programming Styles and Idioms*. Reading MA: Addison-Wesley.

Cox, B., and A. Novobilski. 1991. *Object-Oriented Programming: An Evolutionary Approach*. Reading, MA: Addison-Wesley.

Gamma, E., R. Helm, R. Johnson, and J. Vlissides. 1995. *Design Patterns: Elements of Reusable Object-Oriented Software*. Reading, MA: Addison-Wesley.

Goldberg, A. 1985. *Smalltalk-80: The Language and Its Implementation*. Reading, MA: Addison-Wesley.

Griss, M. February 1995. Software Reuse: Objects and frameworks are not enough. *Object Magazine*.

IEEE. 1994. *IEEE Guide to Software Requirements Specification*. New York: Institute of Electrical and Electronics Engineers.

Jacobson, I., M. Christerson, P. Jonsson, and G. Övergaard. 1992. *Object-Oriented Software Engineering*. Reading, MA: Addison-Wesley.

Jones, C. 1994. *Assessment and Control of Software Risks*. Englewood Cliffs, NJ: Prentice Hall.

Love, T. 1993. *Object Lessons: Lessons Learned in Object-Oriented Development Projects*. New York, NY: SIGS Books.

Marick, B. 1995. *The Craft of Software Testing: Subsystem Testing including Object-Based and Object-Oriented Testing*. Englewood Cliffs, NJ: Prentice Hall.

Martin, J and J. Odell. 1992. *Object-Oriented Analysis and Design*. Englewood Cliffs, NJ: Prentice Hall.

Meyers, S. 1992. *Effective C++*. Reading, MA: Addison-Wesley.

Ousterhout. 1994. *Tcl and the Tk Toolkit*. Reading, MA: Addison-Wesley.

Rumbaugh, J., M. Blaha, W. Premerlani, F. Eddy, and W. Lorensen. 1991. *Object Oriented Modeling and Design*. Englewood Cliffs, NJ: Prentice Hall.

Shlaer, S. 1988. *Object-Oriented Systems Analysis: Modeling the World in Data*. Englewood Cliffs, NJ: Prentice Hall.

Taligent, Inc. 1993. *Lessons Learned from Early Adopters of Object Technology: A White Paper*. Cupertino, CA: Taligent.

Taligent, Inc. 1994. *Taligent's Guide to Designing Programs: Well-Mannered Object-Oriented Design in C++*. Reading, MA: Addison-Wesley.

Taylor, D. 1990. *Object-Oriented Technology: A Manager's Guide*. Reading, MA: Addison-Wesley.

Yourdon, E. 1994. *Object-Oriented Systems Design: An Integrated Approach*. Englewood Cliffs, NJ: Prentice Hall.

Using Fusion on a Hewlett–Packard Medical Imaging Project:
Analysis Phase Retrospective

Ron Falcone, Jacob Nikom, and Ruth Malan

Hewlett–Packard

2.1 Introduction

The medical imaging project documented in this paper faced the exciting but risky proposition of developing a breakthrough product in a new business area. Fusion analysis modeling proved very valuable in exploring the functionality and high-level structure of this first-of-its-kind system. Upon completion of the analysis phase, a project retrospective was held to capture the lessons learned[*]; it led to this paper, which describes the experiences of the project and identifies practices that worked well and pitfalls to avoid.

In the section that follows, we set the context for the project, pointing to the challenges that the project team had to address during the Fusion analysis phase. Next, we describe the organization and process, indicating the importance of role/responsibility allocation and a structured process in achieving a highly productive analysis phase. Lastly, we cover specific technical areas, including a description of how some aspects of the application were modeled, some of the difficulties encountered, and solutions that the team developed during Fusion analysis modeling.

---

[*] The retrospective was held for the benefit of the Advanced Objects Project in Hewlett–Packard Laboratories to help understand real-world project experiences with Fusion and the needs for the evolution of Fusion.

2.2 PROJECT CONTEXT

To provide some insight into the kind of product being developed and the challenges that Fusion helped the project team to address, this section outlines the project objectives and constraints and briefly describes the product and development issues and solution approaches.

Business Objectives

At present, no products combine techniques to acquire images and perform multiple types of measurement to provide a comprehensive examination of an internal human organ for the purpose of medical diagnosis. This project's objective is to be the first to market with such a product.

Product Description

The imaging product under development is comprised of multiple components (Figure 2.1):

- Data acquisition hardware and software
- Database
- Visualization and image processing (VIP) software package (to be discussed in this paper)

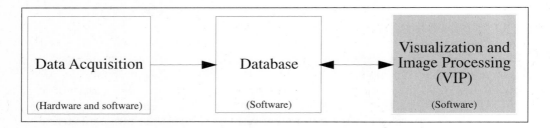

Figure 2.1 Schematic of the Medical Imaging Solution

The VIP application is intended to provide the following functionality:

1. Qualitative analysis of medical images:
   - viewing individual images and images by group sequence
   - changing image viewing parameters (intensity, contrast, brightness, artificial colorization, etc.)

2. Quantitative analysis of medical images:
   - manual procedures for extracting specific regions in the images
   - automatic segmentation procedures for outlining the organ boundaries
   - numerical procedures to support evaluation of the organ condition
   - dynamic graph plotting procedures for representing the results and supporting user interaction with those results

This project presented almost all major software engineering challenges, since it needed to provide

- A sophisticated user interface with the ability to directly manipulate objects on the screen
- Access to a database with the ability to store a large amount of information and the necessity of dealing with persistent and transient objects
- Advanced numerical algorithms containing the clinical knowledge necessary for automating medical analysis
- Complex data structures typical of software dealing with geometrical and multimedia objects

Consequently, implementation of this project created unique requirements for software developers in terms of analysis, design, and implementation.

Project Constraints

Time to market
Completing this first-of-its-kind product in an aggressive, fixed time frame was the top priority. To help address this time-to-market constraint, imaging libraries were chosen to be reused, even though they placed technical and organizational constraints on the product. On the other hand, because this was a new product and time constraints were tight, little priority was given to design *for* future reuse.

Budget constraints
The project's budget was tight. For the software group this came down to a hard choice between getting training in OO design practices or buying a CASE tool. The team chose training.

Technology Choices
The product incorporates the following technologies: UNIX, X/Motif, and imaging libraries. Both X/Motif and the imaging products are C-based libraries. UIM/X was used for user interface prototyping. SoftBench was chosen as the development environment, with ClearCase for configuration management. The project standardized on Framemaker for documentation.

The team recognized that the product would need to be readily adaptable. Because it was revolutionary, new use scenarios would emerge to alter the requirements for future versions or variants of the product. Therefore, object technology was chosen to help design and build a more readily evolvable, flexible system. Moreover, it was anticipated that inheritance could be leveraged to yield efficiencies in developing the product. Since the choice was between C and C++, the latter was chosen for development of the VIP software, even though we had misgivings about the complexity of the language and lack of C++ experience.

OO methodology and CASE tool investigation
The team conducted an initial evaluation of three OO analysis and design methodologies (Fusion, OMT, and Schlaer-Mellor) and three supporting CASE tools.

However, we decided that we needed training to adequately evaluate tools—how can you evaluate a tool fairly if you don't have a comprehensive understanding of the methodology? We also needed a common language to describe our ideas. Thus training had to come first and, as it turned out, it was all we could afford. We could contract internally to HP's Software Initiative (SWI) at a fraction of the cost and carry on a more informal relationship than working with an outside supplier. Since SWI has considerable expertise in Fusion training and consulting, that sealed our choice of Fusion.

Project Issues and Solutions

Acquiring C++ knowledge

While the team members were senior engineers with a lot of C experience, only two had C++ experience. The project chose a multipronged approach to address the lack of C++ experience, including C++ training and adoption of an OO analysis and design methodology.

OO analysis and design method: By first doing OO analysis and design, it was believed that the team would be better prepared to do C++ coding, since they would pick up OO concepts through use of the OO method. Also, by analyzing and designing the system with Fusion models rather than mixing design into implementation, the coding phase would be very focused and would restrict the use of C++ to the necessary constructs to properly implement the system.

C++ training: Two of the team members took C++ courses through a local college. These were full-semester courses with good lecturers and frequent, instructive homework assignments, and they provided an excellent learning mechanism. The team members who took a week-long C++ course and audited a videotaped class did not gain the same solid grounding in C++. Based on these experiences, we recommend that managers provide the time and incentive to take a college class in C++ for credit.

Acquiring OO analysis and design knowledge

While some of the team had attended OMT classes, few had any experience applying an OO analysis and design method. Therefore, Fusion training was a high priority.

Fusion training and consulting: HP's internal software consultancy, the Software Initiative (SWI), was contracted to provide Fusion training and ongoing Fusion consulting. The four-day Fusion workshop that the SWI consultants held on site with the project team was highly successful for a number of reasons:

- It was delivered immediately prior to the OO analysis phase—i.e., "just-in-time."
- It focused on applying Fusion to the team's problem space.
- The entire project team, including the project manager, attended the workshop, so all gained exposure to the Fusion models and process.

To the Software Initiative's credit, the team concluded that their decision to allocate their discretionary funds to Fusion training and consulting was key to their success. The SWI's expertise was very valuable, for example, in helping to clarify aspects of Fusion, working through analysis roadblocks like determining the appropriate level of detail for the use scenarios, and in model reviews. Based on this experience, we recommend that projects transitioning to OO development invest in expert training and consulting.

Acquiring domain knowledge

A few of the team members had a background in related product areas. However, for the most part the software team faced the challenge of learning the domain language and concepts. Team members read relevant books and papers and attended various conferences, seminars, and trade shows to gain background domain knowledge. In the three VIP product application areas, multidisciplinary teams (with representatives from software, marketing, and data acquisition) were formed to work on requirements analysis and issue resolution. These teams visited a number of hospitals to talk with domain experts, watch clinical procedures, and perform task analyses, thereby developing further understanding of the application area and user requirements.

Team building

Because this was a new product area for HP, engineers had to be brought on board from other HP medical divisions and other companies. Thus the VIP software team consisted of a set of engineers with rather diverse backgrounds. Moreover, most of the team had never worked together before. To assist in building a cohesive team, experts from the University of New Hampshire facilitated a two-day team-building exercise. Additional opportunities to help build the team were created, including team celebrations on completion of project milestones.

Summary of Challenges

This team faced a variety of challenges:

- The product was the first of its kind, and although there was experience in the industry in various technologies that the product would bring together, they had not been combined before.
- The time-to-market objective was aggressive.
- Most of the team were new to this product domain, though some had experience in related areas.
- Most of the team were new to object technology, and all were new to Fusion.
- The team members had not worked together before.

As will be seen in the sections that follow, the team completed a very successful analysis phase in spite of these challenges. Along with a combination of management and engineering expertise and ingenuity, Fusion's systematic process and clear model deliverables played a key role in this success.

2.3 PROCESS AND ORGANIZATION

As the project progressed, the organization and process evolved. A principal lesson that the team learned was that structure (in terms of role/responsibility allocation) and discipline (in terms of frequent model inspections on a tight schedule) are important to a highly energized and effective OO analysis phase. For the benefit of those new to object-oriented development in general, and Fusion in particular, the project time line, organization, and process are described in this section.

2.3.1 Project Time Line

Figure 2.2 shows the major project deliverables (shown above the time line) and significant events (shown below the time line) for the project. The phase 1 kickoff meeting was held in March. During the ensuing months, the primary focus of effort was on capturing user needs and producing the requirements documents (a draft version and then the Software Requirements Specification, or SRS, Rev. A). At the same time, a variety of technology investigations were carried out, including assessment of library software, methods, and tools.

With a good draft of the requirements document (SRS Rev. A) in hand by the end of November, the OO analysis (OOA) phase was initiated. Since no his-

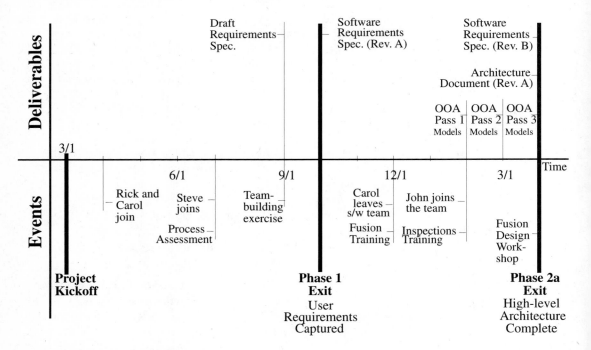

Figure 2.2 Major Project Events and Deliverables

torical OO project data were available for the project to base its OOA phase estimates on, the team essentially guessed at a reasonable time frame for the analysis work. Two intermediate checkpoints were set (at the end of Pass 1 and Pass 2) so that the analysis work would be done iteratively, and progress checks could be made at those intermediate checkpoints. Thus the analysis was conducted in three passes or iterations, with increasingly refined Fusion OOA model deliverables expected at the end of each pass. The analysis phase was completed on schedule and accounted for 15% of the *estimated* total project effort.

During the analysis phase it became clear that the OO modeling was surfacing significant gaps and ambiguities in the requirements document. Therefore, a revised requirements document (Rev. B) was planned to coincide with the end of the analysis phase.

Some of the more notable events in the earlier stages of the project included the two-day team-building exercise, a process assessment facilitated by the HP Software Initiative (SWI), and Fusion and inspections training from SWI. The principal project milestones that had been reached by April (just over a year after the project kickoff meeting) are the Phase 1 Exit (user requirements captured) and Phase 2a Exit (high-level architecture complete) checkpoints.

2.3.2   Evolution of Organization and Process during the OOA Phase

Figure 2.3 shows the primary project activities and responsibilities. For the analysis phase, these are detailed in the subsections that follow. Immediately following the Fusion training workshop, the team continued with the OO analysis phase, indicating that Fusion is easy to learn and apply to good effect.

During the OO analysis phase, the roles and responsibilities of the team members changed. This was not planned up front, but emerged as the team adapted to more efficient and effective ways of working. The informal checkpoints at the end of each pass provided the opportunity to explicitly adopt new modes of operating that had evolved during the previous pass.

OOA Pass 1

Team meetings

During the OOA first pass, the entire team met every day for about six hours to work on the analysis models. The objectives were to foster communication and develop a shared system view, and to have the various individuals' perspectives and expertise reflected in the analysis. The following meeting procedure emerged:

- Discuss the problem and draw the object model on the white board.
- Translate the object model from the white board into Framemaker.
- Next morning distribute the model to participants.
- Start each meeting with discussion of the previous day's model. (This created an opportunity to spot possible problems by seeing the model with a fresh view.)
- After approval of the model, go on to develop the next one.

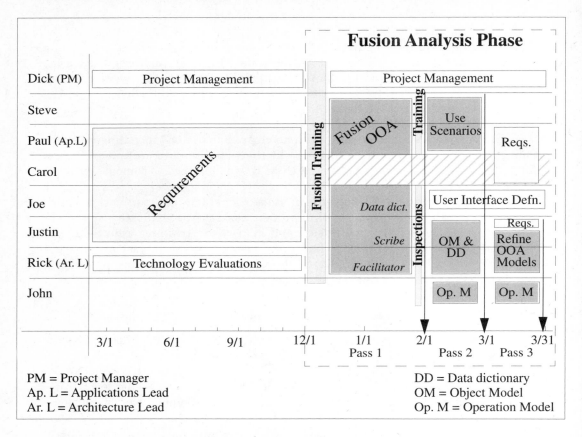

Figure 2.3 Primary Project Activities and Responsibilities

What worked well in Pass 1 team meetings:

Dedicated meeting room: To accommodate this mode of working, a conference room was dedicated to the team. Four white boards provided ample space for drawing diagrams, and because the room was reserved for the team, the models could remain posted from one day to the next.

Issues list: The team maintained an issues list. As issues were identified, they were classified by type (specification, analysis, and design) and priority (low, medium, and high urgency). Each type was associated with an action (specification—try to resolve and record in SRS; analysis—try to resolve and record in analysis model; design—postpone until design phase). Each issue was logged in the issues list, along with the assigned owner and due date. An illustrative segment of the issues list is shown in Table 2.1.

These effective meeting practices were continued through the next passes.

Table 2.1 Segment from the Issues List Dated 2/10

No.	Class	Owner	Due Date	Description	Resolution
3	Design			When do you load images?	Deferred
4	Design			When we update contours on the display or in the database: — Do we send one event containing all contours? — Or do we send one event for each contour?	Deferred
5	Analysis	Rick	3/3	Need a method for tracking Analysis & Design documentation back to the SRS	Open
6	Spec.	Paul, Joe	3/9	SRS describes searching for Exams by Study Type, but they don't have a Study Type.	Open
7	Analysis	Justin	2/6	Is a contour an ROI? If they are different, how?	A contour is used for surface representation and corresponds to a specific anatomical surface of the organ. It should be placed extremely precisely to correctly describe the surface. A region of interest (ROI) is used for measurements of average pixel intensity in any area of the image. The placement does not have any anatomical significance and does not require careful positioning. Moreover, this is a manual procedure, whereas surface-related placement of the contours could be done automatically. Finally, contours are chained to each other to represent a surface, whereas ROIs do not need to be chained.

What did not work so well:

The daylong working meetings did not allow time to mull over approaches. This tended to result in team members "shooting from the hip" rather than advocating well-thought-out ideas.

Roles and responsibilities

The following roles were assigned to help make the process more efficient and effective.

Facilitator: The lead architect most frequently took the role of facilitator, although the applications lead also played this role. The facilitator was responsible for capturing the team's input on the drawing board and for keeping order in the meetings. This was not always easy, given the strong personalities in the team.

Scribe: The role of scribe was assigned to one of the team members for the duration of Pass 1. This person was responsible for capturing the models drawn on the boards, translating them into Framemaker, and distributing the updated models to the team. The role was difficult, because things would change during the course of the discussion and it was hard to manage these changes on paper. Also, closure was not reached on some issues, leaving alternatives unresolved. However, having the updated paper copies of the models distributed at the meetings was important because it gave the team the chance to look them over and verify that their understanding had been captured in the models.

Data dictionary owner: The team member assigned this role was responsible for capturing new terms as they arose, providing definitions for them, and maintaining consistency in the data dictionary.

Accomplishments

By the end of the first pass, the team understood the bounds of the problem well and had developed a shared sense of the overall system and a common vision of the product to be built. For example, during the requirements capture phase, there was no clear understanding of what classes made up derived data. It looked big and amorphous, but through the analysis modeling process it became clear that there was a relatively small set of classes, and the team could be very specific about what needed to be done to create the product.

Transition

The daylong meetings that the team started out with in Pass 1 were too long and not clearly focused. During the first pass the team began to adjust the process, and formally adopted a more disciplined and structured process for the second pass.

OOA Pass 2

Responsibility assignments

During the second pass, responsibilities for different models were allocated to smaller subteams.

OOA responsibilities: Two engineers were assigned responsibility for extending and refining the object model and data dictionary, two were assigned to work on the use scenarios, and one on operation schemata.

UI responsibility: The user interface subsystem was intentionally more independent from the rest of the system. Since a first pass at the interface to the UI subsystem had been defined, further development of the UI definition was spun off as a parallel thread of work during the second and third passes of the analysis modeling.

Inspections

The team received training on how to conduct inspections from the Software Initiative, and a formal inspections process was adopted. This allowed the team to spend less time in group meetings while retaining the benefits of developing a shared system view and getting input from all the developers on the team. In particular, before each inspections meeting, the OOA models were submitted to a desk review by the other subteams. Consequently, the team came to the meeting having already read and commented on the models that the participants had been given to review. At the inspections meetings there was still much discussion, but the discussion was very focused and more productive than in the long team meetings in the first pass.

The second pass was very schedule driven, with frequent due dates and corresponding inspections for completion of models. Because a number of threads of analysis work were being pursued simultaneously (Figure 2.3), inspections meetings were held almost daily. This kept up the pressure to get work done and to review the models developed by the other subteams.

Accomplishments

At the end of the first pass the team had visited all the analysis models once, but things did not quite fit together. During the second pass, the models were revisited and revised. Operation schemata were added, and there was clear convergence on the appropriate solution.

OOA Pass 3

Responsibility assignments

In the last pass, only three members of the team worked on the OOA models. Two continued to refine the object model, resolving outstanding issues and ensuring that the OOA models were consistent. The third engineer elaborated the operation model. Of the remaining team members, one continued to work on the user interface (UI), while the applications lead revised the requirements document (SRS).

Inspections

Those involved in the SRS and UI performed a valuable role in inspecting the OOA documents, providing the richest set of comments, raising important issues, and holding the OOA subteam's "feet to the fire" to get the analysis models right. They had a more objective view, yet understood the system, so they could see gaps or contradictions and how everything fit together. Conversely, through the understanding gained during the analysis modeling, the OOA model subteams were able to offer valuable input during inspections of the SRS and UI documents. They were able to point to gaps, ambiguities, or inconsistencies in the SRS, and had a good sense of the trade-offs and costs involved in the specified functionality.

Accomplishments

Through the process of object-oriented analysis, the team developed a deeper understanding of what this visualization and image processing software package would provide to users, and of the overall structure of the system. At the end of the analysis phase, the high-level system architecture and the refined user requirements were officially signed off, marking completion of Phase 2a, which was a major project checkpoint.

The team faced a number of challenges at the outset. However, over the four-month period during which the Fusion analysis phase was conducted, the team became more structured and made rapid progress as the process was adapted to one that was more disciplined.

2.3.3   Summary of Lessons Learned in the OOA Phase

Practices that Worked Well

The following practices proved highly effective:

- Partitioning of work to be done and assignment of responsibilities
- Conducting desk reviews and inspections
- Maintaining an issues list

Also, conducting the analysis phase as a series of passes, with intermediate checkpoints, was viewed as a key success factor. Not only were the models refined iteratively, but the passes allowed the team to incrementally adapt the process, creating opportunities to formally adjust as they learned better modes of organizing and working through the analysis activities.

2.4   BUILDING ANALYSIS MODELS

We turn now to the more technical aspects of Fusion analysis modeling in this product domain. First, we set further context, providing some additional description of the product and underlying architecture. As is common in the early part of the analysis phase, the team faced the challenge of identifying the objects[*] in the system. We present an illustrative example of the team's approach to developing application objects. To demonstrate how features of the Fusion models were used in this application, we provide some examples of the use of roles in the last part of this section.

2.4.1   Product Requirements

One primary goal of our product was to put clinical knowledge into software. In the first release, there were to be three primary applications: visualization, measurement, and diffusion. Each application provides the physician with different kinds of information related to a diagnostic task. The visualization application creates a picture of the organ in space. The measurement application provides

---

[*] While these may more correctly be called classes, it was more convenient to loosely refer to objects, while being clear on the distinction between object instances and classes.

specific calculations based on manually entered and acquired imaging data. Lastly, the diffusion application derives measurements based on image processing of contrast agents (e.g., agents injected into the bloodstream or organ).

2.4.2   Basic Architecture

A goal of the architecture was to keep the user interface (UI) as independent as possible, to isolate future changes in this area. The imaging platform (including database access and abstract imaging class libraries) was also intended to be maintained separately. The application classes formed the intermediate layer (Figure 2.4).

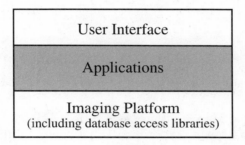

Figure 2.4 Layered Architecture

2.4.3   Developing Application Objects

The following discussion illustrates how we developed useful objects in our system by modeling physiological objects in our application domain. In particular, we decided to model some of the anatomical features of the organs as objects in our system. One such feature is the surface of the organ. The intersection of these surfaces with imaging planes created contours that we could see in our images. A stack of images in space contained a stack or collection of contours. These were our first candidates for application objects (Figure 2.5).

Working with the **contour** object we encountered some problems. A contour could be used for a surface representation, corresponding to a specific anatomical surface of the organ. In this case it should be placed extremely precisely to describe the surface correctly. It could also be used to create a region of interest (ROI), which is used for measurements of average pixel intensity in any area of the image. In the latter case, the placement does not have any anatomical significance and does not require careful positioning. Moreover, this is a manual procedure, whereas surface-related placement of the contours could be done automatically. Lastly, contours are chained to each other to represent a surface, whereas ROIs do not need to be chained.

Evidently the **contour** and **ROI** objects were similar internally, but had different usage. Also, **contour** could be used instead of **ROI**, but not vice versa.

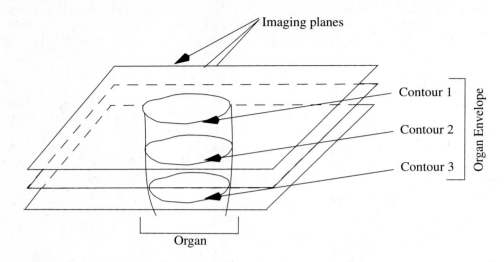

Figure 2.5 Representation of Anatomical Features: Contours and Envelopes in Space

Therefore, we decided to model them as a base and derived class (Figure 2.6a). Now it seems obvious, but we experimented with many different solutions: using an abstract base class that two objects were derived from; having only one object—**ROI**; having **ROI** as an attribute of the **Contour** class; etc.

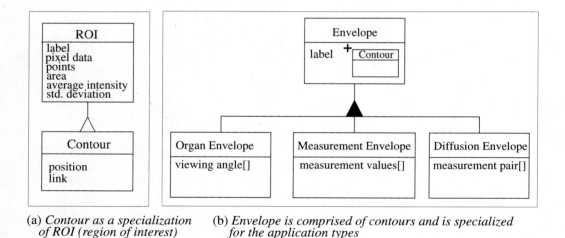

(a) *Contour as a specialization of ROI (region of interest)*

(b) *Envelope is comprised of contours and is specialized for the application types*

Figure 2.6 Representation of Anatomical Features and Use of Specialization

Taking this a step further, we created an **envelope** object which is an ordered collection of contours and may correspond to the real anatomical surface in space, or some "imaginary" surface if one of the parameters is time instead of spatial coordinates. We found that **envelope** is one of the central objects in our system, and it is utilized in all three applications.

We modeled this relation as a disjoint superclass partition or subtyping inheritance (Coleman et al. 1994, p. 257). This allowed us to put the common part—the collection of contours—outside each subclass and concentrate on the application's peculiarities in the specialized class (illustrated in Figure 2.6b). Once we found this basic architectural feature, solving the rest of the puzzle was quite easy. Pieces started to fit together almost automatically.

Modeling physiological objects had another advantage. At first glance all three applications looked very different, and this expanded the scope of the problem that we had to solve. However, because the applications were being performed on the same organ, through the analysis modeling we began to see that we could leverage the underlying physiological commonality to simplify the design. Moreover, although the technologies and use scenarios might change during the lifetime of the product, the human physiology was a constant that we could rely on to give stability to particular areas of our architecture.

2.4.4 Illustrative Use of Roles

Next, two examples are presented to show how roles were applied in this domain. In Figure 2.7, an **Organ** is modeled as an aggregate class that contains a second aggregate class, **Organ Wall**. Physiologically, an organ wall has an outer surface and may have an inner surface. These are represented in the model by two **Measurement Envelope** objects that exist in the **inside** relationship with each other. To distinguish the two, they are assigned the role of inner and outer, respectively.

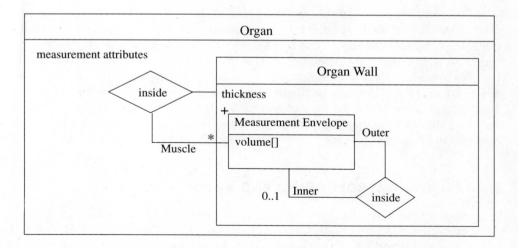

Figure 2.7 Applying Aggregation and Roles to Model an Organ

In the second example (Figure 2.8), we modeled organ masks as a role on an organ envelope. A mask is an arbitrary portion of the image that contains the structure the user wants to see. It is used to reduce the computation requirements of the software by limiting the field of interest. The mask is submitted to a segmentation process that will define the actual structure. We did this simply to show that the mechanism (modeled as **Organ Envelope**) used to define a mask is identical to that used to define a structure.

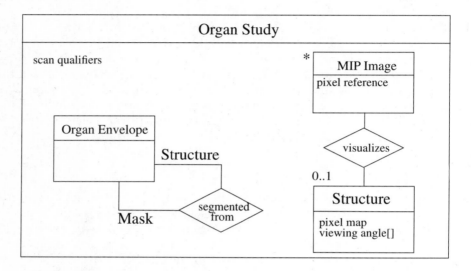

Figure 2.8 Organ Study Example, Showing Use of Roles

Once this was done, we were confronted with an issue that is not well documented in Fusion: what should we do with roles that have unique relationships with other objects? We elected to treat the roles as objects in other (portions of) diagrams that showed their relationship to other objects (as illustrated in Figure 2.8). We considered using generalization/specialization instead, but during analysis there was no difference in the attributes and therefore we could not justify them as unique objects. As we defined methods and got more complete definitions, we thought we would possibly drop the role notation and define **Mask** and **Structure** to be specializations of a generic **Organ Envelope**.

2.5 FUSION: IMPROVEMENTS AND VALUE

In this penultimate section, we pay particular attention to the lessons learned in the application of Fusion analysis models. First, we identify the models that the team used and extended. Next, we describe the problems that the team encountered in using the models and the solutions that they developed. Finally, we identify the benefits that the team believes Fusion brought to the project.

2.5.1   Modified Fusion Models

For the most part, the team used the Fusion analysis process and models as stated in the book (Coleman et al. 1994), but did not do any life-cycle models. The SWI consultants recommended doing some of the use scenarios up front, both to explore user requirements and to help identify classes. Therefore, the team identified and defined a number of use scenarios in conjunction with developing the first-pass object model. The team also extended some of the models, adding an assumptions clause and descriptions to the use scenarios (see, for example, Figure 2.12); and a use scenario reference clause in the operation schemata (as illustrated in Figure 2.9). The latter facilitated cross referencing between the use scenarios and operation model.

Operation:	select images
Description:	Request from the User that identifies a set of images that are the target of user operations.
Use Scenario:	Verify Image Quality, Assess Organ Diffusion, Review Exam Results
Reads:	**supplied** Images
Changes:	Study: selected images
Sends:	User: identify selected images.
Assumes:	Images are displayed.
Results:	A set of Images is selected by the User for operations; the Study retains knowledge of what Images are selected.

Figure 2.9 Operation Schema Showing the Use Scenario Reference Clause

2.5.2   Problem Areas and Solutions

Representing relationships

Of the three types of relationships that can be expressed with Fusion (is-a, has-a, and uses-a), emphasis is placed on the uses-a relationship. This relationship tends to be the most difficult to express concisely on a diagram yet convey a significant concept to the developers. At first we tried to express every relationship, but found most to be common across many objects. This cluttered the diagrams. It was better to express the relationships in words in the operation model. We limited the uses-a relationships that we showed in the object model to those that represented the most important ideas.

Since several pairs of objects may share the same type of relationship, we had the problem of duplicate entries in the data dictionary. We essentially came up with synonyms to nominally show the relationships to be unique. This was not entirely satisfactory and the issue should be taken up in improving Fusion.

Some members of the team found three-way relationships difficult to express correctly and understand. We never really solved this issue, but often one of the objects in the ternary relationship was a product of, or place for, the interaction of the other two. Introducing notation to make these kinds of distinctions in the object model may encourage the use of ternary relationships and give them a clearer meaning.

Fusion text lacks examples and specificity

The Fusion book (Coleman et al. 1994) does not go into enough detail. For example, it was necessary to go to other texts for better explanations of fundamental object concepts like the distinction between classes and instances (e.g., Booch 1994, and Rumbaugh et al. 1991), as well as more advanced concepts such as patterns (Gamma et al. 1995). Also, although all the necessary notation and semantics are covered in the text, generally the brevity and lack of examples leave those who are new to OOA/D and Fusion with too little to go on.

The workshop training and follow-up consulting provided by HP's internal software consultancy, the Software Initiative, were crucial in supplementing the text and helping the team move forward.

Attributes in the data dictionary

We found that having attributes of objects arranged in alphabetical order throughout the data dictionary made it difficult to update and review, so we introduced a variant in the notation to identify an attribute and grouped the attributes of an object immediately following the class entry (Figure 2.10).

Contour	Class	A **Contour** is a **ROI** used to outline an area on an **Image**.
.label	Attribute	The type attribute is used to define what anatomical structure is being described by the **Contour**.
.position	Attribute	The position attribute is used to describe where on the **Image** the **Contour** is located. The position will be the centroid of the **Contour** and can be selected for rotation and movement.
Envelope	Class	An **Envelope** is used to describe a three-dimensional surface described by a set of **Contours**. **Envelope** exists in x, y, z coordinates.
.label	Attribute	The label attribute is used to describe what anatomical structure is described by an **Envelope**.
.volume[]	Attribute	The volume[ ] attribute is used to describe the volume enclosed by an **Envelope**. The value of this attribute only makes sense when the **Envelope** describes a physical structure. It can be interpreted as displaced volume when the **Envelope** describes an Envelope structure.
draw diffusion region	SysOp	Request from the User to place a diffusion region at a specific location on an image.

Figure 2.10 Sections of the Data Dictionary

Representing use scenario variations

When doing use scenarios, we found it difficult not to consider or show key decision path alternatives and optional steps. If the graphical notation were richer, this sort of thing could be done in the use scenarios without either requiring lifecycle models or limiting the range of alternative scenarios considered.

Level for use scenarios

It was difficult to settle on the right level for the use scenarios—at too high a level they had little value, and at too low a level they quickly became mired in details. After a fair amount of trial and error, and with help from the SWI consultant, the team settled into getting the right level of information. Two use scenarios are contrasted in Figures 2.11 and 2.12. The first illustrates a case where some of the operations are at too low a level of granularity, and the second shows the refined use scenario. In particular, the operation "draw diffusion border" in Figure 2.12 corresponds to two operations, "drop points" and "ROI is done," in Figure 2.11.

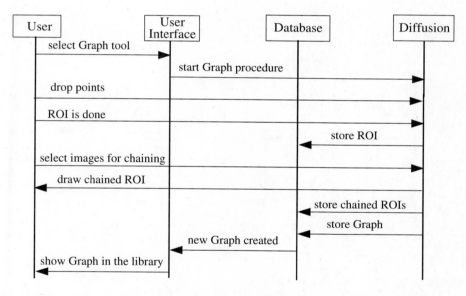

Figure 2.11 Use Scenario for Building a Time-graph (January 13)

User interface considerations

OO analysis and design methods say very little about designing good architectures. They provide little guidance on how to design and work out issues that arise in user interface analysis and design.

To isolate the user interface, it was treated as an agent external to the rest of the system. The database was also treated as an external agent. Since this system has only one human agent interacting with it, treating these two subsystems (UI and database) as external agents also helped to make the use sce-

Use Scenario: Assess Organ Diffusion

Assumptions: Diffusion scan is displayed in the Image Area, in the Default Layout, which
shows all Images on the Screen at once.
Image quality has been verified.
No Graphs have been created for this Exam yet.

Description: The tech first selects the Graph tool and places one Diffusion border on an Image and
chains it to a Selected subset of Images in the Scan. She repeats this for a second Diffusion border,
chaining to the same set of Images. She Chooses a Diffusion Zoom Layout and zooms the Images to
verify the placement of all diffusion borders. Several diffusion borders are found to be incorrectly
placed, and she Moves them to their correct positions. She approves the created diffusion borders
and starts the Graph creation operation, and a Graph entry appears in the Library. She uses the
Library to View the Graph in the Image Area, using the default Graph Layout. She Measures the Signal Intensity at one point on the curve and the Image from which that point was generated is displayed.

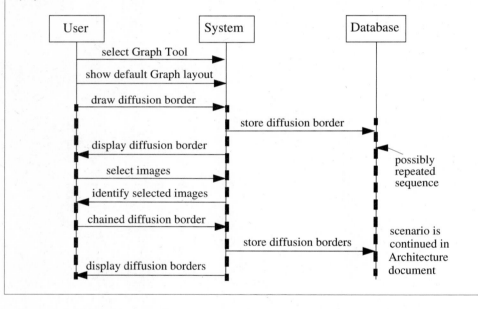

Figure 2.12 Use Scenario for Assessing Diffusion of an Organ (March 23)

narios more valuable. Figure 2.11 shows an early example of a use scenario
(dated January 13), where User Interface is shown as an agent. This is contrasted with a later use scenario (dated March 23), shown in Figure 2.12, where
User and User Interface have been collapsed into one agent (from the perspective of the system *excluding* the UI subsystem).

Good tool support is important but not critical
The team used Framemaker for the analysis documentation, both of the Fusion
diagrams and the text. In hindsight, not having a tool made the task of keeping
updated and consistent models difficult but not impossible. However, as our mod-

els grew and we entered design, the need for a tool became more pronounced. We were fast approaching the point where we would have no choice but to purchase a tool to track all the details and changes. On a larger project, the need for better tool support might have surfaced earlier.

2.5.3   Benefits of Object-oriented Analysis

For this project, the benefits of using an object-oriented analysis method included communication and evaluation of alternative ways of structuring the system (at the analysis level) and documentation of the system use models and structure. The general benefits the team gained from using Fusion include:

- Fusion calls for a clear set of work products around which the team structured its activities to both explore as well as document the analysis of product requirements.
- Using the Fusion notation we learned to express our ideas, as well as select and define terms, in an object-oriented way.
- Through the process of analysis, a number of significant issues (61 specification and 15 analysis) were identified and resolved. Had these only surfaced during coding, they would have resulted in significant rework. Moreover, since the Fusion analysis models could be inspected, a considerable number of defects were uncovered early.

The particular benefits provided by the Fusion models were the following:

Object model: Most of our time was spent on the object model, because it provided a useful medium for exploring, communicating, and documenting ideas about the scope and high-level structure of our system.

Use scenarios: The use scenarios were valuable in exploring functional flow and representing user requirements in the analysis models. Modeling the UI and database subsystems as agents in the use scenarios helped identify subsystem interfaces.

Operation model: The operation model helped link together the object model and use scenarios and exposed significant gaps in the other two models. It specified functionality that the design must accommodate. Unlike OMT, Fusion provided traceability between analysis models and design models, the key link being the operation model; in effect, this made the entire modeling process consistent and seamless.

Data dictionary: The data dictionary played an invaluable role in the project. In the beginning of the analysis phase, the team members would kick around terms as if they were generally understood. After a while it was discovered that the same term meant different things to different people. The data dictionary became very important to ensure common understanding.

In retrospect, the team determined that Fusion had played an important role in addressing the challenges that they faced.

2.6 CONCLUSION

Although the project is not yet complete, by the end of the analysis phase it had accomplished a considerable amount and learned a number of lessons of import to Fusion practitioners (as well as to method developers). By adjusting the process and responsibility allocations, the team achieved a high level of productivity that yielded a good shared understanding of the system functionality and high-level structure in just four months. While this would be a significant achievement under any circumstances, it is all the more notable given that this is a breakthrough product.

Fusion played an important role in the analysis phase successes by providing models that proved valuable in exploring the system functionality, surfacing ambiguities and gaps in the requirements document, and in understanding and evaluating choices in structuring the system. It also established clear deliverables (in the form of models) that the process, responsibilities, and schedule could be structured around.

However, the team did encounter some difficulties with Fusion. Some of these can be attributed, at least in part, to lack of experience in object-oriented analysis and design, but others point to areas where Fusion (or the Fusion text) could be improved. The team also extended the analysis models in useful ways, adding assumptions and description clauses to the use scenarios and a use scenario reference to the operation schemata.

ACKNOWLEDGMENTS

We would like to thank Dave Hempstead, John Hart, Peter Kelley, Jim Grady, and Jeff LeBlanc for their support and valuable suggestions for improvements to this paper. We would especially like to acknowledge all members of the VIP team who contributed to the lessons learned on this project. In addition, we would like to thank the HP Software Initiative consultants, Jean MacLeod, Mark Davey, and Wendell Fields, for their contributions. Bill Crandle, Lew Creary, and Reed Letsinger are also thanked for their suggestions made in reviewing this paper.

REFERENCES

Booch, G. 1994. *Object-Oriented Analysis and Design with Applications*, 2nd ed. Redwood City, CA: Benjamin/Cummings.

Coleman, D., P. Arnold, S. Bodoff, C. Dollin, H. Gilchrist, F. Hayes, P. Jeremaes. 1994. *Object-Oriented Development: The Fusion Method*. Englewood Cliffs, NJ: Prentice Hall.

Gamma, E., R. Helm, R. Johnson, and J. Vlissides. 1995. *Design Patterns: Elements of Reusable Object-Oriented Software*. Menlo Park, CA: Addison-Wesley.

Rumbaugh, J., M. Blaha, W. Premerlani, F. Eddy, and W. Lorensen. 1991. *Object-Oriented Modeling and Design*. Englewood Cliffs, NJ: Prentice Hall.

P A R T

██ 2 ██

Applications

*F*usion was developed for use by technical software developers. Today it is being used in a wide variety of domains, including finance and telecoms. The papers in Part 2 describe interesting applications of Fusion and identify extensions and modifications that have made Fusion successful in practice.

Paul Jeremaes's paper, "Extending the Fusion Design Process for TMN Application Development," deals with issues that arise in applying Fusion in the Telecommunications Management Network (TMN) area. In particular, the presence of the Management Information Base and TMN standards place constraints on system design. Domain-specific constraints in the form of legacy databases or applications that the system must interact with are common in system development. Thus the extensions to the Fusion design process that were developed to deal with "bottom-up" design constraints in TMN application development have a bearing on a broader class of application areas.

Working for a commercial software house that develops custom software under contract, Laurence Canning and Richard Nethercott have gained experience applying Fusion in a variety of domains. They describe approaches to Fusion project planning and execution in "Using Fusion for Commercial Fixed-Price Bespoke Development." For bespoke development, especially on fixed-price projects, the ability to predict and control software development costs may be viewed as a core competency of successful companies. The paper covers such topics as cost estimation and staffing that are critical in bespoke development, but just as vital in any disciplined development project of reasonable scale.

In "An Approach to Process Description using Fusion," Colin Atkinson and Michael Weisskopf develop extensions to Fusion for process modeling. Process modeling has emerged as a crucial activity for organizations that develop, maintain, or rely on software. The paper describes an approach to process description using notations adapted from Fusion. In addition to offering the benefits and maturity of a mainstream object-oriented development technique, Fusion pro-vides notational innovations that the authors believe make it particularly well suited to process description. Chief among these is the *object interaction graph,* which enables the functional and behavioral aspects of a process to be concisely described in terms of interacting objects.

After first describing how Fusion models can be used to capture software processes and then detailing the required enhancements to the notation, the paper applies the approach to a portion of the Domain Maintenance Process developed for use by Rockwell in reengineering NASA's space shuttle support software.

Extending the Fusion Design Process for TMN Application Development

Paul Jeremaes

Hewlett–Packard Research Laboratories

3.1 INTRODUCTION

Fusion is an object-oriented development method that provides a framework of analysis and design models and processes to support the full software development life cycle (Coleman et al. 1994). It was designed as a generic object-oriented method, assuming a *green-field* or *clean-slate* development effort that takes a set of initial requirements through to implementation.

In practice, textbook developments are rare. There will typically be domain-specific constraints placed on the development activity. These may take the form of application design constraints, made explicit in the requirements, or perhaps aspects of the application's embedding infrastructure. No matter what form they take, these constraints will almost certainly influence the way the system is developed and in some cases will require modifications to be made to the development process.

In this paper we investigate extensions to the Fusion design process to support the development of TMN management applications. The Telecommunications Management Network (TMN) is an architecture for the management and control of telecommunication service provider networks (Bapat 1994). A set of international recommendations and standards defines the TMN architecture and the function of certain elements in a telecommunication network (TMN 1992a through e). In what follows, we show how aspects of this architecture affect the way in which management applications are developed, raising the need for additional steps during the design process.

3.2 TMN APPLICATION DEVELOPMENT

The main driving force behind the TMN standardization activity comes from the telecommunication service providers, who wish to ensure the interoperability of management applications obtained from different vendors. To that end, the TMN standards define an architecture, functional components that populate that architecture, and interfaces to those components and provide guidelines for application developers.

     The full details of the TMN architecture are beyond the scope of this paper, but we will consider one aspect that is of central importance to the application developer, namely the Management Information Base (MIB). Conceptually, the MIB contains all the management information about network elements (e.g., transmission/signaling equipment), network configuration, customer services, etc. In practice, the MIB consists of a distributed, heterogeneous collection of data sources. Management applications interact with the MIB to gain access to the structure and content of management information and thus provide the necessary management and control functions (Figure 3.1).

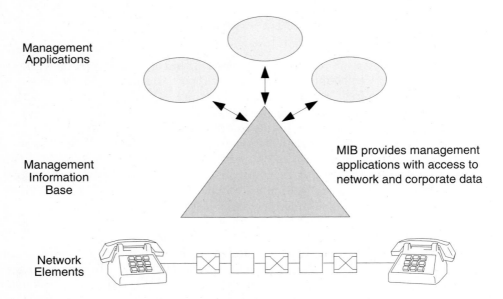

Figure 3.1 Management Applications Gain Access to Network Elements via the MIB

     The MIB is defined in terms of *managed objects,* and the TMN standards use many familiar object-oriented concepts to define these (TMN 1992f). A managed object can represent anything deemed important to the management of the telecommunications network (e.g., multiplexers, switches, subnetworks, and software) and provides a management view of the resource concerned (NCC Blackwell 1992). It is defined in terms of the management operations that can be performed on it, the behavior of these operations, the data attributes that are visible at the management interface, and the notifications that it is allowed to make about events that occur. Note that one network element may be modeled by hundreds, possibly thousands, of managed objects.

Managed objects in the MIB represent the network resources being managed and provide network information to a variety of management applications. Consequently, the developer of a management application has to produce a design with the contents of the MIB in mind. The design cannot proceed based only on the operational and functional requirements of the particular application being developed. It is also constrained by the information that is available from the managed objects in the MIB. This constraint can be looked on as *bottom-up* design information (Figure 3.2). A similar situation exists when a class library or application framework is used on a development project. The existing classes and structures in a framework, for example, have to be utilized in the application design, imposing bottom-up design constraints.

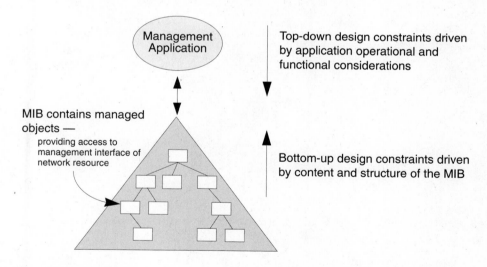

Figure 3.2 The MIB Imposes Constraints on Application Design

The core Fusion method is essentially driven *top down*, with the required *system operations* guiding the design process. The steps outlined in this paper show how the apparent conflict between top-down and bottom-up design constraints can be resolved when developing TMN applications that require access to managed objects in the MIB. We start by considering the analysis and design models that are used in Fusion to establish the information model for an application. We then see how the information model has to be modified to take the MIB into account.

3.3   APPLICATION INFORMATION MODELS

A major output of Fusion analysis and design is the application information model, designed to support the required system operations. This is realized in terms of object classes, data attributes of these classes, and the object-valued attributes, providing visibility links between classes.

Initial attention is given to the information model with the construction of the *object model* during analysis. This captures the static structure of information in the application and its environment. The *system object model* is a subset of this object model and provides the foundation for the information model of the application to be built (Figure 3.3). The dynamic aspects of analysis are captured by the two components of the *interface model*, namely the *operation model* and the *life-cycle model* (not illustrated).

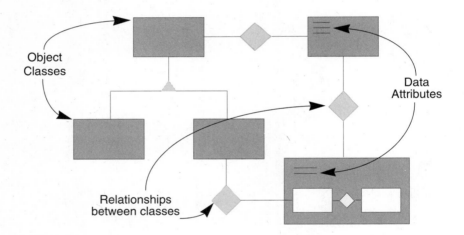

Figure 3.3 System Object Model Captures Static Structure of Information

These analysis models establish a precise description of the requirements placed on the design activity. Although a skeleton of the application information model has been formed at this stage, it is not until the design really gets under way that the structure and content of the information model start to take shape.

The *object interaction graphs* (OIGs) have the greatest influence on this by identifying the need for specific object instances to send messages to other objects. It is this messaging behavior that determines the visibility structures required by object classes, i.e., the object-valued attributes that provide references to object instances to enable message passing (Figure 3.4). These visibility structures *implement* the relationships, required of the design, that were initially identified on the system object model. Data attributes are also introduced during the development of the object interaction graphs to support the algorithms that implement the system operations. These data attributes, together with those identified on the system object model, also form part of the application information model.

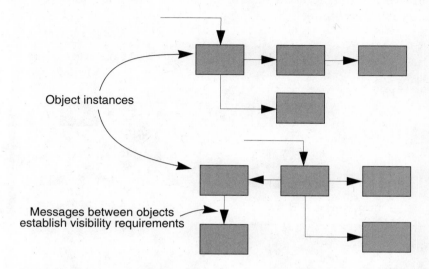

Figure 3.4 Object Interaction Graphs Characterize Part of the Information Model

For TMN application development, the information model has to be designed taking into account both top-down and bottom-up constraints. It has to be designed to adequately support the required functionality and also to derive much of its information from managed objects in the MIB. Cumbersome relationships may exist between an application and the MIB if the design of the information model is poor, leading to inefficient data access (causing unnecessary MIB *traffic*), redundancy, and possible inconsistency of data.

To counter this potential danger, an appropriate stage in the design process has to be established where the top-down and bottom-up influences can be combined. In Figure 3.5 the application information model is represented by the system object model and object interaction graphs. These two models show graphically the possible *points of contact* that may be required between the application information model and the MIB, namely:

- Data attributes—data values obtained from managed object attributes
- Object-valued attributes—derived from relationships between managed objects in the MIB
- Object behavior—application functionality implemented by managed objects in the MIB

Figure 3.5 shows the MIB represented by a containment tree of managed object instances. Note that in the TMN standards the containment relationship is of primary importance in structuring the MIB. This is used as a naming relationship to provide unique names for all managed object instances. Internally, other relationships may also be represented between managed objects in terms of attribute values that refer to the object identities of other managed objects (i.e., object-valued attributes).

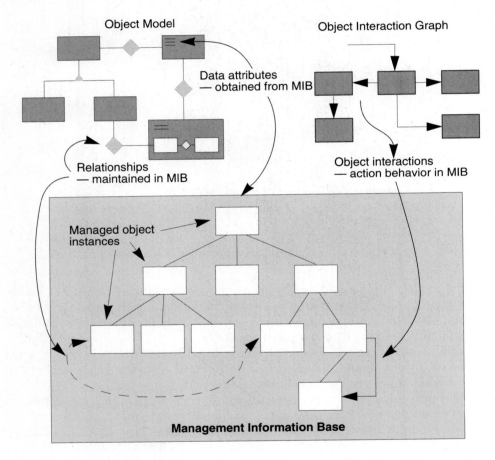

Figure 3.5 Applications Require Access to the Structure and Content of the MIB

3.4 GAINING ACCESS TO THE MIB

It has already been pointed out that the top-down/bottom-up design issue for TMN applications is similar to the design of an application using a predefined class library or application framework. Here there are predefined (managed)

object classes, instances of which have to be used in the design to meet the requirements of the application. For the developer of TMN applications, the MIB imposes a design constraint that has to be factored into the design process.

However, the major difference for the TMN application developer is that the MIB is typically regarded as an *active* information base. Many applications have access to it, and these may change the structure and content of data in the MIB. The network elements are also continuously notifying the managed objects in the MIB of changes in status, network events, error conditions, etc.

There are two main consequences of these MIB characteristics. First, the application developer has to be able to *explore* the MIB to determine what managed objects exist. Depending on the application development environment, appropriate tools are required to discover the data available in the MIB. For example, a browser would be used to explore the structure of the MIB and to obtain details of the data held by managed object instances.

Second, a different computational model exists between the management application and the MIB from that which exists inside the management application itself. Within the application we assume the computational model of, say, C++ or Smalltalk; that is, message passing between object instances is synchronous, and the invocation of an object method corresponds to a procedure or function call in more traditional programming languages, such as C or Pascal.

The TMN standards define protocols and management information services to enable applications to access and modify the MIB data. The computational model employed is asynchronous. This means that for any managed object in the MIB that the management application needs to access, the application has to provide an agent or proxy to manage interactions with that managed object. We refer to these as *proxy objects* in the remainder of this paper. In the Fusion models this is similar to the introduction of monitor or terminal objects to handle asynchronous interactions with agents external to the system interface (Coleman et al. 1994).

Much of the additional design activity that has to be introduced because of the influence of the MIB is concerned with the introduction of proxy objects into the application information model and extending the design models to interact with these objects.

3.5   EXTENDING THE FUSION DESIGN PROCESS

As stated in Section 3.3, an appropriate stage in the design process has to be found where the requirements of the application and the constraints of the MIB can be resolved. We believe that this should take place early on in the design process when the object interaction graphs are being developed. Experience has shown that if the design is allowed to develop too far it becomes difficult to reengineer the application information model, and the cost of repair is greater.

The following process steps give a flavor of the additional design activity required to introduce the influence of the MIB.

1. Develop an initial idea of the structure and behavior required in the application information model (analysis and early object interaction graphs).
2. Identify a data value or behavior that depends, either directly or indirectly, on data or behavior in the MIB.
3 Locate the data or behavior of interest in the MIB and obtain details of the managed object(s) involved.
4. Modify the design of the OIGs and other models as appropriate to accommodate proxy objects providing access to managed objects in the MIB.

This design activity is iterative in nature and the developer may have to design new object classes based on the results of the MIB exploration. There are a number of possible outcomes, which include the following:

- The application information model is modified to accommodate new object classes that (naturally) map onto managed object classes in the MIB. For example, finer granularity object modeling may be required to accommodate the detailed containment relationships in the MIB. This in turn will require rework on the operation model and object interaction graphs.
- The MIB is modified to include new abstractions that contain data more suitable for the management application being developed. Although this is not an option always open to the application developer, the possibility of re-engineering the MIB should not be overlooked. The interested reader should refer to Bapat (1994) to gain further insight into MIB modeling techniques.
- New abstractions are included in the application information model that mediate between the application and the MIB. For example, a required class in the application may have to be formed as a subclass of a more abstract class, instances of which correspond to managed objects represented in the MIB. Conversely, the application may only be required to provide a restricted view of a managed object in the MIB or perhaps to provide a view of data derived from a number of managed objects.

There are clearly other stages during the Fusion analysis and design activity where the influence of the MIB could be taken into account. For example, this could happen early on in analysis when the domain object model is being developed. In this modeling activity, restrictions could be made to use only object classes that correspond to managed object classes in the MIB. However, if the constraints imposed by the MIB are allowed to influence the application analysis too strongly, this can lead to a poor object-oriented design. For example, the dominance of the containment relationship in the structure of the MIB can smother more appropriate relationships required by the application. At the other extreme, if the impact of the MIB is not considered until late in the design activity, this can lead to unacceptable runtime inefficiencies.

3.6 Conclusions

The guidance provided by Fusion establishes an essentially top-down approach to object-oriented analysis and design. The models produced, together with the supporting development processes, are driven by the operational and functional requirements of the application being developed. The method provides a systematic approach, moving from an initial set of requirements through to implementation. In practice, many deviations and iterations are required to investigate alternative design choices and to factor other constraints into the design process. This paper has addressed the issue of domain-specific constraints on the design of the application information model.

The particular domain of TMN application development introduces the MIB as a design constraint. This contains a specialized object-oriented structure, providing the management interface to the network elements and other sources of network data. The goal of the application developer is to design an information model that supports the required management functionality but at the same time minimizes any disparity between the data abstractions represented in the MIB and those required by the application.

Our experience to date has been that, if attention is given to the structure and content of the MIB early on in the design process, then appropriate modifications can be made to the application information model to satisfy both the top-down and bottom-up constraints. However, care must be taken not to allow the structure of the MIB to dominate the design of the application information model and, as a consequence, introduce inappropriate object classes and object visibility structures.

The Fusion object interaction graphs prove to be the most effective models for considering the two design influences. Their initial design, based on the operation model from the analysis phase, provides a suitable foundation for exploring the MIB to discover a source for the required data. Proxy objects are introduced into the object interaction graphs to manage the asynchronous messaging between the application and the MIB. Additional object abstractions are introduced into the application information model and/or into the MIB to mediate between the two potentially different information structures. Further research in this area aims to develop mechanisms to partially automate the development of information model viewpoints of projected data from the MIB.

References

Bapat, S. 1994. *Object-Oriented Networks: Models for Architecture, Operations, and Management*. Prentice Hall.

Coleman, D., P. Arnold, S. Bodoff, C. Dollin, H. Gilchrist, F. Hayes, and P. Jeremaes. 1994. *Object-Oriented Development: The Fusion Method*. Englewood Cliffs, NJ: Prentice Hall.

NCC Blackwell. *1992. OSI Management: Technical Guide*. NCC Blackwell, ISBN 1-85554-187-4.

TMN. 1992a. *Principles for a Telecommunications Management Network*. ITU-T Rec. M.3010.

TMN. 1992b. *TMN Interface Specification Methodology*. ITU-T Rec. M.3020.

TMN. 1992c. *Generic Network Information Model*. ITU-T Rec. M.3100.

TMN. 1992d. *TMN Management Services: Overview*. ITU-T Rec. M.3200.

TMN. 1992e. *TMN Management Functions*. ITU-T Rec. M.3400.

TMN. 1992f. *Management Information Services—Structure of Management Information—Part 4: Guidelines for the Definition of Managed Objects*. ITU-T Rec. X.721.

Using Fusion for Commercial Fixed-Price Bespoke Development

Laurence Canning and Richard Nethercott

Admiral Computing Limited

4.1 Introduction

The primary aim of a commercial software house is to develop successful systems for clients. This success can be measured in many ways. Most importantly, the system should meet the requirements of its users, both in the level of functionality it provides and in its usability. From a commercial standpoint, the project's success is measured by whether the agreed on budget and delivery schedule are met. For fixed-price bespoke[*] software development, the issues of budget and time scale are even more important, because any overrun will mean that the project, and hence the company, may lose money.

Object technology promises to make systems easier and quicker to build through software reuse and will ultimately ensure that such systems become more maintainable. Both factors contribute to reduced costs and shorter development time. However, the adoption of object technology, like that of other new technologies or processes, introduces a number of risks into a software development project. Along with the risk there lies opportunity. There are benefits to be reaped by those prepared to take up and manage the risk.

This paper discusses the management of the risks associated with the use

---

[*] Bespoke or custom software development entails developing application software under contract, usually for a specific purpose and tailored to the customer's needs. When the project is run on a fixed-price basis, the software house agrees up front to develop the system for a fixed cost and probably within a fixed amount of time.

of an object-based approach to commercial software development and how the use of Fusion can aid in accurately planning and executing a project to ensure commercial success.

This paper is presented in three primary sections:

- A background on Admiral Computing and how it is using Fusion
- A discussion of project planning, with subsections on planning the development life cycle, estimating cost and schedule, and planning the staffing profile and work allocation
- A discussion of project execution, with subsections dealing with each of the phases of the development life cycle

Particular attention is paid to issues that arise in fixed-price bespoke development, as well as to insights drawn from our experience of what works well for Admiral Computing and our clients.

4.2 BACKGROUND

Admiral Computing Limited is part of the Admiral group of IT companies, which has offices in the United Kingdom, Ireland, mainland Europe, Singapore, and Australia. Admiral's work covers all aspects of the computing industry, including training and management consultancy as well as bespoke software development. Admiral has customers across all market sectors, including finance, banking, commerce, industry, government and defense. At the time of writing, Admiral Computing has more than 350 IT staff and develops software systems on an assortment of platforms and varying in size, complexity, and application domains.

Admiral Computing has been developing software using object-oriented tools and techniques for several years, and its first Fusion pilot project was in early 1994. Since then, Fusion has been used successfully on several projects and has now been adopted as the method that is the foundation of the Admiral Computing Object Based Approach (ACOBA). ACOBA is a generic process that has evolved over time and comprises a development method (Fusion), guidelines and standards, strategies and metrics, templates, and reusable software libraries. ACOBA is being used on all of Admiral's current OO development projects, ranging from a client/server reporting architecture for a car leasing company, to a real-time network administration system utilizing distributed objects for a telecommunications company, to an electronic banking system for a UK bank. ACOBA has been applied in conjunction with several development platforms, including Microsoft's Visual C++ and IntelliCorp's OMW/Kappa.

Although ACOBA is not discussed explicitly in this paper, the insights that we have gained through its application, and the use of Fusion in particular, on fixed-price bespoke development projects are covered in the sections that follow.

4.3 PROJECT PLANNING

For a software house whose main business is the development of large business-critical systems, upward of 20 development staff typically work on each project. To ensure successful delivery of such systems, project planning and tracking must be far more rigorous than for small[*] projects. The development life cycle needs to be defined and project delivery points negotiated with the client. Also, project resource requirements must be accurately determined in order to establish the price and delivery schedule laid out in the customer contract. These must be competitive yet ensure a reasonable profit margin for the software house. In addition, staff allocations and responsibilities need to be mapped out.

4.3.1 Life Cycle Breakdown

Traditionally, software houses have employed the waterfall life cycle to specify and develop procedural code. Using this approach, the development is split into several distinct phases: requirements capture, functional specification, system design, system implementation, and end-user acceptance. For contract development, it is common for customers to require that each phase be completed and signed off before the next begins. This gives customers control points during the development cycle at which they can validate that the project is on track to meet their requirements.

Functional Specification	Design	Code and Test	System Test	User Acceptance

Time ⟶

To obtain the maximum benefit from Fusion, and object technology in general, it is desirable to overlap these phases quite heavily—using the iterative life cycle as opposed to the waterfall. Thus, while customers tend to exert pressure to employ a waterfall life cycle, the OO paradigm encourages a more iterative approach.

We have found that many of our customers can be persuaded to allow us to merge the functional specification and design phases into one analysis and design phase.

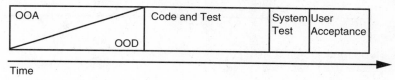

Time ⟶

---

[*] When the project team is small—comprising three or four engineers—management of the project is simplified. For example, because the team is tightly coupled in terms of communication (i.e. they sit next to each other), team members know what others are doing, and planning, coordination, and integration can be more informal.

This combined phase allows us to iterate between analysis and design. By this means, we are able to achieve significant benefit from the iterative approach while still meeting our customers' need for a controlled development cycle.

4.3.2   Evolving Development Process

The nature of software object engineering is such that iteration of the requirements and design should occur, but in a controlled fashion. Today, a number of industry-wide initiatives are working toward this; many under the auspices of Rapid Application Development (RAD). Indeed, the direction of initiatives such as the Dynamic Systems Development Method (DSDM) consortia in the United Kingdom has many strands that match the approach we have developed using Fusion.

Since RAD and iterative development have been promoted as the means to reduce project cost and duration, there is a lot of pressure on software houses to adopt these approaches. Falling prey to this hype without managing the attendant risks can cause projects to fail. Consequently, we are evolving a model (Figure 4.1) that takes advantage of salient RAD and iterative development concepts, but allows us to manage risk through staged delivery of products.

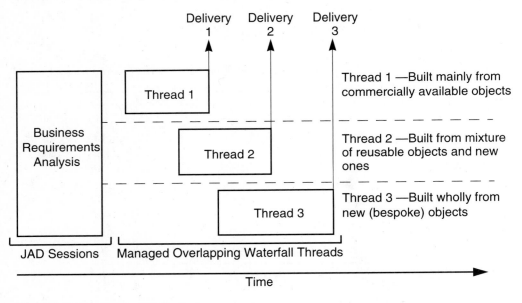

Figure 4.1 Development Life Cycle

The model involves Joint Application Development (JAD) sessions to rapidly identify the business requirements. These keep occurring until the majority of the business is understood. Then the IT planners work with the business to identify "streams" of development work that result in a quantifiable business benefit and so are possibilities for staged delivery. Each thread is then developed using the approach described, but in their entirety they result in a project in which the user is continually receiving new deliveries and gaining business benefit earlier and more effectively.

Ideally, the earlier deliveries should utilize reusable components so that they can be delivered more quickly. Later deliveries can be worked on in parallel with the other threads and will build on these threads. These later deliveries consist more of bespoke code developed specifically for the system concerned.

Obviously extra management problems are caused by the dependencies between threads of development, and there is danger of rework if some of the earlier threads are changed after delivery and after the later threads have been designed based on them.

4.3.3 Estimation

The ability to accurately estimate the effort required to complete a project is critical to the success of fixed-price software development. This is especially the case when bidding for projects that are let by competitive tender, because overestimating the scope and cost of a large development project can make the bid uncompetitive, and underestimating can cause the company to win the bid on a project that will ultimately be unprofitable.

Organizations letting large projects in this way expect a professional engineering approach in which the software house is able to give an accurate estimate for the work up front and stick as closely as possible to it. This approach is similar to that of other engineering disciplines such as civil and mechanical engineering in which estimating is tightly coupled with planning, cost control, and operational procedures.

In most cases, the software house can negotiate to produce a functional specification under one contract and the design and implementation under another. When the business requirements provided up front are not very detailed, it is common for the specification phase to be delivered under a time and materials[*] basis. The delivered functional specification then provides a baseline for the more accurate estimation of the construction effort and hence a fixed-price contract.

Since the development approach determines the way that the work is to be staged, the approach needs to be defined as a step toward establishing the estimate. Other factors that influence the development effort, including the method, tool set, and reusable assets that will be used on the project, need to be identified. These variables determine which data set, based on historical project data, is appropriate for the current estimate. The duration and cost of the project are

---

[*] Time and materials is effectively the opposite of fixed price. Although initial estimates would be provided, the customer pays for the actual number of days' effort that the software house puts into the work. This is less risky for the software house, but potentially not as profitable. It can be cheaper for the customer, because the software house does not need to include potentially large contingency budgets.

then figured using the relevant historical data and scoping estimates based on the overall functionality to be delivered. This process is discussed in more detail in the sections that follow.

Metrics

Since accurate effort metrics are so essential to the success of bespoke fixed-price development, it behooves the organization to capture useful metrics data on all projects. However, with the introduction of new technology, including object technology, the existing metrics datasets may provide less predictive accuracy. For the data set to support reliable estimates, data must be collected from many projects using that technology. As yet, relatively few object-oriented projects have been completed and the data that exist include biases introduced by embedded learning curves and the immaturity of the method (if any) used on the early object-oriented projects. Consequently, during the period of transition to object technology, the degree of uncertainty surrounding the estimates will be somewhat higher than for similarly scoped projects based on technologies with which we have long-standing experience.

Standardizing on Development Method and Tools

Estimates that are based on data from projects that share essential characteristics with the current project are typically more accurate. Therefore, by standardizing on important factors that influence development effort, the base of project data that can be used for future estimation is maximized. The main variable that needs to be fixed is the method to be used for the development life cycle. First-generation object-oriented methods have suffered from being too theoretical and providing too little structured guidance during design. The Fusion method, developed at Hewlett–Packard, overcomes these problems by taking the best parts of the first-generation methods and validating the approach through practical experience.

So, given a method that a software house can rely on to provide sound and seamless support from analysis through design to implementation, it is now possible to use the method, refine it to optimally suit the way in which the software house works, and then collect reusable metrics data from the projects that use the method.

Along with the use of Fusion as the standard method, the adoption of a common development tool set helps to enhance the predictive power of the metrics. For commercial software houses in the United Kingdom, the most popular, and hence most profitable, tool set is currently Microsoft's Visual C++ and the Microsoft Foundation Class (MFC) library. Although this tool set is given as an example throughout this chapter, the same principles would apply equally to other tool sets, including another C++ class library, one of the Smalltalk environments, Borland's Delphi, or IntelliCorp's OMW/Kappa.

The MFC library creates constraints that must be considered during analysis and design of the system. By deciding to use a subset of this class library as our standard tool set, the ways in which the operations are presented to the user are limited to a defined set. We know how to implement this set (and have reusable code to do it) and this constrains the system. More importantly, it enables the estimate to be based on known factors and hence to be more accurate.

Estimation Procedure

Metrics are captured during each project. Rules are defined so that any new job can be sized and estimated based on the historical project data. In the traditional approach, estimates are based on the number of functions identified in the functional specification, each one being assigned a size and level of complexity. The software house's metrics are then applied to these figures to obtain an initial estimate for the effort required.

For example, in a project that principally involves GUI development, the "size" of a function can be gauged from the number of windows that are required and the number of fields on them. In one project, the following size estimates were ascribed to distinct functionality:

1 screen, < 10 fields—small

1 screen, > 10 fields—medium

2 screens, < 15 fields—medium

3 screens, < 25 fields—large

4 or more screens, > 40 fields—very large

Depending on how the screens have been defined, there comes a stage where "large" isn't large enough. For functions this elaborate, it is more desirable to break the function down into multiple "small," "medium," and "large" estimates. For nonscreen-based systems, other metrics must be defined to judge the size of a function.

The complexity can be judged by many factors: the number of action buttons on the screens; whether the screens are read-only or updatable; and the amount of validation and processing identified in the specification. In the project used as an example here, the following complexity measures were ascribed:

1 action button; read only—simple

2 action buttons; updatable—medium

2 action buttons; much processing—medium

5 buttons; much processing and algorithms—complex.

These size and complexity estimates are then entered into a spreadsheet and an algorithm is applied, together with the software house's metrics, to obtain an estimate for the effort. For example,

Size	Metric
Small	5
Medium	10
Large	15

Complexity	Metric
Simple	0.5
Medium	1
Complex	2

Function	Size	Complexity	Result (days)
Users	Small	Medium	5 x 1 = 5
Clients	Medium	Simple	10 x 0.5 = 5
Suppliers	Medium	Simple	10 x 0.5 = 5
Bank Accounts	Large	Medium	15 x 1 = 15
Interaccount Transfers	Large	Complex	15 x 2 = 30
Authorization	Small	Complex	5 x 2 = 10
Administration	Medium	Medium	10 x 1 = 10
Batch Processing	Large	Complex	15 x 2 = 30
Total			110 days

Clearly, this is not the end of the story; many other factors affect the final estimate produced (e.g., the actual staff resources available, the risks involved, even the time of year!). The granularity of functions in the specification is generally coarse, and determining the complexity based on them can lead to inaccurate estimates.

Fusion's interface model can be used in a similar fashion to determine metrics, but has several important advantages:

- The model is supported by an extensive object model.[*]
- The granularity of a system operation is much finer than a function.
- The data dictionary captures detailed requirements information as discrete components that can be assessed individually.

Together, these factors can lead to a much more accurate sizing of the work to be performed. It must be noted, however, that other benefits to an object-oriented approach, though they occur, cannot enter into the sizing process as they cannot be guaranteed (e.g., inheritance is not something that just happens; it is common to have quite flat hierarchies). In time, the software house can adjust the metrics applied to the sizing, based on their experience of the business area, system functionality, and tool set adopted.

---

[*] Essentially an entity relationship diagram, Fusion's object model captures much more information, especially relating to complexity.

4.4 STAFFING

4.4.1 Issues

Staff allocation is a significant factor in the successful planning and execution of a bespoke development; the correct balance and application of skills, knowledge, and experience is essential. It is desirable for a commercial software house to have staff with a wide range of experience on a project. This enables effective utilization of senior staff and allows junior staff to gain experience without impacting the success of the project. Efficient application of project members can make a significant contribution in keeping development costs down.

Although these issues regarding resource planning are relevant to all software development, we have found that paying particular attention to them on Fusion-based developments can contribute to realizing the benefits that object technology promises. The increased granularity that an object-oriented approach achieves, together with a loosely coupled and highly cohesive solution, gives the project management much greater control over resource allocation. For instance, particular and scarce expertise can be applied just where it is needed, without compromising the overall design of the system.

Requirements for project staffing vary from phase to phase, though it is usually essential to have some carryover of developers from one phase to another, even if none work throughout the project life cycle. For each phase, the staffing level should be ramped up over a period of time. When the bespoke development has a fixed delivery date, it can be difficult to accommodate this ramp-up period, but forgoing it could lead to more serious problems later in the development. Where development constraints allow, a smaller development team working over a longer period is more efficient than a large development team working over a short period (i.e., in the first case the total engineering hours is less though the elapsed calendar time is greater).

4.4.2 Analysis

During the analysis phase, it is essential to use analysts with the correct problem domain knowledge. Although the team requires experienced Fusion analysts, it is not essential that all members be experts. Instead, the team can be split between the required skill areas: business analysts, object analysts, GUI designers, prototypers, and so on. If the implementation tool set has already been defined by the business requirements, then knowledge of this tool set is clearly essential (e.g., the GUI designers must be aware of what types of control are available and how they can be used).

An initial core team should be used to produce a first-cut object model and interface model. Once this nears completion, the team size can be increased to the required level to take the model to the necessary level of detail.

For large developments, more than one team of analysts may be required. The work must therefore be partitioned to ensure efficient staff utilization, although consistency becomes more of an issue. Where a system can be split into easily identifiable subsystems, this does not pose a problem. If this is not so obvious, some up-front high-level object modeling should be performed to help identify how the partitioning should be performed. The very nature of object-oriented systems means that there will still be an overlap between two or more parts, but as long as this can be identified initially, it can be managed.

4.4.3   Design

Staffing the development of the design models takes the emphasis away from the business analysts. Some, or even all, can be replaced by Fusion designers.

As in the analysis phase, where the nature of the system being developed dictates, relevant expertise should be used to model specific areas of the system. For example, where a relational database is to be used, experts in this area are required to perform the physical database design.

As the implementation tool set (i.e., the OOPL and class libraries) plays an increasingly important role, the related expertise should also increase. For small projects, it is desirable to have designers who have several or all of these skills in order to keep the staff levels, and hence the costs, down. For larger projects the relevant specialist experience is more important to the project's success.

Ramping up the design team or teams can take place almost immediately, since the analysis models are easily partitioned into work-products. For projects in which multiple teams work concurrently in the design phase, care must be taken (as in the analysis phase) to partition the work so that the dependencies and coupling between the teams' work are minimized.

4.4.4   Implementation

One of the considerations in the staffing of the implementation phase involves the implementation of the core ancestor classes. The ancestor hierarchy must be in place and fully tested before the subsequent child classes are built, because changes in these fundamental ancestors can necessitate rework in the child classes, which can become very onerous and expensive.

Therefore, the development plan for the project must be carefully worked out. Although implementation of the core ancestor classes can begin towards the end of the design phase, the staffing profile must at first be rather shallower than on traditional projects. As a result, the duration of projects in which the ancestors are largely built from scratch may be longer than that of traditional projects. This is a fact of life that some OO evangelists seem to ignore. The solution, of course, is to build up a tried and tested set of ancestors that can be reused on projects. If some or all of these objects can be reused from previous development projects or from class libraries, significant savings in effort and project duration can be achieved. Once the core classes have been implemented, the teams can be ramped up very quickly.

The allocation of the remaining work to the developers is the next issue for the planner of the implementation phase. Two potentially conflicting needs have to be balanced. The first is to maximize efficiency and reduce the development time for the current project. The second is to have staff available for the follow-on maintenance and upgrade work who have a sufficient general understanding of the system. One approach to achieving the first is to apply specialist skills to each technical area. An approach to the second is to ensure that developers have exposure to various parts of the system, thus developing general skills and understanding of the overall system.

In all the systems we are planning to build currently, there are three identifiable layers of software, each of which has an associated class hierarchy (Figure 4.2). These layers are:

1. Presentation layer (largely MFC-based in our systems)
2. Application object layer (the business logic of the system, sometimes comprising C code and database objects, such as stored procedures and triggers)
3. Data access layer (the actual classes that implement the database access routines)

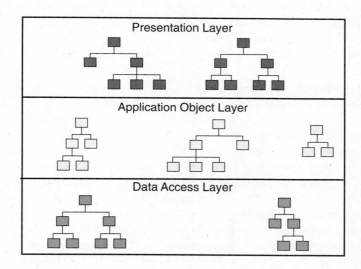

Figure 4.2 Schematic Representation of the Architectural Layers

Any particular operation in the system will involve software at all three of these layers. But the technical knowledge required to build each layer can be different. At best, the layers differ technically because they use different class hierarchies; at worst, the data access and application object layers need a lot of RDBMS knowledge to build triggers and stored procedures.

One approach, which we term the layered approach, involves allocating teams to the architectural layers. In this way, specific skills (e.g., user interface, database, communications, networking, and problem domain expertise) can be applied very effectively, but can lead to integration problems.

For example, given a set of people who know databases and a set of people who know C++, one could allocate the persistent classes to the database special-ists and the C++ intensive layers to the others. However, experience shows that this approach can result in integration problems when the three layers are pulled together. Of course, where specific areas of expertise are required (e.g., for classes that interface with external agents) technical gurus are essential.

Within the layered approach, there are two means to further decomposing the work:

- Each class hierarchy forms a unit of task allocation. This approach should be applied especially at the early stages of an implementation, to ensure that the most used class ancestors are implemented before the project is ramped up. It is also effective for coding the model (business) objects. Class hierarchy development can mean speedy and efficient implementation, maximum reuse, and simple planning, but can lead to integration prob-lems, depending on the level of detail and accuracy of the design models.
- Methods that provide similar behavior (e.g., polymorphic methods) across various classes are allocated to the same individual to implement. Planning and change control can be more difficult in this case, because more than one person works on a class. To avoid the problems of configuration control, it is more efficient to either implement these methods up front or leave them until last.

An alternative to the approach of allocating development staff to the archi-tectural layers is to allocate them to specific operations or scenarios within the system. We call this the functional approach. By organizing work around object interaction graphs rather than the inheritance graphs, the database people and the C++ people (to use the example above) have a clear definition of how the var-ious parts are to integrate together. This approach has the benefit that integra-tion will not be a problem if the separation of scenarios is well chosen, but has the drawback that productivity is reduced as the developers are not being directed at the areas of technology that they specialize in.

Applying resources to functional areas of the system can be the most effec-tive way to ensure that integration problems are minimized, problems with the analysis and design are spotted early, and knowledge of all areas of the system is distributed across the developers. Planning is also simplified. But because devel-opers become generalists in this approach, it inherently means more and longer learning curves and hence leads to longer development times. On the other hand, developers with a suitable overall understanding of the system and gen-eral skills are available to form the smaller team that will maintain and upgrade the system.

Each of these approaches to organizing the work has advantages and disad-vantages and if applied in isolation will cause problems. In practice we have found that a combination of these approaches is both practical and efficient.

4.4.5 Testing and Acceptance

One aspect of object-oriented development often omitted from methodologies is that the system must be formally tested and accepted by the end users. Although many of the principles of system testing and acceptance are common among all developments (i.e., the tests are against the business requirements) there are issues that the development team faces when an object-based approach has been used.

It is inevitable that during formal testing, change requests will be raised to either fix bugs or alter functionality. For reasons of cost, once the implementation nears completion, the staffing levels must be ramped down. The team mix that is left, therefore, is very significant.

As described above, different skills can be applied in different ways to the development. The functional partitioning approach would lead to all developers having knowledge of many or all aspects of the system. Any of them could, therefore, be used for the support team. If specialist skills have been used to implement key areas and if these people are not available to work on the support team, it is important to ensure that the documentation—the analysis and design models—relating to their area are detailed and that any changes identified during the implementation have been applied.

4.5 PROJECT EXECUTION

4.5.1 Analysis

Clients usually communicate their requirements in a collection of vague verbal descriptions or through a document outlining the "wish list" functionality. When approaching analysis from an object-oriented standpoint, the first step is to identify objects that are good candidates to be within the system. We appreciate that this object model is likely to change during the course of the project, so the aim is not to have it complete and perfect before moving on, but to have enough in place to provide a solid foundation for the design work.

Development of the object model obviously follows standard object-oriented principles in that the problem domain—the business—is examined to identify objects and relationships for inclusion in the model. Users have little trouble understanding this approach (after an initial learning curve), and the diagrammatic representation of the model as defined using Fusion notation has proved to be a successful mechanism.

For the purposes of scoping systems that mainly interact with users (usually via a GUI), we have considered the Fusion interface model to consist of the operations that these users (agents) have with the objects within the system (problem domain), together with a definition of how all the operations fit together to form the system being considered. Use scenarios are a very effective mechanism for identifying these agent–system interactions, leading us to a list of operations that we expect the system to provide, together with their relative sequencing. They can also aid in refining the object model.

The identification of scenarios has proved difficult due to the sheer number of scenarios that can exist for any real-life business. Part of the analysis at this stage is to limit the scope of the scenario coverage in order to avoid addressing too much of the users' requirements in one go. Ideally, a software house on fixed-price work will limit the scope of the scenarios to result in only those system operations identified in the bid for the work.

The interface model has to be couched in terms that completely identify the scope of the final system to be developed. To this end we have derived a format for the model that encompasses a definition of all system operations (embellished with life-cycle expressions where necessary to reduce complexity), the associated MFC-style GUI interface, and the processing associated with every operation in the interface.

The development of the interface model is facilitated by prototyping the main objects and the important (or complicated) system operations. We are starting to find that the presentation parts of the prototype (the Views and simple Controllers from the Model–View–Controller architecture) can be reused from previous systems when working on a prototype. This is a consequence of constraining all systems to use the MFC.

Business logic (the Model objects and less generic Controllers from MVC) usually has to be built quickly in a prototype, and the code is rarely, if ever, carried forward and used in a production system.

The resultant interface model ends up as an amalgamation of parts of a prototype combined with documentation identifying the system operations and selected life-cycle models.

Various CASE tools have been used to record the system dictionary and parts of the analysis models. Paradigm Plus has been used for its full Fusion support. Unfortunately, in the version we used the resultant graphical output was difficult to integrate into our other documents. This was a particular concern, given our need to produce polished analysis (and design) documents. These are presented to our clients to satisfy them that we understand their requirements and are on track to meet their needs so that they can sign off that phase of the project.

4.5.2 Design

Design overlaps analysis rather heavily. Prototyping really starts to develop the user interface of the system. If existing ancestors are reused from previous systems to quickly provide the look and feel (or presentation layer) for the prototype, then these are usually of production quality and dictate the design for this part of the system.

Object interaction graphs have proved very important in preventing problems when the full system is integrated. However, rather than religiously produce all of the object interactions, judgment is required to select the ones that are important (based on complexity and where large numbers of objects are involved) and to formally record only those. Common, standard, or similar operations need only be done once.

Visibility graphs have varying usefulness depending on the implementation tool used and the size of the project being undertaken. If a good garbage collection mechanism is available, visibility graphs are mainly a system design aid to help in understanding the full object usage of the system. Rather than falling prey to the "follow all the steps for the sake of it" syndrome, a pragmatic development of visibility graphs for the more complex relationships in the system can be cheap to undertake up front and helps avoid many problems during implementation. Other reasons to spend more time detailing the visibility graphs include performance considerations (both speed and resource utilization), development of reusable components, and development with large project teams.

During this time the system dictionary is updated and expanded. We have found that this dictionary should be ordered and collated by object and by class, rather than by grouping all like types together (i.e., rather than having sections for attributes, relationships, methods, etc.). The class descriptions, therefore, contain all the public and private methods and properties of a class together in one place. These class descriptions refer to the class hierarchies and are presented in the order identified by the hierarchies so that inherited detail is not repeated and specializations are concentrated on. CASE tools obviously make this task less cumbersome, but are not always available for use on projects.

The hierarchy of MFC plays a fundamental role in the design of systems using this library. Sadly, some aspects of the class library change in different versions of the MFC. In particular, we have experienced problems with the data access classes being changed in later versions of the library after we had built our own specializations around the earlier data access classes (because the earlier ones were not robust enough for use in commercial development). This presents problems when upgrading the systems to use later versions of the library. A similar problem will exist for upgrades to any commercially available class library.

The adoption of object-oriented analysis, design, and programming techniques in the commercial sector is far in advance of the use of object-oriented databases. One potential drawback to the use of object-based techniques, therefore, is the need to address the anomaly between object modeling and relational database modeling. Rather than embed the database operations within the classes identified in the object model, we have chosen to extend the Model–View–Controller architecture to include classes that facilitate object persistence in a relational database—MVCPersist. Fusion does not specifically address the mapping between an object model and a physical database. However, the various existing design models—object interaction graphs, visibility graphs, class descriptions, and inheritance graphs—can still be used to capture the design of the objects used to enable persistence, together with additions to the system dictionary which describe the physical mappings between classes, objects, methods, and relationships to tables, rows, stored procedures or triggers, and foreign keys.

Most object-based architectures have elements of the Model–View–Controller (MVC) approach within them (see Figure 4.3) as originated by the Smalltalk environment.

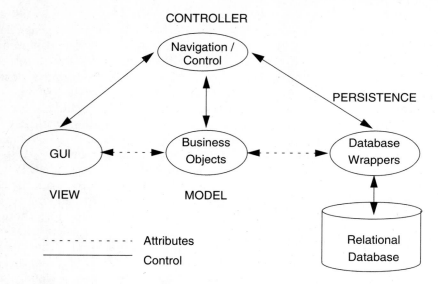

Figure 4.3 MVCPersist Architecture

The MFC is built around a Document–View approach (see Figure 4.4). Taken literally, this loses the advantages of the separate Controller component and can lead to the application domain code, the business objects, being very closely coupled with the code to navigate between the GUI and the application objects. This makes it difficult to reuse the business objects in different systems and also prevents easy reuse of the MFC-based GUI code comprising the views and controllers (documents).

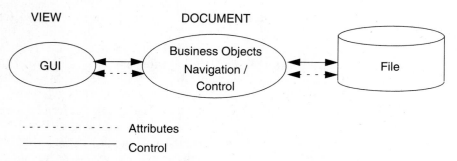

Figure 4.4 MFC Document–View Architecture

It is therefore important for the designer to ensure that an MVC architecture is built by sensible use of the MFC. This can most easily be achieved by separating the business objects—the Model—from the Document and using the

Document purely as a controller. Unfortunately, the MFC is based very strongly around the Document being the application object and is structured around file-based persistence, rather than through an object or relational database.

4.5.3 Implementation

To achieve the maximum benefit from an object-based approach, it is preferable to overlap each phase of the development. As stated in Section 4.3.1, this is rarely possible when a fixed-price bespoke development is being undertaken. We have found that this overlap is more beneficial between the analysis and design phases than between design and implementation.

One of the distinct advantages of the use of Fusion is the seamless move between phases. Traditional, functional developments require a certain amount of design to be undertaken by the developer before coding a unit because of the lack of continuity between the phases. We have found that the information captured by Fusion's design models simplifies the actual process of coding. There are, however, management issues concerning how the phase should be executed.

Plunging into the implementation of the objects in the design models can lead to gross inefficiencies. For a first-time development, where there is no reusable code or mechanisms, it is essential to put in place a foundation for the subsequent development work. We have found it advantageous to develop the life-cycle model first. This provides a framework for subsequent development to build on and can reduce the need for object test harnesses. Building the non-object contents of the data dictionary (e.g., types and functions) should also be performed as soon as possible, together with the physical database.

An important step, which can lead to reduced implementation times, is to stub all classes up front. Where the analysis and design models have been captured using CASE tools, this mechanical process can be made less tedious by generating the code fragments automatically. We have found Paradigm Plus useful here due to its flexibility in generating the code to meet existing style and coding standards. For a GUI system this "stubbing" process should also include the completion of the user interface elements, if they were not all created during the analysis phase.

The extensive information captured by Fusion's design models ensures that the code fragments are not just a skeleton for the developers to use, but a partial implementation of the actual classes. The visibility graphs, especially, resolve reference implementation issues up front (this is one area in particular where we believe other methods, traditional and object oriented, are incomplete).

By the time the actual coding of the objects begins, a significant infrastructure has been put in place. The lower level of granularity that exists within an object-oriented system, compared with traditional approaches, leads to increased robustness and flexibility while attaining reduced maintenance. From Admiral's point of view and that of our customers, this is a fundamental benefit of an OO approach.

4.5.4 Testing

Testing is one area not covered by most object methods. In function-based systems, testing is usually split into three types:

- Unit testing is performed by the developer to test an individual piece of work—a function or a functional area (e.g., an individual screen and all the actions that can be applied to it).
- Integration testing checks that different functional areas work together.
- System testing checks the overall completeness of the system against the original functional specification.

Over the course of our projects we have evolved a set of standard tests for the MFC-based views into the system. Testing of the presentation layer can be approached in a standard reusable way by following a "crib sheet" designed for this purpose.

Testing of the business objects is far more difficult. So far we can see no alternative to low-level path testing, which is extremely labor intensive and mind numbing. Our attempts to leave the testing of the business object code until higher-level system tests has resulted in lots of minor (as well as major) problems appearing with code buried in the objects that is better picked up at low-level unit testing.

The definition of the "unit" in an object-oriented development is not quite the same as that in a traditional approach. We believe that testing a unit should be done in two stages:

- Intra-object testing validates that an individual class is correct and complete. Note, however, that this should test every part of that class, including inherited methods, as well as the new and polymorphic ones. The idea that you only need to test the changed parts of a class is mistaken, as side effects can easily be introduced.
- Inter-object testing validates that a collection of classes works together as designed. The definition of these tests can be based on the conversations identified in Fusion's object interaction graphs in the design. Though similar to the traditional unit testing of functions, this approach can be adopted at various different levels of granularity to test the patterns of objects.

Although this detailed level of testing will ensure that the behavior of the classes is as expected, it can also be very time consuming and complete overkill. In practice a pragmatic approach to the level and scope of testing individual objects and groups of objects must be taken. Objects intended for reuse must clearly be most accurate.

The objectives of traditional integration and system testing are shared by any type of development—to prove that the system is complete and correct. The advantage, however, to testing a system developed with Fusion is that the analysis models provide a clearly defined set of operations that the system must be able to perform and a set of life-cycle expressions to help define the valid ordering of these operations.

4.6 CONCLUSION

Fusion provides a big benefit to software houses building OO systems, because it is based on practical experience and includes design aspects missing from some of the first-generation methods. However, its diagrammatic and, at times, mathematical representation of life-cycle models, scenarios, and the like, can lead to the analysis and design documentation being almost abstracted from the problems of developing an IT system. Consequently, it is difficult for anyone, other than those closely involved in analyzing the system, to understand what the Fusion notation is trying to tell them. Moreover, a CASE tool is required if the Fusion method and notation are to be followed exactly.

It is up to the analysts and designers to identify and use the steps of the method that are of most value in defining the system that they are concerned with. This paper has identified some areas of Fusion that are useful for commercial applications consisting mainly of user functions. Other aspects of Fusion may be useful for other types of systems, such as real-time applications. It is clear to us that Fusion can be adapted to cater to particular design problems, whether it be simply for GUI development or more complex enhancements for designing distributed object systems.

The biggest benefit of Fusion is in helping to standardize the approach to large and small projects and ensuring that all aspects of analysis, design, and implementation are covered. As a standard approach, it enhances communication between the staff involved in the project as well as with the end users—poor communication is probably the single biggest cause of project failures.

Further iteration of the method will help to identify the most useful parts and to add the necessary extensions for different types of projects. In terms of its use for Visual C++ and MFC-based projects, a formal tie between HP and Microsoft would be helpful.

An Approach to Process Description Using Fusion

Colin Atkinson and Michael Weisskopf

Research Institute for Computing and Information Systems
University of Houston—Clear Lake

5.1   INTRODUCTION

In recent years, process modeling has increased in significance as more and more organizations have recognized the importance of controlling and improving their business activities. This is as true in the field of software development as it is in other manufacturing domains. A well-defined and documented process is essential for improving productivity and quality, providing stability in the face of staff turnover, and enabling organizations to demonstrate a certain level of capability to their customers (Humphrey 1989). Moreover, process description is a step toward process-driven environments and the associated goal of automated process enactment.

Many different notations have been used to describe processes. Some approaches have developed new notations for the specific purpose of process modeling, such as IDEF3 (Mayer et al. 1992) and MVP (Rombach 1989), while others, such as ProcessWeaver (Cap Gemini 1992), Arthur (1988), and APPL/A (Osterweil 1987), have used notations adapted from computer science and other engineering disciplines (Petri-nets, data flow diagrams, and the Ada programming language, respectively). Recently, the rise in the popularity of the object-oriented paradigm has fueled an interest in the use of object-oriented methods for process modeling. Riley (1994), for example, has used the analysis method OSA (Embley et al. 1992) for capturing software processes, while Baldi et al. (1994) have developed an approach employing the Coad/Yourdon method (1991a,

1991b). Several other methods, such as ALF (Oquendo et al. 1991) and EPOS (Conradi et al. 1989), employ key elements of the object-oriented approach, particularly "entity-relationship" diagrams.

With its emphasis on modeling real-world entities and its support for powerful abstraction mechanisms such as encapsulation, modularity, and inheritance, the object-oriented approach is naturally suited to process modeling. Objects are usually the most stable elements of a changeable environment, so models structured around objects are likely to be more robust and maintainable than models centered on events or activities (cf. functions). Object-oriented approaches also generally support a larger variety of perspectives and abstraction levels than more traditional modeling techniques.

These advantages notwithstanding, the first generation of object-oriented methods, such as Booch (1993), OMT (Rumbaugh et al. 1991), and OSA (Embley et al. 1992), have a number of deficiencies that reduce their efficacy for process modeling, as well as for software development. One problem is the lack of cohesion and fidelity between their various models, particularly those describing the structural and functional aspects of a system. Another is the loosely defined semantics of their notations, which can lead to confusion and ambiguity.

Fusion (Coleman et al. 1994) was developed to address these deficiencies in earlier object-oriented methods and incorporates many advanced features that promise to be as beneficial for process modeling as they are for software development, if not more so. These advantages include greater cohesion between the models, greater flexibility for exploring and defining relationships between objects before committing to definite architectures, and full support for the description of object creation and flow of control. In this paper we investigate how the features of Fusion can best be leveraged for the purpose of describing software processes and the adaptations to the method's notations that are needed. In particular, we discuss how object interaction graphs can be used to describe the distribution of process responsibilities among the participating objects.

The paper is structured as follows. In Section 5.2 we give an overview of our modeling strategy in terms of a simple everyday process, following in Section 5.3 with a detailed description of the changes we make to the Fusion method to adapt it for process description. In Section 5.4 we provide a detailed description of how we go about building a description of a process using the adapted version of Fusion. Special attention is paid to the construction of object interaction graphs and the various types of object interaction that are typically found in processes. In Section 5.5 we describe the important technique of hierarchical decomposition and the various techniques that can be used to handle complexity. The issue of providing separate views of a process is tackled in Section 5.6, and in Section 5.7 we describe our case study of the Domain Maintenance Process. In Section 5.8 we introduce some enhancements that can be helpful in the description of concurrent processes. The paper concludes with an evaluation of the approach (Section 5.9).

5.2 GENERAL MODELING STRATEGY

The term *modeling* can refer either to the *process* for model generation or to the *representation* of the model in some human-readable form, or a combination of the two. Therefore, to avoid confusion, in this paper we use the term *generation* to refer to the creation of new processes, *description* to refer to the representation of processes, and the term *modeling* to refer to a combination of the two. This paper is concerned primarily with the description aspect of process modeling, rather than the generation aspect.

According to Curtis et al. (1992), any process can be viewed from four different perspectives:

- Informational: what process artifacts are manipulated
- Functional: what operations are performed on these artifacts
- Behavioral: when and how these operations are performed
- Organizational: who performs the steps and where

In our technique these separate perspectives are captured by three types of Fusion model, as illustrated in Figure 5.1.

Process Characterstic	Notation
organizational informational	object model
functional behavioral	object interaction graphs operation schemata

Figure 5.1 Modeling Strategy

The informational and organizational aspects of the process are captured using object models and the functional and behavioral aspects are captured using object interaction graphs and operation schemata.

As in the development of a software system, the data dictionary plays a useful role as a central repository for the definition of the entities in the various models. Although we make no further references to data dictionaries in this paper, we assume that the modeling activities described are accompanied by the creation of a data dictionary in the manner presented in Coleman et al. (1994).

The artifacts, individuals, and roles that feature in the organizational and informational perspectives of a process are objects that can easily be captured in an entity-relationship (ER) style diagram, such as the Fusion *object model*. As an example, consider the process of baking a cake. A simplified textual description of this process might be as follows:

1. *read* **Recipe**
2. *get* **Ingredients** from **Refrigerator**
3. *add* **Ingredients** to **Mixer**
4. *mix* **Ingredients** using **Mixer**
5. *remove* **Mixture** from **Mixer**
6. *bake* **Mixture** using **Oven**
7. *clean* **Oven** and **Mixer**

The organizational and informational aspects of the process can be captured together in an object model of the form shown in Figure 5.2.

Notice that we have to introduce a **cook** object who is responsible for enacting the steps listed. Starting from the top left, this diagram indicates that objects of class **Recipe** are **used_by** objects of class **Cook**. The cardinality constraint * indicates that a given cook may use zero or more recipes and a recipe may be used by zero or more cooks. Each cook may make zero or more objects of class **Cake**, but a cake can be made by only one cook. Objects of class **Cake** are cooked by one **oven** object. Moreover, the totality marker n indicates that every cake must be cooked by an oven. An object of class **Oven**, however, can cook many cakes. Each **cake** object is **made_from** one object of class **Mixture**, which in turn is created by one object of class **Mixer**. Moreover, every **cake** object is made from a **mixture** object, and every **mixture** is created by a **mixer** object. A **mixture** object is composed of several objects of class **Ingredient**. There are three kinds of ingredients: objects of class **Egg**, objects of class **Flour**, and objects of class **Milk**. There are no other **ingredient** objects, and this set of ingredients is disjoint (indicated by the black triangle). **Ingredient** objects are stored in an object of class **Refrigerator**, which has a Boolean attribute **is_empty**, indicating whether it has anything inside.

Because this process is so simple it is possible to include all the affected objects within a single diagram. In general, however, several diagrams will be required to define all organizational and informational aspects of a process.

Our strategy for modeling the functional and behavioral aspects of a process is based on the hierarchic decomposition of operations. At the top level we regard the complete process as a single atomic operation.

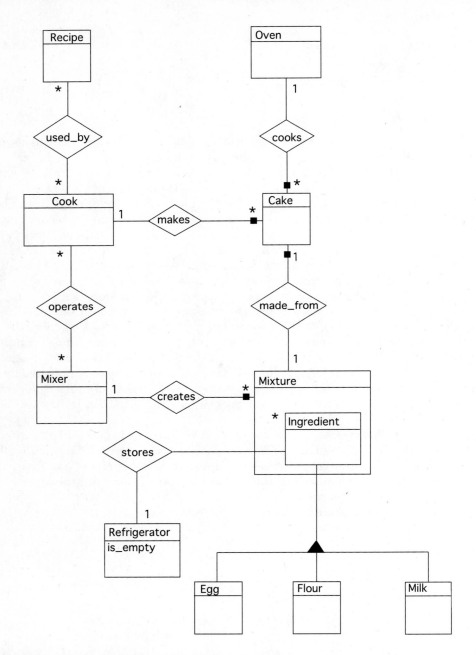

Figure 5.2 Baking Cake Object Model

Figure 5.3 shows a schema for the **make_cake** process.

operation	**make_cake**
description	creates a cake from three ingredients using a mixer and a cooker

reads	**supplied r : Recipe**
changes	**egg, flour, milk, refrigerator**
	new c : Cake
assumes	**egg, flour, milk** exist
	refrigerator.is_empty = false
result	**egg, flour, milk** no longer exist
	refrigerator.is_empty = true
	There is a new **Cake, c**

Figure 5.3 Make_cake Schema

This operation schema defines the effect of the operation in terms of preconditions and postconditions on the entities in the object model. The **assumes** clause states what must be true before the operation can be performed, and the **result** clause states what has become true after the operation has been executed. In this case, the **assumes** clause indicates that, in order for this operation (or process) to have a successful conclusion, objects of class **Egg, Flour,** and **Milk** must be available. Here we are applying the Fusion convention of using the class name, starting with a lowercase letter, to denote a single instance of the class. The **result** clause states that after the **make_cake** operation has taken place the **egg, flour,** and **milk** objects no longer exist, and the **refrigerator** object has moved to a state of being empty. The positive effect of the operation is that a new instance, **c**, of class **Cake** has been created.

The changes clause lists all the objects and relationships that are changed as a consequence of the execution of the operation (process). An extreme form of change is the creation of a brand-new instance of a class, which is identified using the keyword **new**. The **reads** clause lists the objects that are used by the operation but are not changed. In this particular case the object **r** of class **Recipe** is preceded by the keyword **supplied**. This indicates that it is passed as an "in" parameter of the operation.

The schema provides a completely declarative description of the process. An object interaction graph complements this by providing a procedural description of the process in terms of the sequence of suboperations associated with individual objects (i.e., methods). If required, each suboperation in an object interaction graph can be defined declaratively using an operation schema and then broken into lower-level operations using other object interaction graphs (see Section 5.5). This process of decomposition is continued until all the operations have been described in terms of primitive operations which are deemed to require no further decomposition. An interaction graph for the **make_cake** operation might have the form shown in Figure 5.4.

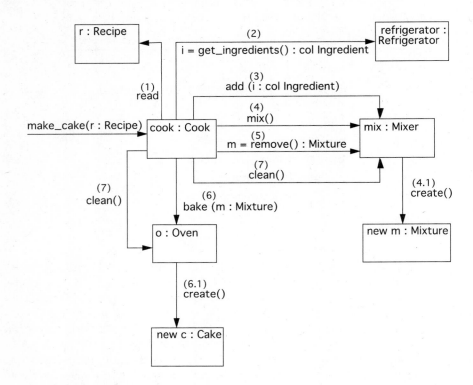

Figure 5.4 Make_cake Object Interaction Graph

The boxes in this diagram represent objects (i.e., class instances), and the arrows between them depict interactions or "messages." The sequence annotations—for example, (3)—next to the arrows indicate the order in which the interactions need to take place. In this case, the object **cook** of class **Cook** first has to "read" the object **r** of class **Recipe** (i.e., invoke the **read** operation of object **r**). The object **cook** then gets a collection of ingredient objects from the **Refrigerator** (2). To generate a new **Mixture** object **m**, the **cook** has to interact with the object **mix** of class **Mixer** in several ways. First, the **cook** adds the collection of ingredients to the **mix** object (3). Then it instructs the object to **mix** the ingredients. The enactment of the **mix** operation (4) involves the enactment of the **create** operation on the class **Mixture** to generate a new object **m** (4.1). The **cook** then removes the resulting **Mixture** object from **mix** (5) and requests the object **o** of class **Oven** to bake **m** (6). The enactment of the **bake** operation involves the enactment of the **create** operation on the **Cake** class to generate a new object (6.1). The final stage of the process is to clean the equipment that is used in the procedure, namely the

Mixer object **mix** and the **Oven** object **o** (7). Because both **clean** operations have the sequence number (7), they may be performed in any order.

This type of interaction diagram has the advantage over the traditional data flow/flow-chart style of describing functionality in that it relates the operations to be performed to the objects that are responsible for performing them.

5.3   NOTATION ADAPTATION

The previous section provided a general overview of how we believe Fusion notations can be used to model a process. Although processes have many similarities to software systems, there are some differences that require some minor modifications to the Fusion models used. Before we go on to describe the modeling rules in detail, in this section we identify the notational changes and extensions that we feel are necessary to make the Fusion models more suitable for describing processes. We have endeavored to keep these changes to a minimum, and to use the Fusion notations and semantics wherever possible.

No environment/system boundary. One of the most important (and difficult) aspects of the Fusion analysis phase involves drawing the boundary between the system to be implemented and the environment. This boundary manifests itself in all the analysis models. First, it appears as a dotted boundary line in the object model (making it a system object model). Second, it drives the definition of system operations and output events — the inputs and outputs to the system, respectively.

This distinction between system operations, output events, and other "internal" operations is inappropriate for process modeling because we are not concerned with building a single software system with a well-defined boundary. Therefore, in our approach there is no notion of a *system* object model, system operations, and output events. Instead, all operations are treated equally and are amenable to description in an operation schema.

No "sends" clause in operation schemata. An immediate consequence of the absence of a system boundary is that the **sends** clause in operation schemata is no longer needed. This clause is used to list all the output events that are sent as a result of the execution of the corresponding system operation and the agents that receive them. Since there is no concept of an output event, there is no need for a **sends** clause. Therefore, the operation schemata used for process modeling differ from those used in Fusion proper in that they have no **sends** clause.

Conditional annotation. Fusion interaction graphs can capture the fact that two operations (messages) are alternatives, only one of which will be chosen at the appropriate point in the sequence of messages. However, on an interaction graph there is no way of showing that an individual operation is optional; that is, the message may or may not be sent depending on a certain condition. Since such conditions are common in software processes, we add a special annotation to interaction graphs to show that an operation is conditional. This conditional annotation takes the form of a question mark, ?, which appears next to the sequencer for the message. Its purpose is to alert the reader to the fact that the operation concerned is only executed under certain conditions. The actual condition is shown in the pseudocode description accompanying the diagram.

Decomposed messages. One of the most useful features of Fusion interaction graphs for process description is the facility for decomposing a message into a lower-level interaction graph. To help the reader of a diagram quickly ascertain that a message is further decomposed in another diagram we graphically distinguish such messages using thicker lines. A *primitive* method is depicted using a normal thin line, while a *non-primitive* message that is further decomposed in another interaction graph is depicted using a thick line.

Parameter modes. A message on a Fusion interaction diagram can return a result with a given name. This works well for methods returning only one value, but cannot handle the return (passing back) of several values. To deal with this situation, we allow message descriptors on interaction diagrams to use Ada-like parameter modes in addition to the value-returning mechanism currently supported. Three parameter modes are allowed: the mode "in," which corresponds to a value passed from client to server, the mode "out," which corresponds to a returned value passed from the server to the client, and the mode "in out," which is passed in both directions. The default mode is "in."

Temporary attributes. A fundamental principle in Fusion is that while a system operation is executing the state of the system is undefined. The objects, attributes, and relationships in the object model only define the state of the system between the execution of operations. However, when modeling software processes, a finer-grained concept of state is required. This is satisfied by the introduction of temporary attributes in object interaction graphs to capture temporary state changes that only last while an operation is executing, but are nevertheless important to its successful conclusion.

5.4 GUIDELINES FOR BUILDING PROCESS MODELS

In the previous sections we gave a general overview of our approach and listed the required notational changes. In this section we discuss the use of these notations in more detail and provide a set of guidelines that can help in the creation of process descriptions.

5.4.1 Object Models

When modeling a process from an object-oriented perspective, everything that plays a role in, or is affected by, the process is regarded as an object. To identify which type of objects are affected by which type of operations and to help in the construction of object interaction graphs, it is useful to define two basic classes of objects:

- Agents
- Artifacts

Agents are objects that actively contribute toward the enactment of a process, but are left unchanged when it is completed. Examples of agents include humans, tools, and roles such as designer and tester. *Artifacts* are passive objects, either changed as a result of the enactment of the process or serving as data for the process. Examples of artifacts include documents, software modules, and process descriptions. It is possible for an object to be both an artifact and an agent, but in the majority of processes objects are either one or the other. It is more common for an agent in one process to be an artifact in another process, and vice versa. For example, the goal of a process may be to produce a software artifact (tool) that will later be an agent in other processes. Similarly, a person, while usually an agent in most processes, may be an artifact in a process concerned with personnel training.

Conceptually, all objects of interest in the process are descendants of either the class **Agent** or the class **Artifact**. Thus we think of all objects in the system as being in an inheritance hierarchy with a root of the form indicated in Figure 5.5. It is usually not necessary to depict this hierarchy explicitly in the object model because the agent/artifact status of objects can be inferred directly from the operation (process) schema, as described later. If a class can be both an agent and an artifact in a single process, however, this must be shown explicitly in the object model of the process.

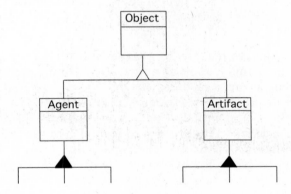

Figure 5.5 Conceptual Class Hierarchy

Other methods for process modeling typically define special classes that play specific roles in the process. For example, Baldi et al. (1994) define five "general" classes (**Role, Person, Tool, Task**, and **Data**), while the Clear Lake Life-cycle Model defines three specific agents (**Transform Team, Quality and Safety Management Team**, and **Project and Configuration Management Team**). These can all be accommodated within our framework and are simply added as subclasses to the hierarchy in Figure 5.5. For example, **Roles, Person**, and **Tools** would be subclasses of **Agent**, while **Tasks** and **Data** would be subclasses of **Artifact**. **Roles** are simply regarded as high-level agents that may have specialized subclasses. Thus the role of the transform team can be played by individual people, and so on.

5.4.2 Process Schemata

The functional and behavioral aspects of the process (Curtis et al. 1992) are defined using two different notations. First, a declarative description of the process is created in the form of an operation schema. Since we are dealing with the description of processes rather than software services we prefer to use the term *process schema* rather than operation schema. However, they are one and the same. Schemata can also be defined for steps of smaller granularity (variously called tasks, activities, substeps, etc.). The process schema describes the effects the process has when viewed as a single indivisible operation.

The most important elements of a process schema are the **assumes** clause and the **result** clause. The first lists all the conditions that must be true for the process to be guaranteed to reach a successful conclusion, while the second lists all the things that become true as a consequence of the successful enactment of the process. Once these clauses have been defined, key aspects are summarized in the **reads** and **changes** clauses. The **reads** clause lists the artifacts that are read in the process but not changed (i.e., inputs), while the **changes** clause lists the artifacts that are changed by the enactment of the process (i.e., products). Thus the process schema lists all the artifacts in a process, and lists only the artifacts. Agents do not appear in process schemata since they are responsible for enacting the process and are not permanently changed by its completion. Any artifact not appearing in the process schema would not be used or changed and so would play no part in the process.

System state

To use operation schemata effectively, whether for software or process description, it is important to appreciate Fusion's concept of system state and how the individual operation schema modifies it. In Fusion, the system state is an abstraction of the object model containing instances of the relationships and classes defined in the object model. Objects and relationships are added to and removed from the abstract state space by individual operations as they execute.

Objects and relationships in the state space that are permanent and limited in number can be identified by unique identifiers. For example, the state space for the **make_cake** process is assumed to contain only one **refrigerator** object, so this can be given a unique name across all schemata that operate in this state space. The convention is to use the name of the class with a lowercase letter.

Other objects and relationships in the state space may not have individual identifiers, however. In this case the objects must have a distinguishing attribute. For example, if in the make_cake schema **r** had been the ID of a **recipe** object rather than the object itself, the schema would have had to specifically identify the **Recipe** object involved using a construct of the form

   recipe with ID = **r** ...

recipe is a local identifier of class **Recipe** that refers to the specific instance of **Recipe** having **r** as the value of its ID attribute. Local identifiers exist only for the duration of the schema's enactment (i.e., during the execution of the operation).

Other local identifiers refer to objects created by the schema, such as **c** in the **make_cake** schema, and those that refer to parameters, such as **r** in the **make_cake** schema.

Objects referred to by global identifiers such as **refrigerator** are assumed to exist automatically.

5.4.3   Object Interaction Graphs

The final task in process modeling is the creation of one or more object interaction graphs that provide a procedural description of the functional and behavioral aspects of the process. The procedural description in the object interaction graphs must conform to the declarative description in the schemata (i.e., it must produce the same effect). Although agents may be temporarily changed while the process is taking place, only artifacts may be changed permanently as a result of the enactment of the process.

The basic primitive for the operational description of the process is the client/server interaction or message exchange.

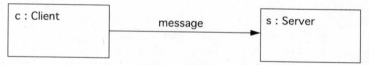

This allows interactions to be modeled in a way that corresponds closely to real life. In particular, the message concept allows us to model appropriate exchanges of information between entities. In all cases, the client of an operation must be an agent. However, the server may be an agent or an artifact.

Object state

Fusion has only the concept of system-level state, as described above. In our approach, this is used to describe the permanent effects of the process as a whole. However, to create object interaction graphs for the purpose of process modeling, it also useful to introduce the concept of object state. The states of objects (as opposed to the system) facilitate the description of the effects of the individual interactions used to implement the process. Once the process has been completed, the individual object states are forgotten.

Every interaction (message) must change the state of one of the objects involved (i.e., client or server); otherwise, it would make no useful contribution to the enactment of the process. Every interaction must therefore have one of the following effects. It must

- Change only the client's state
- Change only the server's state
- Change the state of both client and server

In one sense, the state of every object is changed by its involvement in an interaction, if only in that the number of times it has participated in that particular interaction has increased by one. However, we are interested only in object state changes that have a bearing on the successful completion of the process. We therefore define the following list of things affecting the state of an object:

- Knowledge of another object's internal information or of a data value
- Visibility of another object (i.e., possession of a reference to the object)
- Values of the permanent attributes, or the relationships in which it participates
- Values of the object's temporary attributes
- Creation or destruction of the object

Temporary attributes are like ordinary attributes except that their value is changed only during the duration of the process in question. By the time the process is completed, the value of the attribute must have returned to its original value. Temporary attributes have no effect on the system state and hence do not appear in the object model. We therefore place them within object icons in object interaction graphs.

Interaction Types

To assist an engineer in constructing an interaction graph from a textual description of a process, such as that provided in the **description** clause of a process schema, this section defines several distinct types of interactions. Interaction graphs built from these primitive interaction types are likely to be much easier to construct and understand than those built from haphazard combinations of arbitrary interactions. From the sentence patterns typically observed in textual process descriptions, we believe that the following ten interaction categories are sufficient for the needs of process description.

Table 5.1 identifies the various types of interaction based on whether the server is an agent or an artifact, and on the combination of changes that is induced. Remember that the client object in every interaction is an agent. The table also helps us determine where it is appropriate to decompose interactions into lower-level interaction graphs, as will be described in Section 5.5. In fact, it only makes sense to decompose those interactions listed in the first column (under agent), that is, those for which the server is an agent.

The parentheses on either side of the name of the interaction type indicate the parameter patterns allowed for that type. The parentheses on the left indicate the allowed return values or "out" parameters, while those on the right indicate the "in" parameters. A — corresponds to zero parameters, a **D** defines a parameter of a data type, and an **O** indicates an object of a class type. Thus the entry for the inquiry interaction indicates that it must have an "out" parameter of a data type and can have no "in" parameters of any type. Any option not listed is not allowed. We now describe each interaction type in more detail and discuss how each may be identified from a textual description of a process.

Table 5.1 Interaction Types

Object Server changed	Agent	Artifact
Client only	(D) inquiry (-)	(-, D) read (-)
Server only	(-) delegation (O) (-) update (D) (-) instruction (-)	(-) create (-, D) (-) destroy (-) (-) transform (-, D, O)
Both	(-, O) transfer (-, O)	(-) association (O)

Read interactions

In this type of interaction the server is an artifact whose state is not changed. It is the state of the client that is changed by gaining knowledge of the (internal) information stored by the server or by obtaining a data value associated with the server. A read interaction may be parameterless or may have a parameter of a data value. In the latter case the parameter must be a return value (i.e., an "out" parameter).

In a textual process description, such an interaction usually corresponds to sentences of the form "John reads the book" or "The engineer checks the program."

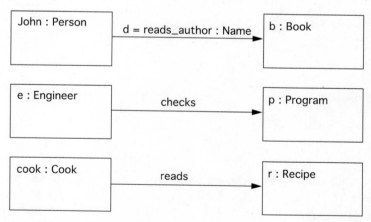

Inquiry interactions

The other type of interaction that changes only the client is an inquiry interaction. In this case, however, the server is an agent rather than an artifact. The message must have a return value (or "out" parameter), which must be of a data type.

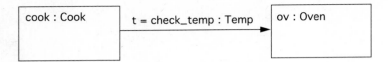

Delegation interactions

In delegation interactions the server is an agent and is the only object that has its state changed. The client asks the server to perform some kind of operation on another object, which is passed as the parameter. Delegation interactions therefore always have an "in" parameter, which is an object of a class type. The state of the server is changed by gaining visibility of the parameter.

In a textual process description, such an interaction usually corresponds to sentences of the form "John asks Norman to clean the book" or "The manager instructs the engineer to check the document." In both cases, the direct object of the sentence becomes the server of the operation, and the indirect object becomes the parameter.

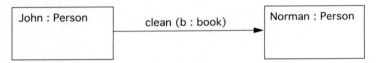

Delegation operations are also useful for capturing situations in which a person performs an action using a tool: for example, John cleans the book using a Cloth. In this case the indirect object becomes the server and the direct object becomes the parameter.

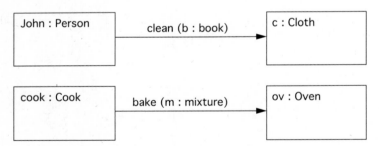

Update interactions

An update interaction is like a delegation operation except that the parameter is a data type rather than an object of a class type. The state of the server is changed by gaining knowledge of the data value passed as the parameter. This kind of interaction is often used to give the server object a value that it uses in several ensuing interactions.

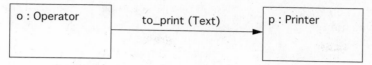

Instruction interactions

An instruction is like an update and delegation operation except that it has no parameters. The state change induced in the server is normally described in terms of changes to a temporary attribute.

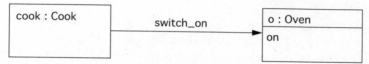

In this example, the temporary attribute **on** is added to the object **o** to record the fact that the **switch_on** instruction has taken place. Another instruction must follow at some later stage to return this temporary attribute to its original value. It would be an error for the process to complete with the temporary attribute in a changed state.

Transform interactions

A transform interaction changes only the server object, but in this case the server is an artifact. This is the type of interaction that ultimately puts the permanent changes required of the process into effect. The interaction may be parameterless or may have an "in" parameter of a data or class type. In the case of a parameterless interaction or an interaction with a parameter of a data type, the state change is achieved through changes to the value of one or more permanent attributes. In the case of an interaction with a parameter of a class type, the change is achieved in terms of the set of relationships in which the object participates.

In a textual process description, such operations usually correspond to sentences of the form "Norman cleans the book" or "The professor grades the assignment."

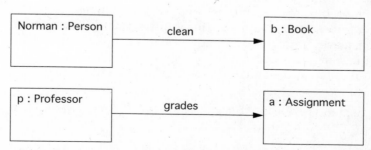

Transform operations are often preceded by delegation operations whose server matches their client. Thus the delegation operation corresponding to

"John asks Norman to clean the book" could sensibly be followed by the transform operation corresponding to "Normal cleans the book," yielding the following interaction sequence:

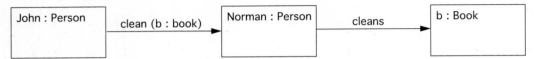

Note that in transform operations the server exists before and after the operation takes places. If this is not the case, the operation must be either a creation or a destruction operation.

Transfer operations

In a transfer operation, the states of both the client and the server object are changed, and an object of a class type is passed from the client to the server. The state of the client changes because it relinquishes visibility of the exchanged object, and the state of the server changes because it gains visibility of the exchanged object.

In a textual process description, such an interaction usually corresponds to a sentence of the form "John returns the book to the library " or "The student collects his assignment from the professor."

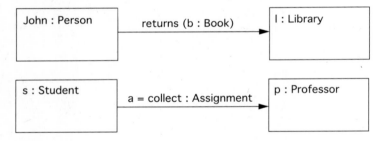

Association operations

In an association operation, the states of both the client and the server are changed, but in this case the server is an artifact. The state of the server is changed because the set of relationships in which it participates is changed. The server either enters into a new relationship with the object passed as the "in" parameter or leaves a previously existing relationship with the object. The state of the client is changed because it relinquishes visibility of the parameter object. All association interactions must have an "in" parameter of a class type.

Creation operations

A creation operation induces a radical change in the server object — it brings it into existence. The server object must be an artifact, and the interaction may have a parameter of a data type that serves to initialize the attributes of the new object.

Obviously, in a textual process description a creation operation corresponds to a sentence of the form "John creates the program." However, there are many synonyms for create, such as "Norman writes the book" and "The engineer draws the diagram."

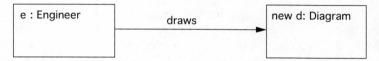

Destruction operations

Destruction operations are the reverse of creation operations. Rather than bringing objects into existence, they destroy them. In all destruction operations the server must be an artifact.

As with creation operations, there can be many synonyms of the word destroy that give rise to destruction operations, for example, "John eats the cake" or "The engineer deletes the file."

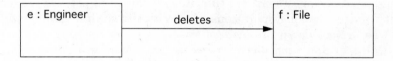

5.4.4   Additional Guidelines

Having introduced the basic building blocks for object interaction graphs in this section, we provide a few additional guidelines for their use.

Server visibility

For a client object to send a message to a server object, the client must have visibility of (i.e., know about) the server. If the server is a globally unique object, its identity is assumed to be known by all potential client objects. If this is not the case, however, potential clients must be passed the reference to the server object through a delegation or a transfer interaction. An interaction graph that does not indicate how clients receive the identity of all non-unique objects is incomplete.

Instructions

Many processes are described textually as a series of instructions. The description of the **make_cake** process in Section 5.2 is one example. In such circumstances an implicit agent is responsible for enacting the process. This must be made explicit in the corresponding object model and object interaction graphs. In

the cake-making example it is obvious that the implicit agent is the cook. However, if the identity of the implicit agent is not obvious, it is always possible to
introduce an object of class **Reader** to satisfy this need. This **reader** object, which
corresponds to the person reading the instructions as they are enacted, is the
controller object in the top-level interaction graph.

Object location

It is easy to get bogged down in the details of object movement when developing
object interaction graphs for processes. Most processes involve the movement of
objects in one form or another, but it is usually unnecessary to describe the
movement explicitly. Changes in location are usually implied by other operations. Thus, in the **make_cake** interaction graph, the transfer operation bake (**m :
Mixture**) implies the movement of the **mixture** object into the **oven**. It would have
been possible to describe the movement operations explicitly, but this was not
appropriate for the level of abstraction used.

   If changes in location are important for a process and need to be described
explicitly, temporary location attributes can be introduced to record the location
of the objects. If the location is an important result of the process, the object
affected should have the required permanent attributes.

5.5 HIERARCHICAL DECOMPOSITION

One of the most powerful features that Fusion brings to process modeling is the
possibility of decomposing operations hierarchically so that complicated interactions can be broken down into sets of lower-level interactions. To illustrate the
hierarchical decomposition of processes, let us consider another example from
everyday life, the task of washing one's clothing at a public laundry facility. As
before, it is first necessary to prepare an object model describing the objects that
appear in the process (Figure 5.6).

   In this example we will require an object that is both an agent and an artifact. As discussed in Section 4, this situation must be depicted explicitly in the
object model as shown in Figure 5.7.

   The next step is to define the schema providing a declarative description of
the process (Figure 5.8). The schema illustrates the use of the type constructor
col to represent a set or collection of objects of a given class.

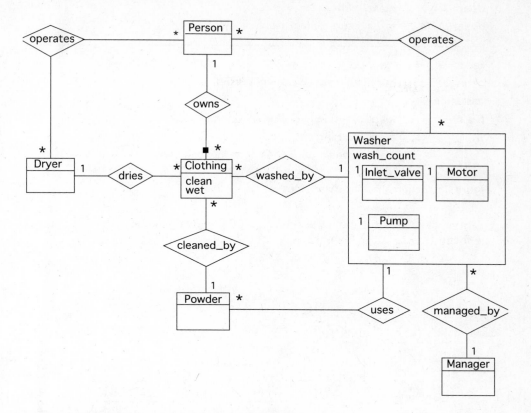

Figure 5.6 Object Diagram for Washing Clothes

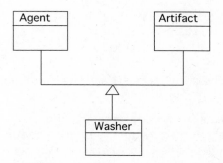

Figure 5.7 Object Diagram Showing Joint Agent/Artifact Specialization

operation	clean_clothes
description	takes a collection of clothing objects and cleans them

reads	
changes	supplied c : col clothing, washer
assumes	
result	for all clothing in c, clothing.clean = true
	for all clothing in c, clothing.wet = false
	washer.wash_count has been incremented

Figure 5.8 Schema for the **clean_clothes** Operation

An associated procedural description of the **clean_clothes** process might be of the form illustrated in Figure 5.9.

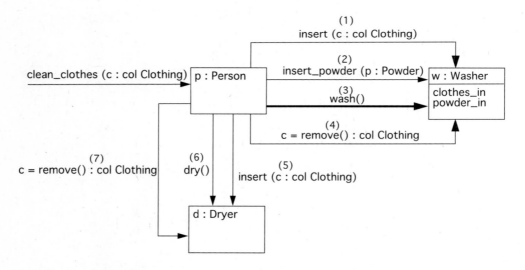

Figure 5.9 Top-level Object Interaction Graph for **clean_clothes**

If all the operations in the interaction graph are primitive, that is, if they are sufficiently simple and well defined to require no further decomposition, the interaction graph would be sufficient to describe the complete process. However, in this particular example it might be helpful to decompose the wash operation and describe in more detail how it is performed. It would be possible to simply add more information to Figure 5.9, showing substeps of the wash interaction. However, to avoid complicating interaction diagrams, it is also possible to illustrate the details in another lower-level interaction graph. In such a case, the arrow corresponding to the decomposed interaction is made thicker than normal to indicate that further information is available in another object interaction graph.

The first step in decomposing the interaction is to write a schema that describes declaratively what it is supposed to do (Figure 5.10).

operation	**wash**
description	washes the collection of clothes in the washer

reads	
changes	**c : col Clothing**
assumes	**washer.clothes_in** = true
	washer.powder_in = true
result	for all **clothing** in **c**, **clothing.clean** = true
	for all **clothing** in **c**, **clothing.wet** = true
	washer.powder_in = false
	washer.clothes_in = true
	washer.wash_count has been incremented

Figure 5.10 Schema for **wash**

The next step is to prepare another interaction graph describing procedurally how this operation will be implemented. Conceptually, this additional interaction graph (Figure 5.11) is a child of the first interaction graph (shown in Figure 5.9).

This process of hierarchically decomposing operations is repeated until all the nonprimitive operations have been expanded. The total set of interaction graphs produced in this way represents the process model.

As mentioned earlier, an important restriction on interaction decomposition is that only interactions in which the server is an agent can be decomposed (i.e., the inquiry, delegation, update, instruction, and transfer interactions). Actions with an artifact as the server cannot be decomposed, because the artifact would have to be the client in the subinteractions, which is not allowed.

When using Fusion to develop a software system, the decomposition is continued until interactions have been reached that can be implemented as a single method (or member function). When using Fusion to describe software processes, however, the decision as to when to stop further decomposing interaction is a matter of judgment based on the level of abstraction at which the process is being described. An interaction is regarded as primitive (i.e., requiring no further decomposition) if the target reader is likely to be able to enact it without any further explanation (e.g., reading a document or submitting a form).

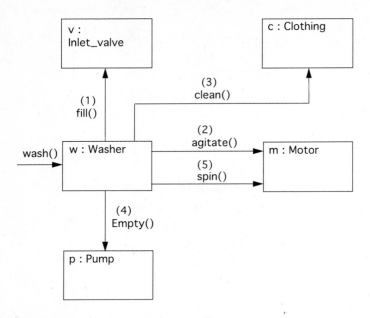

Figure 5.11 Object Interaction Graph for **wash**

5.5.1 Self-referential Interactions

All the interactions illustrated so far have involved a separate client and server. This is the usual situation. However, sometimes it is possible for the client and server to be the same object. The object concerned in a sense interacts with itself in order to change its state in some way. In an object-oriented program this corresponds to the situation in which an object invokes one of its own methods.

This feature becomes very powerful when combined with the facility for decomposing high-level interactions. First, it allows a complex set of interactions among a variety of objects to be grouped together in a convenient way. Second, it can be used to indicate that a complex set of interactions is repeated a number of times as a group.

As an illustration of the use of this feature, suppose that we wish to model the process that a person who is a cook performs in order to complete a set of chores on a Sunday. This set of chores includes making a cake according to the process defined in Section 5.2 and washing clothes according to the process elaborated earlier in this section. The person who performs this process must be a cook; otherwise he or she would not satisfy the object model defined for the **make_cake** process.

We can easily combine the two separate object models into one by defining a "linking" diagram that connects classes from both models. According to the Fusion rules, the two separate object models then become a single, larger object model (Figure 5.12).

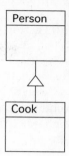

Figure 5.12 "Linking" Object Model for the Sunday Chores Process

Having defined an object model for the process of doing Sunday chores, we now define the schema (Figure 5.13).

operation	**do_sunday_chores**
description	performs a set of Sunday chores: making a cake, washing clothes, and writing letters

reads

changes   **egg, flour, milk, refrigerator, c : col clothing, washer, b: col Blanksheets, e : col Envelope, s : col Stamps**

                     new col Letter, new cake

assumes   **refrigerator.is_empty** = false

result   for all clothing in **c**, **clothing.clean** = true

                     for all clothing in **c**, **clothing.wet** = false

                     washer.wash_count has been incremented

                     egg, flour, milk no longer exist

                     refrigerator.is_empty = true

                     there is a new **Cake**

                     a new collection of **Letters**, **l** has been created

                     a collection of **Blanksheets**, **b** has been consumed

                     for all **envelopes** in the collection **env**

                                      a **letter** has been inserted into **env**

                                      a **stamp** has been placed on **env**

                                      env.posted = true

Figure 5.13 Schema for **do_sunday_chores**

At the highest level, the object interaction graph for this process simply consists of three self-referential high-level processes, as shown in Figure 5.14. Note that the highest-level object interaction graph for the process does not have to explicitly include all the objects read or changed by the process, because they appear in one or more of the lower-level object interaction graphs. The lower-level object interaction graph for the **make_cake** process is exactly the same as in Figure 5.4. However, in the object interaction graphs for **clean_clothes** in Figure 5.9 the **person** object needs to be changed to the **cook** object in order to form proper subgraphs of the **do_sunday_chores** graph.

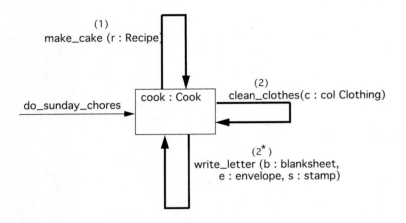

Figure 5.14 Top-level Interaction Graph for **do_sunday_chores**

All that remains to complete the description of the **do_sunday_chores** process is to describe its remaining subprocess, **write_letter**. To do this we must further extend the object model to include the entities involved in this part of the process (Figure 5.15).

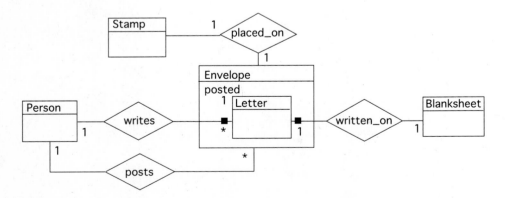

Figure 5.15 Object Diagram for the Letter-writing Chore

Then we must define the schema for the process (Figure 5.16).

operation	**write_letter**
description	creates a new letter from a blank sheet of paper, seals it in a stamped envelope, and posts it

reads	
changes	**supplied b : Blanksheet, e : Envelope, s : Stamp**
	new l : Letter
assumes	
result	a new **Letter**, **l**, has been created
	the **Blanksheet**, **b**, has been destroyed
	l has been inserted into the **Envelope**, **e**
	a **Stamp**, **s**, has been added to **e**
	e.posted has been set to true

Figure 5.16 Process Schema for **write_letter**

Finally, we prepare an object interaction graph that provides the corresponding procedural description (Figure 5.17).

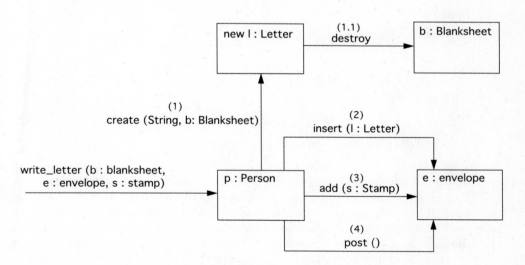

Figure 5.17 Object Interaction Graph for **write_letter**

Note that the process **write_letter** is repeated many times in the top-level interaction graph. Therefore, although this process itself only deals with one letter at a time, its effect in the overall process **do_sunday_chores** is to change collections of the objects involved. This technique is commonly used for describing the repetition of a complex set of operations.

5.6 VIEWS

When describing software processes, it is often important to provide different views of the process which describe the involvement of the individual participants. There are two main ways in which this can be achieved.

5.6.1 Object Participation Diagrams

One way of providing a restricted view of a process from the perspective of an individual agent is to simply extract from the object interaction graph the interactions in which that agent participates, either as a client or as a server. Applying this approach to the **make_cake** process for the **Mixer** object **mix**, we get the interaction graph fragment illustrated in Figure 5.18.

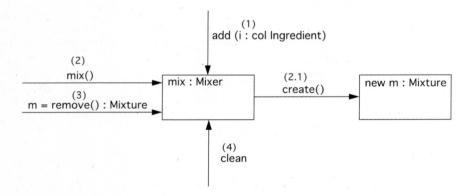

Figure 5.18 Object Participation Diagram for **mix**

   Figure 5.18 indicates that, through its involvement in the **make_cake** process, this object can expect to be the server in four interactions, **add**, **mix**, **remove**, and **clean**, and be the client in one interaction, **create**. The sequence annotations have been localized for the **mix** object, and indicate that the **create** interaction takes place as part of the **mix** interaction. Since the model of communication in object-oriented systems is asymmetric, the objects that are clients of **mix** are not indicated. However, all the servers are depicted because the **mix** object needs to know their identities in order to interact with them.
   Although the components of Figure 5.18 have the same semantics as in an object interaction graph, the diagram itself is obviously not a well-formed object interaction graph. We therefore use the term *object participation diagram* to

indicate that the diagram focuses on one particular object in the system. If an object has only one incoming call (i.e., it only acts as a server in one interaction), its participation diagram will be a well-formed object interaction graph. However, we still refer to the diagram as a participation diagram to record the fact that it is focused on one object.

When creating object participation graphs, it is important to take all the interaction graphs for the process into account, not just one interaction graph at a particular level of abstraction. The participation graph for the **Washer** object **w** is presented in Figure 5.19. It contains more information than could be derived from the individual interaction graphs alone and lists all the interactions in which the object **w** is involved as part of the **do_sunday_chores** process.

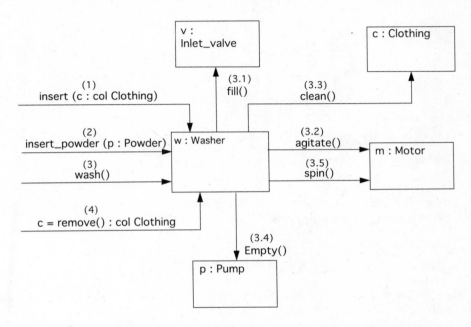

Figure 5.19 Participation Diagram for **w**

5.6.2   Visibility Graphs

Standard Fusion visibility graphs provide another useful view on processes from the perspective of individual objects. Such graphs describe the nature of the communication paths that objects of a given class require in order to participate in the process as a client. For example, the visibility graph for **Washer** objects would have the form shown in Figure 5.20. It indicates that objects of class washer are clients of four other objects. Three of the objects, **p**, **v**, and **m**, are bound to **Washer** objects by virtue of the fact that they are inside the icon for **Washer**. They are also exclusive servers of **Washer** objects by virtue of their double-lined icon boundary. The keyword **constant** in their icons also indicates that these three objects are the only objects of their class to which instances of **Washer** refer. **Washer** objects are also clients of a collection of **Clothing** objects, **c**. The dashed visibility arrow indicates that instances of **Washer** only have visibility of **c** for the duration of a single method call (interaction). The visibility of the other three servers, on the other hand, is permanent.

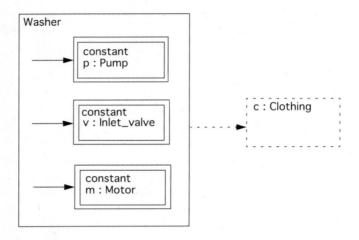

Figure 5.20 Visibility Graph for Class **Washer**

Since artifacts can never be clients in object interaction graphs, it is only possible to have such visibility graphs for agents.

5.7 DOMAIN MAINTENANCE PROCESS

In this section we apply the adapted version of Fusion and the guidelines discussed thus far to a real case study. The example chosen is a portion of the initial domain maintenance process developed as part of the RBSE program for use by the Rockwell Space Operations Company on the ROSE project. We do not show the full process description since this would take up too much space. Instead, we focus on illustrating how the various features discussed in the paper can be used to describe a real process. First, we provide a little background about RBSE (Eichmann 1995), ROSE, and domain maintenance to set the context.

5.7.1 Background

The Repository Based Software Engineering (RBSE) program is a research and development program at the University of Houston—Clear Lake whose goal is to provide state-of-the-art technology transfer mechanisms to improve NASA's software capability. The purpose of RBSE is to support the adoption of software reuse through repository-based software engineering.

An important project in which RBSE technology has been applied is the Reusable Objects Software Environment (ROSE). This environment is being developed at NASA's Johnson Space Center to provide an economical and effective approach to reengineering and maintaining Flight Design and Dynamics (FDD) systems. These systems are used to simulate potential orbits and trajectories before and during flights of the space shuttle.

The software development life cycle employed by ROSE is a domain-centric approach that involves multiple domain development cycles and application development cycles. The domain engineering process deals with capturing, analyzing, and formalizing the abstractions and architectures that are common to the domain as a whole, while the application engineering process concentrates on the differences and idiosyncrasies of individual applications within the domain. Application engineering not only builds on the results of domain engineering to produce concrete applications, but simultaneously feeds back variations to the domain perspective to maintain and evolve the architecture as needed. The role of domain maintenance in this type of life cycle is multifaceted and tightly coupled with application maintenance.

The domain maintenance process developed for the ROSE project has its roots in L. Arthur's work on software evolution (Arthur 1988). Arthur describes a seven-part change management (software evolution) process consisting of

- Change management
- Impact analysis
- Release planning
- Change specifics (corrective, perfective, or adaptive)
- Analyze change(s)
- Design change(s)
- Implement change(s)

The ROSE version of this process begins following delivery of domain products to the repository. It addresses the issues involved in recording, tracking, and implementing changes to domain engineering products and governs the application of the other domain engineering processes in a maintenance setting. The domain maintenance process also provides resources by which maintainers can interact with application engineers during the course of application engineering processes. Such interactions result from the need to synchronize application-specific architecture extensions with possible future domain extensions and the need to correct defects in the fielded domain products. Domain maintenance is the key to keeping control of changes to delivered products, whether or not the complete domain architecture has been delivered.

The following acronyms are used in the description of the process:

DE	Domain engineering
DA	Domain analysis
DD	Domain design
DI	Domain implementation

DM	Domain maintenance
DSSA	Domain-specific solution architecture
AE	Application engineering
AA	Application analysis
AD	Application design
AI	Application implementation
AM	Application maintenance
CCB	Change control board

5.7.2 Fusion Description

The Fusion object model for the domain maintenance process is broken up into several smaller models for clarity. Starting with the object model in Figure 5.21, we observe that the classes **Customer** and **ROSE_Team** are specializations of the class **Stakeholder**. We also see that classes **DE_Team**, **CCB**, and **AE_Team** are further specializations of **ROSE_Team**.

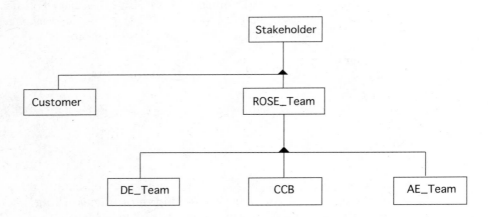

Figure 5.21 Object Diagram for the Domain Maintenance Process

Moving to the object diagram in Figure 5.22 we find that **DE_Team** is composed of potentially multiple instances of the classes **DA_Team**, **DD_Team**, **DI_Team**, and **DM_Team**. Every instance of **DA_Team** must participate in an instance of the **analyze** relationship with an instance of **DA_process** to create an instance of **DA_products**. Every instance of **DA_products** must also participate in the **analyze** relationship. The cardinality constraints show that one instance of **DA_Team** uses one instance of **DA_process** to produce one to many instances of **DA_products**. The possible kinds of **DA_products** are also shown. We see a similar arrangement for the classes **DD_Team** and **DI_Team**. Instances of **DM_Team** can participate in the **maintains** relationship with instances of **DM_process** to maintain instances of **DE_products**. Additionally, instances of **DM_Team** can participate in the **maintains** relationship with instances of **DM_process** to maintain instances of **DE_processes**. Additionally, instances of **DM_Team** may participate in the **inter-act** relationship with instances of **DA_Team**, **DD_Team**, **DI_Team**, and **AE_Team**. Notice that the only reason class **AE_Team** is not described in any depth here is because we are not interested in those details for this process.

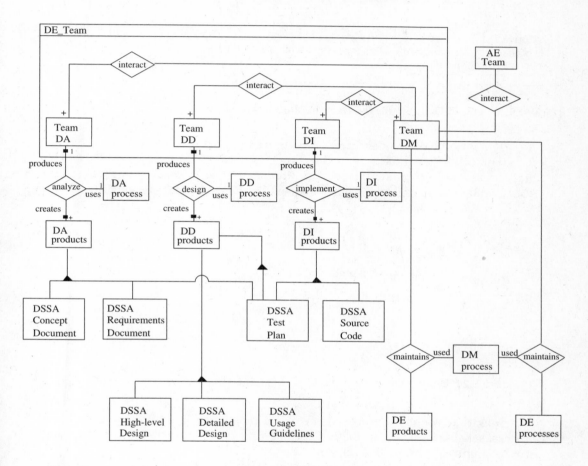

Figure 5.22 Object Diagram for the Domain Maintenance Process

The object model fragment in Figure 5.23 shows that the class **DM_process** is composed of potentially multiple instances of nine other classes (each of which corresponds to a subprocess). Every instance of **DM_process** must participate in the **manages** relationship, as must every instance of **Request**. A given **manages** relationship can have only one **DM_process**, but zero to many instances of **request**.

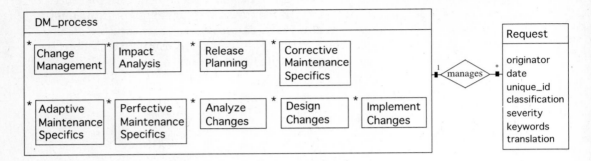

Figure 5.23 Object Diagram for the Domain Maintenance Process

The final object model fragment (Figure 5.24) that we will consider shows the structure of the ROSE repository and the two main types of **ROSE_Artifact** that it stores, **Process_Artifact** and **Product_Artifact**. Notice that the class **ROSE_Artifact** is related to the class **Request** by the **describes** relationship.

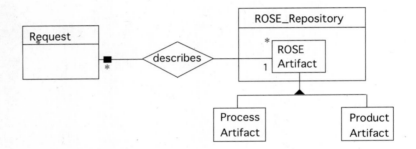

Figure 5.24 Object Diagram for the Domain Maintenance Process

Now that we have examined the object model, we illustrate the associated process schemata (Figures 5.25, 5.27, 5.29, and 5.31) and object interaction graphs (Figures 5.26, 5.28, 5.30, and 5.32).

Because of the complexity of this process, its top-level object interaction diagram is composed entirely of self-referential, high-level interactions, as shown in Figure 5.26. Notice that only one of the three possible alternatives (4), (4'), or (4") will be selected in this top-level object interaction graph. The determination of which to execute is based on the classification made during **Change_Management** (1).

The purpose of the first subprocess, **Change_Management**, is to control change to evolving entities. Two major categories of changes are recorded: change (e.g., enhancement) requests and discrepancy (e.g., problem) reports. The former describe changes to the domain products that are considered desirable by the requester, while the latter are reports of defects or product attributes or

operation	**Process_modification_request**
description	A request for a modification (r) to a base-lined artifact (product, process, etc.) is processed by using the domain maintenance process to control change

reads	**DM_Process**
changes	**supplied r : Request, ROSE_Artifac**t
assumes	There exist base-lined domain engineering **ROSE_Artifacts** to be maintained
result	If the **r** was accepted
	then the **r.approved** = true and the corresponding **ROSE_Artifact** is modified accordingly
	Else
	r was rejected and **r.approved** = false

Figure 5.25 Process schema for **Process_modification_request**

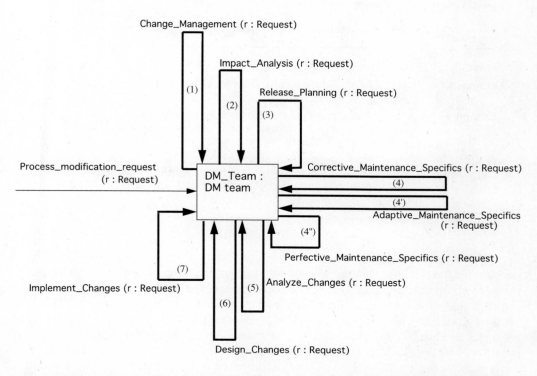

Figure 5.26 Top-level Object Interaction Graph for **Process_modification_request**

behaviors that are out of line with their requirements. This process step concentrates on acquiring the change requests (CR) and discrepancy reports (DR) in a timely and orderly manner. The classification is taken further by specifying the request as corrective (i.e., something is broken), adaptive (i.e., some function needs to be changed or added), or perfective (i.e., some performance or quality improvement needs to be made without change of function).

The next step is to assign the request a problem severity (although adaptive and perfective changes may have no severity, they can be rated by expected benefit). Classification keywords and the products that the request relates to are then identified. Finally, the database of existing modification requests is checked to ensure that the request is not a duplicate. If it is original, it is entered into the database. However, if it is found to be a duplicate, it is not entered and the originator is notified. This step is executed asynchronously from all others in this process on an event-driven basis.

The schema for the **Change_Management** subprocess is shown in Figure 5.27.

operation	**Change_Management**
description	Classifies a Request object according to its type, severity and keywords, and either enters it into the database as an original request or returns it to its originator as a duplicate
reads	**DM_Process**
changes	**supplied r : Request, MR_DB : Modification Request database**
assumes	There exist base-lined domain engineering **ROSE_Artifacts** to be maintained and a request for modification of one or more of those **ROSE_Artifacts** has been made
result	**r** has been classified according to its type, severity, and keywords and has either been entered into the **MR_DB** as an original request or returned to its originator as a duplicate

Figure 5.27 Process Schema for **Change_Management**

The corresponding object interaction graph is shown in Figure 5.28. The decomposition of the **Change_Management** message from the top-level object interaction graph reveals the classification and severity assessment for the request, based on an existing classification scheme. Because the same basic request may have already been made by someone else, the database of existing requests is checked for duplication—as shown by the message with sequence label (3). The result of this message is used to determine which of the two alternatives for message (4) will be called, as indicated in the annotation. None of the messages on this diagram is further decomposed. Note that message (1) is an example of a transform interaction because the server is an artifact and its state is changed, in this case by the classification data value passed in as a parameter.

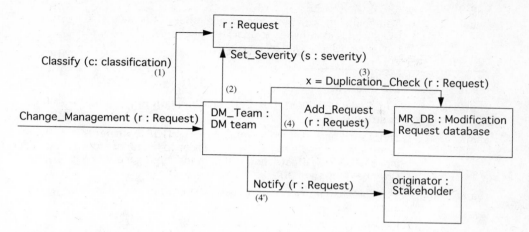

Figure 5.28 Object Interaction Graph for **Change_Management**

The objective of the second subprocess, impact analysis, is to determine the scope of requested changes as a basis for planning and implementing them, presenting these findings to a change control board (CCB), and recording which requests were approved or rejected by the CCB. The impact statement that the CCB uses to make its decision is not only based on the CR's impact on the architecture, but also on its "clients" (e.g., applications built so far). First, the wording of the request is translated into a precise and unequivocal description using the accepted technical terminology. Next, impacts are traced to other subsystems, phases of the life cycle, applications, documents, and user interfaces. Resource requirements are then determined. Finally, the decision is made to approve or reject the request. These requirements have to be captured in the process schema (Figure 5.29).

The corresponding object interaction graph for **Impact_Analysis** is shown in Figure 5.30. The decomposition of the **Impact_Analysis** message (from the top-level object interaction diagram) reveals the activities that take place to accomplish the analysis. Notice that both the **translate_request** message (1) and the **estimate_resources** message (4) are shown to have further decompositions. Note also that message (5) is an example of a transfer interaction in which the passing of the object **r : Request** changes the state of both the client and the server (in this case both are agents). The **DM_Team** relinquishes visibility of the request and the **CCB** gains visibility of the request. Message (5.1) is an example of a read operation, since it involves a change to the state of the **CCB** object, but not the **Request** object **r**. It is questionable whether this particular interaction adds much value to the interaction graph, and it could easily be omitted if it is clear how the higher-level interaction (5) is to be implemented.

operation   **Impact_Analysis**

description   Determines the complete impact of a request, and sets the ob-
                       ject's status parameter to indicate whether it has been ap-
                       proved or disapproved by the CCB

---

reads   **DM_Process**

changes   **supplied r : Request, MR_DB : Modification Request data-
                       base**

assumes   There exist base-lined domain engineering **ROSE_Artifacts** to
                       be maintained and a request for modification of one or more of
                       those **ROSE_Artifacts** has been made and gone through
                       Change_Management

result   The complete impact of **r** has been determined and recorded,
                       and

                       if the CCB approves r

                           then **r.status** = approved

                       else (the CCB disapproves the request)

                           then **r.status** = disapproved

Figure 5.29 Process Schema for **Impact_Analysis**

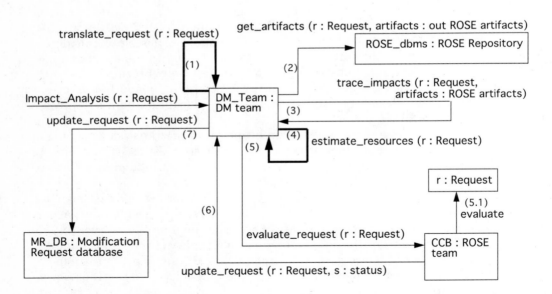

Figure 5.30 Object Interaction Graph for **Impact_Analysis**

We now consider the first subprocess, **Translate_Request**, of **Impact_Analysis**. The objective of this subprocess is to translate the wording of the request into a precise and unambiguous description, using the accepted technical terminology (Figure 5.31). This translation must then be approved before progress can continue.

operation	**Translate_Request**
description	Translates a Request into an unambiguous and precise description that has been approved

reads	**DM_Process**
changes	**supplied r : Request,**
assumes	There exist base-lined domain engineering **ROSE_Artifacts** to be maintained and a request for modification of one or more of those **ROSE_Artifacts** has been made and gone through **Change_Management** and is ready for translation.
result	The translation of **r** has been approved

Figure 5.31 Process schema for **Impact_Analysis**

Finally, the object interaction graph for **Translate_Request** is of the form illustrated in Figure 5.32. The third interaction in this sequence, labeled (3?) is only called if the result of interaction (2) is false (i.e., the originator did not approve the translation).

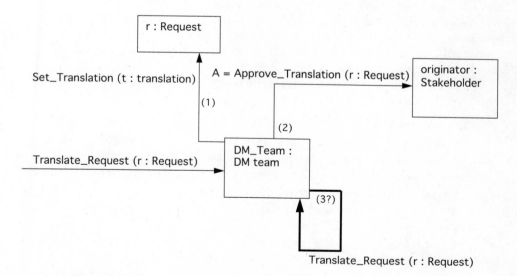

Figure 5.32 Object Interaction Graph for **Translate_Request**

The object interaction graph for **Translate_Request** reveals two interesting points. First, the message marked with sequence (3?) is a self-referential call of the **Translate_Request** message and the thick arrow indicates that it is elaborated in another interaction graph (in this case the same one). This means that the **DM_Team** applies the **Translate_Request** process again (in this case passing in the same request), thus creating a form of recursion. The second interesting point is that the recursive **Translate_Request** (3?) invocation is conditional. The **DM_Team** can therefore iterate through the **Translate_Request** process until it arrives at a translation that is acceptable to the originator.

5.8 CONCURRENT PROCESSES

The examples presented so far have considered purely sequential systems in which only one thread of control can operate at a time. In reality, however, many processes are concurrent and have several threads of control operating simultaneously. In Fusion terms, such a situation corresponds more to a complete system than to a single operation, but with the possibility that system operations may execute concurrently. At present, Fusion has no facilities for handling concurrency within a system. Therefore, in this section we introduce some extensions to the Fusion notation that we have found useful in describing concurrency and timing. These extensions should be considered as a prototype only, because their ramifications have not yet been fully worked through. Moreover, if care is not taken in their use, inconsistent scenarios can easily arise.

Object interaction graphs of the kind illustrated earlier for the wash process describe the sequential implementations of operations. An object that invokes an operation of another object (i.e., sends it a message) must wait until the operation is completed before it is able to proceed with the next operation. In other words, each interaction graph has a single thread of control, and an object can only do one thing at a time.

To use Fusion to describe concurrent activities, several additional annotations are required:

- **Thread symbol.** A small circular thread symbol placed around the beginning of a message arrow on an interaction graph indicates that the operation is to be executed asynchronously with the client. In other words, the client of the operation is able to proceed before the operation has completed.
- **Active object.** When placed inside an object icon, the thread symbol represents an active object that can issue calls to other objects spontaneously (i.e., without any incoming method calls).
- **Time markers.** These can be used to mark the time at which methods are invoked, start executing, or finish executing. A time marker is simply a variable that stands for a particular moment in the execution sequence of an object interaction graph. Placed at the server's end of a message, it indicates the time at which the operation finishes. A time marker placed at the

client's end of an arrow and outside the boundary of the client icon indicates the time at which the operation starts executing. In contrast, a time marker at the client's end inside the icon depicts the time at which the operation is first called.

- **Exception handlers**. These are normal operations that are invoked in the event of an operation failing to be invoked by the specified time or to complete correctly by the specified time. In all cases, the exception handler is identified by annotating a normal sequencer with a ! symbol. If the exception is raised because the operation is not invoked in time, the corresponding exception handler originates from the client object. A failure that arises after the operation has been invoked, however, is handled by an exception handler originating from the server object. Note that the ! annotation originating from the client has the same meaning as the ' annotation. The only difference is that in the former case the execution of the corresponding operation is regarded as exceptional.

A concurrent process can be thought of as a collection of sequential processes that proceed in parallel and interact from time to time. Essentially, our approach is to think of each component process as sequential, but with extra timing conditions describing when individual interactions may take place. Thus object interaction graphs must still be interpreted as describing a sequence of interactions.

The following interaction graph (Figure 5.33) shows all these extensions in use on a modified version of the interaction graph for the **wash** process (Figure 5.11). We do not expect an interaction graph to have as many timing annotations as this in practice.

Note that time markers denote the time at which the stated event actually occurs, not when it is supposed to occur. The constraints that indicate when the events are required to occur are defined as predicates in a corner of the interaction graph.

The t_0 and t_1 annotations to the **fill** operation are variables standing for its start and finish time, respectively. The first inequality on the right side of the diagram, $t_1 - t_0 < 5$ min, indicates that the operation must be completed within 5 minutes of its invocation. Similarly, the t_2 and t_3 annotations mark the start and finish times of the **agitate** operation. The thread symbol at the start of the agitate interaction indicates that it is executed asynchronously with the **w** object. As soon as **w** has sent the request to invoke **agitate**, it may proceed to the next interaction. However, the third condition on the right side of the diagram, $t_2 + 20 > t_5 > t_2 + 15$, places a constraint on when the following operation (3) may start. It states that it cannot start any sooner than 15 minutes after the **agitate** operation has been started, but that it must start within 20 minutes of the agitate operation being started. As with the **agitate** operation, the thread symbol at the beginning of the **empty** operation indicates that it is executed asynchronously. The thread symbol within the **Manager** object, **m**, indicates that it is an active object that may call other objects spontaneously.

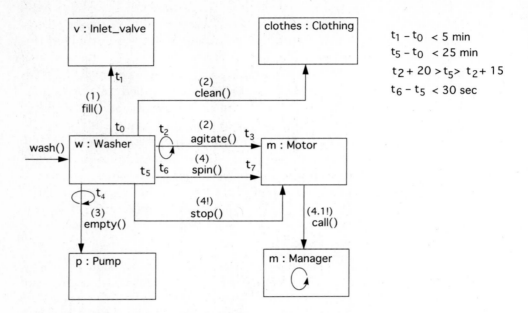

Figure 5.33 Object Interaction Graph for **Wash**, Illustrating Concurrency Annotations

The second condition on the right, $t_5 - t_0 < 25$ min, indicates that the **spin** operation must be called within 25 minutes of the start of the **fill** operation.

The final condition on the right, $t_6 - t_5 < 30$ sec, indicates that the **spin** operation must start within 30 seconds of being called. In Ada terms, this corresponds to a timed entry call, in which the call is abandoned if the rendezvous does not start within the specified period.

The diagram shows exception handlers to be executed if certain constraints are violated. The (4!) sequencer next to the **stop** operation indicates that this is an exception handler for **spin**. Because it originates from the client of **agitate** (i.e., **w : Washer**), the exception handler will be executed if the start constraint is not satisfied, in other words, if the method cannot start executing according to the specified constraints. When originating from the client object, the ! annotation has the same effect as the ' annotation. The sequencer label (4.1!) next to the **call** operation indicates that this is executed if the **spin** operation fails to complete in time or if it is aborted for some other reason *after* it has been activated. When originating from the server, the ! annotation has the same effect as the ? annotation.

Often a thread of control created within an interaction graph results in a call being placed back to the controller of the interaction graph. Although it might be tempting to place this call on the same interaction graph, this is not allowed, because it is no longer part of the sequential execution path that the object interaction graph describes. Messages returned to the controller within new threads of control (i.e., asynchronously executing method) must be described within a separate, dedicated object interaction graph. The same is true of return messages originating spontaneously from active objects. Thus, in our example, if the **Manager**, **m**, at some indeterminate time in the future interacts with the **w** object to fix it, this operation must be defined in its own interaction graph.

Object participation diagrams are also useful in the context of concurrent processes, because they provide the only indication of all the incoming messages that a given object receives. Such diagrams are therefore a good place to describe the synchronization and mutual exclusion properties of the object. Although we currently have no specialized notation for doing this, a simple textual description is usually adequate.

5.9   CONCLUSION

In this paper we have presented an approach to process description using the notations provided in the mainstream object-oriented development method Fusion. We have presented a small set of modifications and enhancements to the Fusion notations to tailor them to the needs of process description, and we have defined a set of guidelines for their use. We have illustrated the approach using several simple case studies from everyday life and a real-life process from the domain of software maintenance. Finally, we delineated some possible enhancements for the description of concurrent processes.

When all facets of process modeling are taken into account, we believe that Fusion, adapted in the way described, is an extremely powerful process description notation, which compares favorably even with approaches based on multiple modeling paradigms. Fusion is able to capture most dimensions of a software process using only three tightly integrated models and scores highly against three common criteria used to assess process notations; namely, support for

- Communication
- Formal analysis
- Enactment

Communication
Fusion brings to process modeling the many advantages associated with the object-oriented paradigm, such as modularity, encapsulation, abstraction, and inheritance. In addition, it provides further features that are not generally found within other object-oriented methods, including

- Complementary declarative and operational descriptions of processes
- Support for hierarchical process decomposition
- Closely correlated notations and models

Formal analysis
The Fusion notations have well-defined syntax and semantics, giving the resulting diagrams a clear, unambiguous meaning that makes them amenable to completeness and consistency checks.

Enactment

There are two aspects to the problem of process enactment. The first is the automation of individual agents that participate in the process. Because Fusion was
designed as a software development method, it is a relatively straightforward
matter to carry objects that might lend themselves to automation through to
implementation in a programming language. Riley (1994) describes how this can
be done using the Ada-like object-oriented language DRAGOON (Atkinson
1991). The second aspect is the development of automatic systems to understand
processes described using the notation. Fusion satisfies an important prerequi-
site by offering notations and diagrams with well-defined semantics.

Another strength of Fusion is its ability to support different views of agents
by means of interaction graphs showing only those interactions that are relevant
to particular agents. This enables a process to be represented from multiple
points of view, each abstracting away unnecessary detail.

The notational enhancements introduced in this paper were motivated by
the needs of process modeling, but many of them may also be applicable to software development using Fusion. Conditional annotations, highlighting decomposed messages, and Ada-like parameter modes, although minor, all help to
clarify the object interaction structures at runtime. Temporary attributes are a
slightly more profound extension that could prove useful in highlighting state
changes, which, although temporary, are nevertheless important to the successful completion of an operation.

Although some guidelines for the use of the notation have been provided,
we have not really addressed the process by which the various models should be
developed. The Fusion process for developing software systems (Coleman et al.
1994) is clearly the best starting point for developing such a process. However
there are several important differences between the process of software development and that of process development, and these need to be addressed further.
Another area needing further work is extensions for the description of concurrent processes. We have suggested a few enhancements in this direction, but
more work needs to be done to find a comprehensive set of enhancements and a
watertight set of guidelines as to their use.

Although the approach presented in this paper is under consideration for
use in the ROSE project, whose domain maintenance process we used for the
case study, it has yet to be applied in earnest in a real project. Obviously, such
real-life testing is important if the approach is to be further developed and
adopted. Our next goal in this work is to apply the approach to the canonical process example defined in the International Software Process Workshops (Kellner
et al. 1991).

ACKNOWLEDGMENTS

The authors would like to acknowledge the contributions of the following individuals to the ideas presented in this paper. Carl Irving, Charles McKay, and Michel Izygon played a large part in the development of the domain maintenance process used as the case study and have influenced several aspects of the overall approach. Several members of the ROSE team at Rockwell have also contributed to development of the domain maintenance process. The authors are also grateful to Dan Drew, Todd Dunnavant, David Eichmann, and Carita Nyholm for their comments on earlier drafts of this paper.

The work described in this paper was supported by the NASA-funded RBSE project under the RICIS (Cooperative Agreement NCC 9-16) and was performed in cooperation with NASA's ROSE project. The authors are grateful to NASA, RICIS, Rockwell, and the University of Houston—Clear Lake for the opportunity to work on this project.

REFERENCES

Arthur, L. J. 1988. *Software Evolution: The Software Maintenance Challenge.* New York: Wiley.

Atkinson, C. 1991. *Object-Oriented Reuse, Concurrency and Distribution: An Ada-based Approach.* New York: ACM Press.

Baldi, M., G. Silvano, M. L. Jaccheri, and P. Lago. July 1994. *An Initial Experiment with Object-Oriented Software Process Modeling.* Dipartimento di Automatica e Informatica, Politechnico di Torino.

Booch, G. 1993. *Object-Oriented Analysis and Design with Applications.* Menlo Park, CA: Benjamin Cummings.

Cap Gemini Sogeti. 1992. *Process Weaver User's Manual.* Cap Gemini Innovation. Meylan, France.

Coad, P., and E. Yourdon. 1991a. *Object-oriented Analysis.* Englewood Cliffs, NJ: Prentice Hall.

Coad, P., and E. Yourdon. 1991b. *Object-oriented Design.* Englewood Cliffs, NJ: Prentice Hall.

Coleman, D., P. Arnold, S. Bodoff, C. Dollin, H. Gilchrist, F. Hayes, and P. Jeremaes. 1994. *Object-Oriented Development: The Fusion Method.* Englewood Cliffs, NJ: Prentice Hall.

Conradi, R., O. Solberg, V. Ambrolia, and M.L. Jaccheri. September 1989. Software Process Management in EPOS. IFIP WG2.4 working paper.

Curtis, B., M. I. Kellner, and J. Over. September 1992. Process Modeling. *Communications of the ACM.* Vol. 35, No. 9. pp. 75–90.

Eichmann, D. 1995. The Repository Based Software Engineering Program. *Proceedings of the Fifth Systems Reengineering Technology Workshop.* Monterey, CA, Feb.7–9.

Embley, D. W., B. Kurtz, and S. N. Woodfield. 1992. *Object-oriented System Analysis.* Englewood Cliffs, NJ: Yourdon Press.

Humphrey, W. S. 1989. The Software Engineering Process: Definition and Scope. *Proceedings of the Fourth International Software Process Workshop*. New York: ACM, pp. 82–83.

Kellner, M. I. 1989. Representation Formalisms for Software Process Modeling. *Proceedings of the Fourth International Software Process Workshop*. New York: ACM, pp. 93–96.

Kellner, M. I., P. H. Feiler, A. Finkelstein, T. Katayama, L. J. Osterweil, M. H. Penedo, and H. D. Rombach. 1991. ISPW-6 Software Process Example. *Proceedings of the First International Software Process Workshop*. Washington, DC: IEEE Computer Society.

McKay, C. W., and C. Atkinson. 1992. The MISSION Approach (Volume II of the MISSION Concept Document). *RICIS Report*. Houston, TX: University of Houston—Clear Lake.

Mayer, R. et al. 1992. Information Integration for Concurrent Engineering IDEF3 Process Description Capture Method Report). *Technical Report* No. ALTR1992-0057. Air Force System Command, Wright–Patterson Air Force Base.

Oquendo, F., J. Zucker, and P. Groffiths. May 1991. The MSP Approach to Software Process Description, Instantiation and Enaction. *First European Workshop on Software Process Modeling*. Milan, Italy.

Osterweil, L. April 1986. Software Process Interpretation and Software Environments. University of Colorado, Boulder, Colorado, CU-CS-324-86.

Osterweil, L. 1987. Software Processes are Software Too. *Proceedings of the 9th International Conference on Software Engineering*.

Riley, J. D. 1994. Applying Object-Oriented Analysis to Software Process Modeling and Definition. *TOOLS USA'94*.

Rombach, H. D. 1989. An Experimental Process Modeling Language: Lessons learned from modeling a maintenance environment. *Proceedings of the Conference on Software Maintenance*. Washington, DC: IEEE Computer Society.

Rumbaugh, J., M. Blaha, W. Premerlani, F. Eddy, and W. Lorensen. 1991. *Object-oriented Modeling and Design*. Englewood Cliffs, NJ: Prentice Hall.

Shlaer, S., and Mellor, S. J. 1988. *Object Life Cycles: Modeling the World in States*. Englewood Cliffs, NJ: Yourdon Press.

Managing Fusion Projects

Both papers in Part 3 deal with topics that managers and developers have recognized as important, but for which there was hitherto little guidance specifically tailored to Fusion. In particular, the first deals with an incremental life cycle for Fusion and the second with metrics and defect tracking specifically targeted to Fusion projects. Both have been developed by practitioner consultants who have applied and improved their approaches over the course of multiple projects.

The analysis, design, and implementation stages of the Fusion development life cycle may seem suggestive of a waterfall life cycle. However, these stages can just as easily be fit into a spiral or incremental approach consisting of multiple mini-waterfall cycles (perhaps better termed "cascades"). Evolutionary development is a variant of the incremental life cycle that involves the delivery of intermediate products to customers at frequent intervals during the project so that customer feedback can be more readily incorporated into the next development stage.

In "Evolutionary Fusion: A Customer-Oriented Incremental Life Cycle for Fusion," Todd Cotton melds evolutionary development and Fusion to form an approach that offers all the benefits of evolutionary development together with the sound technical framework that Fusion provides. This combination is a key success factor for a growing number of Hewlett–Packard projects. Cotton describes the evolutionary life cycle and provides guidance on managing projects using Evolutionary Fusion, including how to prioritize feature sets and decompose the project work so that it can be accomplished in multiple short development iterations. In addition to advice on the evolutionary development process and roles, the paper also presents a variety of insights and heuristics that are useful for Fusion development in general.

In "Method Metrics and Defect Tracking: Measuring and Improving the Fusion Development Process," Kris Oosting presents a process for developing metrics for Fusion projects, together with a set of Fusion-specific metrics. The process is based on the well-tested goal–question–metrics approach and adds a useful device for stimulating questions and identifying metrics called "What Can Go Wrong" lists. These lists also aid prevention by alerting developers to possible challenges in applying Fusion and are useful in identifying analysis and design defects early during model reviews. Defect tracking is also described, and defect registration templates and defect analysis models are provided. In addition, tips on the management of metrics data collection and defect tracking programs are offered.

Evolutionary Fusion:
A Customer-oriented Incremental
Life Cycle for Fusion

Todd Cotton

Hewlett–Packard

6.1 INTRODUCTION

Fusion provides a thorough and consistent set of models for translating the specification of customer needs into a well-structured software solution. For reasonably small projects, the sequential steps of Fusion map well into the sequential
software life cycle commonly known as the waterfall life cycle. For larger
projects, those representative of most commercial and IT software projects today,
an incremental life cycle such as Evolutionary Development provides a much
better structure for managing the risks inherent in complex software development. This paper introduces Evolutionary Fusion, the combination of Fusion,
with its advantages provided by object orientation, and the key Evolutionary
Development concepts of early, frequent iteration, strong customer orientation,
and dynamic plans and processes.

Although based on the best of other object-oriented methods, Fusion is a
relatively new method. The Fusion text (Coleman et al. 1994) was published in
October 1993, and as a member of the Hewlett–Packard software development
community, the author was exposed to preliminary work by Derek Coleman and
his team earlier in 1993. The response from the first few teams to apply Fusion
to their work was extremely encouraging. As members of the Software Initiative,
an internal consulting group focused on further extending Hewlett–Packard's
software development competencies, the author and his colleagues have helped
facilitate the rapid adoption of Fusion within Hewlett–Packard. Fusion is now

used in nearly every part of Hewlett–Packard, contributing to products and services as diverse as network protocol drivers, real-time instrument firmware, printer drivers, internal information systems, and even medical imaging and management products. This paper is based on these collected experiences.

To simplify the presentation of concepts, the paper first discusses experiences gained working with small, co-located development teams. Later sections deal with the extensions that have been made to scale Evolutionary Fusion up for larger teams split across geographic boundaries.

6.1.1   Need for an Alternative to the Waterfall Life Cycle

The traditional waterfall life cycle for software development has served software developers well. By breaking software projects up into several large sequential phases—typically an investigation or definition phase, a design phase, an implementation phase, and a test phase—project teams could move forward with confidence. System requirements were captured through significant customer interaction during the definition phase. Once these requirements were complete, the other phases could progress with focus and efficiency since few if any changes to the specification would be allowed. With limited competition and with products that would remain viable for years, it was safe to assume that the system requirements captured many months or even years earlier would still be accurate. Unfortunately, this is no longer the environment in which software is developed.

Today, our ability as software engineers and project managers to accommodate all risks and accurately schedule projects that may include tens or even hundreds of engineers over several years of development is seriously challenged. Customers' needs, competitive products, and even the development tools we use can change as often as every few months. We have at least two choices. We can try to further refine our estimation and scheduling skills, fixing more parameters of our projects at very early stages of knowledge and experience, or we can look for an alternative development life cycle that better supports the dynamic and complex nature of our business today.

One alternative to the waterfall life cycle is Barry Boehm's (Boehm 1986) spiral life cycle. Actually more of a meta life cycle, the spiral life cycle can be instantiated or "unwrapped" in a number of ways. One instantiation is the iterative life cycle, an approach advocated by industry-leading OO methodologists such as Jim Rumbaugh (1995) and Grady Booch (1994). An iterative life cycle replaces the monolithic implementation phase of the waterfall life cycle with much smaller implementation cycles (Figure 6.1) that start by building a very small piece of the overall functionality of the system and then add to this base over time until a complete system is delivered. Incremental development "determines user needs and defines the system requirements, then performs the rest of the development in a sequence of builds" (MIL-STD 1994).

Another instantiation of the spiral life cycle is Evolutionary Development, proposed by Tom Gilb (1988). Evolutionary Development adds to the iterative life cycle a much stronger customer orientation that is implemented through an

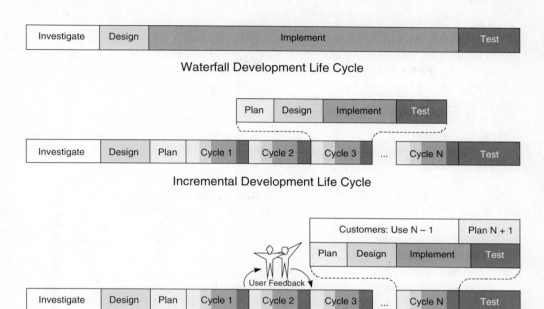

Figure 6.1 Waterfall, Incremental, and Evolutionary Life Cycles

explicit customer feedback loop. Evolutionary Development "differs from the incremental strategy in acknowledging that the user need is not fully understood and all requirements cannot be defined up front ... user needs and system requirements are partially defined up front, then are refined in each succeeding build" (MIL-STD 1994). The Evolutionary Development life cycle has been used successfully within Hewlett–Packard since 1985 and was the natural choice to combine with Fusion when we needed an alternative to the waterfall life cycle.

6.1.2 Evolutionary Development

Evolutionary Development (EVO) is a software development method and life cycle that replaces traditional waterfall development with small, incremental product releases or builds, frequent delivery of the product to users for feedback, and dynamic planning that can be modified in response to this feedback. As originally presented by Gilb (1988), the method had the following key attributes:

1. Multiobjective driven
2. Early, frequent iteration
3. Complete analysis, design, build, and test in each step
4. User orientation
5. Systems approach, not merely algorithm orientation

6. Open-ended basic systems architecture
7. Result orientation, not software development process orientation

Using EVO, a product development team divides the project into small chunks. Ideally, each chunk is less than 5% of the overall effort. The chunks are then ordered so that the most useful and easiest features are implemented first and some useful subset of the overall product can be delivered every one to four weeks. Within each EVO cycle, the software is designed, coded, tested, and then delivered to users. The users give feedback on the product and the team responds, often by changing the product, plans, or process. These cycles continue until the product is shipped.

EVO is thus characterized by early and frequent iteration, starting with an initial implementation and followed by frequent cycles that are short in duration and small in content. Drawing on ongoing user feedback, planning, design, coding, and testing are completed for each cycle, and each release or build meets a minimum quality standard. This method offers opportunities to optimize results by modifying the plan, product, or process at each cycle. The basic product concept or value proposition, however, does not change.

At Hewlett–Packard, we have found that it is possible to relax some of Gilb's ideas regarding EVO (May and Zimmer 1994). In particular, it is not absolutely necessary to deliver the product to real customers with customer-ready documentation, training, support, etc., to benefit from EVO. For instance, customers participating in the feedback loop change during the development process. Results from the early cycles of development are typically given to other team members or other project teams for feedback. Less sensitive to the lack of complete documentation and training materials, they can still give valuable feedback. Results from the next several cycles are shared with surrogate customers represented by members of the broader Hewlett–Packard community. The goal is still to get the product into the hands of actual customers as early as possible.

There are two other variations to Tom Gilb's guidelines that we have found useful within Hewlett–Packard. First, the guideline that each cycle represent less than 5% of the overall implementation effort has translated into cycle lengths of one to four weeks, with two weeks being the most common. Second, ordering the content of the cycles is used within Hewlett–Packard as a key risk-management opportunity. Instead of implementing the most useful and easiest features first, many development teams choose to implement in an order that gives the earliest insight into key areas of risk for the project, such as performance, ease of use, or managing dependencies with other teams.

Benefits of EVO
The teams within Hewlett–Packard that have adopted Evolutionary Development as a project life cycle have done so with explicit benefits in mind. In addition to better meeting customer needs or hitting market windows, there have been a number of unexpected benefits as well, such as increased productivity and reduced risk, even the risks associated with changing the development process.

Better match to customer need and market requirements

The explicit customer feedback loop of Evolutionary Development results in the delivery of products that better meet the customers' need. The waterfall life cycle provides an investigation or definition phase for eliciting customer needs through focus groups and storyboards, but it does not provide a mechanism for continual validation and refinement of customer needs throughout the long implementation phase. Many customers find it difficult to articulate the full range of what they want from a product until they have actually used the product. Their needs and expectations evolve as they gain experience with the product. Evolutionary Development addresses this by incorporating customer feedback early and often during the implementation phase. The small implementation cycles allow the development team to respond to the customer feedback by modifying the plans for future implementation cycles. Existing functionality can be changed, while planned functionality can be redefined.

One Hewlett–Packard project used a variation of Evolutionary Development that also included an evolutionary approach to product definition (May and Zimmer 1994). During the first month, the development team worked from static visual designs to code a prototype. In focus group meetings, the team discussed users' needs and the potential features of the product and then demonstrated their prototype. The focus groups expressed strong support for the product concept, so the project proceeded to a second phase of focus group testing incorporating the feedback from the first phase. Once the feedback from the second round of focus groups was incorporated, the feature set was established and the product definition completed.

Implementation consisted of four- to six-week cycles, with software delivered to customers for use at the end of each cycle. The entire development effort spanned ten months from definition to product release. The result was a world-class product that has won many awards and has been easy to support.

Hitting market windows

To enhance productivity, many large software projects divide their tasks into independent subsets that can be developed in parallel. With few dependencies between subteams, each team can progress at its own pace. The risk in this approach is the significant effort that must be invested to bring all the work of these subteams together for final integration and system test. When issues are uncovered at this late stage of development, few options are available to the development team. It is difficult if not impossible to prune functionality in a low-risk manner when market windows, technology, or competition change. The only option open to the team is to continue on, finding and removing defects as quickly and as efficiently as possible (see Figure 6.2).

With an EVO approach, the team has greater flexibility as the market window approaches. Two attributes of EVO contribute to this flexibility. First, the sequencing of functionality during the implementation phase is such that "must have" features are completed as early as possible, while the "high want" features are delayed until the later EVO cycles. Second, since each cycle of the implementation phase is expected to generate a "complete" release, much of the integra-

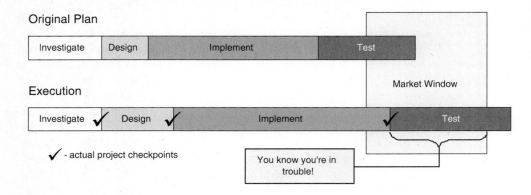

Figure 6.2 Hitting Market Windows with a Waterfall Life Cycle

tion testing has already been completed. Any of the last several EVO cycles can become release candidates after a final round of integration and system test. When an earlier-than-planned release is needed, the last one or two EVO cycles can be skipped as long as a viable product already exists. If a limited number of key features are still needed, an additional EVO cycle or two can be defined and implemented as illustrated in Figure 6.3.

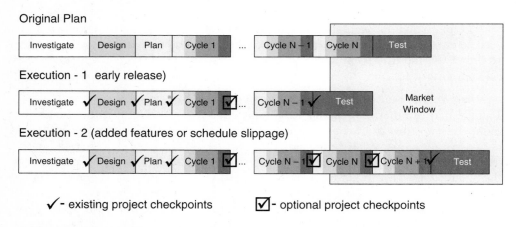

Figure 6.3 Hitting Market Windows with an Evolutionary Life Cycle

Engineer motivation and productivity

Some of the gains in productivity seen by project teams using EVO have been attributed to higher engineer motivation. The long implementation phase of the waterfall life cycle is often characterized by large variations in engineer motivation. It is difficult for engineers to maintain peak productivity when it may be months before they can integrate their work with that of others to see real results. Engineer motivation can take an even greater hit when the tyranny of the release date prohibits all but the most trivial responses to customer feedback received during the final stages of system test.

EVO has led to higher productivity for development teams by maintaining a higher level of motivation throughout the implementation phase. The short implementation cycles keep everyone focused on a small set of features and tasks. The explicit customer feedback loop and the small implementation cycles also allow the development team more opportunity to respond to customer feedback and thereby deliver a product that they know represents their best work.

Quality control

Although software development is in many ways a manufacturing process, software development teams have struggled to apply quality improvement processes such as Total Quality Control (TQC). Unlike the manufacturing organizations that can measure and refine processes with cycle times of hours, minutes, and even seconds, the waterfall life cycle gave cycle times of months or years before the software development process repeated. With EVO, the software implementation cycle is dramatically reduced and repeated multiple times for each project. All parameters of the implementation process are now available for review and improvement. The impact of changes in processes and tools can be measured and refined throughout the implementation phase.

Reducing risk when changing the development process

Many teams experience considerable anxiety as they make the transition to an object-oriented approach to development. The transition to OO usually entails a number of changes in the way a software engineer works. There are new analysis and design models to apply, new notations to master, and new, occasionally eccentric, tools and compilers to learn. There is also valid concern about adopting a new method at the beginning of the development process. Few teams are willing to make a full commitment to a new method when they have little experience with it. There may even be organizational changes anticipated if the organization is looking for large-scale productivity gains through formalized reuse.

Development teams and managers want some way to manage the risks associated with making so many simultaneous changes to their development environment. EVO can help manage the risks. The repeating cycles during the implementation phase provide for continual review and refinement of each parameter of the development environment. Any aspect of the development environment can be dropped, modified, or strengthened to provide the maximum benefit to the team.

Costs of EVO

Adopting Evolutionary Development is not without cost. It presents a new paradigm for the project manager to follow when decomposing and planning the project, and it requires more explicit, organized decision making than many managers and teams are accustomed to.

In traditional projects, subsystems or code modules are identified and then parceled out for implementation. As a result, planning and staffing of large projects were driven by the structure of the system and not by its intended use. In contrast, Evolutionary Development focuses on the intended use of the system. The functionality to be delivered in a given cycle is determined first. It is common practice to implement only those portions of subsystems or modules that support that functionality during that cycle. This approach to building a work breakdown structure presents a new paradigm to the project manager and the development team. Subsystem and module completion cannot be used for intermediate milestone definition because their full functionality is not in place until the end of the project. The time needed to adopt this new paradigm and create an initial plan can be a major barrier for some project teams.

Many development teams lack a well-defined, efficient decision-making process. Often they make decisions implicitly within a limited context, risking the compromise of the broader project goals and slowing progress dramatically. Evolutionary Development forces many decisions to be made explicitly in an organized way, because feedback on the product is received regularly and schedules must be updated for each implementation cycle.

The continual stream of information that the project team receives must be translated into three categories of decisions: changes to the product as it is currently implemented, changes to the plan that will further the product implementation, and changes to the development process used to develop the product. Fortunately, because of EVO's short cycle time, teams have many opportunities to assess the results of decisions and adjust accordingly.

6.2 EVOLUTIONARY FUSION

Fusion and Evolutionary Development are complementary. One of the primary assumptions of EVO is that one can decompose the functionality of a project into small manageable chunks. It is also expected that these chunks will provide some measurable value to the intended user and can thus be given to the user for feedback. Fusion provides the method of decomposition. At the highest level, Fusion decomposes the functionality of a system into use scenarios. *Use scenarios* are defined from the perspective of a user or agent of the system and are expected to capture a use of the system that provides some value to the agent.

EVO also presupposes that an architecture capable of accommodating all the expected functionality of the system can be defined prior to implementation. This architecture must be flexible enough to accommodate new or redefined functionality resulting from customer feedback. Fusion helps create this flexible architecture. The object model provides an architecture that encapsulates common functionality into classes and provides flexibility and extensibility through generalization and specialization. Fusion also accommodates large-scale change through the well-defined linkages between models. If necessary, changes to functionality can be rolled all the way up to the use scenarios and then cascaded back down through the appropriate analysis and design models, replacing guesswork in assessing the impact of a change with a more systematic approach.

Evolutionary Fusion divides a project into two major phases, the definition phase and the development phase (Figure 6.4). During the definition phase, a project's functionality is specified and its viability as a product or system is first estimated. The Fusion analysis models play a key role in this phase. The use scenarios serve to remodel the specification document, checking it for clarity and completeness. They can also be reviewed with customers to validate the development team's understanding of customer needs. The object model captures the initial architecture for the system and provides additional checks of the specification. The data dictionary captures the teams' emerging common vocabulary and understanding of the problem domain. The operation model, through its system operation descriptions, gives an indication of the size and complexity of the project. This information is critical for estimating resource needs and developing the initial plan for the development phase.

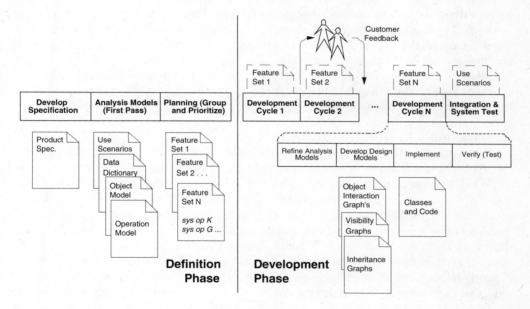

Figure 6.4 Evolutionary Fusion Life Cycle

The second phase is the development phase, in which code is incrementally designed, implemented, and tested to meet the specification. Each development cycle follows the same pattern. First, the analysis models are reviewed for completeness with respect to the functionality to be implemented during that cycle. Next, the Fusion design models are created or updated to support the functionality. And finally, the code is written and regression tests executed against the code. In parallel with the development activities of the team, selected users or customers of the system are working with and providing feedback on the release from the previous cycle. This feedback is used to adjust the plan for the following cycles. To complete the development phase, a final round of integration and system testing is done. The next two sections discuss these two phases in more detail.

6.2.1   Definition Phase

The definition phase is best characterized as a period of significant communication and thought. Communication must occur between all members of the project team to make sure that everyone shares a common understanding of the project's goals. Thought must be put into the specification document to make sure that it is complete and unambiguous and that it meets the requirements. Communication must occur between the development team and the intended users of the system to ensure that the system, at least as it can be specified on paper during this early stage of the project, will meet their needs. Thought must go into defining an architecture capable of supporting the intended functionality of the full system. The goal is to identify and resolve as many issues as possible during this phase. Specification errors that are not resolved during this phase can be extremely costly to repair later.

Our experience has shown that the Fusion analysis models are ideal for stimulating the thought and supporting the communication that must occur during the definition phase.

Analysis Models—First Pass

Like Fusion, Evolutionary Fusion requires some form of system specification as a starting point, and just about any level of detail in the system specification will do. When the specification is at a high level, the analysis models serve to identify large numbers of issues and questions that need to be resolved before development can begin. When the specification is at a more detailed level, the analysis models serve to remodel and recapture high-level structure and functionality that may be lost in the detail. We have yet to define what level of detail in the system specification yields the most efficient definition phase for Evolutionary Fusion. Regardless of the level of specification detail, the analysis models provide the beginning of a common vocabulary and understanding of the problem domain that will serve the team well throughout the project.

The most critical component of the system specification is the value proposition (Moore 1991). The *value proposition* clearly articulates why the intended customer of the system will choose to use it over the other options available. The functionality defined in the specification is the development team's initial best estimate as to how to deliver that value proposition. There are usually countless other ways to deliver it. The explicit customer feedback loop of Evolutionary Fusion will validate the best estimate over time and will suggest better ways to deliver the value proposition. The value proposition itself should remain constant throughout the entire development process. If the value proposition changes during the development phase, it will be quite difficult for the team to make all the modifications necessary to implement a new one and still end up with a coherent set of product features.

Use scenarios

The first analysis model to be created is the set of use scenarios. To provide some structure for this activity, it is useful to first generate a list of all the agents that exist in the system's environment. It can often be a challenge to decide what constitutes an agent. For example, the file system provided by the operating system is clearly part of any system's environment. It can be expected to provide services to and make demands on the system being defined. Representing the file system as an agent does not add any additional clarity to the team's understanding of the system under definition. However, representing specific files, such as configuration files, legacy databases, or data input files, does. In one project, it was useful to model, as an agent, a critical data input file generated externally to the system. A general rule of thumb is that an agent must add to the understanding of the system if it is to be included at this early stage.

Once the list of agents is complete, each agent can be examined with respect to the demands it will make on the system. These demands are captured as use scenarios. As with defining agents, determining an appropriate level of granularity for the use scenarios can be a challenge. Another rule of thumb is that use scenarios should provide complete chunks of value from the perspective of the agent. In the project mentioned above, the system was modeled as providing value to the input file by accepting records of data from the file and translating those records into a format that could be used by the rest of the system. This approach will help avoid the issue of trying to keep all use scenarios at the same level of granularity. It is the agent that defines the appropriate level of granularity, not the system as a whole.

Once the use scenarios have been specified, each is diagrammed to decompose it further into discrete system operations and events. It is also useful to annotate in the margins of the use scenario diagram any time constraints that may exist (see Figure 6.5). For systems of reasonable size, it is difficult to define a correct set of use scenarios on the first try. Building the use scenarios is itself an iterative process of refinement.

Use Scenario A

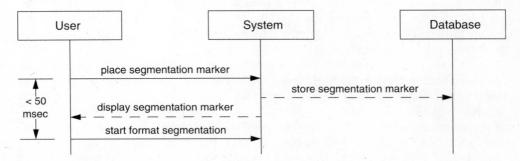

Figure 6.5 Use Scenario with Time Constraint Annotation

Object model

As Ould (1990) states in his text on software engineering strategies,

> *The success of the incremental delivery approach rests on the ability of the designer to create-—from the start-—an architecture that can support the full functionality of the system so that there is not a point during the sequence of deliveries where the addition of the next increment of functionality requires a massive re-engineering of the system at the architectural level* (p. 59).

The Fusion object model, the next analysis model to be created, serves as that architecture.

Once the use scenarios are complete, the development team has a much clearer understanding of the demands that will be placed on the system. The use scenarios are an excellent source of information for building the object model. The use scenario diagrams can be stepped through, making sure that analysis classes exist to support the need of each system operation. It is also quite common that building the object model will generate further refinements and improvements to the use scenarios.

Operation model

The last analysis model to be created during the definition phase is the operation model. It documents in a declarative fashion the change in the state of the system as it responds to a system operation. Each system operation is described using only terms from the use scenarios, object model, and data dictionary.

A complete specification of the system exists when the operation model is completed. The use scenarios capture the intended uses of the system from the agents' point of view. The object model captures the high-level architecture of the system. The operation model documents the effect that each system operation has on the system. The creation of each model has stimulated the thought necessary to identify and resolve issues, while the notation for each model establishes a common communication format for the team.

Managing the analysis process

An appropriate question to ask at this point is how much time should be invested in making a first pass at the analysis models. Although there is no formula that we can offer for Evolutionary Fusion, the application of a progress measurement technique used by many development teams during implementation works surprisingly well at this early stage of development.

During the integration and system test phase, many teams compare the rate at which defects are being identified to the rate at which defects are being isolated and repaired. In the early part of this phase, the rate of defect identification exceeds the rate of defect repair. At some later point in this phase, the rate of repair exceeds the rate of identification, and estimates can be made on when the desired defect density will be reached and the product can be released.

A similar approach can be used to track progress during the creation of the analysis models in Evolutionary Fusion's definition phase. Any issue identified during the creation of the analysis models can be considered a potential defect in the specification of the system. As with testing code, the initial attempts to build the analysis models will generate a large number of potential issues, or defects. As the creation of the analysis models progresses, fewer and fewer issues, or defects, will be found. Once the rate of resolving, or repairing, these issues exceeds the rate of finding new issues, a completion date for the first pass at the analysis models can be estimated.

An additional parameter often assigned to defects is a classification that represents the severity of the defect. Few systems are shipped with known defects that can cause unrecoverable data loss, but many are shipped with known defects that have only limited impact on the system's use. It can be helpful to apply a similar classification scheme to the issues found during analysis (Crough and Walstra 1993). Many issues identified will be of such impact that they must be resolved before moving on to the development phase. Other issues will be of lesser impact and, as such, resolution can be delayed until the development phase. There is also a third class of issues that relates directly to design or implementation. These must be reclassified as design or implementation issues and marked for resolution during that phase.

There is an expectation that a team must complete all the analysis phase models before moving on to implementation. Our experience has shown that this is not the case. It is only necessary to complete a high-level view of the complete system and to resolve the critical and serious "defects" that have been logged against the analysis models. This approach can also help teams avoid "analysis paralysis," the malady that afflicts many teams when they try to resolve every known issue before moving on to design and implementation. The analysis models will be revisited as the first step of each implementation cycle, so further additions and refinements can be made then.

It is difficult to accurately estimate the length of the analysis phase, especially if it is the team's first use of object technology. Fortunately, using the approach described here can provide early indication of progress so that resources can be managed accordingly.

Building the Plan

The last task of the Evolutionary Fusion definition phase is to plan the next phase, development. This task consists of three major steps: assigning ownership for the key roles that must be played during this phase, defining the standard EVO cycle, and determining the sequence in which functionality will be developed (May and Cotton 1995).

Key roles

For the development phase to progress in a smooth and efficient manner, it is helpful to define and assign ownership for three key roles: project manager, technical lead, and user liaison. On large project teams, these roles may be shared by more than one person. On smaller project teams, a person may play more than one role.

Project manager: Many aspects of the project manager's role become even more critical with Evolutionary Development. The project manager must work with the marketing team and the customers to establish the project's value proposition, identify key project risks, document all commitments and dependencies, and articulate how Evolutionary Development will contribute to the project's success. Agreement on the value proposition is critical, as it will help keep the decision-making process focused. The key project risks will be used to sequence the implementation so that these risks can be characterized and addressed as early as possible. The commitments and dependencies will also be a key consideration when sequencing the implementation cycles. It is also important that the project manager solicit and address any concerns that the project team has with the Evolutionary Development approach.

The project manager must also define and manage the decision-making process. Although this is often an implicit task of the project manager, the large amount of information and the increased number of decisions that must be made using Evolutionary Fusion require that this process be made explicit. Based on the kinds of changes anticipated during the project, the project manager must consider how information will be gathered, how decisions will be made, and how decisions will be communicated. With very short development cycles, delayed decisions can slow progress dramatically.

Working with the technical lead, the project manager may also decide to include explicit design cycles in the schedule. For software architectures and designs that are expected to survive many years, supporting multiple releases or even multiple product lines, it is important to invest in the evolution of the architecture. As the development phase progresses, certain isolated decisions that compromise some aspect of the architecture will be made. There will also be new insights into the architecture and its robustness that could not have been anticipated during the definition phase. Design cycles dedicated to the architecture will deliver no new functionality for the user. By including tasks such as architecture refinement, design development, and design inspections, these cycles will deliver to future EVO cycles an architecture that is better equipped to meet the demands that will be placed on it.

Technical lead: The technical lead is responsible for managing the architecture of the project as well as tracking and helping to resolve technical issues and dependencies that arise between engineers and between subsystems. The technical lead also plays a key part in defining the detailed task plans for each implementation cycle. With a broad view of the system, the technical lead can make sure that tasks scheduled for an implementation cycle are feasible and that they all contribute to the stated deliverable for the cycle.

User liaison: The user liaison manages the team's interaction with the users, including setting up the user feedback process by defining expectations of the users, locating and qualifying users against these expectations, and coordinating any initial training that the users will need on the system. Once the development phase is underway, the user liaison will be responsible for collecting feedback, tracking user participation and satisfaction with the process, and ensuring that users are kept informed of the development team's response to their feedback.

It is important to keep in mind that the users providing feedback on the system may change over time. In the early development phase, it may be unrealistic to deliver the system to actual users, since there may simply not be enough functionality in the system. For these releases, other members of the project team or other members of the organization can act as surrogates for actual users.

Defining the standard EVO cycle

The next step in planning the development phase is to define the standard EVO cycle to be used. This task includes establishing the length of the cycle as well as the milestones within the cycle. The general rule of thumb is to keep the cycle length as short as possible. Within Hewlett–Packard, projects have used a cycle length as short as one week and as long as four weeks. The typical cycle time is two weeks (see Figure 6.6). The primary factor in determining the cycle length is how often management wants insight into the project's progress and how often they want the opportunity to adjust the project plan, product, and process. Since it is more likely that a team will lengthen their cycle time than shorten it, it is best to start with as short a cycle as possible.

Monday	Tuesday	Wednesday	Thursday	Friday
Final test of last week's build Review and enhance analysis models for new features	Release last week's build to users Create design models for new features Begin implementation of new features	Incremental build overnight		Weekend build from scratch

Monday	Tuesday	Wednesday	Thursday	Friday
	All user feedback collected	Functionality freeze - no new features added beyond this point Incremental build overnight	Test new functionality Review feedback, determine changes for next release	Test new functionality Weekend build from scratch

Figure 6.6 Example Two-week EVO Cycle

Grouping and prioritizing functionality

With key roles assigned and the standard cycle defined, the last step in planning the development phase is to group and prioritize the functionality into implementation "chunks." The chunks must be no larger than can be delivered in the standard cycle time. Prioritization ensures that critical or high-risk features are completed early and that low-risk features are delivered last. Some of the most common criteria used for grouping and prioritizing functionality will be discussed later in this section.

The deliverable from the planning phase is an implementation schedule that maps all functionality for the system into implementation cycles and provides enough detail for the first three or four cycles so that actual implementation can begin. To help develop this schedule and to maintain a user perspective, the Fusion use scenarios and system operations provide a useful grouping of system functionality. Recall that system operations, which may appear in multiple use scenarios, are grouped together to define use scenarios.

The first step is to divide the system development into four or five major chunks and to group those use scenarios that include top-priority functionality into the first chunk (Figure 6.7). The rest of the use scenarios can then be grouped into the following major chunks, with the use scenarios containing the lowest priority functionality in the last chunk. Each chunk should contain approximately the same number of use scenarios.

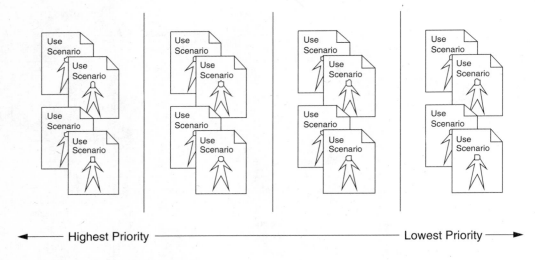

Highest Priority ─────────────────────────────── Lowest Priority

Figure 6.7 Prioritize Use Scenarios

The next step is to order the use scenarios within the first chunk using the same criteria as before (Figure 6.8). When producing this ordering, it is not uncommon to move scenarios between groups to achieve a better balance and sequence. Since system operations may appear in multiple use scenarios, many of the system operations that are contained in the use scenarios of later groupings will be implemented with use scenarios in earlier groupings. Therefore, it is best to have the fewest use scenarios in the first chunk and the most in the last chunk.

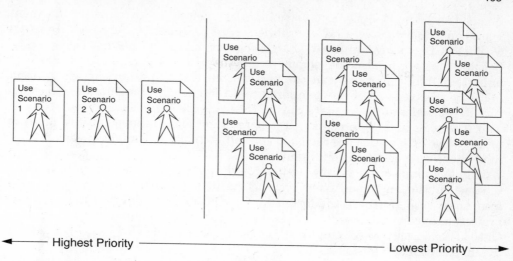

Figure 6.8 Order the First Group of Use Scenarios

The system operations from the use scenarios in the first group can now be grouped and sequenced into the first few implementation cycles (Figure 6.9). Keep in mind that the deliverables from each cycle should be defined in such a way that they can be validated by a user of the system. For these early cycles, the limited functionality may be best validated by another member of the development team. The key concept is that you must be able to validate the success of the cycle in some way.

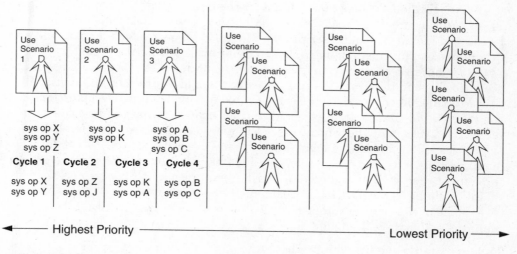

Figure 6.9 First Implementation Cycles Defined

When estimating the number of system operations that the development team can implement in a cycle, experience has shown that taking the common wisdom of the team and dividing that number in half yields the best results. Because this approach to development may be new to the team, it is extremely important from a motivational perspective that these first few implementation cycles be successful. Also, keep in mind that there is a fair amount of infrastructure developed and put in place during these first few implementation cycles as well. The tools and the process will undergo significant refinement during these first few cycles. For these reasons, keep the functionality content of the first few implementation cycles to a minimum.

A technique used widely within Hewlett–Packard is to adopt a naming scheme for the implementation cycles. One team used the names of wineries from their local Northern California region. As they completed each cycle, their project manager would buy a bottle of wine from that winery and store it away. Once several cycles were completed, the team would celebrate by taking the wine to a fine restaurant for lunch.

The final step is to estimate the number of cycles needed for the rest of the intended functionality and to project a final implementation completion date (Figure 6.10). This is accomplished by counting the new system operations that must be implemented in the rest of the chunks and dividing by the number of system operations that can be completed in each cycle to give the total number of implementation cycles. In the example used to illustrate the planning process, the estimated length of the implementation phase is 32 weeks. To facilitate communication, it is useful to assign themes to each of the implementation chunks. The project team and the users will need both a detailed and a high-level view of the project, but there are typically many members of the organization that prefer to see just the "big picture." The themes can help convey that big picture.

With the deliverables now defined for the first several EVO cycles, the technical lead can prepare the detailed task list for these cycles. This detailed task list should include a clear description of the task, an owner for the task, and any dependencies that the task may have on other tasks within the cycle.

It is not necessary to provide any additional detail for the groupings of use scenarios beyond the first. It is only necessary to make sure that all functionality as it is defined at this early stage is accounted for and that an overall estimate of the effort is calculated. It is expected that experiences from the first few implementation cycles will affect future cycles in many ways. These later implementation cycles will be defined in more detail several cycles before their start date. On small projects with one or two co-located teams, detailing the next three or four implementation cycles is adequate. On larger projects, it may be necessary to maintain detailed schedules that reach further out in time.

Some of the criteria commonly used in setting priorities during this initial planning activity are the following:

Features with greatest risk: The most common criterion used for prioritizing the development phase implementation cycles is risk. When adopting object technology, many teams are concerned that the system performance

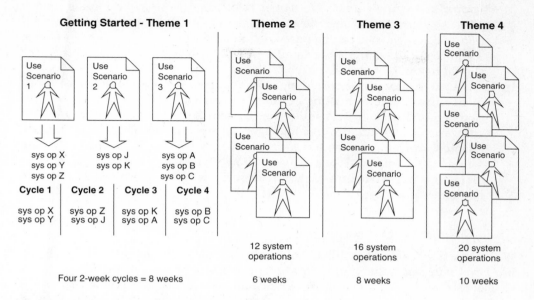

Figure 6.10 Completed Implementation Plan

will not be adequate. Ease-of-use is another common risk for a project. The use scenarios that will provide the best insight into areas of greatest risk should be scheduled for implementation as early as possible.

Coordination with other teams: Most software development teams today have commitments to or are dependent on other teams. For example, firmware development depends on some form of hardware development. Reusable software platforms make a strong commitment to the products that are built on them. It may be necessary to adjust the priority assigned to functionality to accommodate these dependencies and commitments.

"Must have" versus "want" functionality: All product features are not created equal. Some features are considered critical to the success of a project, while some features would simply be nice to have. Some development projects must meet well-defined standards and may even have to pass certification tests of their functionality that are defined by governing regulatory agencies. On these projects, it is often best to complete the required or "must have" functionality before the value-added or "want" functionality. Those use scenarios that capture the required functionality should be given higher priority than those that capture only desired functionality.

This same criterion can also apply to core or fundamental functionality that must be in place before additional functionality can be implemented. It may be necessary to build up in a layered fashion the core functionality that all other functionality will depend on. It is imperative that each cycle contributing to the core functionality be defined so that some validation or feedback may be obtained.

Most popular or most useful features first: If project risks are minor and if project commitments and dependencies are insignificant, then prioritization of use scenarios can be based on value to the intended user. Those use scenarios that are the most popular or will be of the most value to the user should be completed first.

Infrastructure development: A significant amount of development environment infrastructure must be put in place during the first few implementation cycles. The tools that will be used, such as the compiler, debugger, and software asset configuration manager, as well as the processes that are adopted, can be developed in an evolutionary fashion in parallel with the functionality intended for the user. Some teams have found it valuable to make the infrastructure tasks an explicit category in the plan for each implementation cycle.

6.2.2   Development Phase

With both the development phase plan and the detailed plans for the first few EVO cycles in place, the implementation process can begin. Each EVO cycle consists of the same basic steps: refining the analysis models, developing the design models, and writing and validating the code. The customer feedback process is executed in parallel with these tasks. The deliverables from the previous EVO cycle are evaluated by selected users or their surrogates, and decisions are made that shape the content of the subsequent EVO cycles.

Refining the Analysis Models

The EVO cycle begins with a review of the existing Fusion analysis models against the functionality or system operations defined as deliverables for that cycle. For each cycle, new functionality may be defined for delivery and existing functionality may be identified for modification.

The process for moving through the Fusion analysis models remains the same. Use scenarios that include the system operations must be reviewed for changes that were the result of feedback and refinement from previous EVO cycles. The object model must be reviewed for similar changes. Additional detail may be required in the object model. The system operation descriptions are reviewed for any changes and to ensure a common understanding by all members of the team.

The technical lead is a key player during the refinement of the analysis models. Because they represent the overall architecture for the system, any extensions or enhancements of the models must be made without serious compromise to the integrity of the architecture. If compromises must be made, they should be logged as defects against the architecture and considered for possible repair in a later EVO cycle.

Design Models

Based on the clear understanding of the deliverables for the cycle generated by the review and refinement of the analysis models, the Fusion design models can be created or updated. Object interaction graphs will determine the new classes that will be needed or the new methods that will be added to existing classes. The Fusion design models determine what coding must be done for the cycle.

Coding and Validation

In addition to the code that must be generated to implement the design models, any tests needed to validate this work in later cycles must also be completed. Many teams make use of test harnesses to validate their code during the early cycles of development. These test harnesses are software modules or subsystems that can exercise the method interfaces of other software subsystems. They are particularly useful during the early cycles of development when major portions of the architecture have not been implemented. They also provide great value in later EVO cycles as tools for focused and automated regression testing.

Customer Feedback

The customer feedback loop operates simultaneously with the implementation tasks. Beginning with the second cycle and continuing throughout the development phase, some group of users or surrogate users will be validating the product that the team has completed so far. The feedback that they provide must be evaluated against the value proposition of the project for appropriate decision making. It is important that the project manager, technical lead(s), and user liaison(s) allocate enough time during each cycle to review plans, processes, and architectural documents to assess the impact of each decision.

System Test Using Use Scenarios

Although the use scenarios can be helpful in conducting unit and integration testing for each implementation cycle, they can provide the greatest value during system test. Since the use scenarios are not structured along architectural or subsystem boundaries, they tend to provide a broad level of system testing that generates paths of execution through the entire system. They may be augmented to generate boundary and stress-test conditions, and they can also serve as a basis for creating user-level documentation.

6.2.3   Scaling up for Large Projects

In the use of Evolutionary Fusion with large projects, and especially with those that include multiple development teams that may not even be co-located, there are a number of additional issues to consider. It may not be appropriate to integrate the deliverables from all project teams every EVO cycle. It is useful to define a higher-level set of EVO cycles and to integrate all work together at the end of those cycles. To manage these multiple levels of EVO cycles, as well as the broad set of technologies that may be involved, it is also useful to employ multiple technical leads, or architects.

Hierarchical EVO cycles

As the size of a project team grows, a larger and larger portion of the standard EVO cycle is dedicated to integrating the work of the many project team members. To keep the standard EVO cycle as small and as efficient as possible and to let project teams progress in parallel, it is necessary to introduce hierarchical EVO cycles. These hierarchical cycles are essentially a formalized version of the chunks of functionality or groupings of use scenarios introduced earlier in Section 6.2.1, under Grouping and Prioritizing Functionality.

The four or five major chunks or groupings that the use scenarios are initially broken into become the highest-level EVO cycles. As before, the use scenarios for the first chunk or EVO cycle are sequenced and the system operations allocated between multiple teams (Figure 6.11). For large teams, it is also useful to add an integration EVO cycle at the end of each major EVO cycle.

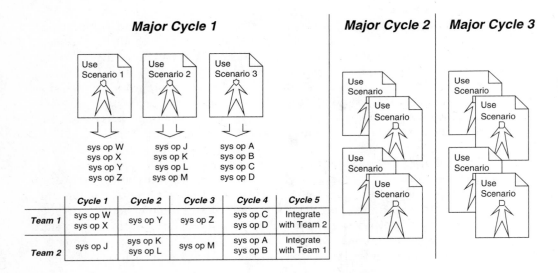

Figure 6.11 Hierarchical EVO Cycles

Each team is expected to define its own user feedback and validation process for its minor EVO cycles. There will also be a feedback and validation process for each major EVO cycle of the system.

Role of Architects

Since it is difficult to define subsets of functionality that are completely independent of one another, it is important to have an identified individual or group of individuals to manage the dependencies throughout each major EVO cycle. This role is best played by the technical leads of each team, the architects. The architects play a key role in allocating system operations among the various teams during each planning phase, and they are best positioned to resolve any technical issues that emerge as a result of the parallel implementation approach. For large projects within Hewlett–Packard, weekly meetings or conference calls are typical for the architect teams.

6.3 CONCLUSION

Much of Hewlett–Packard's success is attributable to the fact that it is a diverse company composed of many independent organizations. However, relatively few software development best practices have achieved widespread adoption in this environment of autonomy and diversity. Fusion appears to be an exception to this rule. Fusion's appeal is largely a result of the respect that its creators have for software development teams. Fusion does not attempt to address every possible nuance of software development with complex notations and model variations. It does provide a reasonably simple, complete set of models that supports a team through most of the development process, acknowledging that software engineers are highly educated and talented professionals and that they are best suited to adapt a method to meet their unique project needs and working styles.

Evolutionary Development has been positioned here as a life cycle for software development, but it really has much broader application to any complex system. Fusion, the method, is changing to better meet user needs using an evolutionary approach. Based on user feedback, we merged Evolutionary Development with Fusion as the deliverable from one evolutionary cycle. There have been a number of other changes to the method, as well as to the method of delivery, again all based on user feedback. As our experience with Fusion grows, so will the method. It is our hope that the Fusion user community will continue to share experiences and to evolve the method in a direction that is both respectful and useful to all software development teams.

ACKNOWLEDGMENTS

It is impossible to thank all those that have contributed in some way to this material covered in this paper, but I must try. First, I would like to thank the many Hewlett–Packard development teams that I have had the privilege to work with. Their unwavering dedication to creating innovative products and to adopting innovative ways of working make Hewlett–Packard a very successful company and an extremely rewarding place to work. Next, I would like to thank my colleagues of the Software Initiative who have worked with me to make Fusion and object technology as easy to learn, adopt, and adapt as possible. I would like to offer a very special thanks to the reviewers of this material, Ruth Malan, Reed Letsinger, Elaine May, and Tom Gilb. Their wealth of knowledge and experience generated insights and suggestions that have added significantly to the clarity and presentation of this material. And finally, to Derek Coleman and his team, for providing us all with the very powerful and useful set of models and notation that we call Fusion.

REFERENCES

Boehm, B. 1986. A Spiral Model of Software Development and Enhancement. *ACM SIG-SOFT Software Engineering Notes*, 11(4).

Booch, G. 1994. The Macro Process of Object-Oriented Software Development. *Report on Object Analysis and Design*, 1(4):11–13.

Coleman, D., P. Arnold, S. Bodoff, C. Dollin, H. Gilchrist, F. Hayes, and P. Jeremaes. 1994. *Object-Oriented Development: The Fusion Method*. Englewood Cliffs, NJ: Prentice Hall.

Crough, R., and R. Walstra. 1993. *Structured Common Sense: A Design Approach for Front-End Software Development*. Hewlett–Packard internal publication.

Gilb, T. 1988. *Principles of Software Engineering Management*. Wokingham, England: Addison-Wesley.

May, E., and T. Cotton. 1995. *Evolutionary Planning Workshop*. Hewlett–Packard internal publication.

May, E., and B. Zimmer. 1994. *Evolutionary Product Development at Hewlett–Packard*. Hewlett–Packard internal publication.

MIL-STD-498. December, 1994. Software Development and Documentation. *Military Standard 498*.

Moore, G. A. 1991. *Crossing the Chasm: Marketing and Selling Technology Products to Mainstream Customers*. New York: HarperBusiness.

Ould, M. 1990. *Strategies for Software Engineering—The Management of Risk and Quality*. Chichester, England: Wiley.

Rumbaugh, J. May 1995. OMT: The Development Process. *Journal of Object-Oriented Programming*.

Method Metrics and Defect Tracking: Measuring and Improving the Fusion Development Process

Kris Oosting

SHARED OBJECTIVES

7.1 INTRODUCTION

Fire fighting but no prevention! Why do we always wait until the coding phase before we start collecting metrics? We exercise prevention when we collect metrics during the design phase and use them to identify problem areas so that we can act.

Much of "object-oriented" software development is still done through coding. Using an OOA/D method appears to be a great deal of work, as does collecting metrics, and it seems better to do something "real." The "real" work—coding—is actually a lot of rework and debugging. Why not move this rework to an earlier phase where changes are easier to make and their impact on the rest of the application is more visible? The time and effort spent constructing analysis and design models and collecting and using metrics based on these models is easily offset by the time saved in code rework.

In this paper we describe metrics that can be used in combination with the Fusion method. We provide an extensive list of metrics, together with an explanation of how to measure and present the metric and how to manage metrics collection. We also discuss defect tracking, describe a complete defect categorization model, and present ready-to-use defect registration and defect analysis models.

This paper is based on work using software metrics and defect tracking on non-object-oriented projects from 1989 onward and object-oriented projects since 1992. The OO-specific experience resulted from work on projects building NEXT-

STEP/OpenStep and OSF/Motif C++ applications. Metrics and defect tracking strategies were used in combination with different OO methods, achieving the greatest success when we started using Fusion early in 1994.

Examples of OO projects that we have measured include projects building a graphical resource planning system, a defect and requirements tracking application, and a radiotherapy treatment planning system. The projects were between 3 and 10 person years. All of these applications have graphical user interfaces (GUIs).

7.2 METHOD METRICS

We use method metrics because they help us to do our work more effectively. *You can't control software development using a method if you can't measure it.*

7.2.1 What Are Metrics?

Let us first determine what metrics are not. The word *METRIC* is not an abbreviation for *Measuring Engineers' Trustworthiness, Reliability, Intelligence, and Correctness*. If it were, then no engineers would use metrics—or they would at least fake the results to their own "advantage"!

Grady and Caswell (1987, p. 4) define a software metric as *"a standard way of measuring some attribute of the software development process."* Size, cost, and defects are examples of such attributes.

When an OOA/D method is used, a specific subset of software metrics, called *method metrics*, comes into play. Method metrics enable us to measure certain aspects of the method and its models. For example, when the *service degree*[*] between two objects is too high (i.e., the objects are too tightly coupled), we might consider finding another way of designing the object interaction graphs that these objects appear in. Again, this is prevention (no code has been written as yet). It would probably be very difficult and labor intensive to discover this type of problem in the source code.

7.2.2 Why Measure?

When there is no benefit, one need not measure. That is why it is important that we know up front what the benefits can be. Method metrics allow us to

- Understand the way the method is actually used
- Evaluate the effectiveness of the method, even per technique
- Control application development
- Find problem areas in analysis and design (to do something about them)

---

[*] The service degree between two objects is the number of different message types sent between the two objects. For example, when object A needs five different services from object B, object A will send five different messages to object B. The service degree in this case is 5.

- Warn the project manager in time if the project goes in the wrong direction
- Evaluate the first OO pilot project
- Establish a basic set of metrics and their norm values
- Make better estimates
- Make the application development process visible

Note that the benefits will also depend on company politics, "religions," and other intangible issues.

7.2.3   What to Measure?

This is the question! It is nice to know what the benefits are, but how does one start? You need to

- Identify what you want to measure
- Define the metric(s)
- Establish how to collect the metrics

The best way to start is with a Goal–Question–Metric (GQM) session (Grady 1992, pp. 23–29) during which you first define your goal(s). For example, your goal might be to minimize design complexity.

For each goal, the project members brainstorm a list of questions that will help them understand whether the goal is being achieved. After agreeing on the usefulness of the questions, metrics can be defined to provide answers to them. For example, metrics such as defect density, McCabe complexity, and lines of source code are all correlated with complexity.

Sometimes the same metric can be used to answer a number of questions. Conversely, one question could need more than one metric to provide the complete answer. Figure 7.1 illustrates the relationship between goals, questions, and metrics.

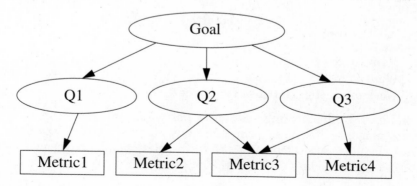

Figure 7.1 GQM Model

For every metric, ask yourself: what do I gain when I have the result, and what do I lose if I do not have it? This allows you to assess whether the information you gain from the metric is sufficient to justify the effort involved in collecting the data.

Before discussing specific metrics, it is very useful to know what can go wrong when using an OO method, OO environment, etc. Knowing what can go wrong will help you ask the right questions about a certain goal. For example, if your goal is to minimize the complexity of design, if you know what can go wrong during design, you can ask the following questions:

- What is the service degree between objects?
- How many objects communicate to support a single piece of functionality?
- Which objects are the main service providers?
- Is there message pass-through?

WCGW lists

What-can-go-wrong lists (WCGW lists) are helpful in generating questions about goals and discovering metrics during GQM sessions. They list what can go wrong during the creation of a model (e.g., a visibility graph). They tell what the method user might do wrong, not where the method is wrong.

Besides being useful aids in GQM sessions, WCGW lists promote

- Prevention—the construction of these lists helps project members understand the method better and aids prevention by alerting everybody to what they might do wrong
- Discovery—problems that arise during modeling can often be discovered through analysis and design reviews[*] and defect tracking (Section 7.3)

The lists can be constructed in a brainstorming session comparable to the GQM session. The participants of this WCGW session should be project members who understand the method and, if possible, who have used the method before on real projects.

The following steps will get you started:

1. Create a WCGW list template and fill in the following:
   - Name of the phases
   - What to model per phase
   - Work product(s) you have to deliver

2. Conduct a brainstorming session to list what you think can go wrong in each phase, model, and technique or work product. For example, in the analysis phase when modeling the static relationship between classes using object models, a class can be a hidden process.

The following tables show enough examples to get you going. Table 7.1 con-

---

[*] Good model syntax checking by CASE tools also aids discovery of problems.

tains examples of WCGW lists created after a brainstorming session for the analysis phase, and Table 7.2 shows the WCGW lists for the design phase. We constructed these lists to find possible metrics quickly and to support defect tracking, and have used them in all of our projects. With these WCGW lists you have a good basis for questions in the GQM sessions. Now it is time to find the metrics to match.

Table 7.1 Analysis Phase WCGW List

What to Model	Work Product	WCGW
Static structure of information in the system	Domain object model and system object model (SOM)	Class is a process. Relationship is dataflow. Class has to be an attribute. Attribute has to be a class. Class not relevant. Relationship not relevant. Relationship incorrect. Too many n-ary relationships. Class should not be in SOM. Class not in SOM. Too many classes in SOM. Invariant incorrect. Generalization not correct. Wrong generalization type. Incorrect aggregation. Incorrect cardinality. Class not described. Relationship not described. Attribute not described.
Input and output communication of the system	Operation model	Incorrect Assumes. Incorrect Result. Incorrect Reads. Incorrect Changes. Incorrect Sends. Model not complete.
	Life-cycle model	Incorrect life-cycle expression. Missing system operation. Missing event. Wrong sequence. Model not complete. Not all scenarios modeled. Not all system operations have a schema.

Table 7.2   Design Phase WCGW. List

What to Model	Work Product	WCGW
Object communication structure	Object interaction graph	Object instead of collection. Incorrect protocol used. Message pass-through. Objects too strongly coupled. Incorrect parameter type. Incorrect return type. Incorrect return value. Too many objects communicate to implement a functionality. Incorrect select predicate. Incorrect stop predicate. Wrong message sent. Incorrect message sequencing. Incorrect object creation. Missing **lib** prefix.
Object reference structure	Visibility graph	Incorrect reference type. Incorrect reference mutability. Incorrect server visibility. Incorrect server binding. Incorrect protocol used. Service degree too high. Missing **new** prefix. Missing **constant** prefix. Missing **lib** prefix. Incorrect use of proxy (distributed objects).
Class inheritance structure	Inheritance graphs	Incorrect generalization type (disjoint, nondisjoint). Incorrect generalization/specialization. Structure too deep. Structure too flat. Incorrect grading.
Class definition	Class description	Incorrect transformation of attributes. Wrong protocol used. Wrong superclass used. List of methods not complete. Incorrect usage of private, protected, and public.
Protocol definition	Protocol description	Incorrect list of methods. Protocol not complete.

Metrics

After defining the goal(s) and the WCGW lists, questions can be written down. To find answers to these questions, we often have to measure certain attributes of the software development process. These metrics will tell us more about the process or technique used.

The metrics have to be defined so that they can be used in combination with the WCGW lists and to support the GQM sessions. The next steps are to

- Make a list of metrics that can assist you in measuring the WCGW items. Some provide early warnings; others provide information you can use to improve your process. Metrics definitions can be found in books or by using common sense.
- Evaluate the results to tune the norm value you use to compare the measurements—otherwise it will be difficult to judge if the results are positive or negative.

Besides the items in the WCGW lists, we are also interested in attributes such as the size of models and code and how much effort or resources we have to assign to get the job done. The more resources involved, the higher the cost. Metrics covering these attributes appear in Tables 7.3 and 7.4.

Note that it is important not to collect too much at once when you start metrics collection. The best way to start is with a small but useful set of metrics. The sooner you can show the benefits, the better it is for your project.

Check each metric against the following criteria to ensure that it is really useful:

- It should be robust (i.e., repeatable, precise, and relatively insensitive to minor changes in tools).
- It should suggest a norm (e.g., a low value for number of defects is best).
- It should be simple (otherwise the metric will be hard to explain and apply).
- It should be predictable and trackable.

WCGW items and metrics

Once you know what can go wrong, it is time to find a metric that can measure each WCGW item to indicate how much it is going wrong. For example, when you are developing an object model, the following can go wrong:

- Too many n-ary relationships—can be measured by collecting the number of ternary or higher-order relationships in a model
- Too many classes in the system object model—count the number of classes
- Classes not described in the data dictionary—can be measured easily by collecting the number of unique classes in the models versus the number of classes described in the data dictionary. CASE tools should provide these metrics.

Interestingly, we discovered that the number of classes or the number of relationships is not a good measure of size. The number of system operations provides more information about how big a system will be or, better still, how long it will take to design.

Our measurements showed that a developer with moderate experience turns three to four system operations into design models (i.e., three to four object interaction graphs with method descriptions, visibility graphs, and class and protocol descriptions) in a day. The amount may seem low, but a lot of thinking and experimentation are involved. You will understand that if many library classes are used the number should be slightly higher. However, developers still need to understand what the library classes offer, and this entails reading the class documentation.

Table 7.3 provides a list of analysis phase metrics that can be used in GQM sessions.

Table 7.3 Example List of Metrics for the Analysis Phase

Work Product	Metric	Motivation
Domain object model	Number of classes	Size and effort
	Number of 4-ary relationships and higher	Complexity and understanding
	Number of invariants	Complexity and understanding
	Number of unique classes on the model vs. number of classes described in the data dictionary	Completeness
	Aggregation level	To measure "over-aggregation" – too much aggregation produces unreadable models
	Number of disjoint and nondisjoint generalizations	Used during reviews
System object model	Same as above	Same as above
Operation model	Number of system operations	Size and effort! (functionality)
	Number of system operations coming from one relationship diamond	Complexity and understanding
Life-cycle model	Number of life-cycle expressions	Complexity and size

What can go wrong during design? The object interaction graph, for example, might have too many objects communicating together to implement some functionality. On the other hand, the model might be too complex (see also the list in Table 7.2). The first we can measure by counting the number of unique objects and the number of messages from one object to another. The second, complexity, can, for example, be measured by a McCabe-like complexity metric for the method descriptions, percentage of reused classes (in this case probably low), and the number of parameters per message (interaction coupling).

Table 7.4 provides a more complete list of metrics that can be collected during the design phase.

Table 7.4 Example List of Metrics for the Design Phase

Work Product	Metric	Motivation
Object interaction graph	Number of objects	Complexity and size of system operation (functionality)
	Number of messages from one object to another (service degree)	Coupling (necessary for regression testing)
	Number of parameters per message (interaction coupling)	Coupling (necessary for regression testing and for simplifying the model)
	Number of if-then-else constructions in method descriptions	Indicator of complexity (high complexity → many defects → high costs)
	Number of case constructions in method descriptions	Indicator of complexity (high complexity → many defects → high costs)
	Number of new classes added	Relation between system object model in analysis and the design
	Number of methods per class	Service provider size; can generate a lot of defects
	Percent of reuse	How much do we use from the library or framework?
Visibility graph	Number of type **new** servers	Indication of dynamic object creation; make sure that they are removed when no longer needed; indicator for finding memory leaks.
	Number of references from client to servers	Service dependence; needs lots of different services; this can give a high chance of problems
	Number of references to one server (in total overview)	If number is high, then this class is an important server; needs extra testing, and sometimes you have to review this high number to see if it is really necessary
Inheritance graph	Generalization/specialization cohesion	How interrelated are the classes? Is the specialization really specialization, or just arbitrary? To locate misplaced classes in the structure
	Number of levels	Indicator of over- or underspecialization
Class description	Number of attributes	Size and effort
	Number of methods	Size and effort

Back to GQM

Now we will demonstrate how to use the WCGW lists and metrics tables with an example. The scenario is as follows: during design and code reviews, complexity was revealed to be very high. According to the developers, this was the best they could do, although they could not prove it. As complex models and complex code tend to have many defects, we decided to hold a GQM session to get a better grip on the situation. The process diagram shown in Figure 7.2 was used to guide this session.

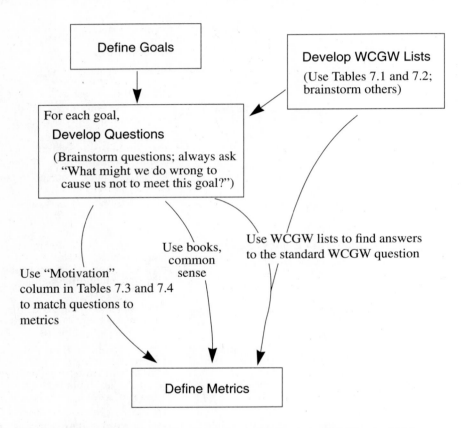

Figure 7.2 Modified GQM Process, Using WCGW Lists and Metrics Tables

Example: Applying the GQM Process

Goal: Minimize the complexity of the design.

Questions

In accord with the GQM process, we asked questions aimed at understanding whether, or how well, we were achieving the goal. First we asked more general questions to avoid jumping to metrics too soon. Then we refined some of these questions with more specific questions that would lead us to metrics. The following is the list of questions generated in our GQM session:

1. What part of the design is too complex? *(A variant of this question is often asked; its purpose is to locate the problem area.)*

2. What do we mean by complexity?

    2.1 Complexity of the messaging structure?

    2.2 Control complexity of method descriptions?

    2.3 Complexity of the reference structure?

3. How high is the complexity now?

    3.1 What is the service degree?

    3.2 What is the control complexity?

    3.3 How many occurrences of message pass-through are there?

4. What are the critical parts of the design?

5. What diagramming techniques are used? *(This question is asked to understand what we used to make the design models.)*

6. How can we predict complexity?

    6.1. Are there norm values for service degree, control complexity, and coupling we can use?

7. How does design complexity relate to the complexity of the coded classes?

    7.1 Is there a relation between complexity of method descriptions and coded methods?

    7.2 How is object referencing really implemented?

8. What are we doing wrong during design to cause the complexity? *(This is what we are really trying to find out. The answers to the other questions should provide an answer to this question.)*

9. What is the experience of the developers; do they need more training? *(This question was asked by the project manager who wanted to know, e.g., if the learning curve was the cause of all the problems?)*

10. Is the complexity always in the same part of the design or the same part of the design process of the OOA/D method?

Metrics (Answers)

Most of these questions have answers that can be measured. By using our common sense, as well as Tables 7.2 and 7.4, we listed the following metrics to help us find answers.

Metrics for Q1

- Model type (e.g., object interaction graph, visibility graph, inheritance graph)
- The subsystem that is too complex
- The system operations involved

Metrics for Q2

This is more about finding the right definition.

Q2.1 and Q2.2: In this case we mean the structure of the diagrams and the structure of the method descriptions of the object interaction graphs (OIGs). Examples are coupling and McCabe-like complexity.

The WCGW list for the visibility graph lists: Service degree too high. This can be measured by collecting the number of different messages between two objects modeled in the OIGs.

Another example is that too many objects communicate to implement a functionality, which can be measured by the number of objects and the number of messages between them in the OIG.

Also, long method descriptions for the OIG and many if-then-else and case-like statements.

Q2.3: In the visibility graph we can measure the number of references to an object. A relatively high number of references indicates a complex design.

Metrics for Q3

Q3.1: Service degree is measured by using the visibility graph to find the reference and the object interaction graph to find the number of messages. See also Table 7.4.

Q3.2: Long method descriptions for the OIG and many if-then-else and case-like statements.

Q3.3: Difficult to find, but the OIGs are the place to look. If there are many occurrences, consider redesign.

Complexity also depends on the type of application and the experience of the developers.

Metrics for Q4:

Version number of the design model. Design review information. Defect tracking information (will be discussed later). Critical parts of a design can be a result of experience or application type. If an application is very complex, there can be more critical parts in the design.

Metrics for Q5

Object communication structure: object interaction graph
Object reference structure: visibility graph
Class inheritance structure: inheritance graph
Class definition: class description
Protocol definition: protocol description

Metrics for Q6

First you need to know what complexity you want to predict: design complexity or code complexity? It is a fact that when the design is very complex, the code is too. And another fact is that complex code generates many defects.

In this case we have to look more closely at the object interaction graphs and visibility graphs to predict the complexity where it will hurt the most, in code. For metrics see "Metrics for Q2." These metrics need *norm values*. For example, service degree lower than 20, complexity of the methods lower than 10, and message pass-through over max 2 levels.

Metrics for Q7

Complex communications often result in complex code. Unclear object referencing also results in complex and unstructured code.

To make the design less complex, we also need to eliminate complex communications to support a functionality. Also, use more library classes. These can be measured by percentage of library classes used in the design models.

Metrics for Q8

Number of objects communicating to implement some functionality. For example, a system operation is supported by 12 objects that communicate together and communicate with themselves. We saw many examples of these forms of over-communication. They also indicate performance problems.

Other answers to this question overlap with those for questions 2 and 3 and are not repeated here.

Metrics for Q9

Systems that they developed before. The training and education that they have. How well do they understand OO principles and how well they can apply the OO principles? This can be tested with little examinations of course. Or was it the first time the OOA/D method was used on a real project.

Metrics for Q10

Areas of specific functionality. The diagram type used to model the solution. Specific classes.

7.2.4   How to Measure

How do we collect the metrics to measure our Fusion development process? The best way would be with tools. Unfortunately, most CASE tools do not supply this kind of information about the method that they support. These are more like computer-aided modeling tools than computer-aided software engineering tools, but the abbreviation CAM was already in use!

Some metrics are easily collected by hand, but others require a tool. Normally, code metrics, like McCabe's complexity, are collected and presented with the help of a tool. However, most method metrics can be collected by the developers themselves or by review teams during design reviews and inspections.

The extra effort involved in collecting these metrics is minimal and gives you good insight into what is really happening and how to improve in the future. Especially today, when competition is strong, we need to produce high-quality software quickly. What would you think if, for example, an object library (e.g., foundation classes) contained a lot of buggy classes you had used to build your strategic product on?

In addition, the project manager needs to understand the meaning of the metrics and how to interpret the results. He or she is more or less responsible for the project and has to justify its status.

7.2.5 How to Present the Results

The best way to present the results of your metrics depends on your audience. For software developers you can keep your presentation technical, but for management you should translate the results to time and money.

This is very useful if managers pressure you to start coding, because they think you spend too much time thinking (i.e., finding an optimal structure for the application). We all know that when management wants a demonstration, we drop our diagrams directly and start to code. Then, after we have shown the prototype, we have to spend ages updating our design and rewriting the code. Pressed to move on, this rework of the prototype is not always done.

Grady and Caswell (1987, pp. 59–81) describe how to sell and present software metrics to your group or company. For example, they suggest that you describe the following: what software process metrics are; how they can help top management, project management, and software engineers, respectively; what software defects rates are and where in the development life cycle most problems are introduced; and definitions of the software metrics you will collect.

Translating the values of the measured metrics to money is not always easy. Sometimes you need to combine metrics to get an answer. This is why the GQM session is so important. You want to find the right answers to the right questions.

Example: Saving Time and Money

During one review we discovered that polymorphism was not used in the right way. The concept was understood, but the use of it was not. 112 lines of code were finally replaced by one line. This fact lowers the complexity and the maintenance effort. Both save money: first, because it lowers the number of defects that will show up; second, because it lowers the effort and time to find out what is happening in the code, it decreases the effort for performing regression testing, and one line generates fewer defects than 112 lines in its class.

To quantify this in monetary terms, you will need to find out what the complexity of the 112 lines was, how many defects this can generate, how much time you will need to maintain 112 versus 1 line of code and how much time it takes to test 112 versus 1 line. The time you will need to find and remove defects and retest the code is called *project spoilage* and will be discussed in Section 7.3.

The object interaction graph (OIG) was instrumental in suggesting the polymorphism problem after the OIG was recovered from the code. A review of the code confirmed the suggestion.

The code was developed using a method other than Fusion, with a less well-defined design phase. That is why we had to recover the object interaction graph and the visibility graphs from code and then review them. During the construction of the object interaction graph, it turned out that a great deal of code was "reused," or rather, copied in more than one place. This code also contained a large number of if-then-else and switch-case statements. Failure to understand polymorphism in the right way resulted in this case in a lot of code with a non-object-oriented structure.

As a result, we learned to look for these cases during the design of object interaction graphs including their method descriptions. We don't want to waste time and money on programming 112 lines of code (with all its testing) and then throw them away.

7.2.6   How to Manage a Metrics Program

Before you can manage this process, you first have to introduce it. Grady and Caswell (1987, pp. 16–18) describe ten steps to successful introduction of a metrics program. These steps can be applied on traditional as well as OO metrics programs.

How you will manage a Fusion project depends on the metrics that you have defined, the way that you collect them, and how the results are presented and interpreted.

Make sure that you don't want to "manage too much" (i.e., want too many metrics at once). Start with a simple and clearly defined set of metrics coming from your GQM model. If metrics don't support any goal, they should not be measured.

As a project manager, you will want to have base-line or reference values for your metrics. One way to get these is to recover metrics data from OO projects that are already finished. Don't worry if you do not have good design models and documentation for these projects. The Fusion method is ideal for recovering design diagrams from code. Giving the complete approach is beyond the scope of this chapter, but this short list will help you to get started:

- Make sure that the code is as structured as possible and is well commented.
- Add headers to each class and to large methods (functions) to describe what each does.
- Group the methods in groups of comparable functionality. For example, group accessor methods together.
- From this improved code, recover inheritance graphs, visibility graphs, and object interaction graphs.
- Review the consistency between the graphs.
- Complete the design documentation (why we did what).

Note that a complete recovery can be too big an investment for large projects. It is about the same as designing and implementing classes for reuse versus for one project. There is always a schedule conflict. Sometimes you just need to find a norm value for the metrics that you have defined. The quickest way is to get them from previous projects. Most of the time we have a lot of metrics data around us, but we just do not take the time to find and collect them. It is like doing projects; we always have the time and budget to do it a second time, but never to do it right the first time.

7.2.7 Metrics Example

In this section, we present some results of measuring methods to compare the outcome. The exercise was performed around the middle of 1994 to justify the use of Fusion over OMT. The size of the project was about 8 person years (compared to about 12 person years if conventional techniques and environments had been used).

Over two years the same NEXTSTEP/OpenStep application was developed, once using OMT and then using Fusion. Although the project teams were not completely disjoint, the first development had little or no influence on the second because of the time interval and because no software or documentation from the first project was used by the second team.

Fusion front loaded the development process, because it requires more models to be developed. However, using Fusion reduced the total development time by 20%.

The metrics are impressive too. By using Fusion we had

- 12% lower complexity in code
- 19% fewer functions needed to implement the same functionality
- 30% less code (for the coding phase 54% less time was needed)
- 40% fewer classes

In the first project, classes and class structures were added whenever the programmer chose to add them. There was no detailed design that could be used to guide the programmer and prevent "hacking."

The final result was that the new Fusion-based system needed less development time—saving money. It is easier to maintain—saving money and irritation. It has a better OO structure—saving money and time in creating changes or extensions and making it easier for the customer to use. We have seen the same trend exhibited in larger projects.

Figure 7.3 shows the percentage of overall development effort spent on each phase for NEXTSTEP/OpenStep projects using Fusion.

In another example, development of an application using NEXTSTEP/OpenStep required 60% less code than if C and OSF/Motif had been used to build the application. This was because many library classes were reused. In the OO approach, design is an important phase, whereas coding consumes much attention in the traditional approach. Coding becomes less time consuming if you make extensive use of class libraries and object kits. Also, the OO programming language used is important. Measurements showed, for example, that C++ code has a higher complexity than Objective-C, and more lines were needed to code the same functionality.

Again, this shows the importance of a good and complete method and the use of metrics to quantify it—to lower the number of defects, good and complete support of design through well-defined diagrams is indispensable.

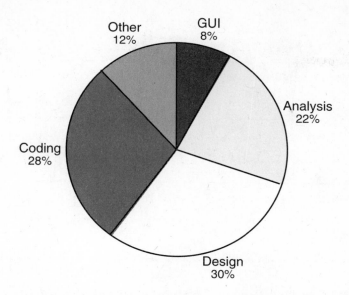

Figure 7.3 Distribution of Effort in NEXTSTEP/OpenStep Projects Using Fusion *(these numbers are average values; GUI means the construction of the graphical user interface inclusive of testing; other includes trying out ideas and other non-Fusion-related activities)*

7.2.8   Method Jump Diagram

The *method jump diagram* provides a way to measure developers' use of a method and is especially useful after the introduction of a new method (often associated with the move to object orientation). We want to know how beginners and experts really use the method. There is a difference in how people use a method to develop different types of applications. Their way of working often differs from the textbook description of the method. We would like to know why and what we can learn from the differences.

Figure 7.4 shows an example of a method jump diagram. The diagram demonstrates how a Fusion beginner used the method to develop a graphical planning application with NEXTSTEP/OpenStep. For the sake of simplicity, a summary is given. A point is recorded in the diagram when the developer makes a change, deleting or adding information. Reading is not recorded; otherwise we would end up doing nothing. Developers who recorded their "jumps" did not view doing so as a very labor intensive task.

The main information you will get from the jump diagrams is as follows:

- How a developer is using the method
- Which models are tightly coupled (indicated by many jumps between them)
- Why the jumps were made. Did they not understand the method, or is the method not complete?

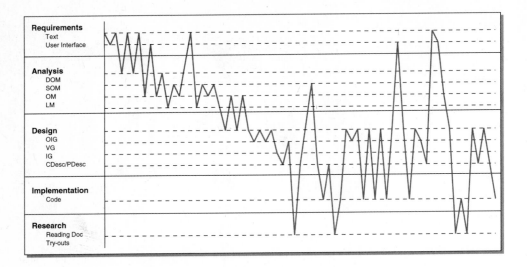

Figure 7.4 Method Jump Diagram *(DOM: domain object model; SOM: System object model; OIG: object interaction graph; VG: visibility graph; IG: inheritance graph)*

- What process was followed. Did the developer try to follow the traditional functional process with an OO method (e.g., can you see a "waterfall")?

The method jump diagram can give some good information about the use of CASE tools during software development. For example, in what sequence are the different modeling tools used? How often is a certain model changed? Can working patterns be recognized?

During the writing of this paper one CASE tool vendor showed an interest in adding this facility to its tool. It would be a good addition to help us understand how we use methods on real projects.

7.3 DEFECT TRACKING

Defects are very expensive, giving rise to much rework and extra testing. If you are building foundation class libraries for your strategic products, you aim for the highest quality. Investing in extra quality is often less expensive than building bad products.

7.3.1 What Is Defect Tracking?

Defect tracking is a technique for describing defects, tracing defects to find their origin ("place of birth"), and maintaining information about their status. This information can be used to understand and improve our OO application development process. Defect tracking tells us a lot about how we do our work. Why? Because a defect is the difference between something promised and what was actually delivered, whether in the specification, analysis, design, or implementation of a product.

7.3.2 Why Use Defect Tracking?

Defect tracking involves good software engineering skills, a clearly defined development process, good project management skills, effective OO methods, and the like. However, even what appear to be costs can be turned into benefits, so you not only invest but you can also gain from it.

Benefits
The benefits of defect tracking include

- Better understanding of your application development process, making it easier to improve
- Better overview of where things can go wrong—prevention, not fire fighting!
- better understanding of how effective certain techniques within the OO methods are
- Evaluation of the method used
- Evaluation of testing strategies
- Evaluation of how effective the method education was
- Good communication model to agree on defect removal strategies for making better products

Costs
Some costs are involved. You have to

- Use easy-to-use tools for defect registration and analysis
- Do design inspections and reviews (maximum of 2 hours per session)
- Assess your way of working
- Use a good and complete method (investment, learning curve)

A useful metric for summarizing the impact of defects on a project is *project spoilage*, which is defined as the amount of time or money wasted during your project on finding, fixing, and testing defects. It is used to convince management that they can spend their money better by investing in prevention (good method and metrics), rather than just throwing it away. A project spoilage of 20% to 25% is common on projects where defect tracking is not used.

The project spoilage equation is

$$Project spoilage = \frac{C_d}{C_t} \times 100$$

Where C_d is the cost of finding, fixing, and testing defects,
        C_t is the total project cost, and
        Project spoilage is the spoilage expressed as a percent of total costs.

The principal benefit of defect tracking is that it helps monitor and contain the effects of project spoilage.

7.3.3 How to Use Defect Tracking

We gained most when we used defect tracking in combination with a clear process and a complete method. The Fusion diagrams describe defined parts of the analysis and design, making the categorization of defects and the use of metrics easier. This is why the Fusion method works well with defect tracking.

Defect identification
Defect tracking begins with the identification of a defect. Many defects are found during reviews and inspections. Design reviews are particularly important; they will help you to find 50% to 70% of the defects. The WCGW lists introduced in Section 7.2 can be used as checklists to help identify defects during reviews.

Defect registration
Once a defect has been identified, it must be registered. Defect registration is simple. Table 7.5 shows an example defect registration template indicating the information that you will need to provide. For registration, specialized tools can be used, although text processors with templates and object-linking facilities are also useful.

Defect analysis
This is the part where all the fun begins. After registering a defect you will need to categorize it and, more importantly, correct it! Even if it is tempting to correct the error right away, it is helpful first to categorize the defect and find out what its real cause is.

This is like the difference between Western and Chinese medicine. When you have a headache, Western doctors give you an aspirin to remove the symptom, whereas Chinese doctors start to examine your back and neck and will attempt to remove the cause of the problem.

With the help of brainstorming sessions and inspections, we try to determine the origin, type, and mode of a defect. These group sessions are short and help us to understand the process and the way we work. Furthermore, they help us to understand the use of methods and tools on the project.

Table 7.5 Defect Registration Template

Number:	Unique number (e.g., 95032)
Defect name:	Name of the defect
Fix priority:	High, medium, low, no fix
Defective item:	Model, code, document, other
Item name:	Name of defective item (e.g., a class)
Version number:	Version number of the class
Date submitted:	mm/dd/yy
Submitted by:	Name of person who entered the defect
Severity:	Low, medium, high, critical
Found by using:	Regular use, during try-out, review, walkthrough, reported by external source, other
References:	Number of a reference document, etc.
Symptoms:	Short but complete description

We have found it useful to develop a *defect categorization model* to help in defect analysis. Table 7.6 shows an example of a defect categorization model for NEXTSTEP/OpenStep development using Fusion.

The Origin column names the process steps and other activities in which a defect could originate. For example, we receive requirements or function specifications, we start with analysis, design, and code, we write documentation, use a specific development environment and tools, communicate with other departments and groups, etc.

The Type column describes the type of defect. For example, a defect would be classified under "functional description" if the design does not effectively convey what the intended class should do. Generally, this is a defect found during design reviews or during coding.

Finally the Mode column describes the reason why the defect occurred. The modes used in Table 7.6 are defined as follows:

- Changed—a change in a work product caused a defect in another
- Missing—information was left out of a work product
- Unclear—information was misleading, ambiguous, or hard to understand
- Wrong—the work product was not correct

Take the following steps to develop your own defect categorization model:

1. Describe the phases of your software development cycle/process. Include
   - Name of the phase
   - What to do in this phase
2. Describe the techniques that you use for creating the work products in the phases described in step 1.

Table 7.6 Defect Categorization Model Example

Origin	Type	Mode
Requirements	Functionality User interface Hardware interface	Changed Missing Unclear Wrong
Analysis	Functional description User interface Domain object model System object model Operation model Life-cycle model Time-line diagram Scenario	Changed Missing Unclear Wrong
Design	Object interaction graph Visibility graph Inheritance graph Class descriptions Protocol descriptions Logic description Error checking Standards	Changed Missing Unclear Wrong
Implementation	Logic Computation Data handling Object interface Protocol Standards Dynamic binding Dynamic loading Reuse DO/PDO communication Version management	Changed Missing Unclear Wrong
Development environment	Analysis and design tools Build tools CASE tools Configuration management Tools Testing tools Metrics workbenches	Changed Missing Unclear Wrong

3. Develop a WCGW list per phase, per technique, and for every work product that can go wrong. Don't make it too detailed!

4. Define the initial defect categorization model. For defect origin, use the phases; for the defect type, use the list under "What to Model" and "Work Product"; and for defect mode start with the given five modes and extend them with modes you identified from "What Can Go Wrong."

Tables 7.7 and 7.8 show an example of a defect analysis form with an associated test template. This template is used in conjunction with the defect categorization model shown in Table 7.6.

Table 7.7 Defect Analysis Form

Date fixed:	mm/dd/yy
Fixed by:	Name of person who fixed the defect
Hours to find:	hh:mm (cost calculations)
Hours to fix:	hh:mm (cost calculations)
Associated test:	Number of the test (description)
Defect origin:	See defect categorization model
Defect type:	See defect categorization model
Defect mode:	See defect categorization model
Description of fix:	Short but complete description

Table 7.8 Test Template

Test identification	Unique number to identify the test
Name:	Name of test
Date added:	mm/dd/yy
Added by:	Name of person who added the test
Date tested:	mm/dd/yy
Tested by:	Name of person who performed the test
Hours to test:	hh:mm (cost calculations)
Purpose of test:	Motivation
Test method:	Incremental, inspection, regression, review, test case, walk-through, other
Test type:	Acceptance, application, configuration, conversion, documentation, functions, installation, interface, integration, method, module, object, performance, portability, procedures, recovery, security, storage, stress, system, usability
Test description:	Description of test; steps, what to test and why, test cases, etc.

Example: Defect Registration and Analysis

During a test of the database we found that the system did not behave according to the specified requirement and its test. The defect was registered as shown in Table 7.9:

Table 7.9 Example of a Registered Defect

Number:	PS95021
Defect name:	Customer fetch detail
Fix priority:	High
Defective item:	Code
Item name:	class CustomerTableController
Version number:	0.8
Date submitted:	24 February 1995
Submitted by:	Simon Roberts
Severity:	High
Found by using:	During try-out
References:	CustomerTableController.[hm] (code)
Symptoms:	When selecting the Fetch Customer button after fetching all customers and selecting one, the wrong customer detail data are displayed in the customer product table.
Date fixed:	01 March 1995
Fixed by:	Yorlady Chica Lopez
Hours to find:	0.5
Hours to fix:	1.5
Associated test:	PS95021A
Defect origin:	Implementation
Defect type:	Object reference
Defect mode:	Changed
Description of fix:	The outlet to the customer detail table was not connected. The outlet variable name was changed, but CustomerTableController.h was not parsed again. (*Normally more detail of the fix is provided.*)

7.3.4 How to Manage Defect Tracking

The management of defect tracking is described in several books (for example, Grady 1992, and Humphrey 1989). It is part of a quality program and therefore has to fit into the quality program that you already have in place. It also requires commitment, otherwise it will not work.

When using defect tracking, you will need metrics. Method and software metrics give clues about where to look for a defect. For example, there is a correlation between complexity and the number of defects. If we cannot identify the complex parts of our design or code, then it is difficult to manage efficient defect recovery and removal. We need to know as quickly as possible why a defect occurred and what caused it to occur.

You also need to measure the effectiveness of the defect tracking and removal process. The old adage "you can't control what you can't measure" also applies to this process. By using defect tracking tools, you can perform all kinds of analyses to assist you in managing the development process. For example, questions that might be relevant to a management decision include "How much time did we spend so far in finding, fixing, and testing design defects?" or "Give me a list of all defects which have mode: Wrong."

7.4 CONCLUSION

Like most other things in life, once started, metrics and defect tracking programs do not turn out to be that difficult. It is *not* necessary to be a "level 3 certified" (SEI) company.

Much can be learned from combining Fusion with metrics collection and defect tracking. We learned the following:

- You should use a method that covers the complete development life cycle.
- You should use a method that has rules for consistency.
- You should use an easy-to-use and complete tool. The tool should not add "funny" diagrams to the method to create a "competitive difference" with other tool vendors.
- You need to collect metrics to understand what you are really doing.
- Defect tracking practices make the development process more visible.
- You can prove the advantages of object orientation.
- There is a schedule conflict between making classes for reuse and making classes for a single product. Make sure that you clear this issue before starting the project.
- Defect tracking can be used to measure the quality of reused classes.
- Don't make it too difficult; start simple.
- This cannot be done in a month. The "old" method and programming languages also took years before everybody understood them (although this is often forgotten).
- After the first few, OO projects need fewer resources and less time to complete. This will likely not be true of your first OO project, although NEXT-STEP/OpenStep projects are very quickly profitable.
- Using a method, a tool, and metrics to support OO application development is great FUN!

REFERENCES

Grady, R. 1992. *Practical Software Metrics for Project Management and Process Improvement*. Englewoods Cliffs, NJ: Prentice Hall.

Grady, R. and D. Caswell. 1987. *Software Metrics: Establishing a Company-Wide Program*. Englewoods Cliffs, NJ: Prentice Hall.

Humphrey, W. 1989. *Managing the Software Process*. Reading, MA: Addison-Wesley.

Extensions to Fusion

*I*n keeping with the desired goal of allowing Fusion to be an open method that the objects community can adopt, adapt, and evolve, Part 4 provides a forum for constructive evaluation of Fusion and proposals for its extension and improvement.

Andrew Blyth's paper, "Requirements Engineering within the Fusion Method," deals with the early phase of the life cycle in which user requirements are elicited and captured. The Fusion method assumes that this phase has already been completed and that a requirements document exists. However, in practice, gathering requirements is often a challenging task for a software development team. Andrew Blyth's contribution shows how the Fusion method can be extended forward in the software development life cycle to support the elicitation, representation, and validation of users' requirements. The suggested extensions are illustrated through a case study.

Howard Ricketts has collected feedback on Fusion from users of the Fusion-CASE tool, as well as from his own experience working as a consultant. In his paper "Proposed Enhancements to the Fusion Method," he discusses three areas of potential improvement to Fusion based on this feedback. Ricketts develops the idea of using object models at design time to support the process of design refinement. He then proposes notational enhancements to the Fusion object interaction graphs to be used in the design of concurrent systems. In the final section of the paper, Ricketts proposes ways that roles can be added to Fusion.

An approach to extending Fusion to address the development of distributed systems is described in Kris Oosting's "Extensions to Fusion Supporting NEXT-STEP/OpenStep (Portable) Distributed Objects." Oosting introduces enhancements to all the design models to capture information about protocols and shows how these changes relate to developing distributed object systems in NEXT-STEP/OpenStep.

Gabriel Eckert's paper "Improving the Analysis Stage of the Fusion Method" is a detailed and thorough survey of problems encountered by computer science students learning Fusion in a university course. Eckert concentrates on the analysis models of the Fusion method, that is, the object model and the interface model. He describes the problems, investigates their causes, and proposes some improvements. Many of the same difficulties can be expected to arise when practitioners first use Fusion on a real software development project. The targeted readership of Eckert's paper includes developers applying the Fusion method during the analysis stage, teachers of Fusion, and researchers interested in object-oriented analysis.

Over several years of consulting and training, Desmond D'Souza and Alan Wills have developed and applied a method for OO development called *Catalysis*, which they describe in "Extending Fusion—Practical Rigor and Refinement." Catalysis proposes some extensions to Fusion, defining systematic refinements from abstract specification to implementation, handling very coarse-grained to fine-grained components, recursively decomposing a component by stages into patterns of collaborating objects, refining the transactions between the collaborating objects, and describing how design objects map to the roles in the specification.

The changes to Fusion described in these papers are proposals derived from the practice of different people in different contexts. The proposals are not necessarily consistent with each other, and some of the authors describe similar ideas but implement them differently. These papers are representative of an ongoing discussion, based on experience applying the method, that will help shape the future evolution of Fusion and of OOA/D more generally.

Requirements Engineering within the Fusion Method

Andrew Blyth

Department of Computing Science
University of Newcastle Upon Tyne

8.1 INTRODUCTION

It has become widely accepted that requirements engineering is vital to the success of any software development project (Davis 1990). The problem is that requirements are prone to misunderstanding and misinterpretation (Gause and Weinberg 1989). The purpose of requirements engineering is to elicit and capture what is required, both at the product and the process level. Based on a clear understanding—shared by the problem owners and the problem solvers—a precise set of interpretations can be derived so that a system that serves its intended purpose can be delivered.

Such a precise understanding of the problem can only be developed through the continual involvement of every relevant party (stakeholder) in the construction and analysis of the requirements specification. Without this involvement, the system is likely to fail (Wiener 1993). All stakeholders, including but not just limited to users, should be involved to some extent throughout the process. By this means, the requisite input for defining the requirements is obtained. Moreover, this inclusion empowers people to make the information technology system work and thus encourages them to embrace the change (Winograd and Flores 1987).

Although Fusion does not address the initial stages of requirements capture, it does provide high-level analysis models (object model and system object model, scenarios, and operation schema) that can play an important part in capturing and refining requirements. Experience using Fusion to capture the requirements of a hospital information system led to several innovations in the Fusion process and to notation that substantially increased Fusion's support for requirements engineering. This paper will (1) present the problem to which the Fusion method was applied and the results that the Fusion method generated, and (2) present a requirements engineering process model that has been derived from this and other case studies.

8.2 HOSPITAL INFORMATION SYSTEM CASE STUDY

8.2.1 Introduction

This case study covers the process used to elicit, represent, verify, and explore the information system requirements for the Jervis Street[*] Accident and Emergency (A&E) department. These requirements are directly related to the applicability and appropriateness of the information system that was proposed.

The case study illustrates how problem owners and problem solvers can begin to investigate and understand both the problem and the solution domains simultaneously through the development of models. These models provide snapshots of the social and organizational system before and after the introduction of the information technology (IT) system. Thus the information system's impact on the organization and the people within it can be assessed. Also, by adopting a dialectic approach, the users and other stakeholders of the system can have a direct impact on the specification and development of the system. This approach makes change a positive force that people embrace, rather than a negative one that they attempt to subvert.

8.2.2 Accident and Emergency Department

The functions performed by the Jervis Street Accident and Emergency (A&E) department are basically twofold. Its primary function, as its name implies, is to provide accident and medical emergency services whenever and to whomever is in need of them. This function has evolved into a second function, which actually consists of the largest proportion of work performed by the department. This function is the provision of low-grade medical services to the local population, where patients use the A&E department as an alternative to general practice. Two factors have contributed to this configuration of work within the department. The first is that the hospital does not charge for its services, unlike private practitioners. Second, the A&E department at Jervis Street has traditionally

---

[*] Jervis Street is an inner city Dublin hospital. A particular aspect of the problem domain is presented in this paper. However, it is worth bearing in mind that it is part of a bigger problem, which in turn fits into, and is influenced by, the social, economic, and political environment of the country.

had an open-door policy toward all patients.

The A&E department is functionally related to a number of other departments within the hospital upon which it relies for services (e.g., pathology, radiology, pharmacy, and the central administration). Internally, it consists of a small set of separate and distinct actors (e.g., senior nurse, consultant, junior doctor, junior nurse, and receptionist).

8.2.3   Scoping the Problem

Requirements engineering commonly begins with the requirements engineer scoping the problem by identifying as many of the stakeholders as possible. Consequently, constructing and validating a precise and accurate set of user requirements begins with stakeholder analysis. Stakeholders are defined as all those claimants inside and outside an organization who have a vested interest in decisions faced by the organization in adopting and utilizing information technology (Mason and Mitroff 1981).

The purpose of the stakeholder analysis is to

- Identify the people, organizations, societies and groups that have a stake in the system
- Identify a set of system boundaries

Systems have failed in the past because the developers did not identify and analyze the views of all of the stakeholders (Wiener 1993). Through the identification and analysis of stakeholders we can build up a clear picture of what exactly is required of the system. We can examine and model each individual stakeholder's perception of the system and of the other stakeholders within it.

Through stakeholder analysis we can begin to construct a set of system boundaries that will be identified and represented by constructing and prioritizing a set of system models and scenarios, where each system model and scenario belongs to a stakeholder. Drawing the boundaries within which the system will operate is a task of immense difficulty and complexity. To draw a line between two objects you are required to say what the difference is between these two objects. Thus by drawing system boundaries a problem solver is partially defining the environment within which the system is required to function.

The system boundaries are established through a user-driven dialectic process in which we identify objects that have a direct relationship to the information system object and objects contained within it. These objects are placed within the system boundary and all other objects are placed outside the boundary.

Stakeholder analysis and the drawing of system boundaries permits us to begin to define a set of contractual relationships that bind the organization and to define what the organization requires of the information system.

When scoping the problem for the Accident and Emergency department, I began by identifying as many stakeholders as possible. Next, I constructed a set of views on the system, each of which identified a set of objects, a set of system boundaries, and a set of relationships between the objects. For each stakeholder,

I constructed and analyzed his or her view of the system using a form of rich pictures (Checkland 1986, Checkland and Scholes 1990).

Rich pictures are a diagramming notation in which people are represented as people, computers as computers, and bits of information as bits of paper. Every single object in the diagram is given a type and a unique name. My experience has shown that stakeholders find such diagrams much easier to understand and draw themselves than the Fusion object diagrams. Moreover, it is easy to derive an object diagram from these diagrams. In doing so, the requirements engineer is typically prompted to ask more questions to clarify aspects of the view being modeled.

The next steps of my analysis consisted of

- Identifying other stakeholders such as individuals, departments, and organizations that existed within the stakeholders' view of the system that I was analyzing
- Using a matrix (a simple spreadsheet) to check that I had asked about the relationships between every object in the diagram

Then I talked to all the new stakeholders that I had identified, constructing and verifying their view of the system. Next, I unified the models by simply merging them together and defining a set of system boundaries. Where I could not merge models, I talked to the stakeholders involved and resolved the conflict.

As a result of this analysis, I identified the following stakeholders: the pathology department, the radiology department, the pharmacy, the central administration (in particular the central administration hospital manager), all the other wards within the hospital, the matron, the staff sister, the senior nurse, the consultant, the senior house officers (SHOs), the junior doctors, the junior nurses, the receptionists, and finally the patients and the patients' next of kin.

The overall workings of the department are complex. Therefore, I will limit my description to two stakeholder views: the view of a citizen using the services of the Accident and Emergency department and the view of a nurse. In constructing and unifying both the citizen's and nurse's views of the system, I will use the Fusion object model as a modeling language. A set of system boundaries will be established for each view, and then both views will be unified to derive a set of requirements. The purpose of modeling at such a high level is to build up a picture of where an information system will be required and what functions it will need to support.

The Fusion method provides a very rich and expressive modeling language that is used to describe and analyze objects, classes, and their relationships within the system. In addition, it provides the means to describe and examine invariants, cardinality constraints, roles, relationship attributes, aggregation, and generalization/specialization.

8.2.4   Citizen's View of the Accident and Emergency Department

Figure 8.1 represents the rich picture from the patient's perspective. Faces above the text show that these objects correspond to people, groups of people, organizational departments, or organizations. Because stakeholders find it easy to identify themselves and their relationships when they are depicted in this way, rich pictures provide a useful framework for building up a shared, validated model of what is going on.

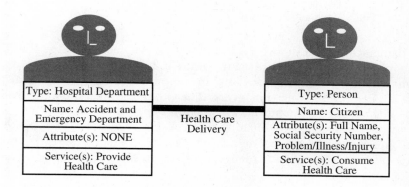

Figure 8.1 A Patient's Rich Picture

In constructing these diagrams, we start by asking two questions

- What type of object is this?
- What is the name of this object?

Once these questions have been answered we ask

- What is this object responsible for and to whom?
- What are their contractual relationships?

We then ask

- Given these responsibilities, what does the object need to know and what does it need to do?

With the stakeholder's answers to all of these questions for each object, we are able to construct a rich picture for that stakeholder. The various stakeholders' views are then unified. In doing so, it is important to ensure that all the responsibilities, attributes, and services for every object in the diagrams are also unified.

Object models are derived from the rich pictures. Figure 8.2 shows the object model of the citizen's perspective. The patient is consuming a service that has already been paid for. The role of the Accident and Emergency department is to provide health care and the role of the citizen is to consume that health care.

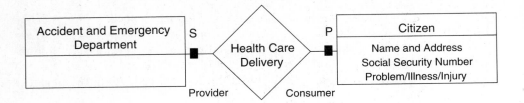

Figure 8.2 The Citizen's Perspective

In translating from Figure 8.1 to Figure 8.2, we need to define the cardinality of the relationship. As annotated in Figure 8.2, we assume that there are only **S** accident and emergency departments in the country and that the total population is **P**. Figure 8.2 tells us that every **Citizen** has the **Health Care Delivery** relationship with every **Accident and Emergency Department**. It also tells us that citizens are not concerned with the various people or systems that make up the Accident and Emergency department; they merely perceive persons within the Accident and Emergency department as deliverers of health care.

8.2.5 Nurse's View of the Accident and Emergency Department

From the nurse's perspective, two very different relationships exist between nurse and patient, and doctor and patient. The nurse perceives the relationship between herself and the patient to be that of health care deliverer–health care consumer and the relationship between the doctor and the patient as that of diagnostician–patient.

Since the rich picture version of the nurses' view is quite large, only the object diagram is shown here, in Figure 8.3. The consumer–provider relationship is used to express the idea of one object consuming a prespecified service, which is supplied by the provider of the service. It is assumed that **P** denotes the total population, that **M** denotes the number of nurses in the Accident and Emergency department and that **Q** denotes the number of doctors in the Accident and Emergency department.

Figure 8.3 tells us that every doctor in the Accident and Emergency department is in the diagnostician–patient relationship with every citizen and that every nurse in the Accident and Emergency department is in the health care provider–consumer relationship with every citizen. The diagram also tells us that the relationship between every nurse and doctor in the Accident and Emergency department is that of colleague. In addition, it tells us that the Accident and Emergency department has a consumer–provider relationship with certain other departments.

In Figure 8.3 we observe that certain objects contain attributes. The patient object is defined to have three attributes. The first attribute is the patient's name and address. The second attribute is the patient's social security number, which is used to identify the citizen uniquely within the national arena

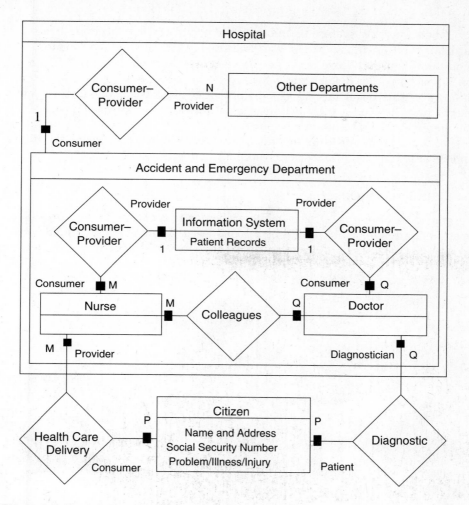

Figure 8.3 Nurse's Perspective

of health care provision. The final attribute is the patient illness or injury. This attribute defines what is wrong with the citizen and why she or he has come to the Accident and Emergency department. The information system object has the attribute of patient record, and through this patient record it provides a set of services to both the doctor and the nurses. This leads us to ask the following questions:

- What are these services?
- What are the differences in the services that the information system provides to both the doctors and the nurses?
- Is there a relationship between the citizen and the information system and, if so, then what is it?

• What interfaces does the information system support?

When we draw system boundaries, we are really identifying all the objects that have relationships with, or are contained in, the information system object. When doing so for Figure 8.3, we can make two interesting observations. The first is that the other departments seem to lie outside the scope of the system. On the basis of this observation, we recommended that the other departments be brought into the scope of the system to ease the flow of information between hospital departments. The second is that the citizen (or patient) also lies outside the scope of the system and thus has no direct access to or control over the information contained in the information system.

8.2.6   Scenario Modeling

In scenario modeling a set of possible scenarios is constructed and presented to the stakeholders for validation. For the purposes of this paper I will only present and analyze one possible scenario—that of delivery of health care to a citizen (Figure 8.4).

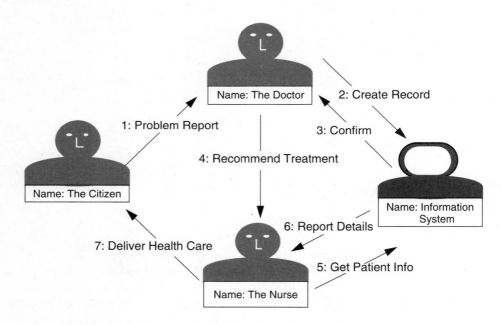

Figure 8.4 Rich Picture of a Scenario

The purpose of scenario modeling is to build up a picture of how the various components within the system are going to interact and what information is going to flow across that interaction. The result of this modeling should be a clear picture of what communication and interaction the information system is required to support. In Figure 8.4 we can see the sequence of interactions. In this diagram each arc is uniquely numbered to show the sequence of interaction. Each arc represents a message sent between objects, and the naming of the arc represents the type of message sent.

In scenario diagrams such as Figure 8.4, we can clearly identify the various stakeholders taking part in the interaction. One question that should be asked of each of these stakeholders is "Does this scenario represent your view of the system?" As a result of this validation, it is possible that additional stakeholders will be identified. If so, they should be consulted too.

When we analyzed Figure 8.4 with the stakeholders, two further questions were useful:

- What information objects flow between communicating objects?
- Are these information objects represented on the object model of the system and, if not, why not?

This type of continual validation with the stakeholders and the use of other diagrams proved very useful in building up a consistent picture of what was going on in the system and thus what was required.

Figure 8.5 shows the same scenario translated into a Fusion scenario diagram.

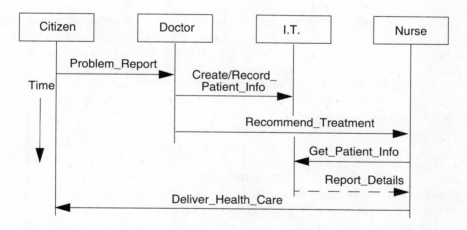

Figure 8.5 Fusion Scenario Diagram for the Scenario Represented in Figure 8.4

In the scenario models depicted in Figures 8.4 and 8.5, the citizen enters the Accident and Emergency department with a problem. The citizen reports the problem to a doctor, who records the patient's details on the information system. While the doctor is recording the information, she is also making a diagnosis of the problem, which forms part of the patient's record. Once the doctor has finished she informs the nurse of the diagnosis and the treatment required. Under Irish law the person who administers a treatment is responsible for its effects.

For this reason the nurse checks the diagnosis to see if she agrees with the doctor. In this scenario she does, and delivers the health care that the patient requires.

8.2.7   Interface Model

Interface models allow us to construct and reason about a set of services that a system will be required to support. The basic idea behind this kind of modeling is that it describes the effects of operations in terms of changes to the state of the system. This assumes the availability of a system object model that describes the data structures maintained by the system. Consequently, we can use this modeling technique as a mechanism to specify and validate the data structures that the information system is required to support. The validation can be done through (1) the comparison and analysis of these models with object models of the system or (2) presentation to the stakeholders.

The outcome of this validation is a unified picture of and agreement upon the interfaces that the system is required to support. The interface models should be derived from and analyzed with the models of the system that already exist so that we can identify when, where, and how these services are being invoked.

From the scenario diagram shown in Figure 8.5 we can identify two services that the information system is required to support. The first is the creation and storage of a patient record, and the second is the retrieval and display of that information. For the purpose of this case study, we shall just model and analyze the service of creation and storage of a patient record through an interface model. Figure 8.6 depicts the service interface model for the **Create/ Record_Patient_Info** service. The model allows us to describe explicitly what the service is, as well as to examine what it reads, changes, sends, and assumes. We can also define and analyze what the results of the service invocation are.

We can observe from Figure 8.6 that the service used to create and record a new patient record only reads information that is supplied by the patient or the doctor. The service changes the patient record by adding the record information to it. In addition, the service sends nothing and assumes that a patient record for the patient does not already exist. Finally, the result of this service invocation is a new patient record containing the relevant information. When we analyze the service interface model (Figure 8.6) and the scenario model (Figure 8.5) together with the object model (Figure 8.4) we observe that the nurses do not have write access to the patient record; they only have read access.

8.2.8   Summary

In this case study, the following activities were undertaken:

- Stakeholder analysis, which involved identifying the stakeholders and creating a matrix to cross-check that all relationships had been captured.
- Modeling, which involved representing individual's views of the system

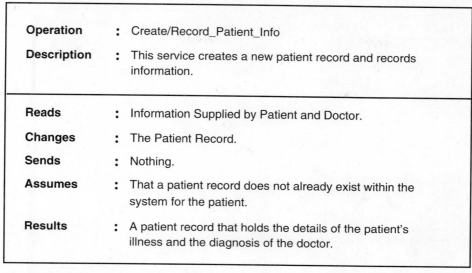

Operation	:	Create/Record_Patient_Info
Description	:	This service creates a new patient record and records information.

Reads	:	Information Supplied by Patient and Doctor.
Changes	:	The Patient Record.
Sends	:	Nothing.
Assumes	:	That a patient record does not already exist within the system for the patient.
Results	:	A patient record that holds the details of the patient's illness and the diagnosis of the doctor.

Figure 8.6 A Service Interface Specification

through a type of rich pictures. These models were integrated into Fusion to provide a system view.

- Scenario modeling, which was also first done with rich pictures and then formalized, and analyzed, in Fusion scenario diagrams for each stakeholder. The Fusion scenario diagrams were then unified and validated.
- Construction and analysis of the interface model (operation schema).

When constructing and analyzing these models, we constantly unified them, checking for any errors, conflicts, or omissions against all the other data that had been collected. These sub-processes were effective in constructing and validating an agreed on requirements specification for the system.

8.3 REQUIREMENTS ENGINEERING PROCESS MODEL

Over the years various process models have been put forward in software engineering (Boehm 1976, 1986). From the Jervis Street case study along with others, I have developed a process model for requirements engineering by examining and classifying what requirements engineers really do. Figure 8.7 outlines a process model for developing a validated set of precise requirements. The process consists of four subprocesses: scoping, system models, user requirements' specification, and scenario structuring.

These four subprocesses are linked together in such a way that from any subprocess it is possible to get to any other subprocess. Consequently, a requirements engineer using this process model may choose to do some systems model-

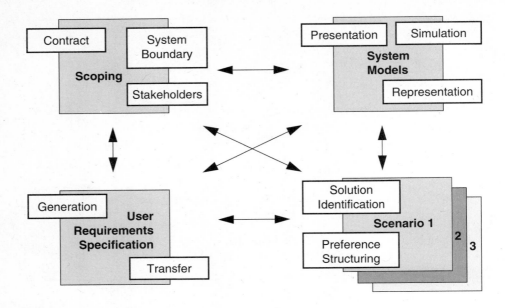

Figure 8.7 Requirements Engineering Process

ing, followed by some scoping, and then finish with some user requirements generation. The process model itself does not impose any order on the execution sequence of the subprocesses; rather, this is left to the requirements engineer.

Based on our experience we have found that all of the subprocesses are vital to the success of the requirements engineering process. The generic process model imposes no sequence on the activities and is inherently iterative. However, our observations indicate that the best place to start is with stakeholder analysis. Once an initial set of stakeholders is identified, scenarios and other models can be developed.

Since certain notations are better for expressing and capturing certain concepts than others, the process model does not prescribe the use of specific methods or notations. However, the Fusion models, supplemented with rich pictures and textual documentation, proved very effective in defining the requirements for the A&E department information system. While the choice is left to the requirements engineer or team, the experience documented in the case study suggests models and notations that will be useful for other projects.

8.3.1 Scoping

The scoping subprocess deals with determining the scope of the requirements and the contractual agreement with the client, establishing boundaries for the contract, gaining an understanding of the purpose and structure of the organizational unit(s) that are to be involved, and identifying the principal stakeholders involved. Some stakeholder analysis is generally useful before moving to the other subprocesses.

Stakeholder analysis allows us to identify the people who will play key roles in the system's life cycle. Systems have been unsuccessful in the past because of a failure to identify and analyze the views of all the stakeholders (Wiener 1993). Through the identification and analysis of stakeholders, we can build up a clear picture of what exactly is required of the system. We can examine and model each stakeholder's perception of the system and the other stakeholders within it. In building up a set of stakeholder perceptions, we can

- Detect possible conflict within the system
- Build up with the stakeholders a shared understanding of what functions the system is required to support
- Identify other stakeholders

The ability to construct and analyze models of the system and models of scenarios is crucial to stakeholder analysis. This modeling and analysis can only be achieved through the use of a shared language and a shared understanding of that language. It is therefore vital that problem owners and problem solvers understand and accept the modeling language(s).

8.3.2   Modeling

The purpose of the modeling subprocess is to represent the current understanding of the system by producing a set of models. These models provide information about the environment in which the system is to function as well as a context for understanding later policy and design decisions. One particularly important use of the description is to act as a focus for discussion. Through the modeling language we can enunciate the problem, reaching consensus through a dialectic process in which the problem is presented and re-presented to both the problem solvers and the problem owners. These models can then be further analyzed and their implications explored through the use of simulation, prototyping or system mock-ups.

The modeling subprocess draws on and contributes to the other subprocesses. For example, it requires that you already have identified an initial set of stakeholders. It also assists in the scoping subprocess by providing models for the determination of further relevant stakeholders and of system boundaries.

This subprocess does not imply the use of any particular notation or set of notations. Consequently, when modeling the system, the requirements engineer is required to select the appropriate notation(s). When making this choice, the requirements engineer should take into consideration the stakeholders' familiarity with the notation. It is our experience that the stakeholders understanding and support of the selected notation(s) are vital to the success of requirements engineering.

8.3.3   User Requirements Specification

The purpose of the user requirements specification subprocess is to identify and specify those requirements that must be observed in any implementation. Scenario modeling has proved itself a very powerful tool for the identification and representation of requirements that must be observed in any implementation, and of requirements in general. Natural language statements of requirements are elicited from problem owners to reach agreement on what the system currently is and what it should be and to identify defects in the current system and how these might be overcome. Statements of requirements are then fed back to problem owners and agreed upon. Requirements are then classified in order to identify conflicts, particularly conflicts in definitions of boundary objects and systems aspects. This subprocess is also concerned with deriving requirements for the models, scenarios, and system boundaries that have already been identified. When conducting this process, it is vital to have an agreed on set of stakeholders and their associated system and scenario models.

8.3.4   Scenario Modeling

Requirements and some priority ordering are used to

- Generate possible design options for the system
- Capture and validate requirements by means of stakeholders' views of the system, with conflicts and trade-offs being resolved with the client

This is achieved through the construction and preference ordering of a set of possible scenarios. A scenario is a representation of one possible set of interactions surrounding the system (see Figure 8.5) or one possible set of system configurations. One of the purposes of stakeholder analysis is to answer the questions:

- How and by what criteria do stakeholders prioritize their options?
- Are different prioritizations needed for different stakeholders?

Scenario modeling also allows for analysis and discussion of the implications of various design options with relevant stakeholders in an iterative fashion. The acceptability of the preferred option can then be agreed to with the stakeholders, ensuring that the option meets the formal model of requirements.

The space in which solution options are discussed is a sociotechnical space, that is, it encompasses possible changes in the organization and new organizational constructs as well as changes in the technical system and new IT constructs. These must be considered together. For example, an organization that wishes to improve its repair service carried out at customer premises might wish to consider making the repair service an integral part of its operations, a separate organization (wholly owned or independent), or a set of independent agents with a common coordinating service to which they all subscribe (the taxi-driver model). Each of these options will place its own distinctive set of requirements on an IT system created to support the requesting, scheduling, use, and monitoring of the repair service.

8.4 CONCLUSIONS

In this paper I have (1) presented a case study and shown how the Fusion method can be extended into the area of requirements engineering and (2) derived and presented a process model through the application of which a set of requirements can be elicited, represented, and validated. This process model is applied to the Fusion method in the case study to show how, through the application of the modeling ideas present in the Fusion method to the process model, a requirements specification can be constructed.

In addition, I have strongly advocated the constant involvement of the stakeholders so as to continually validate the requirements. The use of a form of rich pictures and their mapping down into the various notations used by the Fusion method proved very successful. The stakeholders found the rich pictures much easier to understand than the notations used by Fusion. The problem solvers also found it easy to map the rich picture notation down into the various notations used by Fusion. The case study has illustrated how a clear understanding between the stakeholders and the problem solvers of what exactly is required at product level can be developed.

One very valuable lesson gained from this experience was the importance of using simple but expressive notations. Several of the stakeholders commented that they encountered some difficulty in using the various Fusion notations. With an easy-to-use notation and set of guidelines for building models, the stakeholders quickly began to draw and analyze models for themselves. Another very important lesson was the importance of the empowerment of stakeholders. It is vital that the stakeholders buy into the change and see it as a benefit. The success of this case study came from every stakeholder's involvement in the process of adopting and utilizing Information Technology and consequently contributing a lot of very useful information.

REFERENCES

Boehm, B. W. 1976. Software Engineering. *IEEE Transactions on Computers*, C-25(12), 1226–1241.

Boehm, B. W. 1986. A Spiral Model of Software Development and Enhancement. *ACM Software Engineering Notes*, 11(4), 22–42.

Checkland, P. 1986. *Systems Thinking, Systems Practice.* New York: Wiley.

Checkland, P. and J. Scholes. 1990. *Soft Systems Methodology in Action.* Chichester: Wiley.

Coleman, D., P. Arnold, S. Bodoff, C. Dollin, H. Gilchrist, F. Hayes, and P. Jeremaes. 1994. *Object-Oriented Development: The Fusion Method.* Englewood Cliffs, NJ: Prentice Hall.

Davis, A. M. 1990. *Software Requirements Analysis and Specification.* Englewood Cliffs, NJ: Prentice Hall.

Gause, D. C., and G. M. Weinberg 1989. *Exploring Requirements: Quality before Design.* New York: Dorset House.

IEEE. 1984. *IEEE Guide to Software Requirements Specifications: IEEE/ANSI Standard 830-1984.* New York: Institute of Electrical and Electronic Engineers.

Mason, R. O., and I. T. Mitroff. 1981. *Challenging Strategic Planning Assumptions.* New York: Wiley.

Wiener, L. R. 1993. *Digital Woes: Why We Should Not Depend on Software.* Reading, MA: Addison-Wesley.

Winograd, T., and F. Flores. 1987. *Understanding Computers and Cognition.* Reading, MA: Addison-Wesley.

Proposed Enhancements to the Fusion Method

Howard Ricketts

*Soft*CASE Consulting

9.1 INTRODUCTION

This paper covers a range of suggestions for the improvement of the Fusion software development method. Based on the experiences of *Soft*CASE Consulting and its customers, the suggestions address specific weaknesses that have been identified through the practical application of Fusion.

*Soft*CASE Consulting is a UK company specializing in the development of bespoke CASE tools. In 1993 we were invited to develop a tool supporting the Fusion method, which we set about doing in close collaboration with Derek Coleman's group at the Hewlett–Packard Laboratory in Bristol. The product, *Fusion*-CASE, was launched in April 1994, and over the ensuing months it has grown into a highly successful product. We believe this success is based on our experience developing effective CASE solutions by being particularly receptive to customers' needs.

Comments from customers fall broadly into two categories: (1) changes to or addition of tool features and (2) Fusion method enhancements. The former we have addressed with some vigor; the latter is largely outside our control, although we are not opposed to developing bespoke tools supporting customer-specific method enhancements.

In this paper we present our customers' major concerns together with reasoned responses. The responses take the form of proposed additions to Fusion techniques and modeling notations that fall into three categories:

- Expanded support for moving between different levels of abstraction
- A notation for the design of behavior involving multiple, concurrent control threads
- Support for the concept of roles in design

These enhancements have been applied successfully on two or three consultancy projects, but they still need considerably more road testing. However, they have at least been shown to work in practice and are therefore worth passing on to the Fusion user community. It is my hope that presenting the suggested enhancements will stimulate further discussion which can be fed into the evolution of the Fusion method. In its current form, Fusion is usable on a wide range of projects. By effectively addressing concurrency, levels of abstraction, and roles in design, Fusion will have a far wider appeal and practical scope.

9.2   LEVELS OF ABSTRACTION

The process of analysis and design is invariably iterative—models used to express the system at one level of abstraction are refined to produce more detailed models. The refinement process is driven by our limited ability to manage volumes of complex data. We start with a simplification of the problem and then focus attention on specific aspects of system functionality.

During the early phases of design, we deal primarily with functional requirements that emanate from the requirements specification. At this level, we have a high degree of freedom in our design approach. However, as we move closer to implementation, new constraints materialize from considerations of architecture, performance, reuse, etc. The design decisions we make to address these issues form part of the refinement process and need to be captured.

At present, Fusion provides only limited support for managing the refinement process. The aggregation relation in the Fusion object models can be used to show how objects are composed out of configurations of other objects. However, object models are used only during analysis, and Fusion does not support an analog to aggregation in the design models. Also, in practice, relationships as well as objects need to be decomposed, but Fusion provides no support for refining relationships.

To address these limitations, we use a modified version of the Fusion system object model to capture the refinements of both objects and relationships that occur during design. These models are called *design system object models* to emphasize the fact that they are used during design rather than analysis. The object interaction graphs also need to be modified to provide full support for design through the use of refinement strategies.

9.2.1   Design System Object Models

Consider the following simple requirements statement. A system is to be developed to support a network of client stations, each capable of coordinating a series of instrumentation readings on remote servers. The operator can either schedule a series of operations to take place at some time in the future using the client, or he can enter into an interactive dialogue through the client with equipment attached to the remote server.

At a very high level of abstraction, these requirements can be modeled as shown in Figure 9.1. While not particularly detailed, this abstraction is nonetheless extremely informative and expresses a set of simple system invariants (relationships with cardinalities) which will remain true irrespective of any further refinement, for instance, that clients may use many servers and servers can be used by many clients. Clearly this is a major architectural statement that cannot be ignored—it will have major implications for communication, access to shared resources, persistence, tolerance, etc., all of which will need to be accommodated at lower levels of abstraction.

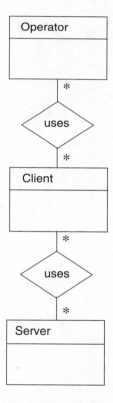

Figure 9.1 Abstract Model

As the high-level architecture is elaborated into a more detailed design, both the objects and the relationships will need to be refined. Object models are useful for capturing these refinements as they occur throughout the design process. At the next level of abstraction, one might choose to elaborate the meaning of the **uses** relationship between **operator** and **client**. From the requirements statement, we can see that this relationship can be refined into two other activities—**schedules** and **uses interactively**. These refinements, shown in Figure 9.2, demonstrate a powerful technique—the introduction of new, more detailed structural elements in support of refined relationships.

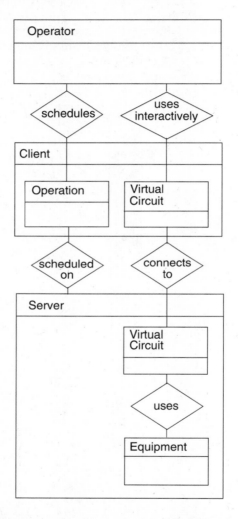

Figure 9.2 Refinement of the *uses* Relationship

Another interesting characteristic of refinement concerns **uses interactively**. The target of the relationship is no longer the client but some equipment attached to the server. The client and server are used to set up what amounts to a virtual circuit across the network. The **uses interactively** relationship has therefore been extended to include not just the client but also the equipment on the server.

The refinement of the relationship **uses** into **schedules** and **uses interactively** causes us to introduce new structural elements within **client** and **server**. One way to represent this is to model the client as an aggregation of **operation** and **virtual circuit** and the server as an aggregation of **virtual circuit** and **equipment.**

Clearly, this model is in no way complete, either with respect to scheduling an operation or to engaging in an interactive session. Both require some initial setup activity and, in the case of **uses interactively**, some way of expressing the setting of controls on the virtual control panel, which then changes the target equipment.

In our example system, the decision has been taken to implement connections between the client and server using CORBA. CORBA allows a client to access objects physically located on some remote server system. This type of connection may be represented as a *virtual* object on one system connected with the *actual* object on the other. The decision as to which system (client or server) holds the actual object is important, since all accesses to the virtual object's methods result in network communication.

The act of setting up a virtual circuit between the client and server for an interactive session involves refining the relationship **connects to** between virtual circuits to include CORBA objects. This refinement is shown in Figure 9.3.

With respect to refining the external agent's interaction with the system, the process of refining object models closely follows the refinement of *use cases* (Jacobson et al. 1992). With respect to refining internal interactions, the motivation is more frequently related to managing complexity or architectural considerations.

It is interesting to ask whether any standard transformations can be identified. To date we have been able to identify the three cases illustrated in Figure 9.4. This list is likely to grow. The refinement relating the diagram in Figure 9.1 to that in Figure 9.2 is a combination of decomposition and extension. The configuration shown in Figure 9.3 is the result of applying an in-line expansion transformation to the **connects to** relationship in Figure 9.2.

A major concern in the practical use of refinement is traceability. Clearly, there is a need for mechanisms that express all types of transformation. However, there are probably many more transformations than those listed above, and it is not particularly useful at this stage to define specific mechanisms for each type of transformation. A good starting point would be to give developers the ability to express the notion that one object model is a refinement of a relationship in another object model. This refinement association would then allow a CASE tool to build up a tree structure of object models that could be walked through, providing a limited form of traceability.

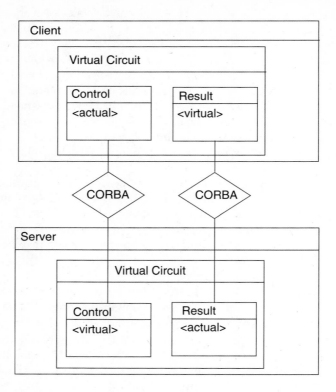

Figure 9.3 Refinement of the *connects to* Relationship

9.2.2 Object Interaction Graphs

Message connections on object interaction graphs (OIGs) are similar in form to relationships, and like relationships they can be refined. Exactly the same transformations should apply, since in many cases a message connection instantiates a relationship on an object model. This leads to the question: what is the equivalent of aggregation on an OIG? The simplest answer is a compound object or subsystem (see later discussion). Once again, the same techniques can be applied—individual message connections can be refined to express more detailed interactions involving constituent parts of an object. To some extent, Fusion already supports the idea of extending interactions through the use of object interaction graphs against individual methods.

9.2.3 Ambiguities in Temporal Scope

One issue that often comes up as a designer moves from higher levels of abstraction to lower levels is a tendency for the temporal scope of relationships to change. At the higher levels, cardinalities on relationships often express time-

Extension

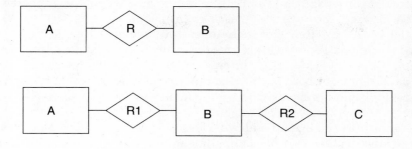

In-line expansion

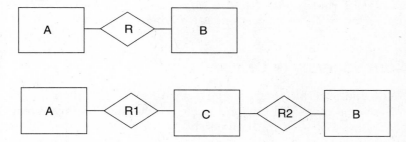

Decomposition

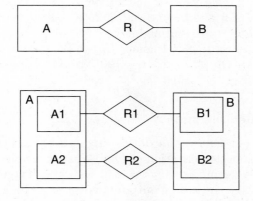

Figure 9.4 Types of Relationship Transformations

lessness; that is, they account for all possible permutations of interaction over an infinite time span. "Operator* uses client*" expresses that, over the life of the system, operators may use many clients and clients may be used by many operators. While this is a useful abstraction, it is also important to be able to model individual sessions, as in "operator schedules operation*." The process of decomposing or refining a relationship into a set of subordinate more detailed relationships often involves shifting from a broad temporal scoping to a narrower one. When we expand the "operator* uses client*" relationship, we are no longer interested in the possibility of many operators using many clients, but in one operator using one client; we are interested in individual "operator schedules operation*" and "operator uses interactively equipment*" events. Refinement allows us to represent both patterns simultaneously. Moreover, both sets of relationships apply simultaneously. The refinement does not replace the higher-level abstraction—it applies as well.

As shown in the example above, classes or relationships at one level may appear at another level with modified meaning. One would like to keep these various abstractions apart while retaining the fact that they form part of the same root. This leads to the idea of classes and relationships having different definitions at different levels of abstraction—in effect, different versions. Maintaining and relating different versions is a challenge for CASE tools.

9.3   CONCURRENCY IN DESIGN

While UNIX and several other popular operating systems have supported concurrency at the process level for some time, the popularity of operating systems such as Windows-NT with its lightweight, multi-threading capabilities makes the prospect of multi-tasking using objects a practical reality. Coupled with the industry's move towards client-server architectures and emerging standards like CORBA, the use of concurrency is being increasingly applied.

Concurrency in its many guises (client–server, real-time programming, etc.) has been the subject of widespread discussion for many years, and the reader is referred to such major contributors as Booch (1994) and Coad and Yourdon (1991a, 1991b). In the context of Fusion, Derek Coleman's paper "Analysis and Design for Concurrent Object Systems" (1993) provides an excellent description of the major methodological issues.

9.3.1   Designing with Concurrency

Fusion is described as a method for developing sequential systems. It is applicable to the design and implementation of event–response driven systems in which each event has a predetermined effect on the system and concludes with a predetermined result (possibly including output events). It is this model that allows us to develop deterministic life-cycle expressions for individual scenarios and then to combine these expressions into a life-cycle expression for the entire system. What Fusion does not accommodate is that the system will act spontaneously, a characteristic of multi-tasking or real-time systems. From time to time a multi-tasking system will undertake some asynchronous activity—deliver results to the operator's console, change some resource, etc.—long after the initiating system operation has concluded.

From a conventional Fusion perspective, this problem can be dealt with by dividing the system into a series of concurrent but internally sequential systems. Each task can then be analyzed and designed using standard Fusion. This explicit concurrency model is effective when the requirements for concurrency are understood and documented as part of the overall system requirements (Coleman and Skov 1993). The process of modeling concurrency is then treated as a prelude to the normal Fusion analysis phase.

Increasingly, however, the motivation to employ multi-tasking arises during design rather than requirements analysis. Software designers faced with architectural and nonfunctional requirements, such as performance, client-server partitioning, CORBA compatibility, persistent data, reuse of existing frameworks, and so on, turn to multi-threading as a major tool in their armory.

The issues surrounding the deployment of multi-tasking are substantially the same whether they are considered during analysis or design. One question is how behavior is to be allocated to different threads of control. Also, with the possibility of multiple concurrent threads of activity, new modes of communication between objects become possible. How are these to be chosen? Threads potentially compete for access to resources, and some threads need to share information with others. How are threads to be synchronized to avoid interference or to make sharing possible?

This section provides a few examples of how practitioners have extended the Fusion modeling notation to help them deal with these issues. It is certainly not intended to be a proposal for everything that would be needed in a method for developing concurrent systems.

9.3.2   Notations for Concurrency

The introduction of multiple, concurrent threads of control most directly affects the object interaction graphs (OIGs), since these are the Fusion models that capture the dynamic flow of communication between objects.

Representing Multiple Control Threads

The first step in treating concurrency is to provide a means for showing the different control threads in OIGs. A natural approach that some projects have adopted is to use different colors for the arcs in the OIG that belong to different threads. While offering excellent visualization of threads in a CASE tool, this approach does not lend itself well to black and white hard copy.

An alternative that works well is to extend the sequence numbers on the arcs with a number, or possibly a name, that labels the thread that the communication event belongs to. For instance, OIG arcs with sequence numbers 2:3.1 and 2:5 belong to the same thread, while 2:3.1 and 3:5 belong to different threads. The first two communication events are constrained by their sequence numbers to occur in a particular order, while the latter two are not.

Distinguishing Different Calling Approaches

When a method is invoked on an object in Fusion, the server object synchronously handles the call, only returning control to the client object when it has finished its task. In undertaking the method call, the server object may send messages to other objects, but in turn these must complete before control flow moves on. This approach is referred to as *call-and-wait* and characterizes synchronous systems. The arrows currently used in Fusion OIGs represent such call-and-wait communication.

When more than one thread can operate at the same time, alternatives to call-and-wait communication become possible and, in many cases, desirable. In the asynchronous *call-and-return* approach, a client sends a message to the server and immediately resumes processing while the server proceeds to service the call concurrently. The client spawns a new thread in which the message is sent and the called method runs.

In real-time systems, the time taken by a server to perform a task is often paramount. From a design point of view, this information becomes an integral part of the method call. Timing constraints lead to a new class of call that may be referred to as synchronous *call-with-time-out*. If the server fails to complete the desired task within the prescribed time, the request will time-out and control will automatically return to the waiting client. This style of call is typically implemented by setting a clock interrupt simultaneously with calling the server; whichever returns first will be acted on.

The notation introduced to represent call-and-return and call-with-time-out communication is illustrated in Figure 9.5. In the case of call-and-return communication, the message in thread **1** with sequence number **1.1** spawns a new thread, numbered **2**, and then returns control of thread **1** to the calling object. The message sent in the call-with-time-out style waits up to **n** microseconds before returning control.

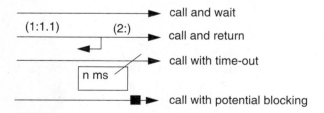

(1:1.1)   (2:)   call and wait
                             call and return
                             call with time-out
n ms
                             call with potential blocking

Figure 9.5 Notation for Different Communication Styles

A further notational addition that is sometimes useful is a marker for those threads that potentially block waiting for a communication to complete. Figure 9.5 shows a filled-in square used for this purpose.

Other communication styles are possible; a common example is interrupts. However, we have found that extending Fusion to support call-and-return and call-with-time-out comminution in addition to call-and-wait has sufficed for at least some projects that need to model concurrency. Undoubtedly, extensions supporting other communication styles will be needed in the future.

Distinguishing Different Types of Objects

Some objects have resources that can be shared by more than one thread. These are called *interface objects*, because they provide synchronization between threads. It is useful to identify interface objects explicitly, since they cannot be relied on to give immediate service to a client, and it may therefore be appropriate to use their services asynchronously. A simple way to mark interface objects is to draw them using bold lines.

When a client object makes a call to an interface object's method, the thread executing on the server may not be able to proceed until it acquires certain of the object's resources. In the case of an asynchronous call, this is fairly irrelevant to the client object. However, irrespective of the calling approach, the server thread may block waiting for some other thread to free up the shared resources. Some threads may never need to block, either because they do not use shared resources or because their callers are effectively masters of the interface object, a common situation in producer–consumer patterns.

Another distinction arising in concurrent systems is between active and passive objects. An *active* object executes substantially autonomously. Once started, it runs indefinitely. Active objects execute in their own thread with a cyclic control structure. Passive objects, on the other hand, only operate when requested to by another object. When they have completed responding to the request, their control thread either returns to the requesting object or it dies.

9.3.3 Synchronization

In a multi-tasking environment, two or more methods of an object may execute simultaneously as parts of different threads, giving rise to contention over the object's resources. If not handled correctly, this contention can lead to corrupted data and/or erroneous functionality. To avoid this problem, the competing threads need to be synchronized so that their access to the common resource can be managed.

Another form of synchronization occurs when one thread requires an object's resources, but only after another thread has usefully updated them. This producer–consumer style synchronization parallels the use of semaphores in conventional programming languages. The producer adds to the supply available to the consumer, and the consumer decreases the supply. If the supply is ever zero, the consumer must block until the producer adds to the supply. The consumer, on the other hand, never has to wait to increment the supply. In this style of synchronization, the control thread running on the consumer object can block because certain resources are unavailable, not because some other thread may possibly interfere with it.

Both thread- and resource-based synchronization will need to be supported by Fusion.

Central to the issue of synchronization is what constitutes the unit of resource. Two possible units will be considered—objects and bags of attributes.

Object-level Synchronization

By making the object the smallest sharable resource, objects effectively become owned by threads during the execution of their methods. A group of objects employed in a thread are by definition synchronous with respect to each other. They may call methods on each other any number of times without blocking, since there is no concern over contention for each other's resources; all are effectively in the same flow of control.

Objects in one thread are always viewed as asynchronous with respect to objects executing in other threads (aliens). Interface objects are those objects where threads intersect.

In this model, each synchronous, call-and-wait message from an alien object will block awaiting control of the object. The object will become unblocked and the method call allowed to proceed when the thread using the object unwinds through the object. In addition to this call-based locking, a thread can take out an explicit lock on an object, thereby locking out access to the object by any other thread.

An object not currently executing a method and not explicitly locked is effectively available and can be called by any object in any thread without blocking; the object then becomes owned by the calling thread.

In the case of an asynchronous, call-and-return message, the calling object spawns a new thread to handle the method call. The caller may therefore proceed without waiting. The spawned thread may need to wait, however, since it is making a synchronous call in a new thread and the called object may be busy processing another thread's request, or it may be explicitly locked.

The simplicity of this design approach is clearly very appealing. Implementation is straightforward using object-level semaphores which must be claimed by each method call prior to execution.

Attribute-level Synchronization

In some applications, an object may be an impractical unit of synchronization. A finer-grain unit would be a *bag* of attributes (one or more). Each bag represents a set of attributes that a method operates on. In this approach, method calls would only be allowed to proceed if they were able to gain control over the bag(s) that they required. This approach requires a minor notational enhancement—a bag identifier attached to each blocked call arriving at an interface object.

Another approach would be to annotate each method call with the names of the bags that it manipulates. While this is more precise and conveys additional information, it produces very cluttered diagrams. The extra information can usefully be described in the method's operation model. It is also conceivable that a method could block on more than one bag, in which case several named bags would need to be associated with a block.

9.3.4   An Example

The recommended notational extensions to the Fusion object interaction graph are illustrated in the OIG shown in Figure 9.6.

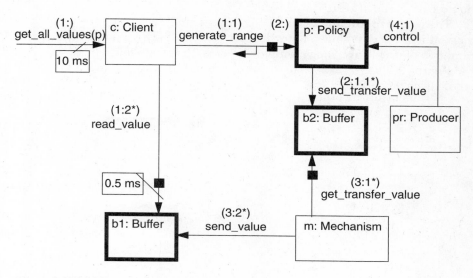

Figure 9.6 OIG for a Concurrent System

The example is based on the classical producer–consumer design pattern. A client object **c** wants to obtain a set of values from some producer object **pr** based on some policy **p**—for example, *odd numbers only*. The producer is only able to supply values intermittently; it may for instance be polling a device or watching a database table. Clearly, a call-and-wait approach is inappropriate here, because there is potentially no limit on the number of results that the producer may produce and hence no guarantee of the timeliness of the response. The interface between the client object and the producer object must therefore deal with coordinating the supply of values from the producer to the client and filtering them according to some policy.

The client object receives a request to obtain a set of values according to a policy, **get_all_values(odd_numbers)**. The client therefore requests the policy to produce these numbers. The policy object may not be able to perform this task immediately, since the producer object may not have delivered any values yet. In this case, the **generate_range** method will block. Sometime later, the producer invokes the **control** method (which does not block), and this immediately releases the lock on the policy object **p**, thereby allowing the **generate_range** method to proceed to deliver values into the buffer **b2**.

Thread 3 then synchronously unloads values from the **b2** buffer and deposits them into **b1**. Thread 1, having returned from the **generate_range** method, proceeds to obtain results from the **b1** buffer, waiting periodically while **b1** is being loaded by thread 3.

The synchronization of access to buffers **b1** and **b2** is characteristic of the use of a counting semaphore. Each call of **send_value** increments the semaphore. The **read_value** method will not have to wait while this semaphore is nonzero. Should it ever reach zero, it will wait.

The objects **p**, **b1**, and **b2** are all examples of interface objects, and the mechanism **m** is an active object, since it runs continuously. To add flavor to the diagram, two methods are shown employing calls that time-out.

Figure 9.7 shows what the example would look like if attribute-level synchronization were used.

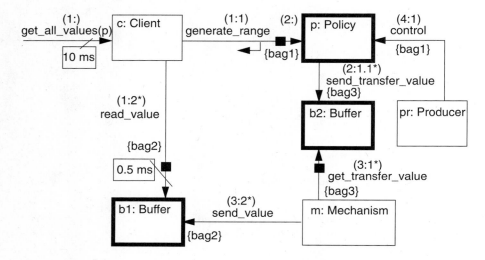

Figure 9.7 An OIG with Attribute Level Synchronization

9.4   USING ROLES IN DESIGN

Visibility in Fusion is represented as a relationship between a design class and design objects. This model of visibility is a direct reflection of the class-based origins of the major OO programming languages—C++, SmallTalk, etc.—in which storage must be preallocated for object references at compilation time.

With the advent of new programming styles such as OLE2 and COM (Common Object Model) in support of systems built from connectable objects, emphasis has passed from the class to the object. In this new model, objects may acquire new capabilities through association with other objects at runtime. Allocation of storage for references is therefore dynamic and transient.

In software engineering terms, the shift to object-based solutions offers the most promising route to achieving true productivity through reuse by supporting the composition of new objects from other objects. This branch of software engineering is already starting to revolutionize domains such as banking and trading floors. From a design point of view, this new model means that it is no longer useful to consider visibility from the perspective of a client class, but rather in terms of a client object.

This section shows how the principle of visibility can be extended to accommodate an object-based view of the world through the notion of object roles. These roles can then be directly tied back into the design system object models to demonstrate how specific temporal relationships are instantiated during design.

9.4.1   Roles

Visibility relationships are derived principally from object interaction graphs. A client object that sends messages to a server object can only do so if it has a reference to the server object. It can only know of the server object if it has been told of it before and remembered the reference, if it has been told of it as part of the current call, or if it created the reference in the first place.

Fusion takes this idea of client–server visibility and provides a set of pragmatic techniques for classifying each client-class/server-object pairing. These classifications—reference lifetime, server visibility, server binding, and reference mutability—have well-defined mappings to OO language structures such as *private, public,* and *constant.*

In reality, the ability of one object to send another a message is not so much a property of its class as of its context. A reference may come into and go out of scope of another object over the course of time as the roles of the two objects and their relationship with each other change.

The role of an object is temporal—it is a capability an object may have at some point in its lifetime with respect to other objects. It is not so much a property of the object as it is a property of how the object relates to other objects. Consider the example object model fragment in Figure 9.8. The roles **employer** and **employee** are transient. Simon is only an employer while Peter is an employee—circumstances have a habit of rewriting these types of relationship. Similarly, Simon might never have employed anyone if his father had not left him the business.

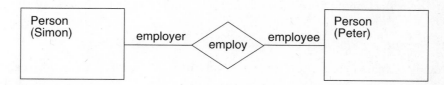

Figure 9.8 Relationship with Roles

It is this transient nature of roles that distinguishes them from classes. In other respects, a role is much like a class. The properties an object has and the methods it responds to depend on the role it is in, as well as the class it belongs to. An employee earns a salary, reports to a manager, has a job title, is eligible for benefits, and so on, because he is in the role of employee. A class preallocates storage for a set of references which all objects of that class have at all times. If one object of the class **Person** is an employee and has all the properties associated with being an employee, then all person objects can have the same properties. While obviously not representative of the real world, it is nonetheless representative of the types of statement that we must make using class-based languages. Roles are a powerful mechanism that can be used for modeling context, a characteristic that is missing from the Fusion object interaction graphs and visibility graphs.

9.4.2 Extending Object Interaction Graphs

In Figure 9.9, an object interaction graph shows how objects could be annotated with their relative roles. It is not necessary to annotate every object with a role. An object needs a role only if it is involved in a transient relationship with respect to some other object. For conformity with object modeling, every object will have a default role, which is its class name. The same object may undertake different roles in different contexts, but these should be represented by separate instances. There is no practical reason why one should not be able to use an object in two or more roles in the same object interaction graph.

Figure 9.9 OIG with Roles

In the case of a client object sending messages to a server collection, annotating the collection indicates that the server collection as a whole plays the role.

9.4.3 Extending Visibility Graphs

Two design objects connected by a message link represent a client–server relationship. At present this fact acts as the starting point for developing visibility graphs. Each pair of client–server relationships is considered in turn. Taking the messages that flow between them as a whole, a developer specifies whether the relationship is permanent or dynamic, exclusive or shared, bound or unbound, etc. These properties are then modeled in terms of client-class/server-object relationships.

Two client objects sharing the same server object may in fact have completely different visibility relationships to the server. This can be modeled in

Fusion by having two instances of the same server object appearing on the visibility graph for the client class. However, this modeling technique is not particularly intuitive, because the contexts giving rise to the alternative visibilities are not shown.

By modeling visibility in terms of client-role/server-role connections rather than client-class/server-object, one carries forward important contextual information. This information can then be used in a variety of ways.

Consider the example in Figure 9.10. The example shows how the various message links on one or more object interaction graphs can be transformed into role–role visibility relationships. Role–role visibility references can be classified using the various Fusion categories of visibility links.

When two or more instances of a role–role reference exist (as in Role1–Role2 S1,S3), the user will need to decide whether both instances can exist at the same time. If they can, it will be necessary to express this—either in the form of a cardinality constraint or by supplying a list of named server instances.

Since an object's role will default to its class, the degenerate case of a visibility reference will be of the form class–class. Again, it may be necessary to consider individual instances to establish the cardinality of the visibility reference.

9.4.4   Roles, Contracts, and Subsystems

As part of the process of developing a visibility graph for a client–server pair, a designer generally produces tables showing all the message connections flowing from the client role to the server role. The set of messages supported by a server role defines a contract that the server will support while in that role. In the same way, the set of messages sent by a client role defines the required interface of the client while in that role.

Another interesting application of roles is in the development of subsystems and composite objects. A composite object is equivalent in hardware engineering terms to a component; it is constructed from a number of simpler objects connected by internal message pathways. It is a real thing in that it has an interface and can be manipulated and described like any other object. While Fusion does not exclude composite objects, there is no support for them in the design models. This problem relates to the separation in Fusion of visibility issues from messaging issues. The representation and use of composite objects would be a major enhancement to Fusion.

A subsystem differs from a composite object in that it does not have an interface or internal logic separate from that of the objects it contains. While it may be convenient to model the subsystem as having an interface, this interface must be implemented directly by services provided by the objects that it contains. In essence, a subsystem is just a bag of objects.

Fusion does not currently support subsystems. A simple extension to object models would be to provide a subsystem node. Borrowing from Coad and Yourdon (1991a, 1991b), this could appear as a box with a dashed border. As a convenience, it may be useful to allow relationships to be drawn between objects and subsystems. These virtual relationships would serve as an abbreviation for

OIGs with Roles

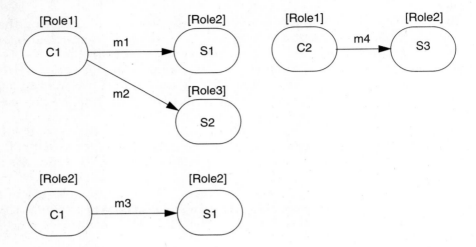

Corresponding Visibility Graphs

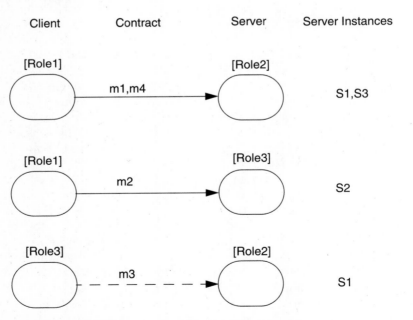

Figure 9.10 OIGs with Roles and Corresponding Visibility Graphs

actual relationships between external objects and objects within the subsystem.

Roles could be used to good effect in defining contracts on the interfaces of subsystems and composite objects. By annotating messages with roles, it becomes possible to group messages to form well-defined contracts. In the case of subsystems, these contracts could then be used to identify appropriate objects inside the subsystem which would be required to service the contract. In the case of composite objects, contracts could be used in the definition of the object's state machine or subinterfaces.

9.4.5   Roles as an Aid to Comparing Design Models

If, as recommended earlier, Fusion is extended to include object modeling during design, then there is good scope for maintaining consistency between the design system object models and the object interaction graphs using roles and role–role visibility references.

The design system object model needs to convey both static and dynamic associations. The static associations are derivable from the inheritance graphs, and the dynamic object compositions are expressed on the object interaction graphs. Dynamic associations follow the path of the links shown in visibility graphs, when these are expressed in terms of roles.

While the design system object model will generally be much larger than the domain object model, it should contain the domain object model as part. The associations expressed on the domain object model should therefore be traceable to the design system object model. Using roles, this traceability becomes relatively straightforward.

9.5   CONCLUSIONS

With an expanding domain of problems to solve and an evolving repertoire of programming techniques that can be employed, it is important that OO methods keep apace. This paper has presented a few extensions to Fusion that have been shown to provide effective improvements in our ability to manage complexity and exploit new technologies.

Levels of abstraction and the process of refinement are powerful software engineering tools not sufficiently employed during design in the current definition of Fusion. Fusion could provide these tools by supporting simple techniques for expressing the notion of relationship and message refinement. The combination of leveled object interaction graphs and design system object models would provide very powerful extensions to Fusion, allowing developers to manage more easily the design of complex systems.

The demand for methods that support the design of concurrent systems is growing. The Fusion notational extensions offered here are purely suggestive and almost certainly need refinement. Furthermore, important issues such as counting semaphores and interrupts have been analyzed only cursorily and are undoubtedly worth further investigation. Before these ideas can be brought into

Fusion, it will be necessary to assess the impact of concurrency on analysis and the related design notations. Clearly, systems which are capable of making spontaneous decisions are difficult to describe using a deterministic grammar, so alterations to the Fusion interface and operation models should be expected.

The use of roles in design provides a powerful abstraction which complements and extends existing Fusion functionality. Roles can be used to identify contracts that assist in the definition of subsystems and component objects. Roles also provide a mechanism for checking the completeness of designs with respect to the analysis models.

There are several other issues needing attention that we have encountered when using Fusion: name spaces, persistent data, the design of client–server architectures, and others. Two significant advantages Fusion has over other OO methods is that it is strongly based on practical experience and that it has been, and hopefully will remain, a team effort.

REFERENCES

Booch, G. 1994.*Object-Oriented Analysis and Design with Applications*. 2nd ed. Redwood City, CA: Benjamin/Cummings.

Coad, P. and E. Yourdon. 1991a. *Object-oriented Analysis*. Englewood Cliffs: Prentice Hall.

Coad, P. and E. Yourdon. 1991b. *Object-oriented Design*. Englewood Cliffs: Prentice Hall.

Coleman, D. 1993. Analysis and Design for Concurrent Object Systems. Sixth International Conference on Software Engineering and Its Application, Paris, November 15–19.

Coleman, D., P. Arnold, S. Bodoff, C. Dollin, H. Gilchrist, F. Hayes, and P. Jeremaes. 1994. *Object-Oriented Development: The Fusion Method*. Englewood Cliffs, NJ: Prentice Hall.

Coleman, D. and D. Skov. February 1993. Analysis and Design for Concurrent Object Systems. *Technical Report HPL-93-18*. Hewlett-Packard Laboratories, Bristol (UK).

Jacobson, I., M. Christerson, P. Jonsson, and G. Övergaard. 1992. *Object-Oriented Software Engineering*. Reading, MA: Addison-Wesley.

Extensions to Fusion Supporting NEXTSTEP/OpenStep (Portable) Distributed Objects

Kris Oosting

SHARED OBJECTIVES

10.1 INTRODUCTION

Distributed (remote) objects for NEXTSTEP became commercially available for building real applications in 1993. At the time, object-oriented analysis and design methods were not ready to provide full support for developing systems using distributed objects. The result was that many decisions were postponed until coding. As you would probably guess, this had ramifications downstream. The weaker support at the design stage undoubtedly led to more defects. Designs were also no longer "in sync" with the code, creating maintenance problems.

There is still much discussion about constructing a completely new method to support the development of client–server applications. A new method must first be tested, and then applied to real projects. After that, the religious method battles are fought, and finally, if we are lucky, another method emerges. Most of the time, existing methods do not support the latest technology. Of course, this is to be expected. It takes some time to discover what the new technology is all about before it can be modeled.

In real life, we have to deliver projects on time, within budget, and with the right functionality. There is no time to wait for the development of another method that might work. So what do we do in the meantime? A solution that worked for us was to take the method framework most suitable for the type of application under development and extend it with some notations and process descriptions to support the new technology—not forgetting quality checks and method metrics. When a method does not support a certain technology, do not blame it for its missing parts, but instead find a way to create a workable solution.

This paper describes some simple and easy-to-use changes in the Fusion method to support the development of applications using the (Portable) Distributed Objects of NEXTSTEP/OpenStep.

10.2   WHAT ARE DISTRIBUTED OBJECTS?

When developing a client–server application, developers rarely want to be bothered with network details. Building a client–server application should be almost the same as building a non-client–server application. Objects themselves are little client–servers anyway. Distributed Objects allow an application to send messages to remote objects using the ordinary Objective-C syntax. This makes it possible to share Objective-C objects, even among applications running on different machines across a network. Even though the use of distributed objects in code is very simple, we still need to model it during design to understand how the application is composed.

While Distributed Objects work between NEXTSTEP/OpenStep computers, Portable Distributed Objects work in a heterogeneous network. The principle is the same, only portable.

In client–server application development, it is not wise to distribute the header files of the server classes to all client applications. Of course, the clients need to know how to communicate with the server to use the services it provides. The best way to do this is through *protocols*. In NEXTSTEP/OpenStep, protocols can be seen as a list of services that are implemented by one or more classes without knowing which classes. This is very helpful for client–server applications since it makes them more secure. Reusing protocols also allows developers to agree early on about the services to provide to each other without having to know the classes that others develop.

The following example demonstrates how easy it is to set up a connection and access objects. Here are the steps to take:

- Register the object that is available to receive messages (on the server). This is called *vending*.
- Set up the connection with the vended object for the services we want to use.
- Start sending messages as if working with objects in one application.

Say we have a database that clients can use. A guard object is added to the server to protect it from clients. This guard object knows how to talk to the server and will be made available to the clients.

```
id guard      = [[ODBServerGuard alloc] init];
id connection = [NXConnection registerRoot:guard withName:
                 "PublicServer"];
if (connection) [connection runFromAppKit];
```

The first line allocates and initializes a guard object. The second line will vend the guard object under the name **PublicServer**. The third line starts the vending.

Through the network name server, clients can find objects that have been vended. When we make a connection with a registered (vended) object, a proxy, acting for the server, will be returned. The code of the client object is

```
id guardProxy =[NXConnection connectToName:"PublicServer"
                onHost:"*"];
```

Now we can use guardProxy in our client application to access the services of the server using normal Objective-C messaging. For example: **[guardObject numberOfObjectsInDB]** returns the number of objects in the database. The "*" for the hostname means that it has to look for **PublicServer** in the netinfo domain. The hostname can, of course, be filled in as well.

We also have to make sure that the client is using the right protocol. In this case, the **ODBServerProtocol** protocol is

```
[guardProxy setProtocolForProxy:@protocol(ODBServerProtocol)];
```

So far programming is easy. The fun really starts when we have to implement encoding and decoding of objects that are passed between applications, but this is an undertaking that falls outside the scope of this paper.

10.3   FUSION EXTENSIONS

To ensure that remote objects, protocols, and client–server aspects are used in the right way, we have to add some notations to the Fusion method. By facilitating representation and design of distributed NEXTSTEP/OpenStep objects in Fusion, these extensions also add a form of defect prevention.

The extensions are as follows:

- A protocol indication is added to the object interaction graphs
- A protocol indication is added to the visibility graphs, as well as an indication for the connection, so that a class can be represented by a proxy for the server class
- A notation is added to the class descriptions
- A protocol description is added to support the protocols

10.3.1   Object Interaction Graph

The protocol indication in the object interaction graphs is as follows:

Message is listed in protocol:

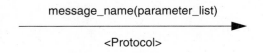

message_name(parameter_list)

<Protocol>

Return value conforms to protocol:

n = message() : Type <Protocol>

Parameter conforms to protocol:

message(param: type <Protocol>)

In the object interaction graph there is no indication that an object is a proxy for another object. Because *proxy* is a visibility indicator, it is shown in the visibility graph.

Many objects from Object Libraries, Object Kits, and Palettes are used in building NEXTSTEP/OpenStep applications. So that we do not describe too much during design, we use a prefix in each object to indicate that it is coming from an object library, kit, or palette. The advantage is that this prefix makes it easy to see which class is reused (for metrics). The method descriptions for reused classes do not contain a description of the method, but instead have information about the reused class (like reference manual page, library location, who is responsible for the class, etc.). CASE tools can provide a mechanism to report on the reuse percentage of a specific design as well.

The notation is as follows:

lib dictionary:
SODictionary

An example of an object interaction graph with protocol and **lib** notation is shown in Figure 10.1. This example is an extension of Figure 4.10 in the Fusion book (Coleman et al. 1994).

Here the reporting facility is designed using the view–controller–model layer approach. A button on a menu in the GUI is initiating the request for a report. **appController** is a controller layer object that communicates with the **depot** model layer object. After the **depot** creates the **report**, it sends it back to

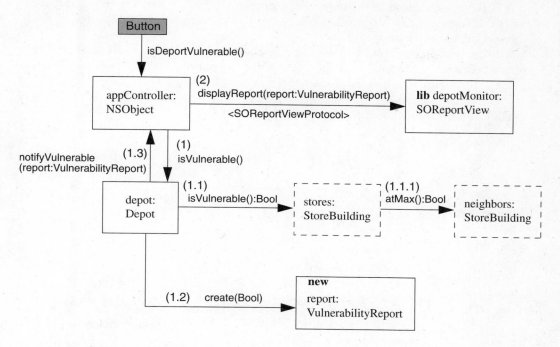

Figure 10.1 Object Interaction Graph

appController. appController uses **depotMonitor** to display the **report. depotMonitor** is a view layer object in the user interface, a scrollable text.

depotMonitor is a library object taken from a palette, hence the **lib** prefix. The services **SOReportView** can provide are listed in the **SOReportViewProtocol** protocol. The descriptions of **SOReportView** and **SOReportViewProtocol** are found in the reference manual. Make sure that **lib** classes always have a clear reference manual page, otherwise no one will use the classes and the benefit will be lost.

10.3.2   Visibility Graph

An example of a visibility graph notation is shown in Figure 10.2.

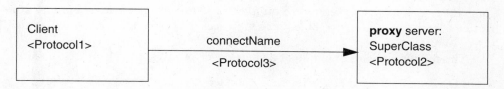

Figure 10.2 Visibility Graph

Client uses **protocol1**. Server uses **protocol2**. The client can communicate with the server proxy by using the services listed in **protocol3**. The name of the connection is **connectName**.

The visibility graph in this example is part of the design of the **Client**. The prefix **proxy** in the server class indicates what the server's visibility is to the client. In the design of the server, the **proxy** prefix is of course removed.

An example where the visibility graph notations are translated to code (NEXTSTEP 3.2) is shown in Figure 10.3.

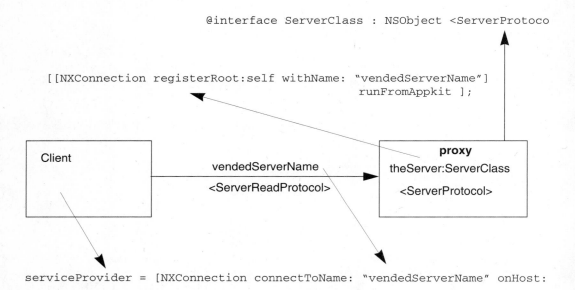

Figure 10.3 Visibility Graph with Translations to Code

Note that this is the extra code a programmer has to add to a standard program to make it work on a network (it searches the netinfo domain). The client will find the host on which the server is running. Code concerning security is not mentioned in this example. The **lib** prefix is also used in visibility graphs.

10.3.3   Class Description and Protocol Description

Class descriptions are extended to support the indication of protocols and connections from user interface objects to view–controller layer objects, called *outlets*.

The following is an example of a class description, showing the extension:

```
class CameraView isa N3DCamera using SOCameraProtocol
attribute
    eyePointX:float
```

```
      eyePointY:float
      eyePointZ:float
      rollangle:float
      renderManager:proxy using RenderManagerProtocol
      rollAngleField:float outlet
  method
      init
      free
      // no more methods listed, because they are in the protocol
         SOCameraProtocol.
  endclass
```

This example shows a class description for a view in a user interface used to display three-dimensional images. The class is a view–controller class using the **SOCameraProtocol** for communication. The class **CameraView** communicates also with a remote object defined as **renderManager**. The **renderManager** is a proxy for a server object, using the **RenderManagerProtocol** to communicate with it. **rollAngle-Field** is a reference to a user interface **TextField** object and is using this text field to display a float value.

The **SOCameraProtocol** protocol can be defined as follows:

```
protocol SOCameraProtocol
    zoomInImage( zoomFactor:float )
    zoomOutImage( zoomFactor:float )
    rotate( angle:float )
endprotocol
```

10.3.4   Summary of the Notations

The notations in this section use the same naming conventions and format as the notations listed in the *Reference Manual* section (Appendix C) of the Fusion book (Coleman et al. 1994). For the reader's convenience, we present the full extended notation in this section and explicitly identify alterations to the Fusion notation.

The standard class definition is listed in Section C-8 of the Fusion book (Coleman et al. 1994). Our extended class definition is as follows:

```
CDesc       ::= "class" Name Inherit* ["using" Protocols]
                Property* "endclass"
Inherit     ::= "isa" Names
Names       ::= Name++ ( "," | ":" )
Protocols   ::= Protocol++ ","
Protocol    ::= Name
Property    ::= Attribute | Method
Attribute   ::= ["attribute"] Mutability Name ":" Sharing Binding
                SpecialType
Mutability  ::= "constant" | ["variable"]
Sharing     ::= ["shared" | "exclusive"]
Binding     ::= ["bound" | "unbound"]
SpecialType ::= Type | "outlet" | "proxy using" Protocol
Method      ::= ["method"] Name CArgList [":" Type]
```

The following expressions were changed from or added to the original class description expressions in Section C-8 (Coleman et al. 1994): *CDesc*, *Protocols*, *Protocol*, *Attribute*, and *SpecialType*. The class description example in Section 3.3, *Class Description and Protocol Description*, demonstrates the use of these changed and added expressions.

The newly added Protocol Description is defined as

```
PDesc         ::= "protocol" Name Inherits* ProtocolList*
                  "endprotocol"
Inherits      ::= "using" Protocol++ ","
ProtocolList  ::= MethodDefs
MethodDefs    ::= ["method"] Name CArgList [":" Type | "("
                  Type "<" Protocol ">" ")"]
CArgList      ::= ArgList   |   PArgList
PArgList      ::= "(" PArg** "," ")"
PArg          ::= Name ":" Type "<" Protocol ">"
```

The class description example in Section 10.3.3 demonstrates the use of the added protocol description notation.

The notation of the object interaction graph, listed in C-5 (Coleman et al. 1994), has been changed as well. In particular, the following expressions have been changed: *ObjectLabel*, *ArrowLabel*, and *Invocation*. The extended object interaction graph notation is

```
ObjectLabel  ::= ["new | lib"] TypedName  ["<" Protocol ">"]
ArrowLabel   ::= [Sequencer] Invocation [Predicate]
                 ["<" MessageProtocol ">"]
Sequencer    ::= "(" [DottedNumber] [Decoration] [Multiplic-
                 ity]")"
DottedNumber ::= Number++ "."
Decoration   ::= (Prime | Letter)*
Multiplicity ::= "*"
Invocation   ::= [ResultName "="] Name [ActualArgList]
                 [":" Type ["<" TypeProtocol ">"]]
ActualArgList::="(" ActualArgs ")"
ActualArgs   ::= TypedName  |  Type
Predicate    ::= "[" SelectCondition [";" StopCondition] "]"
```

Where

> *Protocol* is used to indicated that an object conforms to this protocol.
>
> *MessageProtocol* is used to indicate that the message is part of this protocol.
>
> *TypeProtocol* is used to indicate that the return type or the parameter in the message conforms to this protocol.

Section 10.3.1 contains an example that shows the use of the changed expressions.

The notation for the visibility graph, listed in C-6 (Coleman et al. 1994), has been changed as well. The following expressions have been changed or added: *ServerLabel*, *ClientLabel*, *RefLabel*, *DynamicRef*, *PermanentRef*, and *ReferenceName*. The extended visibility graph notation is

```
ServerLabel    ::= ["new | lib"] Mutability [TypedName | "proxy"]
                   ["<" ServerProtocol ">"]
Mutability     ::= "constant"  |  ["variable"]
ClientLabel    ::= TypedName ["<" ClientProtocol ">"]
RefLabel       ::= DynamicRef  |  PermanentRef
DynamicRef     ::= [ReferenceName["<" ProtocolForReference">"]]
PermanentRef   ::= [ReferenceName["<" ProtocolForReference">"]]
ReferenceName ::= Text
```

Section 10.3.2 demonstrates the use of the new and modified visibility graph expressions.

10.4 WHAT WE LEARNED

Fusion is easy to extend without having to add new graphs. A completely new method for Portable Distributed Objects was not necessary. The technology did not change much. In our minds, these concepts tend to seem more complex than they really are. In practice, the extensions we created worked well enough. It was a practical and minor change for developers.

Discussions about distributed objects and computing now take place during design and no longer during implementation. This is positive, because it is easier to change a diagram than pieces of source code in several files. Previously, discussions always occurred during implementation, because the design notations did not trigger any questions. Now they do.

The **lib** prefix turned out to be quite practical when using a tool. The percentage of reused classes is easily calculated. We found it helpful always to start design with "shopping" for classes to reuse. We found that, for example, two days searching for classes in object libraries, reference manuals, and the like, was much more profitable than developing them ourselves—even if we sometimes have to buy them.

REFERENCES

Coleman, D., P. Arnold, S. Bodoff, C. Dollin, H. Gilchrist, F. Hayes, and P. Jeremaes. 1994. *Object-Oriented Development: The Fusion Method.* Englewood Cliffs, NJ: Prentice Hall.

Improving the Analysis Stage of the Fusion Method

Gabriel Eckert

Swiss Federal Institute of Technology

11.1 INTRODUCTION

Our software engineering course, taught to third-year students, is based on the Fusion method and its application to a complete project. The project follows the classical waterfall model and students, working in groups of five, produce a complete application including documentation. On average, each group spends more than 10 personmonths on the project and produces about 8,000 lines of "delivered" source instructions throughout the seven-month development schedule. While it would be a small project in the "real world," it is a major task for our students and, we believe, a realistic approach to current software development practice.

At the beginning of the project, all groups get the same short problem statement. Subsequently, they must clarify it, establish the precise requirements, define the user interface, and design, implement, and test their application. Compared with the size of the project, the groups are rather too large; this intensifies communication and managerial issues, providing students with valuable experience. Students experience competition not primarily as individuals—the common student situation—but as members of a group having its own strengths, but also its own internal conflicts.

Projects given to the students include an electronic diary, a simple database management system, a simple spreadsheet application, a conference registration system, and more recently two games: Monopoly™ with computer-simulated players, and Risk™ over a network of workstations.

This account is based on our own practice with the Fusion method and on its application by students for the development of the Risk™ game. We describe problems teaching staff and students encountered applying the Fusion method on this project. We share experience gained during the analysis stage of the project, mention potential pitfalls, and suggest ways to avoid them.

The body of this paper is divided into five parts. Following this introduction, Section 11.2 describes what led us to choose the Fusion development method for teaching. Section 11.3 provides a short account of the feedback and reactions we got from our students and introduces the problems we observed.

The next three sections are devoted to a more detailed discussion of the problems encountered, including how to avoid or overcome the identified defects and limitations. In each of these sections, the discussion follows the order used in the Fusion book (Coleman et al. 1994) and provides many references to its content. More precisely, Section 11.4 discusses what we consider to be the major difficulties for the software developer, that is, the pitfalls every Fusion practitioner should be aware of. Section 11.5 attempts to clarify less important—but also less difficult—issues, and to provide interpretations or constructive advice regarding specific aspects of the Fusion analysis models. Finally, the last section is targeted at methodologists and people interested in improving the Fusion modeling notations. Fusion users can easily skip this part, which discusses many specific issues, some of them rather minor.

11.2   CHOICE OF A DEVELOPMENT METHOD

For six years, we used our own refined version (Strohmeier and Jean 1990) of the development method proposed by EVB (EVB 1987), itself related to the early work of Booch (Booch 1983). An account of our experience in teaching this object-oriented method has been published elsewhere (Jean and Strohmeier 1990).

After years of teaching and using EVB, many shortcomings became apparent to us; for example, the very poor support for the analysis stage, the absence of behavioral descriptions, and a strong bias toward the Ada programming language.

We therefore evaluated ten development approaches in order to select one and apply and teach it. Our choice was based on the following main criteria: the method should be general (not oriented toward specific areas) and embrace all development activities; it should have sound and explicit foundations; it should be appropriate for teaching; and a suitable textbook covering the full method without unnecessary details should be available.

The following six methods were eliminated during the first round for the reasons given:

- Responsibility-Driven Design (Wirfs-Brock et al. 1990)
  No coverage of analysis and modeling; too informal.
- Shlaer-Mellor method (Shlaer and Mellor 1988, 1992)

Rather low level; design phase lacking.

- Coad–Yourdon–Nicola method (Coad and Yourdon 1991a, 1991b, and Coad and Nicola 1993)

  Insufficient distinction between analysis, design, and implementation; laconic design phase; lack of behavioral descriptions; superficial textbooks.

- Object-Oriented Information Engineering (OOIE) (Martin and Odell 1992)

  Confused and poorly documented approach; too specific; many irrelevant aspects in the textbook.

- Object-Oriented System Development (de Champeaux et al. 1993)

  Insufficient distinction between analysis and design; poorly documented process.

- Object-Oriented Conceptual Modeling (Dillon and Tan 1993)

  No coverage of design and implementation; set of techniques without proper process.

Four approaches were shortlisted and underwent a more detailed assessment:

- **Objectory** (Jacobson et al. 1992)

  An interesting approach, including aspects largely neglected by other methods. Although extensive, the available textbook unfortunately remains too general. As such, it is not appropriate for teaching a development method and should be extended with specific material.

- **Booch method** (Booch 1994)

  Although improved in the last few years, this approach is more a (rich) set of notations than a proper development method. The origin of the approach and the (intentional) lack of distinction between analysis and design leads, in our opinion, to an implementation-oriented view, not well suited for analysis and modeling. However, the textbook is of good quality and includes a worthwhile description of object-oriented concepts.

- **Object Modeling Technique (OMT)** (Rumbaugh et al. 1991)

  A rich and serious approach, with a good book and a documented process. Unfortunately, the method is perhaps too rich and the coherence between the three models (object, dynamic, and functional) is dubious. As its name implies, it is primarily a modeling approach and the design phase is insufficiently supported. Nevertheless, we considered OMT to be the second best among the evaluated methods.

- **Fusion** (Coleman et al. 1994)

  We finally selected this method because it has

  - Sound foundations, including many established principles and techniques.
  - Complete and concise description of the process and of the products to be developed.

- Clear conceptual and practical separation between analysis and design.

We also identified the following negative characteristics:

- Large amount of documentation required, could discourage students.
- Implementation phase does not cover the adaptation to an object-based but not object-oriented programming language like Ada 83, our implementation language for the project.

We envisaged applying the lightweight version of Fusion (Coleman et al. 1994, Section 10-3.1, p. 236) in order to address the first point, but finally decided instead to carefully plan the development in order to spread out the required work evenly over the schedule.

The second point was considered minor, and we could address it on the basis of our experience with our former development method.

We decided not to simultaneously introduce a new method and a supporting tool, and therefore let the students use their usual word processing and drawing tools to develop the required models and documents.

For course preparation, we used the content of the NTU Fusion video course (Coleman and Jeremaes 1993) and extended it with a number of small modeling exercises and short examples, as well as one larger example that was used over the whole course. We advised students to buy the Fusion book (Coleman et al. 1994), which, surprisingly, turned out to be a major problem as copies were not available for months.

11.3 STUDENTS' FEEDBACK AND PROBLEMS ENCOUNTERED

Overall, students reacted positively to the Fusion method. They appreciated the approach and showed more self-confidence during development than students in previous years. They especially valued the systematic process and the lean and powerful notations provided. Compared to previous years, we perhaps had more questions to answer, but these questions were definitely more precise, related to some specific aspects of the method, instead of being open ended and vague as had been the case before.

During the preparation of the lectures and exercises on the Fusion approach and while experimenting with the method on small examples, we noticed several unsatisfactory aspects of the method. Later, we also observed that students were hesitating and having difficulties that related to many of these same aspects.

Students were encouraged to express their doubts and difficulties. We appreciated the direct questions that candid students often raise. In many cases, these raised issues that we feel are not well handled by the method and helped identify its most unsatisfactory features.

The remaining parts of this paper aim at identifying and describing these shortcomings, explaining and illustrating their relevance, and suggesting possible improvements. We think that these improvements could provide stronger foundations for the Fusion method, facilitate its application, and have a positive impact on learning and training.

As stated in the introduction, this contribution addresses only the analysis models of the Fusion method, that is, the object model and the interface model. Overall, and compared to previous years, we found that students addressed the analysis task more thoroughly and produced better documents. They had relatively few problems with the object model, but the interface model—especially the operation model—caused several problems. Schemata were often incomplete, inconsistent, or too vague. We believe that there are various causes for this situation:

- Object modeling is close to entity-relationship modeling, a subject taught in a separate database course. Therefore, students had better training for this part of the analysis phase.

- Groups started with the object model and spent more time on it while neglecting the interface model until pushed by the deadline. Towards the end of the phase, they had to hurry to submit the whole analysis document and did not spend enough time on the operation model.

- The project involved a dynamically changing collection of agents, evolving roles for these agents, and therefore an evolving set of input and output events for a given agent. The modeling constructs used in the interface model are not well suited to this kind of situation, and most groups could not establish an appropriate model for dealing with this issue.

- Object modeling is quite intuitive, and most students can rely on observations and common sense to check that the object model conforms to reality. On the other hand, it is more difficult to give concrete expression to sequences of events and operation schemata.

- Object modeling is not a precise science, and different aesthetic tastes can lead to various models. Our grading of this model was therefore more lenient. On the other hand, many formal checks can be carried out on the operation model and students have to apply more effort merely to reach consistency, so our grading was more strict.

We will return to some of these points and discuss various questionable syntactic and semantic aspects of the Fusion analysis models and mention common mistakes and areas of confusion. More precisely, we will consider the following issues in the rest of the paper:

- Aspects of the use of relationships in the object model
- Interaction between aggregation and relationships in the object model
- Interaction between subtyping and aggregation in the object model
- Moving from the object model to the system object model: myths and pitfalls
- Types, classes, and collections in the analysis models

- Using relationships and aggregation in operation schemata
- Extending the set of predefined expressions in operation schemata
- Suggestions for improving the life-cycle model

11.4 MAJOR DIFFICULTIES FOR THE SOFTWARE DEVELOPER

In this section, we briefly remind the reader of the Fusion analysis models and describe the main problems encountered while working with them. Unfortunately, the most important issues are also the most difficult ones—and often the most neglected as well! Our aim is therefore to make Fusion practitioners aware of these pitfalls, even if we cannot provide recipes for dealing with them.

In the first part of this section, we raise two issues that we believe are not properly handled by the current development method because they are related to essential difficulties, that is, difficulties inherent in the nature of analysis. Therefore, it would be futile to look for detailed prescriptions on how to handle them, and we can only attempt to contribute to the awareness, flair, and experience of practitioners.

Nevertheless, Fusion provides specific constructs for dealing with these difficult aspects. We are convinced that it is important to realize how these problems are addressed by Fusion constructs and what the limitations of these constructs are.

In the final part of the section, we also mention the most common difficulties encountered by our students.

11.4.1 Fusion Analysis Models

Fusion has no requirements phase (Coleman et al. 1994, Section 1-4.2, p. 9). Following requirements capture, the first phase of the Fusion process is *analysis*, in which the following models are produced:

- **Object model:** model of the problem domain expressed in terms of classes and relationships
- **System object model:** part of the object model that relates to the system to be built
- **Operation model:** description of the behavior exhibited by the system object model
- **Life-cycle model:** description of the permitted sequences of system operations

Recall that the operation model and the life-cycle model together form the interface model.

11.4.2 From the Object Model to the System Object Model: Myths and Pitfalls

According to the Fusion method, the *object model* presents "a model of the problem domain" while the *system object model* is "a subset of an object model that relates to the system to be built" (Coleman et al. 1994, Section 2.4, p. 23). It is suggested that drawing one or several closed dashed curves on an object model is sufficient to establish the boundary between the system and its environment, taking into account the constraint of a well-formed submodel.

It is acknowledged that the extent of the system object model depends on the functionality of the system. However, the book example (Coleman et al. 1994, Figure 2.17 p. 24) and its related explanations suggest that the underlying object model remains unchanged when the functionality changes. The system boundary would merely adapt to include more classes and relationships or to exclude some of them.

This is a very naive vision. It does not take into account the fact that the classes inside the automation boundary (the *system*) change their nature (Hoydalsvik and Sindre 1993). *Inside* the system boundary, information objects are needed, reflecting corresponding real-world objects that remain *outside*. Classes and relationships may therefore appear and disappear as a result of setting up an automation boundary.

The Fusion method recognizes the importance of determining what is inside and what is outside, and we appreciate this concern. But this distinction is proposed in a too-simplistic view, especially with regard to the process of establishing the boundary.

The following example should illustrate this problem. We consider an elevator problem domain (Figure 11.1). The task is to develop the control system for the elevator.

Starting from this problem domain, we naively attempt to model it and develop a simple object model (Figure 11.2). Note that all relevant physical objects of the problem domain are represented here, including the control unit that is to be developed.

The next phase is to find the system boundary. On the one hand, it is clear that the system being investigated is the control unit for the elevator, that is, the class **Control** in Figure 11.2. The other classes could be considered as external agents interacting with this system. On the other hand, we see that we will need both the external agents and some internal information about their state. Inside the system, we will keep images of the real agents that remain outside. As a consequence, our system object model will be completely modified with regard to the domain object model. Moreover, we will adapt it to the expected functionality and simplify it in order to avoid unnecessary classes. Figure 11.3 illustrates a possible system object model for the elevator control system.

Here we notice that some external classes are being represented inside the system, but in a modified form: the attribute **movement** has been moved from the motor to the cabin, which itself has totally lost its button components. All the information related to both the buttons in the cabin and on the floors is now

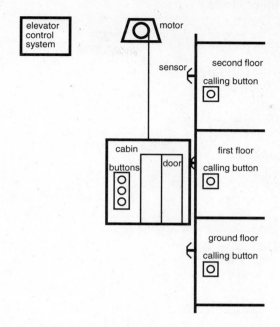

Figure 11.1 Elevator Problem Domain.

being stored in the attribute **cabin called**. We suppose that we are no longer interested in the button states, but rather in the next floor that the cabin should go to (because of a call from this floor, or because of an order given in the cabin).

Note that Figure 11.3 represents only the system, i.e., the **Control** class of the previous object model (*inside* the system boundary), but is rather similar to what was represented *outside* of this class according to the naive system boundary.

Finally, Figure 11.4 illustrates the event interactions between this control system and the agents in the environment.

Of course, this is a simplistic example, but we believe that it shows the kind of problems that arise when moving from the problem domain to the system view.

It could be argued that the analyst should *not* make all the changes that were made between Figures 11.2 and 11.3, and should preserve as much information about the original domain as possible. We believe that this does not reflect the way most analysts work. We observed that, in practice, analysts tend to start with the *system* object model, even if they pretend to be working on the object model! They start with some *implicit* representation of what is inside the system and attempt to develop the simplest model for it, such as the one represented in Figure 11.3. Later, this model is extended with peripheral information (the environment) to become the alleged object model.

Genuine attempts to first develop the object model of the domain usually

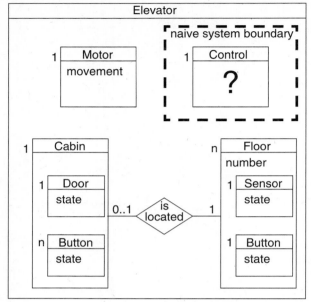

n = number of floors in the building

Figure 11.2 Simple Object Model for the Elevator Problem Domain

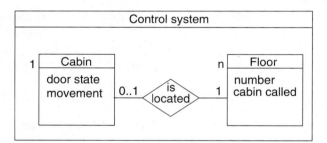

Figure 11.3 System Object Model for the Elevator Control System

lead to intricate models that seem artificial for the sole purpose of describing the system and are not likely to be accepted without revision.

This example illustrates the frequent confusion that arises when there are both agents in the environment and classes inside the system that reflect the external agents. The confusion often begins at the terminology level (are we talking about the agent or about the class?) and later diffuses into other areas.

Other practitioners confirmed that setting up system boundaries can be the

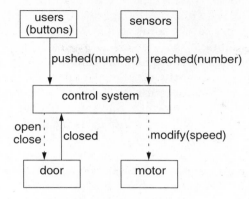

Figure 11.4 Control System and Its Environment

most difficult part of the analysis phase. This is especially true for developments where the system procurers, users, and software developers adopt different views of the role of the system in its environment. It is important to realize that the analysis stage of the Fusion method does not help to resolve these contradictory views.

However, there are many cases where the system extent is already known at the beginning of a project—at least implicitly. Often, analysts know roughly what the system will include and can adopt a system viewpoint; the domain is considered as if the future system were already part of it. The model of the problem domain will then contain these implied assumptions about the system that is to be developed. The domain is described from a system viewpoint and therefore can be represented as a system surrounded by its environment.

This is the expected situation in the Fusion method. Under such circumstances, it is possible to merely draw a closed dashed line on the object model in order to represent the system boundary.

We also believe that analysts should question the nature of information represented in the system object model. Is it *domain information* that agents deal with and that crosses the system boundary, or is it *internal state information* that remains hidden from agents but is merely needed by the system itself to perform its tasks? We suppose that domain information (typical of information systems) can be easily organized into structures that map to the real world, while modeling internal state information (typical of process control systems) is more arbitrary.

11.4.3   Life-cycle Restrictions versus Operation Preconditions

We missed guidelines for choosing the right balance between life-cycle restrictions and operation preconditions. One extreme would be to fully neglect the life-cycle model and express all sequencing constraints in the operation model using appropriate preconditions. The other extreme would be to put a lot of effort into the life-cycle model and simplify the operation model by reducing the operation preconditions. In practice, the solution lies in between, but we were embarrassed by our inability to define it more precisely. It seems that the life-cycle model can always be enriched, but will become more and more unreadable, while the operation model will only be slightly simpler. We know that there is a difficult trade-off to be made, but we lack practical guidelines for evaluating it.

Moreover, there is the risk of redundancy between the pre- and postconditions of the operation model and the life-cycle model because both can be used to express the same behavior. With respect to the notion of internal state information that was introduced in the previous subsection, we see that expressing sequencing constraints in the operation model requires this information to be *explicitly* defined in the system object model. On the other hand, the life-cycle model can be used to express the same sequencing constraints without keeping any explicit state information in the system object model. In other words, the life-cycle model introduces *implicit* internal state information. For the same system behavior, a very detailed life-cycle model will therefore cause information to disappear from the system object model, while a very basic life-cycle model will require additional information to be included in it.

11.4.4 Common Mistakes and Difficulties Encountered by Students

Textbooks usually include typical examples and illustrations of common situations, and the Fusion book complies with this practice. However, it is also of interest to show examples of common mistakes because people often learn more from errors than from correct examples.

We suppose that many beginners experience similar problems and therefore we would like to cite a few difficulties that were common among our students. Contrary to what is detailed in the remaining part of this paper, the following problems are not primarily related to specific technical aspects of the method. Instead, they represent a catalog of typical difficulties and areas of confusion that, in our experience, commonly show up during the learning process:

- For many students, it was not clear from the beginning that the system object model is persistent. Thinking in terms of implementation, they wanted to add system operations "for saving it on the disk," for example, although such operations clearly cannot be expressed in a schema based on this model itself.
- Similarly, some students wanted to have a first system operation for "loading the software" and a last one for "quitting."
- Object identification issues were often included prematurely; that is, students added artificial attributes with identifiers, numbers, or names even when they were not needed. In other words, they did not assimilate the notion of object identity during analysis.
- For some students, it was not obvious that all communication with the

environment must be done with events and that events cannot be output spontaneously by the system. More specifically, they had trouble understanding that it is always necessary to use event arguments in order to exchange data with the environment.

- They often tended to consider concrete, low-level events like "mouse click" or "single keyboard input" carrying very little information, instead of envisaging more abstract events at a higher level, each event carrying much more information. The consequence was a large number of system operations and a complex life-cycle model.

- More generally, they had difficulty in differentiating between inside (the system) and outside (the environment). Although this distinction is very clearly made in the Fusion method, we noticed again and again that it is a difficult step for beginners. As mentioned, we believe this step is not well supported in current analysis methods, especially with regard to the process of establishing system boundaries.

11.5 IMPROVING THE FUSION ANALYSIS PRACTICE

This section addresses many practical issues for analysts applying the Fusion method. We report on our experiences and provide practical and constructive advice regarding specific aspects of the various Fusion analysis models, starting with the object model.

11.5.1 Object Model

Object modeling is the first activity of the analysis process. With Fusion, object modeling is similar to entity–relationship modeling. The emphasis is on modeling the *data structure* of the domain and of the system to be developed.

Students usually liked this part of the project and did not experience major difficulties. Among the ten groups of students, the system object models were largely similar.

In the next three subsections, we discuss minor adaptations to the object model notation that we suggested or that students spontaneously adopted.

Class Multiplicity

It is often beneficial to constrain the total number of object instances belonging to a class. This subsection describes a minor extension that we found useful: multiplicity constraints on classes. The object model notation of Fusion does not allow this unless the class is a component of an aggregation. However, in this latter case, the meaning of the cardinality is to restrict the number of instances within an aggregate object and not within its own class. We feel that both aspects are worth specifying.

Of course, such a constraint can be written as an assertion in the data dictionary; in practice, the students did not retain this solution. Confusing cardinality within an aggregation with global class multiplicity, they expressed both in the object model in a nonsystematic way. Therefore, we suggest a distinct convention for expressing class multiplicity constraints in the object model: the allowed range of class instances can be written as a constraint *within* the class box, as illustrated in Figure 11.5. This notation differs from cardinalities attached to classes in aggregations, which are written on the outside top left of the component class box (Coleman et al. 1994, Section C-2.1 p. 265).

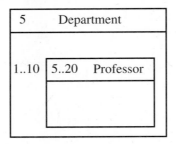

Figure 11.5 Class Multiplicities and Aggregation Cardinality

It must be remembered that a class may have multiple appearances in the same diagram (Coleman et al. 1994, Section C-2.2 p. 268). We suggest that at most one appearance of a given class can have a multiplicity constraint. As with relationship cardinality, but contrary to aggregation cardinality, we propose a default of "*."

In this example, we use class multiplicity to express the fact that there are always 5 different departments, and a total number of professors varying between 5 and 20. Simultaneously, professors are aggregated together within departments into bunches of 1 to 10.

The choice of the word multiplicity instead of cardinality will be explained in the next subsection.

Relationships

We found several confusing aspects in the object model notation for relationships. To illustrate these points, we will use a simple relationship between two classes, as shown in Figure 11.6.

Figure 11.6 Relationship Using Standard Fusion Notation

According to Fusion, this models a situation where:

- There exists a binary relationship **teaches** between a class **Professor** and a class **Course**.
- A professor *may* participate in this relationship and will play the **Teacher** role if he or she does so (because there is no total marker on this role). If a given professor participates, then he or she must teach one to three courses.
- All courses *must* participate in the relationship and will play a role that happens to be called **Course** (because there is a total marker on this role, named after the class). A course is related to exactly one professor by the **teaches** relationship.

Distinction between relationships and tuples

We do not understand why the Fusion convention for naming classes and objects (Coleman et al. 1994, Section C-1.2, p. 263) was not also adopted for relationships and tuples. We think it is beneficial to keep the same kind of clear distinction between relationship types (or just relationships for short) and relationship instances (tuples) that we have between classes and objects. Therefore, relationship names should start with an uppercase letter and denote the current set of tuples, whereas a name starting with a lowercase letter is used to denote some member of the relationship (i.e., a tuple).

Imposing constraints on relationships: proper use of cardinality constraints and total markers

We challenge the total marker notation and claim that it is unnecessary and confusing. We believe that the familiar notation for *relationship multiplicities* is well suited to imposing constraints on relationships (Bapat 1994). Multiplicity notation combines the notion of optionality (is an object obligated to participate in a relationship) and cardinality (how many other objects are related to a participating object). The classical view is that a relationship is either optional or mandatory, and its cardinality is either one-to-one, one-to-many, or many-to-many. What is important here is that a cardinality constraint cannot interfere with an optionality indication. In other words, a cardinality range cannot have a lower limit of zero.

Unfortunately, Fusion mixes both aspects because its cardinality ranges may be used to specify an optional relationship, while at the same time total markers may require the relationship to be mandatory. Note that this aspect is neither clearly explained nor well illustrated in the book, but was spelled out by one of the authors of the method (Dollin 1994).

According to this understanding, each relationship is optional unless a total marker explicitly says the opposite. Consider again our simple example, using the standard Fusion notation, but this time without total markers (Figure 11.7).

Because there are no total markers, the meaning is that any professor may teach 0, 1, 2, or 3 courses and that a given course is taught by at most one professor, but perhaps by none.

Figure 11.7 Optional Relationship

Exactly the same meaning is conveyed by Figure 11.8, although other cardinality ranges are given here.

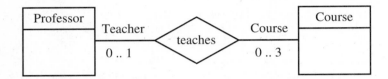

Figure 11.8 Another Notation for the Relationship in Figure 11.7

We consider it disturbing and confusing to have two different cardinality notations for the same meaning. Furthermore, the notation is different from the usual convention of entity-relationship diagrams, without clear benefits.

With the Fusion convention, it seems that cardinality ranges of binary relationships should always have a lower bound of one or greater, a mandatory relationship being specified separately by means of total markers, as shown in Figure 11.9.

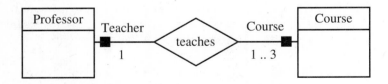

Figure 11.9 Mandatory Relationship

This diagram expresses the fact that any course is taught by exactly one professor (due to the total marker on the **Course** role) and that any professor teaches at least one course (since there is a total marker on the **Teacher** role). Unfortunately, we must also note that information regarding multiplicity is not only divided into optionality and cardinality but also dispersed between two opposite locations: for a given relationship direction (**teaches** or is **taught by**), the total marker is drawn on one end while the related cardinality range is written on the other end. Moreover, these two pieces of information can contradict each other, as illustrated by Figure 11.10.

Figure 11.10 Inconsistent Relationship

Figure 11. 10 is inconsistent because both total markers are contradicted by the lower boundary of their related cardinality ranges. What is the meaning of a teaching relationship where all professors *must* participate in teaching, even if they teach *zero* courses? There is therefore some harmful redundancy between cardinality ranges and total markers.

The solution is straightforward: suppress total markers, and consider a single constraint that expresses not only cardinality but multiplicity (i.e., cardinality *and* optionality), as is common in many entity-relationship approaches. By the way, this is what our students did spontaneously, probably owing to training received in their database course.

However, it should be noted that the conjoint use of total markers and cardinalities allows the specification of multiplicities of zero or a given range, which is more expressive than a simple range that can start at zero. It can be answered that nothing prevents us from generalizing multiplicity constraints and allowing multiple ranges or arbitrary expressions using variables. Indeed, it would sometimes be useful to relate multiplicity to, say, an object attribute value.

A formal discussion and a comparison of the relative power of various notations can be found in (Liddle et al. 1993). This paper also deals with n-ary relationships, which were not discussed here.

11.5.2   Interface Model

Once the structure of the system has been established and documented in the system object model, the system behavior is described in the interface model. This description is based on interacting agents in the environment sending and receiving events. The allowable sequence of events is defined in the life-cycle model, while the precise effect of input events is stated in the operation model.

In the following subsections, we discuss some limitations and present several improvements or adaptations that we applied.

Summarizing the Interface

One example shown in the Fusion book uses a helpful way of summarizing the interface by means of a diagram representing the system, the agents, and the input and output events (Coleman et al. 1994, Fig. 2.18, p. 25). The elevator example shown in Figure 11.4 used a similar representation.

We found such a graphical summary to be very valuable and recommended it to our students, even though it does not seem to be formally part of the method. There is no mention of the technique in the notation summary or in the reference manual.

Specifying the Initial State

It is not clear how to impose an initial system state. We can think of an initialization operation or of the use of assertions in the data dictionary.

Defining an initialization operation by means of a schema is probably more appropriate, but this solution leads to two difficulties:

- **Input event**. Formally, an initialization operation must be activated by an input event sent by an agent in the environment, like any other operation. However, this is quite an artificial constraint for the initialization, and it does not make much sense for the system environment.

- **System object model constraints**. If we assume that there is an initialization operation activated by an event, there must be some undefined system state before. Consequently, this undefined system state cannot conform to the constraints expressed in the system object model. Suppose, for example, that the initialization operation creates the initial objects and tuples with specific attribute values. This means that some cardinality constraints expressed in the system object model cannot be satisfied before the operation invocation, since the involved objects and tuples do not exist. This is clearly unsatisfactory.

Therefore, we suggest that a specific schema be used to specify the initial system state. This schema is used to create all objects and tuples and does not include the **Reads**, **Sends**, and **Assumes** clauses. We must admit that it is not a proper schema because it is not activated by an event and no precondition can be expressed in it (the "before" state is totally undefined).

Changing Number of Agents

The global system behavior is expressed in terms of events sent to or received from agents. The Fusion method requires that agents be *statically* defined; they must be listed in the data dictionary together with their related events. The **Sends** clause of operation schemata must indicate agents that could receive events. This becomes very restrictive if the system deals with a dynamically changing set of agents.

In our student project, the system was communicating with a varying number of agents. The particular events that an agent sends or receives depend on the role it is playing, and agents change their role during the play of the game. We could not model this situation in a satisfactory way without introducing variables to designate agents, for example, in operation postconditions.

This was a major modeling problem for our students, and most groups did not come up with a sensible and systematic solution. The best solution we saw was to consider a single modeled agent and add to each event a parameter carrying a source or destination mark. This mark indicates from which underlying real agent the event comes or to which agent the event is sent. Unfortunately, the result is somewhat unnatural since there is only one agent left in the model, although there are clearly many independent agents in the modeled environment.

Using Relationships in Operation Schemata

In Fusion, relationships are not treated as consistently as classes. There are unexplained differences between relationships and classes that we ignored with our students. To describe the approach we took, we use Figure 11.11, which is taken from (Coleman et al. 1994, Fig. 2.8, p. 18). here we use our own convention according to which relationship names start with an uppercase letter and designate the (changing) set of all relationship tuples.

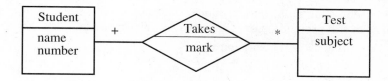

Figure 11.11 Relationship with an Attribute

Named relationship tuples

In Fusion, we can name individual objects, but there is no standardized notation supporting variables for individual tuples because relationships are not considered as types in a typed name definition (Coleman et al. 1994, Section C-1.2, p. 263). Thus **Reads** and **Changes** clauses of schemata do not allow tuples to be introduced (Coleman et al. 1994, Section C-3.2, p. 270).

Similar to class instances, a given tuple should be denoted by a name starting with a lowercase letter. We found it useful to introduce tuple-type expressions, as illustrated in the following definition of variables:

    student : Student *with* student.name = "John"
    test : Test *with* test.subject = "Biology"
    takes : Takes = (Student : student, Test : test)

This declaration of **takes** is inspired by the anonymous use of tuples suggested in Coleman et al. (1994, Section C-4.8, p. 279). Note that this definition does not add a new tuple to the relationship, but just gives a name to an existing tuple. In this context, it can be redundant to mention all the participating objects because cardinality constraints often allow one to identify a given tuple just by giving one participating object instance. Of course, such a definition must be consistent with the current system state in order to be valid, but this is true for any variable definition. In this example, there must exist a student called John in the class **Student**.

We could also envisage defining a named tuple satisfying a condition by means of the **with** operator, as illustrated above. Incidentally, these declarations show the possible confusion between the two overloaded **with** infix operators. First, **with** can be used to provide a local name for an identifier satisfying some condition (Coleman et al. 1994, Section C-3.2, p. 270). Second, **with** can also be used to add a tuple to a relationship (Coleman et al. 1994, Section C-4.8, p. 279). These two uses of **with** are not ambiguous, merely confusing.

Use of relationship attributes

The Fusion book does not suggest a way of reading or modifying the value of a relationship attribute. It is not even mentioned that a system operation could possibly modify such an attribute. The **Reads** and **Changes** clauses of schemata only allow object attributes to be introduced (Coleman et al. 1994, Section C-3.2, p. 270).

We decided to use the notation for object attributes for relationship attributes as well, that is, the dot notation in conjunction with an anonymous tuple, or a name that must be introduced for the concerned tuple. Returning to the example of the previous paragraph, we can write either:

(Student : student, Test : test).mark = B^+

or

takes.mark = B^+

Invariants and Operation Preconditions and Postconditions

We do not follow the authors of the Fusion method when they explicitly include system invariants in both operation preconditions and postconditions (Coleman et al. 1994, Section 3-6.2, p. 57). Actually, the reference part of the Fusion book does not require the inclusion of invariants in **Assumes** and **Result** clauses, but this is done in the example illustrating the process of developing the operation model. It could be considered a pedagogic convention, but we found it to be rather disturbing.

Of course, we agree that system operations must respect any invariants on the system object model. However, we argue that invariants are implicitly part of preconditions and postconditions and need not be explicitly repeated. The justification is that invariants are just constraints that could not be expressed graphically on the system object model, for example, by means of cardinality (Coleman et al. 1994, Section 3-4, p. 41). Therefore, they are written down informally and put in the data dictionary. There is no reason to regard invariants coming from the data dictionary differently from constraints expressed in the system object model. We consider that the whole system object model and the related assertions in the data dictionary together form the implicit invariant of any system operation. We see no reason to explicitly include only a part of it in the **Assumes** and **Result** clauses.

Another related issue concerns items appearing in operation preconditions. According to Coleman et al. (1994, Section C-3.2 p. 270), these items must be mentioned in the **Reads** clause of schemata. Again, it could be argued that any item appearing in an invariant must also be cited in the **Reads** clause because invariants are part of the precondition of any operation—at least implicitly. Since the whole system object model can be considered as an invariant of the system, the conclusion we must draw is therefore that it should then be part of the **Reads** clause, which is clearly nonsense. We prefer to list only those items actually used in the operation postconditions, that is, those items needed by the operation and on which a result depends.

Expressions in Operation Schemata

Fusion provides conventional notations for typical expressions appearing in operation schemata. Nevertheless, we identified several common situations that, we feel, are not properly supported by the method. Hereafter, we present these situations and our suggestions for dealing with them.

Deletion of class instances

While creation of new instances of a class is explicitly considered, deletion of objects is not treated in the operation model and not even considered as a possible effect of system operations (Coleman et al. 1994, Section 2-5.1, p. 26). This is surprising since there is a notation for the deletion of relationship tuples (the **without** infix operator defined in Coleman et al. (1994, Section C-4.8, p. 279). Moreover, we found that it is very common to have to remove an object from the system state, and we do not understand why this is not treated in Fusion.

Of course, it is very easy to define a **delete** operator that can be used to form predicates, and this is what we did. We used it informally, relying on intuition and common understanding for its semantics.

We believe that it would be beneficial to carefully investigate all the consequences of such an operator. Deletion can lead to some difficulties because of the convention that unmarked variable names used in a schema refer to the system state *after* the completion of the operation, that is, once the designated object has been suppressed. Furthermore, deletion can be conditional, and we should be able to specify that the final state either includes an updated object or the absence of this object.

Quantifiers

It is common to have to express sentences such as "There exists ..." or "For all ...," that is, to use existential and universal quantifiers. Again, we standardized a textual notation for them and relied on intuition for their semantics. They proved useful when applied over classes or arbitrary sets of objects as well as over relationships and arbitrary collections of tuples. Again, it would be beneficial to precisely define their meaning and allowed applications.

Local name definition

Fusion provides the following convention for defining a local name for an identifier satisfying some condition:

person : Person *with* person.name = "John"

Such "with-descriptions" can only appear as part of the **Reads** or **Changes** clauses of schemata (Coleman et al. 1994, Section C-3.2, p. 270). We found two problems with such definitions:

- **Needless names:** Suppose that we just want to modify the person name in the above example. We should not define the name **person** in the **Changes** clause because it is only the attribute **person.name** that is modified and not the whole object. What we really need here is to introduce a local name for the attribute in this clause, for example in the following manner:

  person.name : Text *with* person : Person *and old* person.name = "John"

  Note that the prefix **old** is needed if we intend to modify this name in the **Result** clause and want to refer to the person name before the operation invocation. (Unmarked names refer to the final values.)

  By analogy to Coleman et al. (1994), Section C-3.2, p. 270, typing is not necessary for an attribute, and we can use implicit typing for the object **person**. We can envisage rewriting the above sentence in the following way:

  person.name *with old* person.name = "John"

- **Other local names:** Often one needs a local identifier in an **Assumes** or **Result** clause in order to express some condition on an item in a concise way. In many cases, the referred item has already been—indirectly—mentioned in the **Reads** or **Changes** clauses. It may be part of another item— an attribute of an object or tuple, an instance of a class or collection, or a component of an aggregate. For dealing with such cases, we extended the use of "with-descriptions," allowing them to appear in **Assumes** and **Result** clauses in order to define a convenient local name.

Life-cycle Model

The life-cycle model is formed by life-cycle expressions that generalize the scenarios. They can express repetition, alternation, optionality, sequencing, and interleaving.

Familiarity with regular expressions leads to mastering life-cycle expressions without much effort, and this is what most of our students found. Some of them spontaneously added features or applied suggestions that are described hereafter.

Ranges

There is a similarity between short forms for ranges as found in cardinalities and the unary postfix symbols for repetitions (+ and *). The latter symbols can also be considered to mean the ranges $1..\infty$ and $0..\infty$. It is therefore straightforward to extend the life-cycle expression notation in order to be able to specify any range by using the same conventions as for cardinality expressions (Coleman et al. 1994, Section C-2.2, p. 267). We can then express more precise expressions. For example:

$R^{1..2}$ one or two repetitions of R

R^3 exactly three repetitions of R.

Graphical representation

Life-cycle expressions are not very intuitive and readable to the uninitiated. By using diagrams similar to the syntax charts (common for expressing programming language syntax rules), it is possible to give a graphic representation that is sometimes preferred, especially by beginners.

State diagrams

Unlike many other analysis methods, Fusion does not use state machines during analysis. The reasons are that Fusion analysis objects do not exhibit dynamic behavior, that state machines are too close to design, and that they do not fully overcome the state explosion problem (Coleman et al. 1994, Section 8-8.1, p. 208).

While we agree with these arguments, we make the point that they mostly refer to the use of state machines for modeling individual objects. We feel that it is sometimes worth describing the system state—or just a part of it—by using state machine diagrams. Such diagrams represent system events (especially input events) and *abstract* system states. An abstract system state is related to the state of the system object model, but abstracts away from it. Instead of being based on a single definite state of the classes, relationships, and their attributes, an abstract state can be a generalization of the system state (a set of system states) or a more informal notion used to convey some intuitive meaning about a possible system situation.

We used such state diagrams in order to document both the life-cycle model and the operation model. We kept state diagrams partial and informal, and applied them merely to illustrate certain sequences of events leading to specific situations. In some cases, students also used such diagrams merely to illustrate the evolution of a single attribute over the life cycle. Nevertheless, such diagrams helped in acquiring a much clearer overview of the system life cycle, and we suppose that other projects could benefit from them as well.

Named substitution

It is desirable to explicitly differentiate events from named substitutions (local names) in life-cycle expressions. While the examples in the Fusion book do use local names starting with an uppercase letter (as opposed to event names starting with a lowercase letter), this rule does not seem to be imposed by the method. We recommend adopting it or using some other graphical way of distinguishing substitutions from events (name with emphasis, etc.).

Output event sequencing

Life-cycle expressions in the Fusion book use the sequencing operator (dot) between the output events of a given operation (Coleman et al. 1994, Section 3-6.1, p. 51). We believe that this is confusing because system operation postconditions (the **Result** clauses) usually do not specify any order on the output events. The textual ordering of predicates in the **Result** clause does not imply a related time sequence. We suggest using the interleaving operator | | between events that are being output by a given operation when no *explicit* sequence is stated in the schema postcondition.

11.6   IMPROVING THE ANALYSIS PART OF THE FUSION METHOD

This section is targeted at methodologists or experienced users interested in clarifying and improving the Fusion modeling notations. People seeking to adapt the Fusion method and add customized constructs may also find this section of interest. Other Fusion users can easily skip this part since it concentrates on specific issues, some of which are rather minor.

We express our methodological views on some aspects of the Fusion models, and discuss many aspects that we feel are not properly documented. Here, we raise more questions than we provide answers. We also suggest some improvements but do not evaluate them in detail.

In this section, we proceed by following the process of analysis starting with the object model and then continuing with the interface model.

11.6.1   Object Model

The object model of the Fusion method is primarily used to represent a *data structure* by means of entities, attributes, and relationships between entities. Technically, the object model has very little to do with objects because it is *not* based on objects in the usual sense (a grouping of data and operations acting on that data), but on data alone. The object model of Fusion is used to express a *global state* that will be acted on by system operations and is based on an extension to the well-known entity–relationship notation (Chen 1976), essentially including aggregation and generalization.

Even if the Fusion analysis objects were fully fleshed objects with operations, "class model" would be a more appropriate denomination than "object model," because this modeling phase is based on classes (sets of objects) and not on specific object instances. We suppose that nontechnical reasons imposed the "object model" designation: it has already been used in other methods and therefore an alleged object-oriented method must include it.

At this point we must insist that we understand and largely agree with the choice of having an analysis view of objects that is similar to entities in traditional entity–relationship modeling (i.e., without operations). In Fusion, it is a cornerstone of the clear distinction between analysis and design—a distinction that is a very desirable property lacking in many other methods.

11.6.2   Representation of Relationships in the Object Model

It is unfortunate that, although being based on a well-established modeling technique, the object model notation for relationships does not adhere to rigorous foundations, but remains rather vague, even adding confusing notions, as we discussed in the previous section. We return to this point and use the simple relationship example (Figure 11.12) introduced previously.

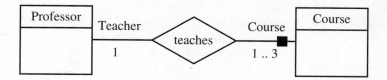

Figure 11.12 Relationship Using Standard Fusion Notation

Apart from the issues raised in the previous section, we question the need for a single relationship name and an additional role name for each connected class, the latter being the same as the class name if omitted. It would be more useful to designate each relationship *direction*, usually by a verb specifying its semantics. Not only would this convention add semantic content to the model, but it would also avoid the rules that relationships are read from left to right and from top to bottom, an artificial and annoying constraint when it comes to modifying and reorganizing diagrams. A binary relationship is bidirectional, each of these two directions being potentially of equal importance. Figure 11.13 illustrates how this could be done.

Figure 11.13 Alternative Notation for Relationships

Unfortunately, this convention only works for binary relationships. We do not deny that higher-arity relationships are sometimes useful, although we seldom found two persons agreeing on the precise interpretation of a given example, especially with regard to cardinality constraints. Perhaps we should challenge the use of higher-arity relationships, as other modeling notations did. This will certainly remain a very controversial issue.

11.6.3 Clarifying the Meaning of Aggregation in the Object Model

We value the fact that aggregations have many purposes in the object model. They can be used to model "part of" and "has a" relationships (with or without underlying physical containment semantics), but also more generally they provide a structuring mechanism.

However, we found several cases—especially involving both aggregation and relationship—where it was not clear whether a given model is legal, and what its conveyed meaning is.

Inclusion of a Relationship in an Aggregation

Is there any difference in meaning between Figures 11.14 and 11.15?

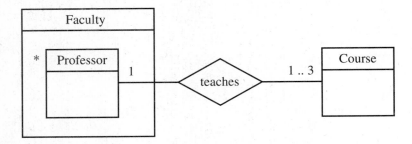

Figure 11.14 Aggregation over a Class

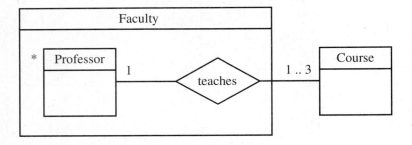

Figure 11.15 Aggregation over a Class and a Relationship

Note that there is no notion of "well-formed" aggregation. This contrasts with the fact that a system object model must be a well-formed object model. In other words, there is more flexibility in delimiting aggregation than in defining the system boundary.

According to Coleman et al. (1994, Section C-2.2, p. 267), a relationship contained in an aggregate class restricts the component objects of each aggregate object. In the above examples, we assume that (1) any professor object can be a component of a faculty object in Figure 11.14, and (2) only those professor objects that participate in the **teaches** relationship can be components of a faculty object in Figure 11.15.

In the above interpretation, we also assume that the meaning of the cardinality of the **teaches** relationship is not modified by the aggregation. In other words, we suppose that cardinality constraints of relationships always relate to the participating classes (set of all objects of the class), and not to the class subsets corresponding to each object of the aggregate class.

Relationship between Aggregate and Components

According to our understanding, it is possible to define a relationship between an aggregate class and its component class, as well as with other classes on the same level. Figure 11.16 illustrates the former situation.

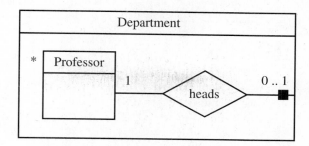

Figure 11.16 Relationship between an Aggregate and Its Component

We could neither find such an example in the Fusion book nor find any reason for not allowing it. However, we do not know the precise meaning conveyed by such a diagram. We can suppose the following: for each department object, there is exactly one professor object that is at the same time a component of the department and a participant in the **heads** relationship. Note that we came to this conclusion merely by reading the relationship constraints (total marker on the department role, cardinality constraint of one on the professor role). As a consequence, it seems that the aggregation cardinality on the **Professor** class could be strengthened and set to **1** instead of *****. Alternatively, it could be the case that aggregation and relationship constraints contradicted each other, a situation analysts should be aware of.

Again, according to the previous section, we can similarly envisage another modeling alternative, shown in Figure 11.17. Here the meaning could be that for each department object there is exactly one professor object that participates in the **heads** relationship. However, it is no longer the case that each department object includes exactly one professor object. The given aggregation cardinality is adequate: there can be professor objects that are not components of a department, or we may find many professor objects aggregated together in a single department object. The one professor object (say John) that is related to a given department (say mathematics) by the **heads** relationship must not be the same as the professor that is enclosed in it as its component object, because the relationship **heads** falls outside the aggregation.

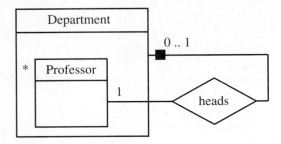

Figure 11.17 Relationship between an Aggregate and its Component

Multiple Appearances of Component Classes

An aggregate does not own its components (Coleman et al. 1994, Section C-2.2, p. 268). According to the model in Figure 11.18, it is therefore possible that the same professor object is a component of many different department objects.

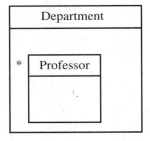

Figure 11.18 Simple Aggregation

Is it also possible that some professors are not components of any depart- ment? We assume that it is not allowed unless the class **Professor** additionally appears elsewhere, outside of the **Department** class, as in Figure 11.19.

However, this latter case is not free from ambiguity because two class boxes appearing on the same diagram with the same name are supposed to denote the same set (Coleman et al. 1994, Section C-2.2, p. 268). Does this mean that there is no semantic discrepancy between the two preceding representations, but only a minor graphical difference? This is the case if we assume that "unattached" professor instances are allowed even if the **Professor** class box happens to be within an aggregation.

11.6.4 Clarifying the Meaning of Subtyping in the Object Model

Subtyping, also called generalization, is used to model the "kind of" or "is a" rela- tionship. There are many possible definitions for such a relationship, and Fusion

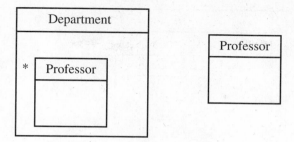

Figure 11.19 Simple Aggregation with Multiple Appearances of a Class

adheres to the subset view of subtyping based on the extensional aspect of a classification.

Among the four possible ways of restricting the subtyping (exhaustive, possibly incomplete, disjoint, and possibly overlapping), Fusion collapses the choices into two (Coleman et al. 1994, Section C-2.2, p. 266): exhaustive *and* disjoint (represented by a solid subtype triangle) or possibly incomplete *and* possibly overlapping (represented by an empty subtype triangle). While these two choices are frequently sufficient, there are also modeling cases for which expressing the other combinations would be valuable.

However, the most problematic aspect of subtyping is found in connection with aggregation. It seems that possible interactions between subtyping and aggregation were not fully anticipated—or at least not perfectly documented.

More specifically, we could not find a precise description of the effect of placing within an aggregation a class participating in a subtyping relation. It does not seem to be forbidden, since we found an example of such a case in the Fusion book (Coleman et al. 1994, Figure 3.4, p. 42). In this figure, the **Store_Building** subclass is part of the **Allocation_List** aggregate class.

What about the reverse case, that is, the placement of a superclass within an aggregation? What would the consequences be for its subclasses? Would it make any difference if the related subclasses were within the aggregation or if they were left outside?

Let us consider in more detail the two cases in Figures 11.20 and 11.21. Is there any difference in meaning between these two examples?

An obvious—but rather unimportant difference—is the fact that it is only possible in the first representation to add some cardinality constraints **C_1** and **C_2** on the subclasses, provided that they are consistent with the cardinality constraint **C** of the superclass and the kind of subtyping used (partition or possibly overlapping).

In the second representation, a cardinality constraint **C** can only be given to the superclass **Super**. Since the subtypes partition the superclass (filled triangle), the superclass **Super** is abstract and therefore has no direct instances (Coleman et al. 1994, Section C-2.2, p. 266). What is the meaning of the cardinality constraint **C** on such an abstract class? It can only apply to subclass instances that

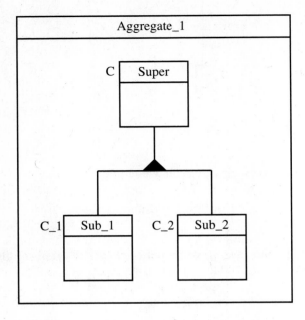

Figure 11.20 Subclasses within the Aggregate

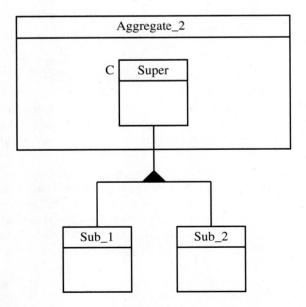

Figure 11.21 Subclasses outside the Aggregate

are outside the aggregation.

Apart from this minor consideration, we could not find a satisfactory inter-pretation for selecting one or the other modeling approach.

On the other hand, it seems clear that an aggregate class can itself be spe-cialized into different subclasses. Again, the same figure in the Fusion book shows an example in which the aggregate class **Allocation_List** is a superclass (Coleman et al. 1994, Figure 3.4, p. 42). The next figure illustrates the opposite case, in which the aggregate class **Status_Report** is a subclass, therefore adding its components to the inherited attributes (Coleman et al. 1994, Figure 3.5, p. 43).

The reference part of the book does not describe such cases. In both the object model syntax and semantics parts, only classes and relationships are explicitly mentioned as possible components of an aggregate.

We believe that such issues should be more thoroughly investigated and documented, especially with regard to their resulting semantics.

Finally, neither the notation summary nor the reference part of the Fusion book mention the convention of having a default cardinality of **1** for aggregation (mentioned in Coleman et al. 1994, Section 2-2.3, p. 19).

11.6.5 Dealing with Types, Classes, and Collections in Operation Schemata

There is much confusion about classification constructs in many current object-oriented analysis approaches, especially with regard to the two following notions (Eckert 1994):

- The **intensional** aspect of a classification (*intent* or *intension*), that is, the description of classification characteristics.
- The **extensional** aspect of a classification (*extent* or *extension*), that is, the finite set of objects that feature such characteristics.

Fusion avoids much confusion by clearly stating that the analysis view of a class is a (varying) set of similar objects. In other words, the method adopts an extensional view of the class construct, close to its meaning in the database or data modeling areas, but different from the usual programming view. This has important consequences for the definition of aggregation and specialization.

However, there is still some confusion between types and classes. In Fusion, types are primarily used to designate sets of values, not objects. This is important for the attributes of classes and relationships that are not allowed to be objects. However, the notion of typed names is used to refer to both types and classes; a typed variable represents a value of a type or an object of a class.

According to Coleman et al. (1994) Section C-4.5, p. 278—as far as we can decipher it! —a type identifier designates one of the following:

- A class, that is, a defined set of objects (class-based type)
- The powerset of a class, that is, the set of all the class subsets (also consid-

ered a class-based type
- A set of values, with various and partially obscure ways of defining them (nonclass type)

Note that there is some confusion between type identifier and typed variable in the section mentioned (i.e., Coleman et al. 1994, Section C-4.5, p. 278). The general form of a typed variable declaration is

typed variable : type identifier

It means that the declared variable designates a (possibly changing) member of the given type, which is itself basically a set of something. In other words, a type identifier must be a set while a typed variable will be one arbitrary element of that set. If we wish to have variables that designate not only objects but also collections of objects, that is, arbitrary sets of objects, we must define a type identifier which itself designates the set of all possible sets of objects, that is, the powerset of the related class. Unfortunately, this is not described clearly in the section of the reference manual mentioned above.

Nevertheless, we are convinced that it is necessary to offer all these constructs, and even to generalize them, since analysts often deal not only with classes and objects but also with various other sets of values, objects, or even relationship tuples. With respect to the latter point, we observe that classes are allowed to act as types in a declaration and do not understand why relationships cannot act in the same way.

We will return to this point later. For the time being, we mention that the definition of **supplied** items for a schema allows objects and relationships, but not classes or tuples, to be arguments of events (Coleman et al. 1994, Section C-3.2, p. 270), which we consider an unnecessary restriction.

Let us summarize the possible declarations. Suppose that **Any_class** denotes a given class.

Any_class   the set of objects forming the whole class Any_class

We can think of different ways to refer to an object of the class:

object : Any_class   one object of the class Any_class (explicitly typed name)
any_class   one object of the class Any_class (implicitly typed name)

To refer to any set of objects (subset of the set **Any_class**), we can think of various notations:

objects : *col* Any_class   is this the meaning of Coleman et al. 1994, Section C-4.5 p. 278?
objects : *set* of Any_class   avoids the unnecessary use of the word collection
objects : P Any_set   powerset of Any_set

It is perhaps unnecessary to introduce the specific term collection since we can think of collections as being just arbitrary sets unless we maintain a precise distinction between collections and sets. Arguably, it is probably not necessary to introduce specific kinds of collections at analysis time.

We think it important to note that a class name can be used both in an expression (in order to designate the current set of objects) and in a variable declaration as type name (in order to constrain the declared object reference). Both uses are meaningful, but students—and other practitioners as well, we suppose—have problems understanding that.

11.6.6   Using Relationships in Operation Schemata

We have already mentioned that relationships are not treated as consistently as classes in Fusion. In the previous section, we mention unexplained differences between relationships and classes that we ignored with our students. Here we add some comments and suggestions, illustrated by the same simple situation taken from Coleman et al. (1994, Fig. 2.8, p. 18):

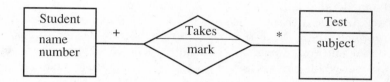

Figure 11.22 Relationship with an Attribute

Again, we use our own convention according to which relationship names start with an uppercase letter and designate the (changing) set of all relationship tuples.

Collections of Tuples

We have already discussed the difference between types, classes, and collections. We believe that we need the same distinction in the context of relationships. In other words, we need to be able to declare a typed variable to designate either an arbitrary relationship tuple or an arbitrary set of tuples (collection). Such an arbitrary set should not be confused with the relationship itself (a defined set of tuples) because it is only a subset of it.

A typical case is to consider all tuples linking a given object in a specific role. For example, consider all tuples including the student John in the following example:

    student : Student with student.name = "John"
    student_take : set of Takes *with* (student, test)

According to the relationship cardinality, **student_take** is a possibly empty set of student-test tuples where all tuples include John in the student role. Note that it would be valuable to introduce the set of all tests taken by John in the above definition.

Expressions Involving Relationships

The conventions suggested for expressions involving relationships are rather unsatisfactory. Basically, only tuple addition and removal (**with** and **without**) and test of object participation (**has-role**) are available (Coleman et al. 1994, Section C-4.8, p. 279). Of course, Fusion does not restrict the kinds of expression used in schemata, but very common situations are not covered by the existing notation. Apart from the already mentioned extensions (tuple expressions, collections, and attributes), it seems that the more frequent need is to traverse relationships, to navigate through their tuples from one participating object to the others. It would be beneficial to have an agreed on notation for such expressions.

Relationship Tuples as Event Parameters

We were confronted with several cases in which relationship information must be sent to or received from the environment. It is not clear how relationships and tuples can be passed as event arguments. According to Coleman et al. 1994, Section C-4.5 and C-4.6, pp. 278–79, Fusion does not support including relationships as event arguments, although Section C-3.2, p. 270 mentions relationships as possible supplied items. Note that according to this reference tuples cannot be supplied but whole relationships (set of all tuples) can, whereas objects can be supplied but not whole classes (set of objects). The reference part of the book just adds to the confusion by defining supplied variables in the same way as objects, which themselves can be *values* of any types (Coleman et al. 1994, Section C-3.2, p. 270)! In our view, this illustrates the fact that relationships were not systematically treated at both the set and instance levels, leading to confusion in the book.

11.6.7   Using Aggregations in Operation Schemata

We have already discussed the use of aggregation in the object model and just recall here that there is no notion of an aggregate owning its components. In the Figure 11.23, the same professor object may be a component of many different department objects.

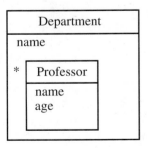

Figure 11.23 Simple Aggregation

Operations on relationships are defined in the Fusion method (Coleman et al. 1994, Section C-4.8, p. 279), but unfortunately operations on aggregates are not. For example, how can we concisely express the fact that a given professor object is a component of a specific department object? How do we move a professor object from one department to another? How can we add the object to another department without removing it elsewhere?

A simple solution consists of the application of the relationship operators **has**, **with**, and **without** for aggregates as well. To say, for example, that a given professor **p** is a component of a given department **d**, we can write

> d : Department
> p : Professor
> d *has*-Professor p

And to move **p** from one department **d1** to another **d2**,

> d1 = *old* d1 *without* p
> d2 = *old* d2 *with* p

Because aggregation is such an important and frequently used modeling construct, we would expect the Fusion method to provide conventions for handling such familiar uses in operation schemata.

To cover this need, we extended the dot notation used for attributes in order to apply it to aggregation as well. For example, we can write **department.professor.age** to refer to the attribute **age** of the object **professor** that is a component of the object **department**. Note that this simple solution overlooks aggregation where the same class appears multiple times in different roles.

Finally, there are also some obscure points related to the convention of the **Reads** and **Changes** clauses in schemata:

- If we mention a department object in a **Reads** clause, does this mean that component objects (professors) can also be read, or is the clause restricted to the explicitly mentioned aggregate without its components? We suppose that all component objects are also readable, but we did not find the precise definition of the effect of such a clause.

- Is it allowed to override the **Reads** clause with a **Changes** clause? For instance, suppose that in the above example we mention a professor object in a **Reads** clause. Would it be valid to mention the attribute **professor.age** in the **Changes** clause of the same schema? Again, we could not find a precise definition but assumed that it is allowed. Indeed, it is often useful because it avoids the need to list all object attributes.

11.6.8   Object Identity

Fusion acknowledges that each object is uniquely identified and that this identity cannot be changed (Coleman et al. 1994, Section 2-2.1, p. 13). However, very few consequences are drawn from this hypothesis, apart from the fact that there is an available operator for comparing identities (Coleman et al. 1994, Section C-4.8, p. 279). For example, it is not clear what happens to the identity of an object sent to the environment as an output event parameter.

In the programming language area, one differentiates objects from object references, the latter being sometimes considered equivalent to pointers or to object identifiers. However, this is very much an implementation view. Identity must remain abstract at analysis time, and it has nothing to do with references or pointers. The system environment cannot handle object identities or references. Arguably, the very notion of an object (in the Fusion sense) is foreign to the environment. Therefore, we cannot suppose that a mere reference is sent, so there must be some kind of object copy made (with a new identity?) and passed as a parameter. What happens if this object is returned later as a supplied parameter of an input event? Would its identity change once inserted in the system state? Would the "same" object then have different identities if supplied later by another input event? It seems that this must be the case, but this would mean that event parameters are not really objects and therefore should not be called such. Perhaps we should restrict event parameters to arbitrary groupings of values, rather than proper objects. Or at least we should precisely define what happens to object identity in such situations. The only mention of this issue we found is terse and unclear (Coleman et al. 1994, Section C-3.2, p. 271).

Returning to the issue of relationships as event arguments, we must also mention that it is not clear what must be known by the environment in order to supply a relationship or a relationship tuple. Since a relationship denotes some subset of the Cartesian product of the classes it relates, it seems necessary to know all related objects in order to supply a relationship. But knowing an object implies knowing its identity, by definition and because two objects can have the same attribute values. Again, it is unclear how the environment could possibly know the identity of objects belonging to the system state.

11.6.9 Syntax Constraints in the Life-cycle Model

We do not fully agree with the restrictions mentioned for life-cycle expressions (Coleman et al. 1994, Section C-3.3, p. 273), or more precisely we do not understand them. We agree that the syntax must enforce the notion that output events are generated by system operations and that a system operation cannot start until the previous one has completed. However, we do not see why the following example should violate these two rules:

PressButton . (#Bleep | ReleaseButton)

We understand the above expression in the following way: either the operation **PressButton** did send the output event **Bleep** and no other system operation is then available, or it did not send **Bleep** and the operation **ReleaseButton** may be activated.

We can think of other cases expressing reasonable life-cycle expressions that seem to violate the above constraints—as far as we understand them:

(PressButton | ReleaseButton) . #Bleep

Is this a valid expression? We interpret it as expressing the fact that either **PressButton** or **ReleaseButton** will be activated and that both would send the output event **Bleep**.

We feel that there is some confusion between the notion of a sequence as

consisting of a system operation name and all the output events immediately following it (as used in the definition of interleaving) and the notion of a sequence
as consisting of any input or output event or combination of them (as used in the
definition of other operators).

11.6.10   Limits of the Method

It would be interesting to establish a catalog of domains and applications for
which the Fusion method is ill suited or does not apply. More specifically, the
description of each model could express its limits, what it cannot be used for, and
report some typical misuses (the "do's" and "don'ts").

11.7   CONCLUSION

Although Fusion is an intrinsically excellent method, through classroom use and
student projects we identified a number of areas that need improvement. In this
paper we have delineated these weaknesses and provided various suggestions
for improving the analysis phase of Fusion.

We acknowledge that the greater the shortcomings in a method, the more
difficult it is to conceive an improvement; the less significant they are, the easier
and the more tempting it becomes to detail a possible fix. We have identified and
proposed solutions to many of these lesser flaws. It is much more difficult to con-
structively address fundamental questions, like the transition from the object
model to the system object model. Moreover, among the unsatisfactory aspects of
the Fusion method that we have discussed at some length here, many are only of
narrow relevance.

We appreciate the Fusion method and realize that many problems that we
discussed in this paper only arose because the method is quite precisely
described. We could not have been so meticulous with many other current analysis approaches, and we respect the precision and established foundations that
the Fusion method brought to object-oriented analysis.

The Fusion book is concise and concentrates on the method, avoiding irrelevant content. However, many of the problems we discussed originate in incomplete and even partially contradictory definitions and explanations. There are
many mistakes in the original edition; we anticipate that they will be corrected
in the next edition and look forward to its improved support for software development.

ACKNOWLEDGMENTS

Many of the problems we identified surfaced during discussions with students
trying to apply the Fusion method or with colleagues trying to teach it. I thank
them all here. This paper especially benefited from the remarks and suggestions

of Dorothea Beringer, Robb Nebbe, and Alfred Strohmeier at the Swiss Federal Institute of Technology and Reed Letsinger, Chris Dollin, and other anonymous referees working with Hewlett–Packard.

REFERENCES

Bapat, S. 1994. *Object-Oriented Networks—Models for Architecture, Operations, and Management*. Englewood Cliffs, NJ: Prentice Hall.

Booch, G. 1983. *Software Engineering with Ada*. Menlo Park, CA: Benjamin/Cummings.

Booch, G. 1994. *Object-Oriented Analysis and Design with Applications*, 2nd ed. Menlo Park, CA: Benjamin/Cummings.

Chen, P. 1976. The Entity-Relationship Model—Toward a Unified View of Data. *ACM Transactions on Database Systems*. 1(1):9–36.

Coad, P. and J. Nicola. 1993. *Object-Oriented Programming*. Englewood Cliffs, NJ: Prentice Hall.

Coad, P. and E. Yourdon. 1991a. *Object-Oriented Analysis*, 2nd ed. Englewood Cliffs, NJ: Prentice Hall.

Coad, P. and E. Yourdon. 1991b. *Object-Oriented Design*. Englewood Cliffs, NJ: Prentice Hall.

Coleman, D., P. Arnold, S. Bodoff, C. Dollin, H. Gilchrist, F. Hayes, and P. Jeremaes. 1994. *Object-Oriented Development—The Fusion Method*. Englewood Cliffs, NJ: Prentice Hall.

Coleman, D., and P. Jeremaes. 1993. *Video Course: Object-Oriented Development—The Fusion Method*. NTU Course MC931005A1.

de Champeaux, D., D. Lea, and P. Faure. 1993. *Object-Oriented System Development*. Reading, MA: Addison-Wesley.

Dillon, Tharam and Poh Lee Tan. 1993. *Object-Oriented Conceptual Modeling*. Englewood Cliffs, NJ: Prentice Hall.

Dollin, C. October 1994. Fusion questions. Messages in the "comp.object" Internet newsgroup.

Eckert, G. 1994. Types, Classes and Collections in Object-Oriented Analysis. In *IEEE International Conference on Requirements Engineering*, Colorado Springs: CO, pp. 32–39.

EVB Software Engineering, editor. 1987. *Object Oriented Development for Ada Software*. EVB Software Engineering, Inc.

Hoydalsvik, G.M. and G. Sindre. 1993. On the Purpose of Object-Oriented Analysis. In *OOPSLA*, pp. 240–255.

Jacobson, I., M. Christerson, P. Jonsson, and G. Övergaard. 1992. *Object-Oriented Software Engineering—A Use Case Driven Approach*. Reading, MA: Addison-Wesley.

Jean, C. and A. Strohmeier. 1990. An Experience in Teaching OOD for Ada Software. *ACM SIGSOFT Software Engineering Notes*, 15(5):44–49.

Liddle, S. W., D. W. Embley, and S. N. Woodfield. 1993. Cardinality Constraints in Semantic Data Models. *Data & Knowledge Engineering*, 11(3):235–270.

Martin, J. and J. J. Odell. 1992. *Object-Oriented Analysis and Design*. Englewood Cliffs, NJ: Prentice Hall.

Rumbaugh, J., M. Blaha, W. Premerlani, F. Eddy, and W. Lorensen. 1991. *Object-Oriented Modeling and Design*. Englewood Cliffs, NJ: Prentice-Hall.

Shlaer, S., and S. J. Mellor. 1988. *Object-Oriented Systems Analysis —Modeling the World in Data*. Englewood Cliffs, NJ: Yourdon Press.

Shlaer, S., and S. J. Mellor. 1992. *Object Lifecycles—Modeling the World in States*. Englewood Cliffs, NJ: Yourdon Press.

Strohmeier, A., and C. Jean. 1990. Conception par objets de logiciels Ada. Département d'informatique—Ecole Polytechnique Fédérale de Lausanne.

Wirfs-Brock, R., B. Wilkerson, and L. Wiener. 1990. *Designing Object-Oriented Software*. Englewood Cliffs, NJ: Prentice Hall.

CHAPTER 12

Extending Fusion: Practical Rigor and Refinement

Desmond D'Souza and Alan Wills

ICON Computing

12.1 INTRODUCTION

What spurred this work... During several years of consulting and training, the authors have applied a number of existing object methodologies to system development, beginning with OMT and Booch. In doing so, we encountered problems in traceability to requirements, semantics for consistency checking, levels of granularity and clear notions of refinement, and distinction between domain models, system models, and architecture (D'Souza 1993, 1994). Most other development methods in use today have similar drawbacks. We evolved and successfully applied an integrated toolkit of techniques for developing object systems, together with development heuristics and a supporting process. The method, called CATALYSIS, began in 1991 as a formalization of OMT, influenced by DisCo (Kurki-Suonio and Jarvinen 1990), VDM (Jones 1986), and Fresco (Wills 1993). Influenced further by second-generation methods like Fusion (Coleman et al. 1994) and Syntropy (Cook and Daniels 1994), CATALYSIS extends these by combining strengths in analysis and specification with a systematic treatment of refinement and architectural design.

Fusion strengths. Fusion (Coleman et al. 1994) was published in late 1993 and quickly made an impact on the landscape of object-oriented methods. The Fusion authors introduced several features that distinguished the method from others. They recommend that system developers

- Explicitly separate the domain model from system models
- In analysis, describe the behavior expected from the system using the system operation schema as the primary vehicle and a life-cycle model as a secondary vehicle
- In design, describe internal behavior expected between objects, clearly capturing mutual visibility and lifetime decisions
- Use aggregation to visually contain compound relationships
- Use programming by contract as the underlying model for the implementation; this approach results in better understood and documented interfaces at all levels

Fusion suggests a recursive process of designing interactions and object modeling, provides reasonably clear guidelines for checking models informally for consistency, and provides guidelines for the development process, with a discussion of reuse.

Fusion weaknesses. Although the method has many strengths, there are some areas in which we felt Fusion could be improved.

- The domain model itself describes "static" information in the domain. In any description there is actually a continuum between persistent and transient, and the separation depends completely on the interaction granularity being considered.
- The life-cycle model describes permitted sequences of events. However, the sequence expressions are quite limited in the presence of certain common kinds of multiplicities and interleavings and consequently do not help with checking of consistency and completeness.
- The operation schema contains some elements of formal description, but the method does not develop this basis far enough to allow thorough consistency checks.
- The method does not produce state models of any objects, probably because of the very design-like interpretation other methods place on state models, using them to discuss internal interactions between objects. However, there is a lot to be gained from using state-diagram views while *still* remaining focused on the system as a component and interpreting the state diagrams as simplified projections of the otherwise compound state of the system.
- While the models and notations for capturing interactions and visibility are reasonable, the guidelines for good design are inadequate.
- Despite the use of programming-by-contract, the notion of contracts was not utilized effectively in the design activities.
- The notion of aggregation could have been pushed further, starting with an interpretation of the system as an aggregate component. To understand the behavior of this component, we need to build a model for it so that we can express the behavior in terms of that model (operation schema). This would

lead quite naturally to a very recursive process for partitioning and design.

- In complex systems there may be significant transformations between analysis models and design. This is particularly true when striving for highly parameterized, configurable implementation components or when tight performance constraints must be met. However, the method does not permit these, since some of the consistency checks on design require simple mapping back to the analysis models.
- There is no direct support in the method for defining multiple views on a complex system. Most complex components have multiple interfaces, and each interface potentially justifies a different model.
- In design, Fusion does not adequately address issues of system architecture. These include issues such as platform, mapping to databases, local versus remote processing, and the corresponding mapping of the analysis and/or design models to this.

12.1.1 CATALYSIS: Main Features

Distinguishing features of CATALYSIS. In developing CATALYSIS, we have adapted the best-known practical techniques for developing object systems and added a degree of rigor to gain clarity and reduce their ad hoc nature. The distinguishing features of CATALYSIS are as follows:

- *Clear separation of concerns*: we make a clear conceptual separation of descriptions into three layers of *what, who*, and *how*.
- Support for *incremental development* and *mixed description levels*: despite the underlying rigor, we do not mandate a rigid, formal process. Rather, we define the essential relationships between the models produced, and then build a pragmatic process to support some of the realities of development. We also encourage combining formal and informal descriptions at any time.
- Integration of important forms of *abstraction* and *refinement*: specification of collaborative behavior separately from localized behavior, multiple views or "roles," synthesis of such views based on *collaboration/design patterns*, deferral of message protocols, distinction of design types ("components") from model types, support for refinements and implementations beyond the current programming language notion of class, and support for architecture and design patterns in the recursive transformation of models from domain to implementation.
- Use of several proven *descriptive models and visual notations* with strong semantic *consistency and completeness criteria*, based on a fairly small set of core constructs. We provide heuristics for choosing appropriate constructs to depict specific views of a system.
- Potential for systematic *mechanical support and checking of semantics*: due to the underlying rigor, it would be possible for a tool to provide important

support with type checking, consistency checking, and test-case generation.

- Support for both *forward-engineering and reengineering* of systems, thanks to the recursive relationship between models and the clear separation of specification types from design types at any level of the process.
- Distinction between the scope of development efforts for *projects* (an application), *products* (an application over its lifetime), and *product families*. We try to characterize the variability factors across each and use these to define units of reuse and configurability and to drive the system architecture.

Rigor, used properly, is very valuable. In this paper we present an overview of the method, examples of its key constructs, and some of its underlying formalisms.[*] We have found that a rigorous basis is valuable in many situations and is essential to a scalable method. However, despite its rigorous aspects, CATALYSIS does *not* prescribe blind formalisms.

How to read this paper. This paper is organized as follows: Section 12.2 provides a summary of terms and process, core constructs, refinements, and design. Section 12.3 describes application of the concepts to modeling a domain. Section 12.4 onwards extends the concepts to modeling and design of a software system. We suggest reading the summary of terms in Section 12.2, and then returning to it as you read the subsequent sections. Paragraph summaries are presented as bold in-line headers at the start of each paragraph; they provide an overview of each section. We urge you to read any formal expressions as a complement to the informal text that accompanies them as an integral part of the specification.

---

[*] More detailed coverage of the method can be found in several reports that are available from the authors (Catalysis 1995a, 1995b, 1995c).

12.2   CATALYSIS OVERVIEW: TERMS AND PROCESS

12.2.1 Basic Terms and Definitions

Term	Definition
Class	A programming language construct for defining how the state and behavior of a set of *objects* is implemented. A class may implement multiple *types*, and vice versa.
Collaboration	A set of *transactions* with some common purpose and a common level of abstraction or detail, involving objects playing different *roles*; often corresponds to a temporal relation between a set of finer-grained transactions that meets the specification of some higher-level transaction.
Component	An *object*, possibly complex, with definite responsibilities assigned to it and which will have an implementation to support one or more interfaces. Not all components will be implemented as instances of classes.
Design	A recursive process of refinement and decomposition of transactions; a distinct level of description that addresses how the required behaviors will be provided by some pattern of lower-level *collaborations* and finer-grained *components*.
Design pattern	A proven design technique, presented with a discussion of its applicability and trade-offs, which suggests a transformation from a specification to the next level of design or from one design to another.
Design type	A *type* introduced to circumscribe some portion of the (next level of) implementation, with an interface of *service transactions*; design types take part in transactions. Members of this type will be identifiable *components* in the implementation.
Model type	A type introduced as part of a specification model, purely to support a specification. Model types do not take part directly in transactions, but they can have *queries*, invariants, etc. Also called *specification type*.
Object	An individual with identity and behavior; a member of some types; an identifiable *component* with an interface; an instance of a *class*.
Query	A hypothetical model of the state of an object used only in pre- and postconditions; often depicted as a diagrammatic link or a typed attribute.
Role	A place for a participant in a *collaboration*; a *view* of an object from the perspective of some other object which collaborates with it. The mapping from design object to role is many-to-many at any point in time and is dynamic.
Snapshot/ Instance diagram	A diagram of an instantiation of a type model at some instant in time, showing the interesting aspects of the objects and the results of their specification queries (depicted as links and attributes).

Specification	A description of guaranteed behavior of some object, together with the conditions under which that behavior is guaranteed; often described with pairs of preconditions and postconditions in terms of a specification model, sometimes with an associated temporal constraint.
Specification model	A set of queries supporting some specification; often depicted as types, attributes, and associations in a set of diagrams.
Specification type	See *model type*.
Transaction—joint and service	A unit of interaction or information exchange between participant objects playing some roles, with a specified effect on those objects. We support both *joint* transactions (multiple participants, described symmetrically with no distinguished receiver) and *service* transactions (attached to a distinguished receiver assigned responsibility for that transaction). Transactions can be refined in several ways. Our transactions do not require the atomicity and serializability properties required of traditional database transactions.
Type	A specification of externally visible behavior of objects (members of that type are all objects that conform to its behavioral specification). A type makes absolutely no statement about implementation.
Use case	A transaction that accomplishes a meaningful objective to an external user of a system; often a *joint* transaction, refined to describe the roles that the different participants play in the *collaboration*.

12.2.2 Development Process Philosophy

No single development process can be suitable to all situations. The development process used on a project depends on several factors, including the project team, the nature of the problem domain, the schedule, familiarity and development maturity, and external constraints. We do not mandate a single development process to be followed under all situations.

We define deliverables and a straw-man process. We focus on clearly defining the different work products, their relationships to each other, heuristic and informal tools to use in constructing these work products, and rules for checking them for consistency and completeness. Within this framework, we define one possible development process and provide guidelines for adapting this process to specific project needs.

12.2.3 Overview of Development Principles and Process

A thumbnail sketch of our development principles. We apply a set of principles across all levels of description. When constructing any *component*, we first broaden our scope to describe its joint behavior with other objects in its environment. We then negotiate the interface between the component and objects in its context and localize the responsibilities of each. At this stage we are defining the scope of responsibilities and services of the component. Separately, we design finer-grained objects and interactions within the component that will implement these services, including specific internal objects appointed to "receive" external requests on behalf of that component.

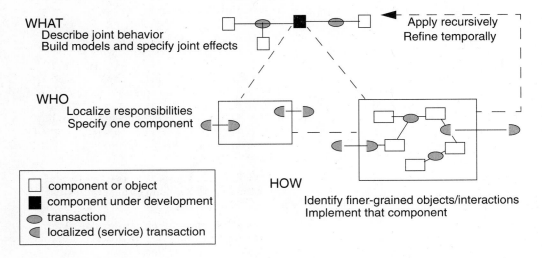

Figure 12.1 Development Process Levels: What, Who, and How

We distinguish three levels: what, who, how. Hence, we are always recursively describing one of the following at a particular level of granularity, and not necessarily in this strict sequence:

- *What*: describe the combined behavior of a group of objects that participate in some joint transaction. To describe any single component, we must first broaden our scope to understand the context in which it operates. Describing joint behavior requires at least a hypothetical model of each participating component. This level of description often represents a particular *design* for some higher-level transaction.
- *Who*: assign and localize responsibilities among the participants in a joint transaction, and design the interactions that will provide the required joint effects. This will eventually define the services provided by each and compose those services in collaborations to implement the joint transaction.
- *How*: identify finer-grained objects that provide the services on behalf of any component, and refine the time-granularity of interactions. The resulting description can be recursively refined into further what, who, and how.

The levels formalize use cases. These three levels formalize the notion of use case (Jacobson et al. 1992). A *use case* describes the joint behavior of a set of objects. It may be refined in terms of the granularity of interactions, as well as in terms of the actual objects providing the required services.

The process covers domain models to implementation. Our overall development process includes the following activities, illustrated in Figure 12.2. There is no strict sequence between the activities, but the deliverables produced have clearly defined and consistent relationships to each other.

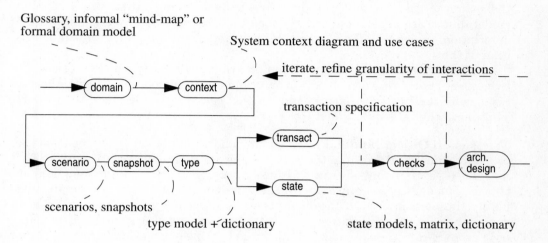

Figure 12.2 Development Process: Major Steps

This process requires us to

- Understand the application environment, including domain terms, concepts, and metaphors. Build a glossary and an informal or formal model of the domain.
- Sketch out the system boundary and scope by building a system context model. This activity is the start of business (re-)design, since it redefines roles and responsibilities, and may involve identifying deeper concepts and new metaphors.
- Build formal models of the system that support the needed interactions and specify required behavior. Refine the granularity of interactions as needed.
- Develop architecture for implementation. Possibly transform the models, and trace and validate the changed models against the original models and specification.

12.3   COLLABORATIONS—"WHAT" AT THE DOMAIN LEVEL

We will illustrate the key points of CATALYSIS with an example of a software system for a vehicle fueling station, with customers purchasing gas, and suppliers refilling the station's storage tanks. For a fuller description of a related problem statement, the user is referred to Coleman et al. (1994).

In this example, we begin by understanding the context within which the software system will be used and by modeling the objects in that domain and their transactions. We will introduce constructs as we use them in the domain model, but these constructs are applicable recursively at any level of system description. In general, the degree of rigor useful at the domain level will be less than at the system level.

The emphasis in this section is on describing what happens, or is required to happen, jointly between objects in this domain. We do not necessarily allocate responsibilities to specific objects and may not even fully understand the responsibilities of the target system at this stage.

The Fusion Object Model. Fusion recommends building an object model of the problem domain to capture the "static" objects and their relationships. The model is essentially an E-R model. It describes the structure of problem domain objects, but does not capture any of the behaviors in the problem domain that justify those structures in the first place. For developers faced with a task of describing a business operation or process, it would probably serve the same purpose as an E-R model. We address this issue by considering collaborative behaviors in the problem domain even before attempting to model it.

12.3.1 Objects and Transactions

Objects interact through transactions. An object-oriented world is described as a network of interacting objects. The interactions are often a combination of essential interactions and "design" decisions, including design at a business or domain level. A transaction is a unit of interaction between objects. Figure 12.3 depicts an occurrence of the sale transaction in our domain. In different occurrences of a transaction, each of its roles—the *slots* for its participants—can be played by different objects. The details of the outcome depend on their states and types. Each transaction is specified in terms of its effects on the participating objects. Conversely, each object can be characterized by the transaction it can participate in.

Abstract transactions may be composed of other transactions. A transaction may encompass a complete dialog of smaller transactions. The common object-oriented programming notion of a *message--response* pair is one special case of a transaction. In Figure 12.4, sale is an abstraction covering some sequence of authorize, dispense, pay. It may well turn out that sale and refill-storage do not occur as messages anywhere in the implemented system, but only as abstractions.

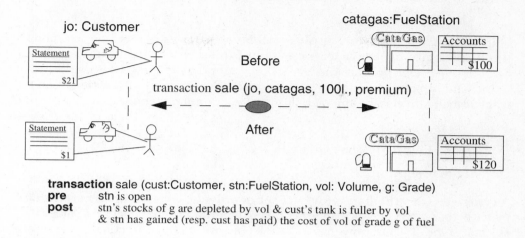

transaction sale (cust:Customer, stn:FuelStation, vol: Volume, g: Grade)
pre   stn is open
post   stn's stocks of g are depleted by vol & cust's tank is fuller by vol
              & stn has gained (resp. cust has paid) the cost of vol of grade g of fuel

Figure 12.3 Transaction Example

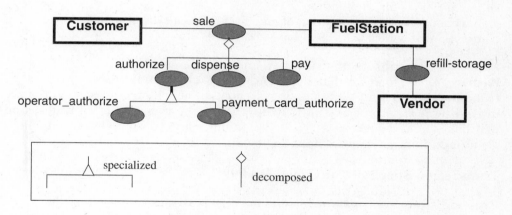

Figure 12.4 Transaction Decomposition and Specialization

Transactions may be specialized. A transaction may also be specialized. A specialization guarantees that all behaviors of the more abstract transaction are also true of the specialization. Specializations of authorize (which switches on the pump motor) include operator_authorize and payment_card_authorize (where the customer inserts a card or cash into a machine beside the pumps).

Objects can be abstract. Just as a transaction may be abstract, so can an object. The word *object* describes any identifiable component, or indeed a whole system, with a definite boundary that will be crossed by transactions in its implementation. An abstract object may be represented by a cooperating group of less abstract objects, without requiring a distinguished element to be the "head."

Objects and transactions apply at all levels. These concepts of objects and transactions are applied to entire systems, to subsystems, and to any components in the design down to the level of programming-language classes. We use a refinement process through which abstract objects and transactions can be transformed into classes and methods of a programming language.

12.3.2 Specifications

Object Specification

A type specifies the behavior of a set of objects. Objects are characterized by their types. A type **T** is a specification of externally visible behavior of a set of objects. Type **T** constrains the possible histories of transactions that these objects—*members* of **T**—can participate in. We write jo:Person to state that object named jo is a member of type Person and conforms to the specification of Person. An object is a member of as many types as it conforms to; but membership of a type is for the lifetime of that object.[*] A type does not make any statements about the implementation of an object. Thus a type is specified by a set of transactions in which the object can participate.

Subtypes are subsets of objects. A subtype is a subset of objects. We write Woman⊆Person to mean that $\forall$ x • x:Woman $\Rightarrow$ x:Person. We draw $\boxed{\text{S}}\!\!-\!\!\triangleright\!\!-\!\!\boxed{\text{T}}$ to indicate that S is defined so that it is a subtype of T. If any transaction is specified with the supertype as a participant, then the guarantees of that transaction will hold for any subtype as well. Subtyping makes absolutely no statement about inheritance of implementation.

Transaction Specifications Need Models

Preconditions and postconditions specify transactions. Each transaction is specified with at least one precondition/postcondition pair. The postcondition is a relation between the states of the transaction participants immediately before and after any occurrence of the transaction. The precondition states under what circumstances this postcondition may be relied on.

A rigorous specification needs a model. Figure 12.3 includes an informal specification of the transaction sale. The semiformal style is readable but potentially ambiguous. In general, we encourage complementing informal descriptions with formal specification so that any informal clause may be rendered formal if

---

[*] We use the notions of state-types and roles to describe more dynamic aspects of an object.

required. For this we need a precise vocabulary in which to describe the effects on the participants, called a *specification model*.

Interpreting models as queries. Our approach to modeling differs somewhat from Fusion's approach. Our primary interest is in describing *behavior*. To describe some collaborative behavior, we need to understand the effect of that behavior on the components involved and on subsequent behaviors. We need at least a hypothetical conceptual model of those components in order to do this. These models are sets of typed *queries*, which we can depict visually as types, associations, and attributes. We prefer these models to be based directly on domain concepts. We then specify the behaviors in a rigorous way in terms of this model. Attributes in our specification models do *not* represent stored data or instance variables.

Specification Models

Models are sets of queries. Since transactions are specified in terms of changes to objects' states, we need precise descriptions of the states. An object's state is modeled by a set of hypothetical read-only queries or "attributes." The implication of "modeled" is that the queries need not necessarily be directly implemented in the final design (although they should certainly be computable in any correct design): their only purpose is to help describe how the transactions affect the object's state and hence how transactions interact across time.

Models define precise mutual vocabularies. Nothing in a model is directly callable by any client code. Thus a model does not violate encapsulation. In fact, it helps provide a clear shared understanding of behaviors *without* exposing implementation. Figure 12.5 shows one type model for specifying the transaction sale.

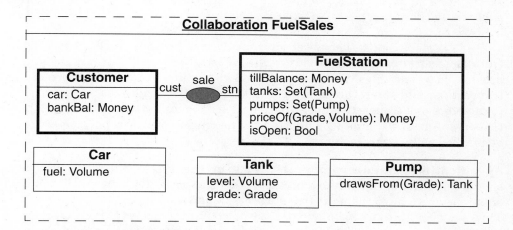

Figure 12.5 Type Model for a Collaboration

We can informally read this model as follows:

We can describe a sale between a customer and a fuelStation if we have a notion of the bank-balance and car of a customer, and the notion of fuel in that car, and notions of the tillBalance in the station, and the priceOf some volume of each grade of fuel at that station, and the tank being drawn from by a pump, ...

Queries can themselves yield interesting types. A type-box such as Customer shows the signatures of queries in its model. It may additionally show the transactions that it takes part in. The results of queries are themselves of other types and may be shown in their own boxes (e.g., Car & Tank).

Formal Transaction Specification

Transaction specs use predicate logic on queries. Using these model queries enables us to specify transactions much more precisely. We usually complement informal explanations with formal precision:

Sale to cust from stn of v units of fuel of grade g.
transaction   sale (cust:Customer, stn:FuelStation, g: Grade, v: Volume)
pre   The results apply only if the FuelStation is open for business.
            stn.isOpen
post
        If a refers to the FuelStation's current price for volume v of grade g,
                $\exists$ a:Money $\cdot$ a == stn.priceOf(g,v)
        volume v of grade g has been transferred from a tank to the customer's car
            $\wedge$ stn.tanks[grade==g].level $-$= v $\wedge$ cust.car.fuel += v
        and amount a has been transferred from the customer's pocket to stn's till.
            $\wedge$ stn.tillBalance += a $\wedge$ cust.bankBal $-$= a

Postconditions relate before and after states. The $\overline{\text{bars}}$ in a postcondition refer to the results of the queries in the objects' prior states. The postcondition is effectively a test that must be met by the designer; it does not imply any order of execution. The == signs are equality constraints, not assignments. x+=y is an abbreviation for x == x + y (so stn.tillBalance == stn.tillBalance + a), and ! is an abbreviation for *not*.

If s is a set, s[p] is the subset (or the only member) for which predicate p is true. Thus stn.tanks[grade==g] is the tank whose grade is g. $\exists$ ($\equiv$ there is some...) declares local variables which may take a single value in any occurrence of the transaction, and their values are constrained by the conditions specified. The parameters of a transaction spec are temporary names for the transaction's participants. Any of them may be affected by the transaction. Any parameters may be marked as **out** parameters.

Specification versus design types. Some of the types in Figure 12.5 are shown in lightly outlined boxes because they are *specification types:* that is, the only reason we have them (at this stage) is to understand the result of a query. Thus the above model only mandates the existence of objects of type FuelStation and Customer. Car and Tank are artifacts used for convenient specification and are not required to actually exist in an implementation. The former two types are *design types:* we know that objects of those types definitely exist because they take part in transactions. In contrast, specification types have no assigned operational responsibilities at this level and no transactions. Their sole purpose is to help understand the specification of some design types.[*]

Multiple pre/post pairs may be combined. We may have several pre/post pairs for one transaction, often in separate parts of a document. This enables different clients to express their individual views of some transaction in terms of a model that is suitable to their view. It allows a subtype to strengthen the specification provided in a supertype and allows multiple supertypes to specify the same transaction (the designer has to create an implementation which satisfies them simultaneously). It also provides an elegant way to describe many *exceptional* situations.

Specialization of transactions (such as authorize in Figure 12.4) uses the same idea. The composition of two specs of the same transaction can be thought of as another spec which guarantees each postcondition under the respective precondition. Below, postcondition R1 is guaranteed if P1 is true; R2 is guaranteed if P2 is true.

$$\frac{\textbf{transaction } \text{trans } \textbf{pre } \text{P1 } \textbf{post } \text{R1} \qquad \textbf{transaction } \text{trans } \textbf{pre } \text{P2 } \textbf{post } \text{R2}}{\textbf{transaction } \text{trans } \textbf{pre } \text{P1} \lor \text{P2 } \textbf{post } (\overline{\text{P1}} \Rightarrow \text{R1}) \land (\overline{\text{P2}} \Rightarrow \text{R2})}$$

Transactions. In Fusion, an operation schema describes the pre-/postconditions of an operation. The method permits more than one schema for each system operation. However, with more than one schema the implied behavior is unclear, especially with the use of an explicit *changes* clause for framing, describing which parts of the model will and will not be modified by a transaction. Fusion examples seem to use an "if-else" structure to describe postconditions, tending to force consideration of many alternate paths at the same time.

We exploit multiple pre/post pairs actively to deal with exceptions and variations in behavior through subtypes. For example, if some of our customers were regular visitors, and they received a free drink each time they purchased fuel, we would simply add another spec for subtype VIPCustomers, implicitly satisfying the original sale:

transaction   sale (cust:VIPCustomer, stn:FuelStation, g: Grade, v: Volume)
post   a free drink has been given by stn to cust ...

---

[*] There is a similar distinction in Syntropy, although Syntropy uses operations in specification types (Cook and Daniels 1994). We have a different semantics for operations on specification types (Catalysis 1995b).

Two Kinds of Transactions

There are two main kinds of transactions. One important feature of a transaction is its locality, that is, which object(s) are responsible for which parts of it. Our method uses two broad kinds of transaction: joint and localized.

Joint transactions specify combined effects. A joint transaction describes an interaction that happens between one or more parties in a symmetric style: it contains no information as to who does what[*]. During the development of a system, this provides a way to state the effects of a collaboration before assigning responsibilities and working out the supporting interactions. Figure 12.5 shows the sale transaction as a symmetric transaction. Note that this transaction, being nonlocalized, would admit an implementation in which the FuelStation sought out unwilling customers and relieved them of some money, as long as it dispensed the appropriate amount of fuel into their cars!

Localized transactions represent services of an object. A localized transaction is provided by one object as a service to others. A separate design decision can localize a joint transaction by assigning responsibilities to objects and defining a corresponding collaboration to achieve the combined effects. Thus we may decide that a customer must request fuel from a FuelStation, or that an Attendant must dispense the fuel. A localized transaction is always qualified with the type of object that executes it (e.g., FuelStation :: sell_fuel).

Both transactions may be refined temporally. In both styles, we may specify a transaction before refining it in terms of finer-grained objects and/or transactions, further separating *what* from *who* from *how*.

Associations

Model queries can be depicted as associations. When the result of a query is itself of a type with its own set of queries, it is convenient to show this query as an association in a diagram. In Figure 12.6, we have shown all queries from Figure 12.5 in this style, yielding a very familiar-looking diagram. In practice, certain queries are best depicted as attributes.

Associations can be navigated by name. The label is written near the *destination* end of the association, as read. We use simple default naming rules for unlabeled associations, using either destination type names or prefixing a ~ to traverse an association in the opposite direction.

($\forall$ cust:Customer· cust.car:Car $\wedge$ cust.car.~car==cust)
$\wedge$ ($\forall$ c:Car · c.~car:Customer $\wedge$ c.~car.car == c)

---

[*] In many situations, being able to elide details of initiator and receiver improves abstraction.

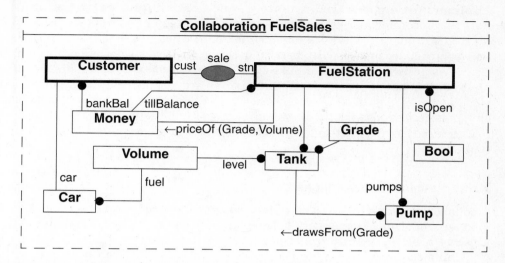

Figure 12.6 Type Model with All Queries Shown Visually as Associations

The semantics are still the same as for model queries. For every cust:Customer object, an object cust.car could be found or created, which is a member of type Car and for which we can identify cust uniquely using an attribute called ~car. Remember that we are defining an abstract vocabulary here: there is no implication that there is a function called car or ~car in any implementation. The same can be said for every member of Car (swapping car and ~car). In this expression, a==b means that the two expressions refer to the same object; that is, their identities are equal or behaviorally indistinguishable.

Queries can return sets and NIL. An association of multiple cardinality ─● implies that the result of the corresponding query is a *flat* set.[*] An optional link ─○ means that the query may have a value of NIL. A query definition may be prefixed with [precondition], which limits the conditions under which that query is defined.

Queries can be parameterized. Even parameterized queries can be shown visually (e.g., FuelStation::priceOf(Grade,Volume) with result type Money). This usage stretches the notation somewhat since the parameter lists are generally different in each direction; hence we annotate the query with an arrow to indicate its direction. Thus a pump draws from several tanks; however, for any specific grade, a pump draws from a single tank.

---

[*] Flat sets are a very convenient variant of sets, which have the useful property that there can only be one level of containment: $\{1,\{2,3\}_F,4\}_F == \{1,2,3,4\}_F$; navigating two multiple connections gives a flat set rather than a set of sets. We also coerce freely between $\{x\}_F$ and x and distribute queries over flat set members: $\{x,y\}_F.q == \{x.q,y.q\}_F$. In a postcondition, if s is a (flat) set, s+=x means s == s∪x.

Implementations are encapsulated; specification queries do not have to be. Specification queries need not be encapsulated: a pre-/postcondition may refer to any query of any type to which it can navigate. In fact, from a specification perspective, it is usually best to describe the logical net effect desired as clearly as possible. One major purpose of encapsulation is to make implementation independent of specification, and queries are not necessarily implemented. However, the length of a specification expression like customer.car.manufacturer.president.spouse.hair_color would suggest that the specification should be restructured. Well-structured specifications will localize queries within model types.

12.3.3 Refining Collaborations

A collaboration is a set of transactions with some common purpose and a common level of abstraction or detail. The transactions in a collaboration may refine those of a more abstract transaction. Consider refining our models to permit pipelining the usage of a pump so that a second customer can begin using the pump before the first customer has completed payment for his fuel. In this refinement we distinguish three steps: enabling the pump (authorize), dispensing the fuel (dispense), and paying the amount due (pay).

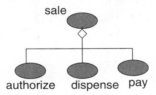

Refining a transaction induces refinement of the model. All transactions of a collaboration use the same models of their participants in their specification so that the effect of each transaction on its successors can be understood. The transactions of the collaboration operate at a finer level of detail than the transactions that they refine, so more detail is needed in the model to be able to understand them; in particular, we need to add some attributes to Pump.

In this case, we refine the model with SaleRecord. As shown in Figure 12.7, to describe this interaction granularity, our model must also include some notion of a SaleRecord that exists (at least) until a transaction has been paid for. The composition of authorize, dispense, and pay transactions is a refinement of sale. Because the heading states that this collaboration refines the more abstract version, we need not restate the previously defined attributes of Pump nor the other parts of the model.

Pump::isOn represents whether the pump's motor is running. SaleRecords abstract the idea that we want to remember the details of the sales that are happening or have happened. This keeps details of the sale apart from the pump itself, allowing a new sale to start before the previous one is paid for. It also

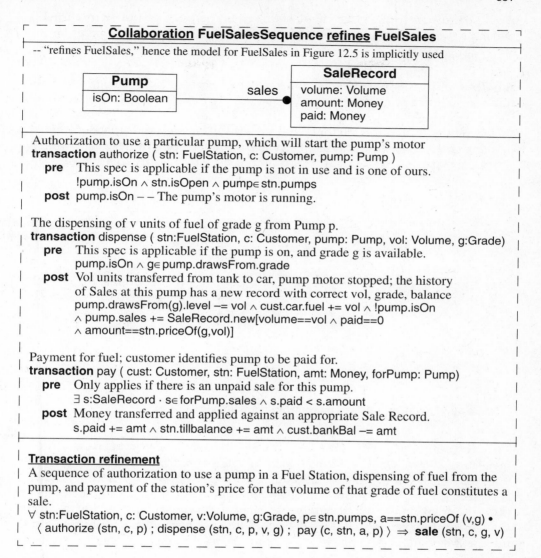

-- "refines FuelSales," hence the model for FuelSales in Figure 12.5 is implicitly used

Collaboration FuelSalesSequence refines FuelSales

Authorization to use a particular pump, which will start the pump's motor
transaction authorize (stn: FuelStation, c: Customer, pump: Pump)
   pre   This spec is applicable if the pump is not in use and is one of ours.
      !pump.isOn ∧ stn.isOpen ∧ pump∈ stn.pumps
   post pump.isOn − − The pump's motor is running.

The dispensing of v units of fuel of grade g from Pump p.
transaction dispense (stn:FuelStation, c: Customer, pump: Pump, vol: Volume, g:Grade)
   pre   This spec is applicable if the pump is on, and grade g is available.
      pump.isOn ∧ g∈ pump.drawsFrom.grade
   post Vol units transferred from tank to car, pump motor stopped; the history
      of Sales at this pump has a new record with correct vol, grade, balance
      pump.drawsFrom(g).level −= vol ∧ cust.car.fuel += vol ∧ !pump.isOn
      ∧ pump.sales += SaleRecord.new[volume==vol ∧ paid==0
      ∧ amount==stn.priceOf(g,vol)]

Payment for fuel; customer identifies pump to be paid for.
transaction pay (cust: Customer, stn: FuelStation, amt: Money, forPump: Pump)
   pre   Only applies if there is an unpaid sale for this pump.
      ∃ s:SaleRecord · s∈ forPump.sales ∧ s.paid < s.amount
   post Money transferred and applied against an appropriate Sale Record.
      s.paid += amt ∧ stn.tillbalance += amt ∧ cust.bankBal −= amt

Transaction refinement
A sequence of authorization to use a pump in a Fuel Station, dispensing of fuel from the
pump, and payment of the station's price for that volume of that grade of fuel constitutes a
sale.
∀ stn:FuelStation, c: Customer, v:Volume, g:Grade, p∈ stn.pumps, a==stn.priceOf (v,g) •
⟨ authorize (stn, c, p) ; dispense (stn, c, p, v, g) ; pay (c, stn, a, p) ⟩ ⇒ **sale** (stn, c, g, v)

Figure 12.7 Transaction Refinement: <authorize ; deliver ; pay > ⇒ sale

leaves an audit trail for historical or reporting purposes.

New objects may exist in postconditions. In the postcondition of dispense,
we use the construction Type.new[predicate], which asserts the existence of an
object that did not exist before the transaction occurred and for which the predicate is true.

A collaboration may refine a transaction. An important part of the collaboration definition is the refinement claim in the bottom section of Figure 12.7, which provides a very strong form of traceability:

⟨ authorize ; dispense ; pay ⟩ ⇒ sale.

A collaboration constrains its transaction sequences. Although this looks like a sequential program, it is really just a temporal constraint.[*] It asserts that if a "compatible" sequence is followed for any (∀) combination of fuel station, customer, pump, fuel grade, volume, and amount of money, and provided that the amount is the appropriate price, then that sequence constitutes what we have previously specified as a sale. It is straightforward to simplify this syntax.

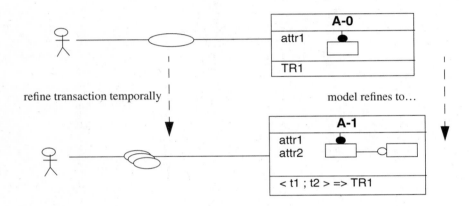

Figure 12.8 Refined Interactions Induce Refined Models

This refinement is traceable and can be checked for correctness. Careful inspection shows that the various parts of sale's specification have been distributed among the three finer transactions, strongly suggesting that the assertion is correct. A completely formal proof would require us to verify a number of other things. For example, we normally use the informal assumption that a correct implementation is one that does not make changes beyond those required to fulfill the relevant postcondition(s), without using framing clauses to explicitly limit which parts of the model may be modified by a transaction. However, in certain critical applications we recommend explicit framing clauses.

Refinement in Fusion. Fusion does not use a strong notion of refinement. An operation schema in Fusion describes the system behavior at a single fixed level of granularity. Although lower levels of granularity are sometimes best deferred, there are times when it is imperative to describe the system at more than one level. However, Fusion does not encourage the analyst to describe such refine-

---

[*] An extension of the Fusion life-cycle expression (Coleman et al. 1994). We express certain temporal constraints using such extended regular expressions.

ments on the grounds that they are implementation dependent.

CATALYSIS treats refinement as an essential part of development. In fact, the temporal refinement described in this example is just one of several useful refinement steps that we support, strengthening traceability. In general, any transaction may be refined in this manner. The model is refined as well, and a sequence expression imposes a temporal constraint on the collaboration.

Fusion uses a more explicit form of "framing." An operation schema has a **changes** clause, which lists those parts of the model that may be modified by the operation. If a schema has its preconditions satisfied, then only the part of the system that will change is identified in its **changes** clause; all others are guaranteed unchanged.

12.3.4 Roles and Collaboration Patterns

Objects play many roles; each collaboration may need a different model.   The participants in the transactions of a collaboration are called its roles. One object may play several roles, in one or more collaborations. Each collaboration in which an object takes part may be described using a different model. These different models represent different views of the object. Each model represents a mutually agreed on conceptual view of transactions by the collaborators.

For example, the FuelStation's dealings with its customers (Figure 12.9) can be described separately from its dealings with suppliers. Moreover, the retailer–supplier collaboration may be expressed in a generic way, independent of the precise kind of item being exchanged. We exploit this by building a separate model to show replenishment of stocks by suppliers (Figure 12.9). The model is *parameterized* by the actual type of the Retailer, Supplier, and Item, and can be reused in a variety of different modeling contexts by instantiation using appropriate types for the parameters.

Transactions and collaborations vary across views. Note that in this view we have introduced two transactions: deliver and stock_depletion. The latter specifies that an order is placed whenever inventories drop below a certain threshold. It appears as a "spontaneous" transaction in this view, even though it is explicitly initiated by a customer in Figure 12.7. The model shown is incomplete, and actually describes a more complex composition of transactions including cancellation and delivery, refining a very high-level transaction for the supply-business itself.

Temporal constraints are complex and do not impose concrete sequences. We now capture more complex sequence constraints, for example, in Figure 12.7. f;g within a sequencing constraint ⟨...⟩ means that f must be *eventually* followed by g; any intervening transactions are not permitted to change the result of g. ||* var:Type · f(var) means any number of interleaved (concurrent) occurrences of f with different values of var. This is used in Figure 12.9 for ||* item∈ materials. <f | g> means that either f or g occurs.

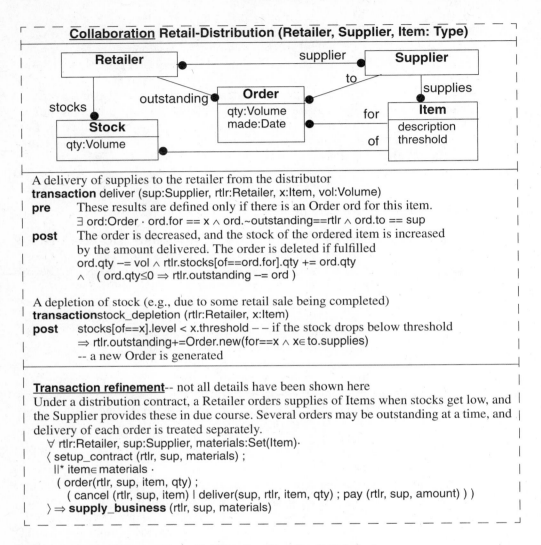

Figure 12.9 A Different View: The Retailer–Supplier Collaboration

We can compose these two views. Of course, we now must describe how these two views of a FuelStation are composed together. We instantiate the type parameterized collaboration by defining Items to be a Grade and Retailer to be a FuelStation. We construct a joint collaboration, with FuelStations playing roles of both supplier and consumer, by composing the resulting model with our original model for a FuelSalesSequence. The result, shown below, can also be depicted visually as a composition of two views. The □ depicted is an *invariant*, that is, a condition that should never be violated.

Collaboration FuelRetail

Instantiate the parameterized distribution model, and compose with retail model
refines FuelSalesSequence
refines Retail-Distribution (FuelStation, FuelSupplier, Grade)
Relate the types and associations of the two models to each other
☐ ∀ fs:FuelStation · fs.stocks == fs.tanks
☐ ∀ t:Tank · t.of == t.grade
A "dispense" transaction (in the retail model) also guarantees a "stock_depletion"
transaction dispense (cust, fstn:FuelStation, g:Grade, v:Volume) ⇒
   transaction stock_depletion (fstn, g)

The two models are combined, subject to stated constraints. This collaboration implicitly has all the definitions of its parents, subject to renamings, like Retailer to FuelStation. We relate the two models, identifying stocks with tanks. The main parts of the resulting joint model (Figure 12.10) could be generated automatically by a tool if necessary.

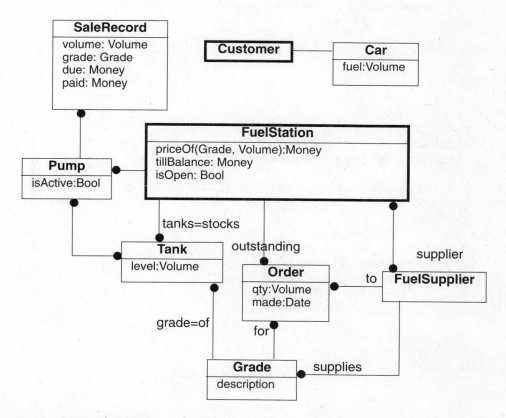

Figure 12.10 Composite View and Model

Transactions in the different roles must interact. We need to specify that the stock_depletion transaction spec is observed whenever a sale occurs, in particular, whenever dispense occurs. This is done by asserting that, in addition to all pre-/postcondition pairs stated in the FuelSalesSequence collaboration, dispense must also observe all those of stock_depletion stated in Retail-Distribution.

This refinement retains all previous guarantees. Notice that none of the previous specifications in the model or transactions is superseded: anyone who has only read the FuelSalesSequence collaboration will still be able to understand those aspects of the FuelStation's behavior it deals with—although it may be necessary to read also the collaborations it refers to. Refinement of collaborations retains previous guarantees.

We combined views and instantiated a parameterized model. Roles   are composed by composing collaborations—whose models describe interrelated types—and relating the types together by further constraints.[*] We have illustrated a composition in which a key step is the instantiation of a type-parameterized collaboration. We might have composed a less powerful variation using unparameterized collaborations, creating within the composition a type that is the common subtype of types selected from the different collaborations.[†]

Multiple views on an object are essential to support *Design Patterns*. A component offers multiple interfaces, each supported by a different model if necessary. This approach is essential to support the integration of *design patterns* (Gamma et al. 1994) into a development method. Using this approach, which is based on objects playing multiple roles, designs are synthesized from known interaction patterns. A significant extension to modeling capabilities, this is also in line with trends in complex components, such as in Microsoft OLE (Microsoft 1993), OpenDoc (1995), and Java (Sun 1995).

Fusion and multiple views. Since CATALYSIS is based on describing collaborative behaviors and using those behaviors to induce supporting models, it is quite natural for us to utilize multiple views of a component. Fusion, like most other existing methodologies, does not support this approach.

Fusion's life-cycle model. Fusion's life-cycle expressions are somewhat limited in the presence of certain common kinds of multiplicities and interleavings. For example, it would be very difficult to describe the fact that multiple cancellation/delivery/payment cycles could be interleaved, although not for the same

---

[*] Loosely speaking, this is the specification equivalent of a framework.

[†] We are developing a richer model of role playing in which many instances of the same type of role can be played by one object (e.g., one person can be an employee of several companies) and in which an object can dynamically change the roles that it plays.

order. The extended life-cycle model of CATALYSIS alleviates many of these limitations.

12.3.5 Specifications, Collaborations, Roles, and Design

A quick review of the constructs we have used so far. The discussion so far has used the domain—the real world outside any computer system—to illustrate the theoretical principles involved, including

- Specification of transactions using pre-/postconditions and a type model
- Use of collaborations (sets of transactions between collaborators with a common model) to capture interactions between members of a set of types
- Refinement of collaborations to a finer level of temporal detail, in which one abstract transaction turns out to be composed of several smaller ones
- Definition of multiple views of a component, each with its own collaborations
- Composition of collaborations to make one type of object play several roles

These principles can be applied inside a software system, as we show in the next several sections. They also apply down to code (see Section 12.5.2).

12.4 SPECIFYING SERVICES—"WHO"

12.4.1 Services

We can effectively localize responsibilities after understanding joint behaviors. When the joint transactions of a component have been identified and specified, we can *localize* them; that is, decide which parts of the precondition and postcondition will be met by the component and which by the other participants. We illustrate this with our fuel station system, but it is equally applicable to any participant in collaborations. In practice, it means refining joint transactions to localized *services*.

Localizing behaviors defines services. A *service* is a transaction for which the responsibility of achieving the required effect has been assigned to one participant (see Figure 12.1), the *receiver* in standard terminology; another participant is the sender; and yet others become involved through services invoked in turn by the implementation in the receiver. Just as with a transaction, a service may be refined to a sequence of transactions.

The name of a service is prefixed with the type of objects that provide it; for example, FuelStationSystem:: selectGrade might represent the selection of a grade of gasoline at a pump. The services a type provides can be listed in its type box. Only design types represent components that provide services. Recall that design types are indicated by dark-bordered boxes. In this case, we have decided that the FuelStationSystem will be a separately implemented component in its domain.

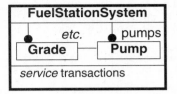

To define a component's services, we need a model of it. It is useful to show the entire model of a component, including associations, inside the model section of the type box to distinguish types representing the real customers from the system's internal model of those objects. This visual containment is also useful in representing certain invariants: navigating links that do not travel outside the type box always lead to the same containing object. Thus a pump at a station can only be associated with a grade of gasoline available at that station.

We distinguish system specification types from their domain counterparts. Notice that at this stage we are specifying the behavior of the component providing the services, and not of any of the objects within its model. For example, although there may be a specification object representing a physical Pump within the system's model, we do not assign the service of recording an event such as the replacement of the pump nozzle (onHook) to that object, but to the system as a whole, with an identification of pump as a parameter. Moreover, as long as the pump parameter in this service remains a specification type, we even defer the means by which the identification of this pump is conveyed. The design of the internal structure of the system and assignment of responsibilities to its components are design steps, although they may be taken early in some situations.

This model is drawn from the domain model. This model represents the view the component needs of its domain concepts in order to adequately specify its services. It is based, as far as possible, on the domain model. In determining the complete list of transactions in which the system takes part, we must take into account all the roles that it plays. In this example, the *software system* that runs the FuelStation has a model that just extends the domain model we have developed so far.

12.4.2 Snapshots

Snapshots depict configurations of objects. A snapshot provides a picture of linked objects at a given instant, with the links all conforming to the associations of a given model. It is a useful tool for discussion, especially to aid understanding of the implications of a transaction spec. Often the best way of formalizing a spec is to draw a two-color before-and-after pair of snapshots (Fig-

ure 12.11), or several superposed snapshots (resembling a filmstrip) illustrating
the evolution of a system's state through a sequence of transactions. The corresponding type model is described in more detail in Figure 12.13.

**Scenarios, with accompanying snapshots, depict sequences of transac-
tion occurrences.** Snapshots accompany interaction diagrams, which illustrate
a particular sequence of transaction occurrences, called a *scenario* (Figure
12.12). Each role in a collaboration is shown as a vertical bar, and transactions
are shown in sequence down the page. Flow of control follows a path vertically
down the page, as each transaction performs its tasks. The initiator of each
transaction is indicated by a darkened oval. It is easy to see how responsibilities
for an overall task are divided between the roles of system and external objects
and to determine whether to shift responsibilities from one to another by shifting
part of a vertical segment sideways. The corresponding snapshots express how
the instance configuration evolves.

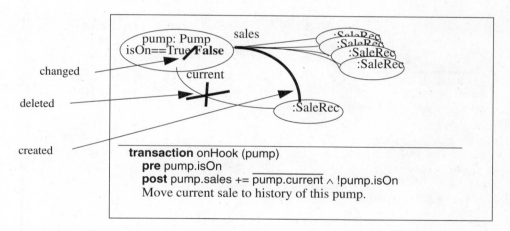

Figure 12.11 Snapshots: A Thinking Tool

All the models can be derived from scenarios and snapshots. As   Figure
12.12 illustrates, the type model abstracts all the snapshots, and each snapshot
is an occurrence of the type model. A transaction specification abstracts all the
pre/post pairs of snapshots for any of its transaction occurrences in any scenario.
A state diagram for any model type is a projection of the snapshot progression
onto a single model type. Each state constrains some portion of the snapshots,
and the transitions correspond to transaction occurrences.

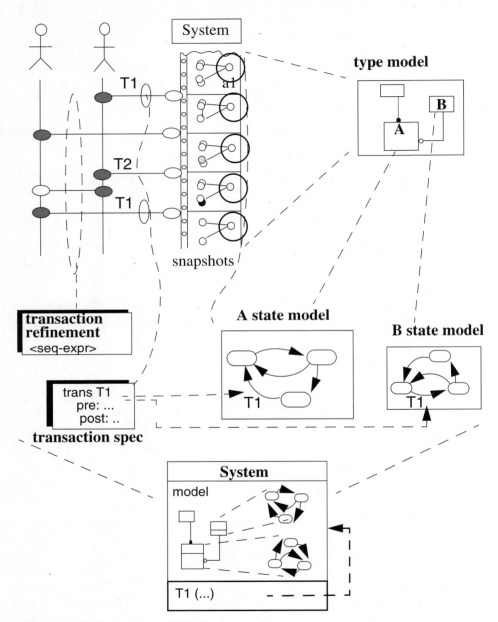

Figure 12.12 Scenarios and Models

Snapshots also help in understanding model consistency. The   snapshots
provide a vivid filmstrip metaphor for clear consistency rules between the models (D'Souza 1993), depicting configurations of model objects before and after

transaction occurrences.[*] Thus, at any level of refinement, we can check that

- The type model admits every snapshot required at the current level of refinement
- The states in the state model must reflect pre-/postconditions on the snapshots
- The states of a model type must be defined in terms of the model queries
- The transitions on a state model are triggered by transactions on the system
- The transaction specification is expressed in terms of the type and state models
- Every part in the type model is created and read by some transaction

CASE tools can readily support snapshots. Some of the available CASE tools for CATALYSIS illustrate a sequence of snapshots as a filmstrip and check the links that you draw against the type model. Of course, snapshots and interaction diagrams only depict a specific trace of interactions at a time and cannot be considered to be complete descriptions. Transaction specifications and state models account for the general cases.

Fusion scenarios, system interface, and models. Fusion utilizes scenarios to define the system interface. CATALYSIS uses a similar approach, except that we can have mixed levels of description. The usage of snapshots as a metaphor to relate all the models is unique to CATALYSIS. Describing the state of a complex component in terms of state models of its model types, without resorting to the design of design internal messaging and intermediate computational states, has also proved very useful in CATALYSIS.

12.4.3 System Model

System models should follow the domain. Specification types (depicted in diagrams with light borders) are used extensively in describing transactions. At the start of the development process, the only "real" objects we know about are the system we propose to develop (or component within a system) and the objects with which it interacts. These are "design objects" at the business level, since they represent specific responsibility allocations made in that context. We will need some queries (specification attributes and associations) to define the transactions. Since queries are hypothetical and defer details of implementation, we prefer to make them relate as closely as possible to the domain. Our initial specification of the behaviors required of a system and the supporting model of the

---

[*] This filmstrip view actually forms a strong basis even for how we teach Fusion and OMT. We have found that our strict interpretation of the snapshots has a very positive effect on the clarity and value of the models produced, because it provides beginners with an intuitive tool for a rigorous approach.

system itself therefore draws strongly on a model of the concepts in the domain; many system specifications may be based on one domain model.

Design models should ideally follow the domain, but will not always do so. In the subsequent design phase, the network of transactions between collaborating objects may remain faithful to the layout of associations in the specification model; this provides for rapid response to domain changes, because the classes in the implementation correspond closely to the types identified in the domain. But where performance or reuse of existing components is important, the model may go through a number of local refinements first, rearranging the model to be closer to a practical implementation, yet still providing the required behavior.

Some development heuristics for system modeling. We have found the following steps useful in generating a specification model of a system, although we will not illustrate all of them in detail in this paper:

- Analyze and model the domain, either informally or formally, to build a well-defined vocabulary and understand relevant domain transactions. (In our example we have created a fairly rigorous model to illustrate the concepts.)
- Write informal scenarios or storyboards of system use, identifying the points at which the outside participants interact with the system. Event charts (or interaction graphs) are often helpful at this stage. Treat the system as a single object, even if it will be eventually designed as a distributed system.
- Next write down the overall responsibilities of the system informally, in terms of the collaborations in which it takes part.
- Describe the identified transactions informally at first and then more formally as you create a system model. The system model should draw on the domain model as far as possible. The transactions are with the system as a whole at this stage, and pre- and postconditions are written in terms of the links and attributes of the model as a whole. You may refine transactions temporally and specialize them.[*]
- Describe what the system needs to know about the world around it in order to behave as required in the system model. It can be derived, beginning with a blank sheet, by adding just those types needed to help describe the system's influence on the objects external to it. (When we need a type, we prefer one chosen from the domain model; in this way, the system model grows as a selection and extension of the domain model.)
- Use snapshots, which depict the effects of a transaction on the model queries and are very useful for understanding and exercising the model

---

[*] These refinements are a formalization of the notion of use case in Jacobson et al. (1992).

through a scenario and to help formalize the transaction specifications.

- Use state charts (only briefly illustrated in this paper, but described well elsewhere, for example in Cook and Daniels 1994) to clarify the states of some model types within a complex component; they will help you understand the states of the complex component.

Inputs and Outputs of the System

Services and their inputs have specified effects on the receiver's model.   When a joint transaction (specified as part of a collaboration, but without a specific receiver) is refined to a sequence of services, it is necessary to specify the effects of each service on its receiver. However, if the receiver is human or outside the scope of our modeling, we may omit it. To specify a system that interacts with human users, it is usual to concentrate only on specifying the services that the system receives—the stimuli from the outside world. Each incoming service transaction has a specified effect on the model of that system.

"Out" parameters might affect the sender's model. We deal with system outputs in several ways. A service may have **out** parameters that define results returned to the sender—implemented in a programming language by output parameters or by return-values with procedure-call semantics.

Outputs can be specified by the desired postcondition on external objects. Services invoked *by* the system can be specified both in terms of an effect on the sender's model (the system model) and on the receiver's model. A state change on the sender records the completion of a task, such as passing information to a user, should that knowledge be significant for subsequent behavior of the sender. For example, a postcondition of a selectGrade request may require that "the operator has been informed of the customer," reflecting a state change in the external object itself.

Outputs can also be specified by requiring output events to be generated.   There might also be a corresponding output invocation, called notifyOperator, invocable by the system upon the operator alarm, which might guarantee the same postcondition, and we might know the system will be wired to the operator's alarm. However, it would normally be left to the designer of selectGrade to choose to satisfy its specified postcondition by using the second operation. In other circumstances, such as in the context of certain "open systems" (Lea and Marlowe 1995), we might prefer to require that specific services be invoked by the system without requiring that specific effects be achieved.

Invariants can relate system model states to states of external objects. The FuelStationSystem's model of a Pump has an isOn status that represents whether the motor is on; transaction specs for the system can refer to it without worrying about making the real motor and the attribute conform; an operation that can be specified with an invariant that crosses the boundary of the system.

GUI presentations can be defined by such invariants. The same applies to user displays of all kinds, which would initially be treated as a separate user-interface domain with its own set of models. We would use invariants to relate them to each other. For example, we might say

$$\forall\ p{:}Pump \bullet p.isOn \Rightarrow p.GUI\_Icon.isHighlighted$$

Implementing such invariants is an issue for architectural design. The protocol and mechanics to control any external objects which are directly reflected in the system model are usually a design step. For example, we might make architectural decisions about the connectors between the system model and the "real" domain objects (e.g., using *model-view- controller* to connect the objects in the system's type model to the user through a graphical user interface) and about the communication of object-ids across this interface by visual or software means.

Refinement of a Joint Transaction to Services

A transaction may be refined to a specific protocol of services. The dispense joint transaction between Customers and FuelStations, which accomplishes transfer of the fuel from an active pump (Figure 12.7), is refined here to a service protocol of select a grade, squeeze the nozzle for some time, and hang up the nozzle. In partitioning responsibilities, we decided that the customer must explicitly select a grade[*] and that a sequence of pulses will be sent to the system by some flow-metering device. We show both originator and receiver for each service using

originator → receiver.service(parameters)

Either one may be omitted if irrelevant, as used below for the meterPulse service. Assertions that should be true at any point in the sequence are shown in brackets.

A temporal constraint specifies this protocol. ∀ stnsys:FuelStationSystem, pump:Pump, grade:Grade, vol:Volume ·
⟨   [pump.isOn]
    cust →stnsys.selectGrade (pump, grade); -- cust selects Grade
        →stnsys.meterPulse (pump)* ; -- measurement pulses sent
    cust →stnsys.onHook (pump) -- cust hangs up
    [!pump.isOn]
⟩   ⇒ **dispense** (stnsys.stn, cust, pump, vol, grade)

We are bridging the gap from domain to system specification. In refining the joint transaction to this service protocol, we refer to several objects from the domain model. These include cust, pump, and grade. In addition, we have now introduced the FuelStationSystem as a "real" object in the domain and relate it to the actual fuel station itself by stnsys.stn. As we will see, some of these domain

---

[*] Once again, this constitutes an external "business design" decision. An intelligent system might choose a grade by recognizing the model of the customer's vehicle.

objects will be reflected in the specification model of the new FuelStationSystem component so that we may describe its services unambiguously.

Refinement induces a more detailed model of the system. As usual, the refined sequence needs a more detailed model, as shown in Figure 12.13.

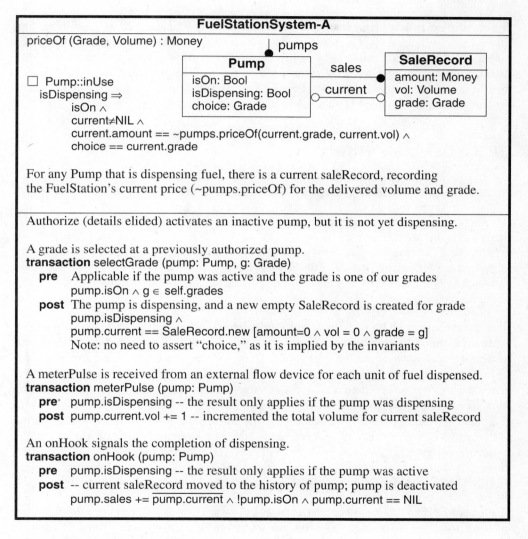

For any Pump that is dispensing fuel, there is a current saleRecord, recording the FuelStation's current price (~pumps.priceOf) for the delivered volume and grade.

Authorize (details elided) activates an inactive pump, but it is not yet dispensing.

A grade is selected at a previously authorized pump.
transaction selectGrade (pump: Pump, g: Grade)
   pre   Applicable if the pump was active and the grade is one of our grades
         pump.isOn $\land$ g $\in$ self.grades
   post The pump is dispensing, and a new empty SaleRecord is created for grade
         pump.isDispensing $\land$
         pump.current == SaleRecord.new [amount=0 $\land$ vol = 0 $\land$ grade = g]
         Note: no need to assert "choice," as it is implied by the invariants

A meterPulse is received from an external flow device for each unit of fuel dispensed.
transaction meterPulse (pump: Pump)
   pre pump.isDispensing -- the result only applies if the pump was dispensing
   post pump.current.vol += 1 -- incremented the total volume for current saleRecord

An onHook signals the completion of dispensing.
transaction onHook (pump: Pump)
   pre pump.isDispensing -- the result only applies if the pump was active
   post -- current saleRecord moved to the history of pump; pump is deactivated
         pump.sales += $\overline{\text{pump.current}}$ $\land$!pump.isOn $\land$ pump.current == NIL

Figure 12.13 Localized Services

Since selectGrade is a separate transaction, whereas previously grade was simply an input parameter to the abstract dispense transaction, we now add the notion of the selected grade to the SaleRecord. In this model, FuelStationSystem::authorize activates the pump, and FuelStationSystem::selectGrade creates the new SaleRecord with an amount due of zero and records the selected grade. To specify the effect of meterPulse, we require SaleRecord to track the volume of fuel based on meter pulses and the amount due based on the selected grade. The model allows us to specify both the current and previous sales on a pump. Some details are elided in the figure.

The refined model has its own invariants. The   model   also   includes   an invariant indicated by □ Pump::inUse. It describes a Boolean condition which must always be true when any pump is in use: it must have a current sale, and the amount due on that sale must reflect the volume pumped and the chosen grade price. In general, invariants may be anchored in this manner to any type in the model. Invariants may remain unnamed.

12.5   DESIGN—"HOW"

12.5.1 Transformations in Design: Reification

Design might rearrange the model. During design we often have to rear-range the information in the model to factor in implementation concerns, for example, distribution, efficiency, and reuse of existing components. Such a step is called a reification, and it may even involve the introduction of entirely new types into the model, in anticipation of patterns of internal collaborations in the design.

We rearrange this model, looking ahead to decoupling pumps from sales. In the design we are envisaging, named FuelStationSystem-B, pumps will not need to know about sale records; they will maintain volume and amount information for the current sale while the pump is active and will have this information transferred to a new SaleB object when the pump becomes inactive. We adapt our model toward this end by adding vol and amount attributes to PumpB.[*] We also decide to keep details of filled but unpaid sales in one queue and completed sales in an archive, and add two new associations for this. The rearranged model, shown in Figure 12.14, is more suitable for distribution between separate processors in pumps and the main station since it only involves the transfer of values from the pump to the new SaleB upon onHook.

We can verify this rearrangement formally. How is this new model trace-able to our previous models? How do we know it is a correct change? Strictly speaking, all the transactions on FuelStationSystem should now be respecified for

---

[*] This makes no difference to the specification itself, as PumpB is still a model type, and not a true component to be implemented. However, we are thinking ahead to an implementation in which Pump will become an encapsulated and implemented design object.

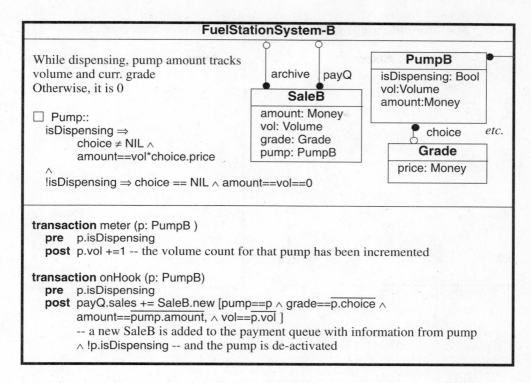

Figure 12.14 A Re-arranged Model, More Suitable for Distribution

FuelStationSystem-B. And (strictly), we should check that the transactions specify at least what they specified in the more abstract vocabulary. Formally, we describe these guarantees by a retrieval or abstraction function. A *retrieval* defines how each query is defined in a design, retrieving the information we expect from it. Since we claim FuelStationSystem-B ⊆ FuelStationSystem-A, we should be able to define the relationship between queries on the two models.

Traceability by Retrieval

We can show that the rearrangement is valid and establish traceability. Since every query on the abstract model FuelStationSystem-A should be traceable from the next design, FuelStationSystem-B, we can define the invariant relationships between their models. We can depict this on a combined diagram to visually depict the retrieval, as shown in Figure 12.15. The double-crossed lines relate the types from the two models and provide traceability between models.

We can combine formal and informal descriptions of traceability. Informal relationships are straightforward. rSale relates a SaleB to a SaleRecord, rPump relates a PumpB to a Pump, rGrade relates the two grades trivially, and

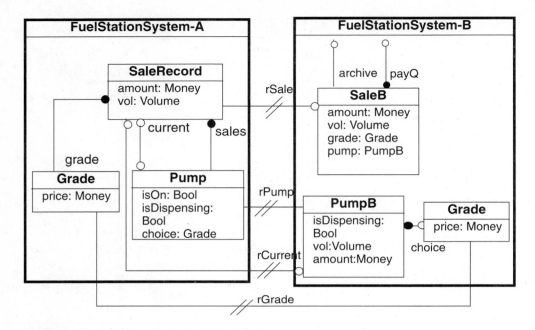

Figure 12.15 Combined Model Showing Traceability (Retrieval) Relations

rCurrent relates a PumpB to a SaleRecord, since a PumpB (with its vol and amount attributes) represents a SaleRecord until the dispensing is completed (hence the "optional" association). These links are formally described below. Note the combination of informal with formal, and start by reading the informal:

PumpB:: -- A PumpB represents both Pump and its current SaleRecord (if any).
-- either there is no ongoing sale, in which case there is no corresponding SaleRecord
        rCurrent==NIL ∧ choice==NIL
-- or PumpB attributes match the current SaleRecord on its corresponding Pump
        ∨ rCurrent.grade==choice ∧ rCurrent.amount==amount ∧ rCurrent.vol==vol
            ∧   rCurrent.~current==rPump

SaleB:: -- SaleB captures a completed SaleRecord in the abstract model
-- the attributes must match up
        rSale.amount==amount ∧ rSale.vol==vol ∧ rSale.grade==grade ∧
-- and the pumps match up, for any completed SaleRecord (~current == NIL)
        rSale.~sales==pump.rPump ∧ rSale.~current== NIL

-- SaleRecord is represented either by SaleB or, if current, by PumpB attributes.
Sale::   ~rSale≠NIL ∨ ~rCurrent≠NIL ∧ current≠NIL

-- A Pump's sales are represented by the current Sale that the PumpB
-- represents, together with all the archive and payQ sales for this
-- FuelStation, which refer to (the PumpB equivalent of) this pump.
Pump::
       sales== { ~rPump.rCurrent } ∪~pumps.payQ[pump==~rpump].rSale
        ∪ ~pumps.archive[pump==~rpump].rSale

This approach supports a variety of architectural choices. This approach
to traceability works even if we choose a very different architecture in design.
For example, we could have decided that the fuel station would itself be built of
three major components, one for managing the pumps themselves, another for
the payment of sales, and a third for archiving historical information. These
three components would have mutual interfaces and models, and the original
specification model could be retrieved from this design as well.

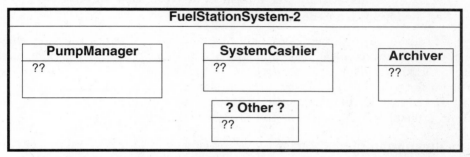

The rigor is available for use when needed. Note that formally establishing
traceability can be cumbersome and impractical without strong support from a
CASE tool. However, like many aspects of CATALYSIS, the rigor is available for
use when appropriate. The informal versions of the formal relationships are both
applicable and very valuable in most situations. In some safety-critical systems,
this degree of formal traceability might be justified.

12.5.2 Stepwise Refinement and Relocalization to Implementation

We have discussed several refinement steps so far... As our running example illustrates, we recommend the following approximate sequence of development steps:

- Build a collaboration model of the domain with more than one view and
  several refinements. Understand the interactions between the "real components" in the business or problem domain. (We used joint transactions and
  did not happen to describe localized services in our example.)
- Identify a tentative system boundary and partition some responsibilities
  between the external actors and this software system. This is actually a
  design step, albeit at the level of domain or business design.
- Build a model of the system that permits description of the service transactions that are being localized to that system. Wherever appropriate, ade-

quately describe the behaviors that the system will provide in terms of this model, rather than designing internal components and their interactions prematurely.

- Bias the model toward anticipated design choices, for example by localizing and partitioning parts of the model. Check that the model is still accurate.

And we can apply them recursively... In the next few sections, we will have gone full circle and will be back to a set of "real components," except that they will now be inside our software system:

- Decompose the type model into internal "real components." Partition the responsibilities between them. If the components are complex, build models of the components so that the interfaces between them can be clearly specified, understood, and negotiated by all developers.

Of course, the pragmatics of a specific development effort will vary widely depending on the true (explicit and hidden) goals of that effort. For example, within the same modeling framework, we would follow a somewhat different progression for well-understood domains versus projects that were truly novel in nature, and we would also approach things differently for projects that were building reusable frameworks as their primary objective.

Even down to implementation... The principles of stepwise refinement and localization can be applied further and the same tools and techniques utilized down to the level of implementation code in an object-oriented programming language.

Localizing before Temporal Refinement

Development could progress along different paths. We will next illustrate briefly how localization of responsibilities and temporal refinement can be freely mixed and matched. In the previous section, we localized behavior only to the level of the FuelStation, but did temporal refinement down to the level of meter pulses. We could decide to stop at a coarser temporal refinement, then directly do the design of some internal components by assigning behavior to them, and then proceed with the temporal refinement.

We could have localized very abstract services, like "dispense." For example, FuelStation must deal with the dispensing of a given volume of a given grade of fuel at a particular pump. Suppose that we had this behavior localized only to the level of the FuelStation and that our model was analogous to FuelStationSystem-A (Figure 12.13), with the addition of a cashLimit on dispensed fuel.[*] We might specify dispense as

---

[*] We have added the detail of a cashLimit on the pumps to illustrate some interesting subsequent design issues. Dispensing cannot exceed the cashLimit for that pump.

transaction FuelStation:: dispense (vol: Volume, g: Grade, pump: Pump)
    pre   pump.isOn   -- pump was authorized
    post   pump.current.amount < cashLimit   (pump) -- sale within cash limit
             ∧ pump.current.amount == vol * g.price -- correct price on the Sale
             ∧ pump.dispensingDone   -- pump changed state

We used a model of Pump with exclusive states isOn and dispensingDone.

Localization within FuelStationSystem

This service could be localized on Pump. We may decide to localize this behavior on the Pump itself, thereby introducing a *design object* for Pump, with specific responsibilities to be implemented within it.

transaction Pump:: dispense (vol: Volume, g: Grade)
This design component Pump will be implemented with real responsibility for "dispense"
    pre   self.isOn
    post   self.current.amount == vol*g.price
            ∧ self.dispensingDone
            ∧ self.amount < ~pumps.cashLimit (self)

Here supporting services have been only partially localized to the pump. We localized isOn, current, and dispensingDone. By localizing behavior to Pump, we have decided that it is now a design type, that is, a component to be implemented as such. It will have a definite implementation boundary (perhaps even as a single instance of a class), and it will control this transaction on behalf of the FuelSystem. Note that SaleRecord is still being used as pure specification type, while Pump will now definitely be implemented to support this interface (or some refinement of it).

And other parts of the design localization have been deferred. However, notice the use of ~pumps.cashLimit(self), instead of self.cashLimit. We may not have decided whether the pump itself will have a notion of its cashLimit, so we merely specify in terms of "the station's notion of the cashLimit for this pump." The cashLimit query is **not** localized. That is, we have not yet decided whether the pump itself will know the cash limit or if will be elsewhere in the system. We might even localize cashLimit to some other object that checks the limit and stops the pump when needed, as we will proceed to do next.

Operations: The Last Transaction Refinement

By applying another refinement... We next decide that dispense itself refines to a sequence of finer-grained operations, conforming to the following life-cycle expression:

Pump:: dispense (v: Volume, g: Grade)
    post   < offHook ; meter*; onHook >
    where v == the count of the number of occurrences of "meter" * some unit volume

And get the sequence <offHook;meter*;onHook> by a different development path. In this refinement, offHook and onHook signal that the delivery nozzle has been removed and replaced, and meter signals the dispensing of some small unit of volume measured by some physical flow-measurement device. Note that we have arrived at a similar internal design by a different refinement path. Both paths are traceable to the specification and back to the domain models.

In certain architectures, transactions that are refined may disappear in the implementation. Whether dispense will now appear explicitly in our code or not depends on our architecture. If we are using co-routines or one process per object, dispense might well be the name of the sub-routine that listens for the events of the dispense life cycle. However, if the transactions translate into function calls, then dispense is not explicitly visible: it is just a mode/protocol used for calling the meter and on-hook functions.

Similarly, specification types may also disappear. In an analogous manner, specification types might also sometimes not be directly represented in an implementation, although we always prefer to retain a direct representation wherever possible. However, design types will always have a clear boundary in the implementation, whether or not it corresponds to a *class*.

And messages, at last! As finer transactions are specified, we eventually arrive at a level that will be directly implemented in a programming language. We change transaction to operation to indicate services that may be invoked by message-sends and that will not undergo any further temporal refinement.

```
operation Pump::offHook (g:Grade)
    pre     isOn                              -- pump had to be authorized
    post    isDispensing ∧ grade == g         -- changed state, and current grade
recorded
```

```
operation Pump::meter
    pre     isDispensing                      -- pump had to be delivering
    post    current.vol += 1 ∧ current.amount == current.vol*grade.price
            -- price and volume updated
            ∧ (current.price > cashLimit (self)) => isDone -- and cashLimit not exceeded
```

```
operation Pump::onHook
    pre     isDispensing
    post    isDone
```

We specify operations down to messages and continue to use specification types. We are using a *model* of Pump with exclusive states isOn, isDispensing, and isDone for the Pump. Each meter pulse increments the volume and price during isDispensing. Note that up to this point we have not implemented these operations, but have simply specified them in terms of localized specification queries. Also, note that we use the notion of current sale record; we have not yet decided whether or not SaleRecord will be a *design* object, implemented with its own responsibilities and services.

Implementing Operations

Objects and operations are finally implemented in an OO language.
Finally, we can actually **implement** our first few behaviors (e.g., Pump::meter).
Note that implementations appear syntactically different from specifications and
that we distinguish imperative assignments to variables from the equality
checks of our specifications. We reify the model type SaleRecord into an actual
implemented class and provide Pump with instance variables for vol, grade, and
sale. Pump will track the current volume and grade, but the amount due will be
tracked within SaleRecord:

```
class Pump {
     data: vol: Volume; grade: Grade; current: SaleRecord;
     services: meter();
}
```

```
Pump::meter () { vol := vol + 1; current.updateAndCheck (vol,grade); }
```

And these operations can also be *specified*. This requires an operation on
SaleRecord, which we may **specify** as

```
SaleRecord :: updateAndCheck (vol: Volume, grade: Grade)
     post amount == vol * grade.price ∧ (price == cashLimit(pump) ⇒ pump.isDone)
```

Until they are all implemented as methods. We might then localize cashLimit
as an attribute on SaleRecord itself, presumably initialized by the FuelStation
when that sale was created for that pump. Eliding details, our decomposed system had at least the two design components shown in Figure 12.16 when we proceed with implementing SaleRecord by implementing its model:

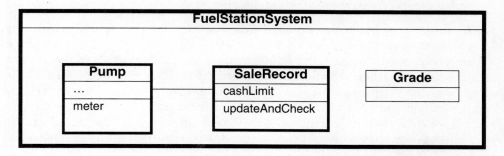

Figure 12.16 Type Model Showing Design Components

```
class SaleRecord {
     data: amount: Money; cashLimit: Money; pump: Pump
     services: updateAndCheck (vol: Volume, grade: Grade);
}
```

```
SaleRecord :: updateAndCheck (vol: Volume, grade: Grade) {
    amount := vol * grade.price;
    if (amount > cashLimit) then pump.stop();
}
```

Note that we have again used the same techniques of refining the interactions, refining the specification model required to describe it adequately, and then assigning responsibilities to new design objects and proceeding recursively.

12.6 ROLE OF REFINEMENT IN DESIGN

Clear refinement steps support traceability. To refine (verb) means to make a design decision, carrying development a step toward an implementation. In theory, separating what, who, and how decisions leads to a step-by-step process of constructing models. Refinement (noun) means the relationship between two descriptions, in which it is claimed that one correctly fulfills the other. A refinement should be documented with some explanation of why the designer believes that this claim is justified and why these decisions were made rather than others. Any development can be thought of as a string of refinements, from tentative specifications at the beginning to solid code at the end.

Actual development is rarely traced to elementary refinement steps. Any refinement can be understood as a sequence of elementary refinement steps falling into a number of different kinds, some of which we will discuss below. In practice, no one ever performs a refinement step by step, but it should nevertheless be possible to understand a refinement in those terms; and it should be clear to designer and reviewers that it *could* be pulled apart into those elementary pieces should any critical uncertainty about it arise.

Refinement can incorporate significant architectural transformations. It is important to appreciate that refinement is often based on the discovery of existing components or patterns of interactions that fit the needs of the application, rather than their creation from scratch. For example, architectural decisions may be a strong force in some refinement steps, as major existing components or patterns of interacting components may be reused. In the next section we illustrate an example of this. The main task, then, is to capture the justification—i.e., to verify that the components discovered, configured, or newly invented perform as required.

In reality, there are several valid and useful refinements. This paper illustrates a few of a repertoire of refinements, which include

- Strengthening a specification
- Transaction decomposition: adding temporal detail to a transaction
- Localization to role: assigning responsibilities to the participants in a transaction
- Signature reification: refining specification types in transaction signatures

- Role composition: one object playing several roles, often based on design patterns
- Object decomposition: implementing an object by a set of objects whose transactions fulfill the original object's assigned responsibilities
- Localization to specification types: using specification types as convenient hangers for services, instead of attaching all behaviors at the system level
- Reification of *connectors*: the mechanisms that will support interactions

And elementary refinement steps will rarely be documented separately.   Of course, real development may use larger steps that are compositions of these refinements, iterative changes to specifications, and so on. Second, separate documents are not produced for every little step, but only for the main ones—initial specification, major design decompositions, specifications of components, and smaller designs.

Design will apply these constructs recursively, addressing several concerns.   Our entire design process is recursive and addresses the following issues:

- Specify and "implement" (by decomposition) recursively: We start with a set of design objects at the business level, with joint behaviors and specification models. We then assign responsibilities, possibly adding new design objects. We decompose some or all of these design objects into component design objects, specify their joint behavior, and then apply the same principles recursively.
- Identify essential dependencies across these design components and then strive to parameterize these components so that the essential dependencies can be realized simply by a specific configuration of the generic components. We arrive at a set of *directed* associations between these design components, representing query connections that must be "remembered" at that level of refinement granularity.
- Design by contract: Each joint or service transaction uses pre- and postconditions and invariants, even at the design and implementation levels. We exploit concepts analogous to polymorphism and late binding for both specification and implementation. We also use multiple views and multiple types per design object.
- Consider design criteria: Responsibilities and interactions are designed based on coupling, cohesion, and reliability. We factor in OO-specific forms of coupling and solutions to them and exploit objects for exception handling.
- Apply design patterns and heuristics: Each step of decomposition might incorporate known interaction patterns as part of the architecture at that level.
- Construct using frameworks: Frameworks define "plug points" for extensibility and provide flexible compositional mechanisms in implementations.
- Make decisions about *technical architecture*: hardware and software plat-

forms, local processing capabilities, communication topology and band-widths, and the mapping of domain objects to this architecture.

The Fusion Design Process. Fusion addresses the design of object visibility carefully in the design process and produces two models: an interaction graph that describes object interactions (including creation) for specific behaviors and a visibility graph that describes the nature of inter-object connections.

Interaction Graphs. CATALYSIS uses a notation similar to the interaction graph, sometimes preferring the time-line version used with scenarios. In CATALYSIS the sequences of interactions can themselves be constrained by extended sequence expressions describing protocols, allowing specific interactions graphs to be automatically checked against this. In addition, we have identified several heuristics for good distribution of responsibilities and clean interaction design, including patterns for flexible and configurable objects. We use pre- and postconditions and mutual models even at this level of work and carry this approach down to implementations in C++ and Smalltalk. These techniques are used quite uniformly in CATALYSIS from domain description to code, varying mainly in the degree of rigor that is practical or recommended at each level.

Visibility Graphs. The Fusion visibility graph captures several aspects of inter-object connections. Due to the nature of refinement and the clear notion of time granularity in CATALYSIS, not all of these are necessary. Where helpful, they can frequently be generated automatically from the refinement relationships themselves.

Persistent versus transient is a matter of granularity. Fusion distinguishes between dynamic and permanent references. However, at the analysis level, Fusion only describes static properties in the system object model, that is, things needed to describe the pre- and postconditions of operations. Since CATALYSIS can describe many levels of refinement, what is a temporary model association (and hence not even shown in the model) at a coarser level of granularity might be a permanent association at a finer level of time granularity, even without decomposing to internal interactions.

Fusion identifies objects that can be referred to by more than one server (shared) and also identifies lifetime dependencies between objects (e.g., delete dependencies). CATALYSIS combines these notions into one. There may be directed associations between the "components" at any level of description, from domain to code. These associations may be annotated with multiplicity symbols and invariants (helping define exclusivity) and with const. Together, these seem to cover common usage of exclusive access and of lifetime dependencies.

12.7 CONCLUSIONS

We have described the principal features of CATALYSIS, an object-oriented analysis and design method that makes significant extensions to methods like OMT and Fusion. The major characteristics of the method are as follows:

- Clear conceptual separation of descriptions into three layers of *what, who,* and *how*
- Support for incremental development and mixed description levels
- Integration of several important forms of abstraction and refinement
- Support for architecture and design pattern transformations in the recursive nature of the process from domain to implementation
- Support for multiple roles per object, enabling support for synthesis based upon design patterns
- Very strong support for traceability based on a variety of refinements
- Suitability for automated tool support and mechanical semantic checks
- Support for both forward-engineering and reengineering of systems
- Use of several proven descriptive models and visual notations with clear semantics
- Customized approaches for the scope of development efforts for projects, products, and product families; we try to characterize the variability factors across each and use these to define units of reuse and configurability

In particular, we illustrate some of these features by carrying an example through the following major steps:

- Build a collaboration model of the domain, with more than one view and several refinements. Understand the interactions among the "real components" in the business or problem domain. Use joint transactions until it is appropriate to localize responsibilities for services.
- Identify a tentative system boundary, and partition responsibilities between the external actors and this software system (actually a design step, albeit at the level of business design).
- Build a model of the system that permits a clear description of the service transactions being localized to that system. Wherever appropriate, specify the behaviors of this system in terms of this model, rather than prematurely design internal components and their interactions.
- Bias the model in the direction of anticipated design choices, for example by localizing and partitioning parts of the model. Check that the model is still accurate.
- Decompose the type model into internal "real components." Partition the responsibilities between them. If the components are complex, build models so that the interfaces between them can be clearly specified and understood.

Several other aspects of CATALYSIS are beyond the scope of this paper. These include heuristics, deliverables, recommended process, transition and training issues, tool support, reengineering systems, characterizing variability, and others (Catalysis 1995a, b, and c, and D'Souza et al. 1996).

Current work includes integrating seamless support for meta-types, adopting a more uniform notion of pattern to describe most aspects of the modeling, richer treatment of role modeling, and exploiting the "rely-guarantee" basis for concurrency.

ACKNOWLEDGMENTS

The authors would like to acknowledge extremely useful comments and insights provided by Doug Lea, Petter Graff, and Vladimir Bacvanski. Thanks also to Derek Coleman for his helpful comments on an earlier version of this paper.

REFERENCES

Booch, G. 1994. *Object-Oriented Analysis and Design with Applications*, 2nd ed. Redwood City, CA: Benjamin/Cummings.

Catalysis. 1995a. CATALYSIS: *The Meta Model*. Report available from authors and at URL: http://www.iconcomp.com/reports

Catalysis. 1995b. CATALYSIS: *A Complete Case Study*. Report available from the authors and at URL: http://www.iconcomp.com/reports

Catalysis. 1995c. CATALYSIS: *Summary of Notation and Process*. Available from the authors and at URL: http://www.iconcomp.com/reports.

Coleman, D., P. Arnold, S. Bodoff, C. Dollin, H. Gilchrist, F. Hayes, and P. Jeremaes. 1994. *Object-Oriented Development the Fusion Method*. Englewood Cliffs, NJ: Prentice Hall.

Cook, S. and J. Daniels. 1994. *Designing Object Systems with Syntropy*. Englewood Cliffs, NJ: Prentice Hall.

D'Souza, D. 1993. A Comparison of OO Methods. *OOPSLA '93 Tutorial Notes*. Available at URL: http://www.iconcomp.com/reports.

D'Souza, D. Sept. 1994. OMT Model Integration. *Report on Object-Oriented Analysis and Design*. Available at URL: http://www.iconcomp.com/reports.

D'Souza, D., A. Wills, and P. Graff. To be published as a text in Spring 1996. *Catalysis: Rigorous Object Development*. Prentice-Hall.

Gamma, E., R. Helm, R. Johnson, and J. Vlissides. 1995. *Design Patterns: Elements of Reusable Object-Oriented Software*. Reading, MA: Addison-Wesley.

Jacobson, I., M. Christerson, P. Jonsson, and G. Övergaard. 1992. *Object-Oriented Software Engineering*. Reading, MA: Addison-Wesley.

Jones, C. B. 1986. *Systematic Software Development Using VDM*. Englewood Cliffs, NJ: Prentice Hall.

Kurki-Suonio R., and H. M. Jarvinen. 1990. Object-Oriented Specification of Reactive Systems. *Proceedings of the International Conference of Software Engineering*.

Lea, D., and J. Marlowe. 1995. PSL: Protocols and Pragmatics for Open Systems. To appear in *Proceedings of European Conference on Object-Oriented Programming*.

Microsoft. 1993. *Object Linking Embedding, Version 2.0*. Microsoft Release Notes and Technical Specs.

OpenDoc. *What Is OpenDoc?* URL: http://www.info.apple.com/dev/du/intro_to_opendoc/iod0_index.html.

Rumbaugh, J., M. Blaha, W. Premerlani, F. Eddy, and W. Lorensen. 1991. *Object-Oriented Modeling and Design*. Englewood Cliffs, NJ: Prentice Hall.

Shlaer, S., and S. Mellor. 1992. *Modeling the World in States*. Englewood Cliffs, NJ: Prentice Hall.

Sun. 1995. *The Java Language Specification*. Sun Microsystems.

Wills, A. 1993. Refinement in Fresco. *Case Studies in OO Refinement*, K. Lano (ed.). Englewood Cliffs, NJ: Prentice Hall.

Fusion Process Summary

The Fusion method is presented in this book as a rational development process (Parnas and Clements 1986). Each notation used has been introduced in turn outlining its logical purpose and its relation to other aspects of analysis, design, and implementation. It must be remembered, however, that the method presented is an "idealized" view. It describes a logical and systematic way of developing object-oriented software. In practice, development does not proceed in such an orderly manner. Individual aspects of the system may be explored and developed before expanding on other parts. Requirements may not be fully known before development beginning. Presenting the development process in a rational manner makes it easier to illustrate the dependencies and relationships between different phases in the development. The reader should realize that actual software development does not mirror such a rational process but that the documentation produced reflects, and in some sense "fakes," the rational process.

In this appendix[*] all of the process steps which have been introduced for analysis, design, and implementation are summarized. Figure A.1 provides a route map for the method and shows the dependencies between the models produced.

---

[*] This appendix is taken directly from Appendix A, Fusion Process Summary, of Coleman et al. 1994.

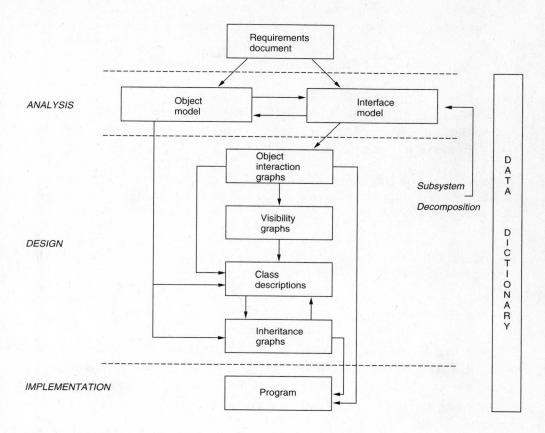

Figure A.1 The Fusion Method

A.1 ANALYSIS

Analysis is about describing *what* a system does rather than *how* it does it. Separating the behavior of a system from the way it is implemented requires viewing the system from the user's perspective rather than that of the machine. Thus analysis is focused on the domain of the problem and is concerned with externally visible behavior. Full details of the analysis process are given in chapter 3 of Coleman et al. 1994.

Step 1: Develop the Object Model
The purpose of the object model is to capture the concepts that exist in the domain of the problem and the relationships between them. It can represent classes, attributes, and relationships between classes.

1. Brainstorm a list of candidate classes and relationships.

2. Enter classes and relationships into data dictionary.
3. Incrementally produce object model looking for

*   Generalizations modeling "kind of" or *is-a* relationships.
*   Aggregations modeling "part of" or *has-a* relationships.
*   Attributes of classes.
*   Cardinalities of relationships.
*   General constraints that should be recorded in the data dictionary.
*   Derived relationships that should be recorded in the data dictionary but that do not appear on the object model.

Step 2: Determine the System Interface

A system cooperates with active agents in its environment. Agents invoke system operations that can change the state of the system and can cause events to be output.

The system interface is the set of system operations to which it can respond and the events that it can output. An entry is required in the data dictionary for every agent, system operation, and output event.

1. Identify agents, system operations, and events.
2. Produce the system object model. The system object model is a refinement of the object model developed in the first step of analysis.

*   Using information from the system interface, identify classes and relationships on the object model that pertain to the state of the system.
*   Document system boundary to produce the system object model.

A useful technique for establishing the interface boundary is to focus on scenarios of usage. For each scenario consider

1. The agents who are involved.
2. What they want the system to do.

Timeline diagrams can be used to represent scenarios. Note that timeline diagrams are a helpful tool for identifying the system boundary, but they only provide a snapshot of system behavior.

Step 3: Develop an Interface Model

The interface model is made up of a life-cycle model and an {operation model.

Life-cycle model

The life-cycle model defines the allowable sequences of interactions in which a system may participate. The life-cycle model is defined in terms of regular expressions that are a means of describing sequence patterns.

1. Generalize scenarios and form named life-cycle expressions.
2. Combine life-cycle expressions to form life-cycle model.

Operation model

The operation model defines the semantics of each system operation in the system interface.

For each system operation

1. Develop the **Assumes** and Results clauses.

    • Describe each aspect of the result as a separate subclause of **Results**.
    • Use the life-cycle model to find the events that have to be output in **Results**.
    • Check that **Results** does not allow unwanted values.
    • Add relevant system object model invariants to **Assumes** and **Results**.
    • Ensure **Assumes** and **Results** are satisfiable.
    • Update data dictionary entries for system operations and events.

2. Extract **Sends**, **Reads**, and **Changes** clauses from the **Results** and **Assumes**.

Step 4: Check the Analysis Models

There are two aspects to checking the analysis models; they should be complete and consistent. A model is complete when it captures all the meaningful abstractions in the domain. Models are consistent when they do not contradict each other. A model can be checked for internal consistency and also for those areas where it overlaps with other models.

Note that the following checks are not exhaustive but provide guidelines for checking the analysis.

1. *Completeness against the requirements*. Reread the requirements document carefully. Check that

    • All possible scenarios are covered by the life cycle.
    • All operations are defined by a schema.
    • All static information is captured by the system object model.
    • Any other information (e.g., technical definitions and invariant constraints) are in the data dictionary.

2. *Simple consistency*. These checks deal with the areas of overlap between the models of analysis. Check that

    • All classes, relationships, and attributes mentioned in the object model appear in the system object model. All other concepts (e.g., predicates) must be defined in the data dictionary or some referenced source.
    • The boundary of the system object model is consistent with the interface model.
    • All the system operations in the life-cycle model have a schema.
    • All identifiers in all models have entries in the data dictionary.

3. *Semantic consistency.* These checks attempt to ensure that the implications of the models are consistent.

- Output of events in life-cycle model and operation model must be consistent. The schema for a system operation must generate the output events that follow it in the life-cycle model.
- The operation model must preserve system object model invariant constraints. If there is an invariant concerning a relationship or class, then any operation that can change them must respect the invariant in its schema.
- Desk check scenarios using the schemas. Choose examples of scenarios and define the state change that each should cause. Then "execute" the scenarios, using the schemas to define the behavior of each system operation. Check that the result is what is expected.

A.2   DESIGN

During design, software structures are introduced to satisfy the abstract definitions produced from analysis. Full details of the design process are given in chapter 4 of Coleman et al. 1994.

Step 1: Object Interaction Graphs
Develop object interaction graphs for each system operation in the operation model. The object interaction graphs show how functionality is distributed across the objects of a system.

1. Identify relevant objects involved in the computation.
2. Establish role of each object in computation.

- Identify controller.
- Identify collaborators.

3. Decide on messages between objects.
4. Record how the identified objects interact on an object interaction graph.

Check the following:

1. *Consistency with analysis models.* Check that each of the classes in the system object model are represented in at least one object interaction graph.
2. *Verification of functional effect.* Check that the functional effect of each object interaction graph satisfies the specification of its system operation given in the operation model.

Step 2: Visibility Graphs

For each class define a visibility graph. These show how the object-oriented system is structured to enable object communication. Visibility graphs are constructed as follows:

1. All the object interaction graphs are inspected. Each message on an object interaction graph implies that a visibility reference is needed from the client class to the server object.
2. Decide on the kind of visibility reference required taking into account:

   - Lifetime of reference.
   - Visibility of target object.
   - Lifetime of target object.
   - Mutability of target object.

3. Draw a visibility graph for each design object class.

   Check the following:

1. *Consistency with analysis models.* For each relation on the system object model check that there is a path of visibility for the corresponding classes on the visibility graphs.
2. *Mutual consistency.* Check that exclusive target objects are not referenced by more than one class and that shared targets are referenced by more than one class.

Step 3: Class Descriptions

Class descriptions are the specifications from which coding begins. They specify the internal state and external interface required by each class.

Extract information from the system object model, object interaction graphs, and visibility graphs to build class descriptions.

Each class description records the following:

1. Methods and parameters from the object interaction graph.
2. Data attributes from the system object model and the data dictionary.
3. Object attributes from the visibility graph for the class.
4. Inheritance information (included after next stage) from the inheritance graph.

   Check the following:

1. *Methods and parameters.* Check that all methods from object interaction graphs are recorded.
2. *Data attributes.* Check that all data attributes from the system object model are recorded.
3. *Object attributes.* Check that all visibility references are recorded.
4. *Inheritance.* Check that all inherited superclasses are recorded.

Step 4: Inheritance Graphs

Here we build the inheritance structures, looking at the classes to identify commonalities and abstractions.

Identify superclasses and subclasses. Construct inheritance graphs. Look for the following:

1. Generalizations and specializations in the object model.
2. Common methods in object interaction graphs and class descriptions.
3. Common visibility in the visibility graphs.

Step 5: Update Class Descriptions

Update the class descriptions with the new inheritance information. Check the following:

1. *System object model*. Check that the subtype relations are preserved.
2. *Object interaction graphs*. Check that all classes are represented in an inheritance graph. A naive assumption is that each class in the object interaction graph is in the inheritance graph. This is generally the case, but we also need to consider that the class structure may be reorganized because of the introduction of new abstract classes.
3. *Visibility graphs*. Check that all classes are represented in an inheritance graph. Abstract classes can be defined for common structure between classes in the visibility graphs.
4. *Class descriptions*. Check that updated class descriptions implement all the functionality of the preliminary ones and respect the inheritance graphs.

A.3   IMPLEMENTATION

The final stage of Fusion is mapping the design into an effective implementation. This transition is relatively straightforward as the majority of complex design decisions have already been made. Full details of the implementation process are given in chapter 5 of Coleman et al. 1994.

Step 1: Coding

System Life Cycle

For life cycles with no interleaving

1. Translate life-cycle regular expression into a (nondeterministic) state machine.
2. Implement the state machine.

   For life cycles with interleaving

1. Implement interleaving-free subexpressions.
2. Link the resulting state machines.

Class descriptions

1. *Specify representation and interface of the classes.*

   - *Attribute declaration.* The attributes of the class descriptions will usually be slots of the named class. Attribute qualifiers are added to specify the *mutability* and *sharing* as appropriate.
   - *Method declaration.* The methods of a class description are implemented by code in the class named (i.e., as member functions, routines, etc.).
   - *Inheritance.* The **isa** clauses of class descriptions name the parents of classes.

2. *Implement method bodies.* Most of the information required for the implementation of method bodies is contained in the object interaction graphs and the data dictionary. The main issues to deal with are *error handling* and *iteration.*

   - *Error handling.* An error is defined as *the violation of a precondition.* Each method promises to achieve its postcondition if it is invoked with its precondition **true**. It is also obliged to invoke any further methods with their preconditions **true**.

   Appropriate code has to be written to manage both *error detection* and *error recovery.*

   - *Iteration.* Code to deal with iterations that arise from invoking methods on collections will have to deal with two cases:
     - A method is invoked on all the objects in a collection.
     - A method is invoked on a subset of the objects in a collection.

Data Dictionary

1. Implement functions, predicates, and types that are both found in the data dictionary and used by methods.
2. Ensure assertions are respected by adding any necessary code to all affected methods.

Step 2: Performance

This is not strictly a step in the implementation process. Remember the following:

1. Performance cannot be obtained as an afterthought. It must be considered throughout the analysis, design, and implementation process.
2. Optimizing rarely executed code is ineffective.

   So,

1. Profile your system in as many ways as you can.
2. Optimize the "hot spots."

Storage Management

Unless the implementation language provides *garbage collection*, you must ensure that when there is no further use for an object, any resources it uses can be reclaimed by the system.

Step 3: Review

1. *Inspections*. A cost-effective technique for the detection of defects in software. Remember that in object-oriented software the static analysis of the flow of control is complicated by the following:

   - Object-oriented languages emphasizing the inheritance relationship rather than the control relationship. There is no direct mapping between functional requirements and high-level functions.
   - The smaller size of data structures, access functions used to implement classes, and classes as a whole.
   - The dispersal of method specifications and implementations among the classes.
   - Dynamic binding making it difficult to determine which code is actually executed for a method invocation.

   Inspections should, in addition to tracing the flow of control, focus on detecting typical flaws in object-oriented systems. Confirm that all subclasses implementing a specific method conform to the method specification.

2. *Testing*. Complementary technique to inspections for exposing defects in software. Test cases for classes should include the following:

   - Checking state observation and manipulation.
   - Applying algebraic properties such as associativity and identity preservation to member function invocation.
   - Checking that destructors in C++ are consistent with the corresponding constructors.
   - Checking proper use of initialization.
   - Checking that casting in C++ is being used in safe ways.
   - Trying to trigger exception-handling capabilities via extreme boundary value inputs.

REFERENCES

Coleman, D., P. Arnold, S. Bodoff, C. Dollin, H. Gilchrist, F. Hayes, and P. Jeremaes. 1994. *Object-Oriented Development: The Fusion Method.* Englewood Cliffs, NJ: Prentice Hall.

Parnas, D. L. and P. C. Clements. February 1986. A Rational Design Process: How and Why to Fake it. *IEEE Transactions in Software Engineering*, 12(2):251–257.

Fusion Notation Summary

Object Model Notation

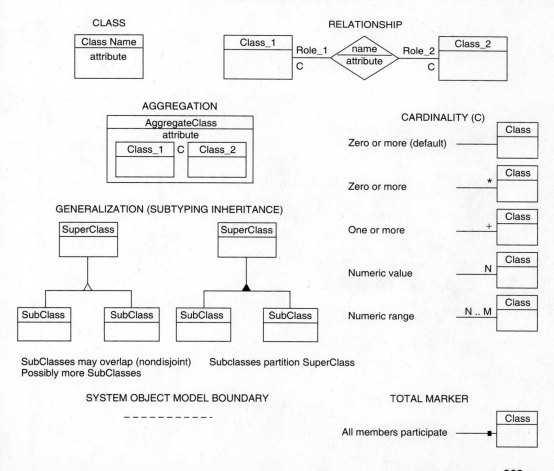

Interface Model Notation

Life-cycle Model

life cycle [Name:] *Regular_Expression*
(*LocalName = Regular_Expression*)*

Regular_Expressions: Name	Any event name (operation), local name, or output event
Concatenation	x,y
Alternation	x │ y
Repetition	
Zero or more	x*
One or more	x+
Optional	[x]
Interleaving	│ │
Grouping	(x)

Operation Model

Operation	*operation identifier*
Description	*<text>Description of operation*
Reads	*<supplied values> <state components>*
Changes	*<supplied values> <state components>*
Sends	*<agent communication>*
Assumes	*<assertions> (preconditions)*
Result	*<assertions> (postconditions)*

Object Interaction Graph Notation

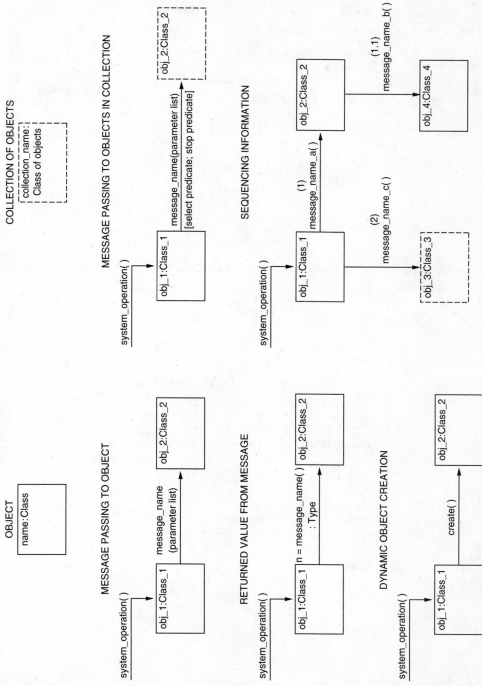

OBJECT

name:Class

COLLECTION OF OBJECTS

collection_name:
Class of objects

MESSAGE PASSING TO OBJECT

system_operation( )

obj_1:Class_1

message_name
(parameter list)

obj_2:Class_2

MESSAGE PASSING TO OBJECTS IN COLLECTION

system_operation( )

obj_1:Class_1

message_name(parameter list)
[select predicate; stop predicate]

obj_2:Class_2

RETURNED VALUE FROM MESSAGE

system_operation( )

obj_1:Class_1

n = message_name( )
: Type

obj_2:Class_2

SEQUENCING INFORMATION

system_operation( )

obj_1:Class_1

(1)
message_name_a( )

obj_2:Class_2

(1.1)
message_name_b( )

obj_4:Class_4

(2)
message_name_c( )

obj_3:Class_3

DYNAMIC OBJECT CREATION

system_operation( )

obj_1:Class_1

create( )

obj_2:Class_2

Visibility Graph Notation

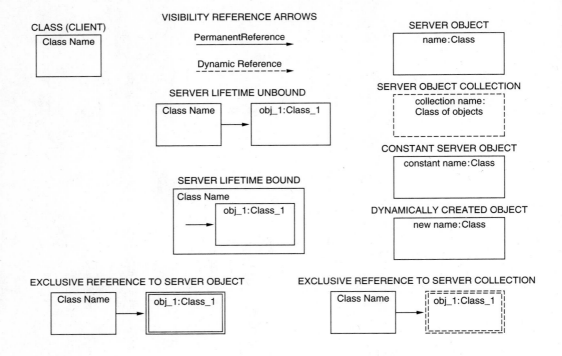

Class Description Notation

class *<ClassName>* [**isa** *<SuperClassNames>*]
//**for each attribute**
[**attribute**] [*Mutability*]*<a_name>* :[*Sharing*][*Binding*]*<Type>*

.
.
.

//**for each method**

[**method**] *<m_name>* *<arglist>*[:*<Type>*]

.
.
.

endclass

Inheritance Graph Notation

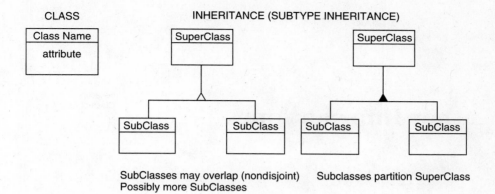

CLASS   INHERITANCE (SUBTYPE INHERITANCE)

SubClasses may overlap (nondisjoint)   Subclasses partition SuperClass
Possibly more SubClasses

ACKNOWLEDGMENTS

Appendices A and B are taken from
    Coleman, D., P. Arnold, S. Bodoff, C. Dollin, H. Gilchrist, F. Hayes, and P. Jeremaes. 1994. *Object-Oriented Development: The Fusion Method.* Englewood Cliffs, NJ: Prentice Hall.

Author Information

Derek Coleman

Derek is a co-author of "Object-oriented Development: the Fusion method" published by Prentice-Hall. He is currently manager of the Application Engineering Department in HP Laboratories Palo Alto. Prior to this he was manager of the team that developed the Fusion method. Derek is an active member of the object-oriented research community and the author of many papers on software engineering and formal methods. He has co-authored papers presented at OOPSLA and other conferences. He has presented tutorials at object-oriented conferences including OOPSLA, ECOOP and Object World.

> Application Engineering Department
> Hewlett-Packard Laboratories
> 1501 Page Mill Road
> Palo Alto, CA 94304
> Tel: (415) 857-2060
> Fax: (415) 852-8488
> Email: dc@hpl.hp.com

Reed Letsinger

Reed is managing a project in Hewlett-Packard Laboratories extending the Fusion method to support the development of large, distributed information systems. He has worked for HP Labs for 13 years on the role of modeling in software engineering. He received a M.Sc from Stanford in Computer Science, and a Ph.D. from Stanford in Philosophy.

Application Engineering Department
Hewlett-Packard Laboratories, MS 1U-14
1501 Page Mill Road
Palo Alto, CA 94304
Tel: (415) 857-5974
Fax: (415) 857-8526
Email: letsinger@hpl.hp.com

Jerremy Holland

Jerremy is a Technical Architect at Hewlett-Packard's Telecom System Division (TSD) in Scotland. At TSD, he pioneered the use of object technology through a successful pilot project and went on to successfully apply OT on a large-scale distributed telecommunication monitoring application. Besides pioneering the use of objects at Hewlett-Packard, Jerremy has been actively promoting the use of OT throughout Scotland as a co-founder of the Scottish Object Technology Group.

Prior to moving to Scotland, Jerremy and his wife lived in California. Jerremy led key areas of distributed system development while working for Trace Products and Mountain Computer. Prior to that, he was one of the Lead Instructors at the Texas Instruments Learning Center in San Francisco, California. Jerremy received his bachelor of science degree in computer engineering from the University of California at Santa Cruz. His professional interests include distributed, object-based systems, simulation, telecommunication system monitoring/management, and data mining.

Hewlett-Packard Limited
Telecom Systems Division
South Queensferry, West Lothian
Scotland   EH30 9TG
Tel: 44-131-331-7941
Fax: 44-131-331-7987
Email: jerremy@hpsqf.sqf.hp.com

Ronald Falcone

Ron received a B.S. from the State University of New York at Albany in Physics. He has 12 years experience in software and systems engineering, the last 4 years being at HP Medical Products Division as Software Architect and Technical Leader. He recently joined Wang Laboratories' Federal Systems Group.

Wang Laboratories
600 Technology Park C27-122
Bilerica, Massachusetts 01821
Tel: (508) 967-6149
Email: ronald.v.falcone@mailoff.wang.com

Jacob Nikom

Dr. Nikom received his MS (Cum Laude) in Mechanical Engineering in Institute of Automotive Engineering (Moscow, 1972) and MS in Computer Sciences in Institute of Electrical and Computer Engineering (Moscow, 1977) and Ph.D. in Artificial Intelligence from the Russian Academy of Sciences Institute for Machine Studies (Moscow, 1983). He worked for many years at Russian Academy of Sciences Earth Physics Institute, Moscow, developing algorithms for signal processing in geophysics.

Before joining HP in 1994, he worked at UMASS Medical School Imaging Center developing software for image processing of living cells, and at Applicon Inc. where he developed constraint-based geometric modeling software providing customers with "design intent capture" capabilities.

Medical Products Group
Hewlett–Packard Company
3000 Minuteman Road
Andover, MA 01810-1099
Tel: (508) 659-2754
Fax: (508) 975-7324
Email: nikom@an.hp.com

Ruth Malan

Ruth obtained a B.A. in Mathematics and English from the University of Natal, South Africa, in 1983. She worked as a software engineer and then as a technical software consultant for a number of years before doing an M.B.A. at Virginia Tech (1990), and a M.Sc. in Operations Research at Stanford University (1993). She joined Hewlett-Packard Laboratories in 1993, and is currently working on enhancements to the Fusion method to better support the development of large, distributed information systems.

Application Engineering Department
Hewlett-Packard Laboratories, MS 1U-14
1501 Page Mill Road
Palo Alto, CA 94304
Tel/Fax: (603) 632-7223
Voicemail: (415) 857-7909
Email: malan@hpl.hp.com

Paul Jeremaes

Paul is a researcher at HP Laboratories. His research over the past 11 years has focused on the development of software engineering methods and on formal specification techniques. Prior to joining HP, Paul worked in the telecommunications industry as a lecturer in software engineering. He was a member of the research and consultancy team responsible for the development of the Fusion method and is a co-author of the Fusion book.

Paul has a B.Sc. in Computer and Microprocessor Systems from the University of Essex.

Hewlett–Packard Laboratories
Filton Road, Stoke Gifford
Bristol BS12 6QZ
United Kingdom
Tel: +44 (0)117 922 8058
Fax: +44 (0)117 922 8972
Email: pgj@hplb.hpl.hp.com

Laurence Canning

Laurence is a member of Admiral's Technology Group and is a recognized Object Technology expert within Admiral. Laurence is the principal architect of ACOBA, Admiral's object-oriented development process.

Laurence has a degree in Computer Science from Liverpool University and has worked for Admiral since graduation. He has gained extensive experience in delivering systems utilizing object technologies, including analysis and design methodologies, database management systems and distributed objects (CORBA). He provides consultancy and technical assurance both internally within Admiral and for clients.

Admiral Computing Ltd.
1 Anchorage Court
Caspian Road
Altrincham, WA14 5HH, UK
Tel: +44 (0)161 927 7888
Fax: +44 (0)161 927 7889
Email: canni_l@admiral.co.uk

Richard Nethercott

Richard is manager of the Technology Group within Admiral Computing. The Group consists of senior technical staff and is responsible for identifying major new technologies and to ensure that the company learns how to apply these in the most pragmatic and efficient manner.

Richard has a degree in Electronics from the University of Manchester Institute of Science and Technology (UMIST), is a member of the Institute of Electrical Engineers and is a Chartered Engineer. He has spent the last 12 years working with software systems of all types, the last 9 of which have been in a commercial software house environment.

Admiral Computing Ltd.
1 Anchorage Court
Caspian Road
Altrincham, WA14 5HH, UK
Tel: +44 (0)161 927 7888
Fax: +44 (0)161 927 7889
Email: nethe_r@admiral.co.uk

Colin Atkinson

Dr. Atkinson is an Assistant Professor at the University of Houston Clear-Lake (UHCL) where he teaches courses related to object-oriented development and software engineering. He was co-principal investigator of the NASA-funded project, MISSION, exploring the use of object-oriented technology in the construction of large safety critical systems, and is currently a researcher on the NASA-funded RBSE project concerned with repository-based software reuse.

Before joining UHCL, Dr. Atkinson worked at Imperial College, London, where he participated in the DRAGON project looking at ways to support the distribution, reuse and dynamic reconfiguration of Ada applications.

University of Houston— Clear Lake, Suite 3-521
2700 Bay Area Boulevard
Houston, Texas 77058
Fax: (713) 283 3869
Email:

Michael Weisskopf

Michael is a Senior Research Associate at the University of Houston-Clear Lake, working primarily in the area of software process development and enactment. He has been a member of the Repository Based Software Engineering (RBSE) project and has worked with Rockwell on the ROSE project to reengineer large portions of the space shuttle support software. This work has involved many aspects of software process capture, development, introduction, prototyping, measurement, and evaluation.

University of Houston— Clear Lake
2700 Bay Area Boulevard
Houston, TX 77058
Tel: (713) 283-3833
Email: weisskop@rbse.jsc.nasa.gov

Todd Cotton

Todd is a Consulting Project Manager with HP's Software Initiative. Todd has been responsible for introducing Fusion into many projects and showing how the method can be integrated with other software engineering best practices. Prior to this, Todd was a software engineer and a software development project manager for a variety of HP's products. Todd holds a B.S. in Mathematics and an M.S. in Computer Science from Stanford University.

Hewlett-Packard Company
1501 Page Mill Road, MS: 5MS
Palo Alto, CA 94304
Tel: (415) 857-3244
Email: cotton@ce.hp.com

Kris Oosting

Kris is responsible for OO project support at SHARED OBJECTIVES in the Netherlands. His work concentrates mainly on supporting NEXTSTEP projects using the Fusion method. Kris is an active member of the object-oriented community with special interest in measuring and improving the quality of object-oriented software development. He tutors courses concerning software quality, software metrics, the Fusion method, and NEXTSTEP/OpenStep.

Kris has also been a guest speaker at universities and several conferences and seminars in The Netherlands, Denmark and the US. He was a speaker at the NEXTSTEP ExPO 1993 and 1994 in San Francisco, and The International Hewlett-Packard User Conference 1994 concerning object metrics and Fusion.

He has written several papers on software metrics and object-oriented methods.

Shared Objectives
P.O. Box 566
NL-1420 CB UITHOORN
The Netherlands
Tel: +31 297 5 31 658
Fax: +31 297 3 31 668
Email: koosting@pimsord.knoware.nl

Andrew Blyth

Andrew received his B.Sc. in Computing Science in 1988 and his M.Sc. in Computer Software and Systems Design in 1989 both from the University of Newcastle Upon Tyne. He then worked for four years on an ESPIRT funded project called ORDIT (Organizational Requirements Definition for Information Technology), and for one year on a DTI/EPSRC funded project called SHEMA. On the 1st of January 1995 he took up the appointment as the Department of Computing Science Research Officer, where his responsibilities include teaching and research. His research interests include enterprise modeling, change management, requirements quality management and organizational requirements capture, definition and validation.

Department of Computing Science
University of Newcastle Upon Tyne
Newcastle Upon Tyne, NE1 7RU.
England
Tel: +44 191 222 8504
Fax: +44 191 222 8232
Email: A.J.C.Blyth@newcastle.ac.uk
WWW: http://www.cs.ncl.ac.uk/a.j.c.blyth

Howard Ricketts

Howard received a BSc(Eng) Hons in Computing Science from Imperial College, London University in 1981. He spent the next decade learning the trade as a software engineer specializing in anything which paid well (RDMBs, X-11, OO design, etc.) with companies such as Shell, Marconi CAE, Plessey DataComms and Systematica (RIP excepting Shell). His genuine interest in OO led to involvement with HOOD User Group. In 1992 he formed a partnership in *Soft*CASE Consulting specializing in the development of tailored CASE solutions. He and his colleagues at *Soft*CASE have successfully completed projects worldwide for customers which include Paranor AG (on behalf of Swiss PTT), N&P Building Society, Norwegian Telecom, Hewlett-Packard and TRW. *Soft*CASE are the developers of the successful FusionCASE and SyntropyCASE products. Howard is currently providing consultancy on OO analysis and design, tools and effective OO project management processes.

*Soft*CASE Tools Ltd.
The Loft, 13 Ravine Road
Canford Cliffs, Poole
Dorset BH13 7HS, UK
Tel: +44 1202 700415
Fax: +44 1202 700416
Email: 100115.1215@compuserve.com
http://www.softcase.co.uk

Gabriel Eckert

Gabriel received B.Sc. degrees in both electronics and electrical engineering and holds an M.Sc. degree in Software Engineering from the University of Aston in Birmingham, UK. He worked many years in several Swiss companies and joined the Software Engineering Laboratory at the Swiss Federal Institute of Technology in 1992. He is pursuing research on object-oriented requirements analysis and specification.

Software Engineering Laboratory
Department of Computer Science
Swiss Federal Institute of Technology
EPFL-DI-LGL
CH-1015 Lausanne
Switzerland
Tel: +41 21 693 5292
Fax: +41 21 693 5079
Email: Gabriel.Eckert@di.epfl.ch

Desmond F. D'Souza

Desmond is the President of ICON Computing, Inc., and a member of the faculty of the Software Quality Institute at the University of Texas at Austin. Desmond has worked with object technology since 1985, and has taught courses and consulted internationally. His interests are in object and component technologies, practical rigorous methodologies, change characterization, design patterns, and re-use. He is the author of the "Education and Training" column in the Journal of Object-Oriented Programming, and contributes regularly to the Report on Object Analysis and Design.

ICON Computing, Inc.
12343 Hymeadow Drive, Suite 3C
Austin, TX 78750
Tel: (512) 258-8437
Fax: (512) 258-0086
Email: dsouza@iconcomp.com

Alan Wills

Alan is a consultant in OO design, specializing in rigorous methods. He is based in Manchester, UK. During the eighties, he took part in academic/industrial research projects in formal methods, and took a Ph.D. in their practical application in OOD. He has since worked with clients in a wide variety of application areas.

24 Windsor Road
Manchester M19 2EB
UK
Tel/Fax: +44 161 225 3240
Email: alan@icon.demon.co.uk

Fusion Services

D.1 HEWLETT-PACKARD TRAINING AND CONSULTING SERVICES

D.1.1 Hewlett-Packard Customer Education

The HP Customer Registration Center can provide you with price, scheduling, catalog, and enrollment information, as well as information about on-site delivery of Fusion training.

To order Hewlett-Packard Customer Education classes in the U.S., call 1-800-HPCLASS (1-800-472-5277). In Canada, call 1-800-563-5089.

Outside the U.S. and Canada, contact your nearest HP office.

D.1.2 Hewlett-Packard Consulting Services

HP offers extensive consulting services in the areas of client/server, distributed computing and object-oriented computing. For more information in the U.S. call (415) 691-3839. Outside the U.S., contact your nearest HP office.

Africa/Middle East
Hewlett-Packard ISB
Bue de Vayrot 39
P. O. Box 364
CH-1217 Meyrin–Geneva
Switzerland
(22) 780 41 12

Europe
Hewlett-Packard S.A.
150 Route du Nant-d'Avril
CH-1217 Meyrin 2
Geneva, Switzerland
(22) 780 81 11

Australia/New Zealand
Hewlett-Packard Australia, Ltd.
31-41 Joseph Street
Blackburn, Victoria 3130
Australia
(3) 272 2895

Latin America
Hewlett-Packard
Latin American Region Headquarters
5200 Blue Lagoon Drive
Miami, FL 33126
(305) 267-4220

Canada
Hewlett-Packard Ltd.
5150 Spectrum Way
Missisanga, Ontario L4W 5G1
(905) 206-4725

D.1.3 Hewlett-Packard Consulting Services in Asia Pacific and Japan

The HP Professional Services Organization offers OO transition services, including seminars and workshops for executives and managers, hands-on workshops for developers and testers, project setup assistance, and analysis and design mentoring. For more information, please contact your local HP office.

Asia Pacific
Hewlett-Packard Asia Ltd.
22-30 Floor Peregrine Tower
Lippo Centre
89 Queensway, Central
Hong Kong
(852) 848-7777

Japan
Yokogawa-Hewlett-Packard-Ltd.
3-29-21 Takaido-Higashi
Suginami-Ku, Tokyo 168
(03) 3335-8079

D.1.4 NTU Fusion Video Course

A Fusion video course, available from HP, has been produced by the National Technological University (NTU) in the United States. The course covers all aspects of the Fusion method. For more information contact Kellee Noonan:

Tel: (415) 857-4568
Email: noonan@hpcea.ce.hp.com

D.2 TOOL VENDORS AND CONSULTING SERVICES

D.2.1 ProtoSoft Inc.

Developers of Paradigm Plus, an object-oriented CASE tool supporting Fusion
and other popular object-oriented methods. Paradigm Plus is a configurable and
customizable Meta-CASE tool.

Headquartered in Houston, ProtoSoft sells direct in the United States and
has distributors and/or re-sellers in Europe (The Netherlands, Germany, Italy,
The United Kingdom), Canada, Australia, and Japan.

ProtoSoft Inc.
17629 El Camino Real \#202
Houston, TX 77058
Tel: (713) 480-3233
Fax: (713) 480-6606
Email: sales@protosoft.com

D.2.2 *Soft*CASE Tools Ltd.

*Soft*CASE develop and market the highly successful *Fusion*CASE CASE tool.
Designed to exclusively support Fusion, *Fusion*CASE provides unparalleled
method support featuring an integrated data dictionary, automatic error checking, design change propagation and extensive navigational facilities. As active
Fusion practitioners, *Soft*CASE staff offer practical analysis and design consultancy, Fusion training and consultancy world-wide.

*Soft*CASE Tools Ltd.
The Loft, 13 Ravine Road
Canford Cliffs, Poole
Dorset BH13 7HS, UK
Tel. +44 1202 700415
Fax. +44 1202 700416
Email: fusion@softcase.co.uk
http://www.softcase.co.uk

D.2.3 Advanced Software Technologies, Inc.

Developers of the Graphical Designer, a multi-method software design tool supporting a wide variety of design methods and generating a variety of output languages including C++ and C. Extensive Meta-CASE support is provided as well
as reverse engineering for creating design diagrams from existing code.

Advanced Software Technologies, Inc.
7800 S. Elati Street, Suite 300
Littleton, CO 80120
Tel: (303) 730-7981

Fax: (303) 730-7983
Email: info@advancedsw.com

D.2.4   Mark V Systems

ObjectMaker supports Fusion notations, syntax, semantics, consistency, publishing, and code generation, on PCs and UNIX. Fusion support can be extended, or combined with other design and process notations. For sales, training, and consulting information, worldwide, contact

Mark V Systems
16400 Ventura Blvd., Suite 300
Encino, CA 91436-2123
Tel: (818) 995-7671
Fax: (818) 995-4267
Email: fusion@markv.com

D.3   TRAINING AND CONSULTING SERVICES

D.3.1   Arthur D. Little, Inc.

Arthur D. Little is one of the world's premier management and technology consulting firms. ADL offers mentoring, consulting, and courses in Fusion Plus through its Object Technology Group. It also offers consulting services in Object-Oriented Change and Learning™. OOCL is an OOBPR extension of Fusion Plus developed by ADL for modeling and managing business processes. For more information contact Ed Swanstrom or Peter Weiss:

Arthur D. Little, Inc.
1755 Jefferson Davis Highway
Suite 200
Arlington, VA. 20877
Tel: (703)416-7900
Fax: (703) 416-7910
Email: swanstrom.e@adlittle.com

D.3.2   Advanced Methods and Tools

AM&T is the software engineering division of Knowledge Base Services Ltd. AM&T provides a range of services chosen to provide balanced support for all components of the system development life cycle including specific technology training and consultancy for Fusion. For more information contact John Robinson or Eric Hymas:

Tel: +44 (0)1274 736895
Email: info@acronym.co.uk

D.3.3   ICON Computing, Inc.

ICON Computing specializes in education and consulting services in object-oriented technology. They offer a series of courses covering analysis, design, introductory through advanced implementation, and project management. The analysis and design courses include Fusion and other popular methods.

Headquartered in Austin, Texas, ICON provides services to clients across the United States and Europe.

ICON Computing, Inc.
11203 Oak View Drive
Austin, TX 78759
Tel (US): (512) 258-8437
Fax (US): (512) 258-0086
Tel (UK): +44 (0)161 225 3240
Email: info@iconcomp.com

D.3.4   ObjectSpace Inc.

ObjectSpace, a recognized leader in object technology, provides object-oriented training, mentoring, consulting and products. Our mentors can lead your organization from analysis and design through to implementation, while the ObjectSpace training curriculum offers a wide variety of classes including "Object-oriented Analysis and Design using Fusion."

ObjectSpace software products include:

- ObjectCatalog™, an enterprise-wide reuse tool that allows developers to locate and reuse components.
- ObjectSystems™, a complete C++ framework for development on a variety of platforms.
- STL Toolkit™, a Cfront compatible, ANSI standard template library, available for all popular C++ compilers, allowing cross-platform development.
- ObjectMetrics™, a metrics gathering tool for Smalltalk.
- ObjectSockets™, a Smalltalk class library for TCP/IP, using the WinSock standard.

For more information, contact
ObjectSpace Inc.
14881 Quorum Drive, Suite 400
Dallas, TX 75240
Tel: (214) 934-2496
Fax: (214) 663-9099
Email: info@objectspace.com
www.objectspace.com

D.3.5 Semaphore

Since 1987, Semaphore has been meeting the growing demand for technical training, consulting and mentoring in Object Technology. Semaphore specializes exclusively in the rapid and effective transfer of critical Object Technology skills to software developers and development groups seeking to reduce the learning curve and advance their software engineering productivity. We have trained over 35,000 students in a curriculum of 35+ courses. Our services span management, development (analysis/design, language, database, etc.), or virtually any customized needs through workshops, classes and mentoring activities. Semaphore supports each phase and transition of your project. Semaphore offers Fusion mentoring/consulting as well as the following Fusion courses:

- OOAD with Fusion (5 days)
- OOA with Fusion (3 days)
- OOD with Fusion (3 days)

> Viktor Ohnjec, Director of Technical Services
> Semaphore
> 800 Turnpike Street
> North Andover, MA 01845
> Tel: 800-937-8080 or 713-998-7419
> Email: semaphorhq@aol.com or vo@neosoft.com

D.3.6 Software Design and Build

One of the first British software consultancies to commit publicly its support to the Fusion method. Based in Bristol, close to the HP Labs, they have a broad range of consultancy services, covering every stage of the development and implementation of information systems. In particular they are active in the object-oriented, human computer interaction, and business process modeling fields. For more information contact John Cato:

> Software Design and Build
> Mariner House
> 66 Prince Street
> Bristol, BS14QD
> United Kingdom
> Tel: +44 (0)1179 308668
> Email: sdb_bristol@cix.compulink.co.uk   or   cato@cix.compulink.co.uk

D.3.7 SHARED OBJECTIVES

SHARED OBJECTIVES is a European based Project Support company dedicated to assist its clients, wherever they may be operating, to manage the change to Object Technology. Whether it be courses, tools or project support, all SHARED OBJECTIVES activities center around a broad knowledge of implementing the technology which is transferred through the practical experience of a live project environment. SHARED OBJECTIVES has proven the efficiency of the Fusion method with many implementational environments and will be involved with a funded European project extending the method to incorporate requirements engineering and retrieval.

SHARED OBJECTIVES
P.O. Box 566
NL-1420 CB UITHOORN
The Netherlands
Tel: +31 297 5 31 658
Fax: +31 297 3 31 668
Email: koosting@pimsord.knoware.nl

D.3.8   QA Training

QA Training provides a wide range of technical courses in Client/Server, Windows, Windows NT, Unix, Databases, Networking, and Groupware. QA is a leader in Object-Oriented technology and offers courses in Fusion as well as other methods.

QA offers over 120 scheduled training courses in London and Cirencester, UK, and onsite courses in the Unites States, Europe, Middle east, and elsewhere around the world.

QA Training Ltd.
Cecily Hill Castle
Cirencester, Glos GL7 2EF
UK
Tel: +44 (0)1285 655888
Email: HELPDESK@QATRAIN.MHS.COMPUSERVE.COM

QA Training
2490 Minnesota World Trade Centre
30 East 7th Street
St. Paul, MN 55101
Tel: +1 612 225 9722

D.3.9   Action Software Inc.

PRODUCT: MOOM Tutor (Mastering Object-Oriented Methods)

MOOM Tutor is a highly sophisticated multi-method learning environment. MOOM Tutor introduces you to several object-oriented methods, presented in depth, initially including Fusion and others. MOOM Tutor teaches you concepts and techniques, applying the concepts, comprehension-validating exercises, and a full case study. The visual metaphor is the most advanced and effective in the industry. The product runs on Windows 3.x and Windows 95 platforms.

Action Software Inc.
3950 Cote-Vertu, Suite 211
Montreal (Quebec)
Canada H4R 1V4
Telephone: (514) 331-2210 or (800) 667-9916
Fax: (514) 331-7507